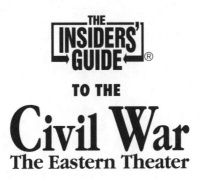

THE INSIDERS' GUIDE®

TO THE

Civil War
The Eastern Theater

TO THE

Civil War
The Eastern Theater

by
Michael P. Gleason

The Insiders' Guides, Inc.

Co-published and marketed by:
Richmond Newspapers, Inc.
333 East Grace Street
Richmond, VA 23219
(804) 649-6000

Co-published and distributed by:
The Insiders' Guides, Inc.
P.O. Box 2057 • Highway 64
Manteo, NC 27954
(919) 473-6100

•

FIRST EDITION
2nd printing

•

Copyright ©1994
by Richmond Newspapers, Inc.

•

Printed in the United States
of America

•

ISBN 0-912367-41-5

Richmond Newspapers, Inc.

Manager
Ernie Chenault

Account Executives
**Jack Barbee, Heidi Crandall
Peg Lewis, Mike Morrison**

Project Coordination
Bonnie Widener

Ronnie Johnson, Susan Reilly, Sean
Contreras, Chuck Nilles, Chris Novelli,
and Ben Shulte artists

The Insiders' Guides®, Inc.

Publisher/Managing Editor
Beth P. Storie

President/General Manager
Michael McOwen

Vice President /Advertising
Murray Kasmenn

Creative Services Director
Mike Lay

Partnership Services Director
Giles Bissonnette

Fulfillment Director
Gina Twiford

Sales and Marketing Director
Julie Ross

Controller
Claudette Forney

Special thanks to:
Dale Gallon, courtesy
of Dale Gallon Historical Art,
P.O. Box 4343,
Gettysburg,PA17325,
phone (717)334-0430
and Don Troiani,
courtesy of Historical Art Prints,
P.O. Box 660, Southbury, CT 06488,
phone (203)262-6680
for providing their unique and
dramatic historic paintings.

Table of Contents

Directory of Maps

Photo: Richmond Newspapers

The anchor of the CSS Virginia, the ironclad Southern warship that fought a historic battle with the USS Monitor, now resides in Richmond, Virginia.

Foreward — How To Use This Book

A number of years ago, I was invited to a rural Virginia elementary school to speak with a class about the Civil War. The teacher was introducing local history to her young students, and the war seemed a likely topic to inspire and excite the class. My talk came at the end of a week-long project in which the youngsters read books and narrated excerpts from family diaries to their classmates. They reviewed collections of Mathew Brady photographs. The class was prepared. I wasn't.

In the question period following my talk, I was stunned when a young girl threw me a seeming innocent curve. "When," she asked, "did the world go to color?" It took a few moments before the question fully registered. Of course, I finally realized, this youngster was a child of color television and video recorders. Having just reviewed the black-and-white Brady photographs associated with the Civil War, her question was quite natural: when did the grass become green, and the sky blue, and blood red?

I don't remember my answer. I know Civil War history never again seemed the same to me. In one brief question, a youngster taught me that the history of that war — indeed, history in general — is a matter of

perspective. I learned that each of us absorbs and appreciates history quite differently. It set me on a quest to "humanize" history, and to make it more appealing and interesting.

A number of educators and historians have turned from "academic" history to "popular" history in an attempt to make the subject more "real" and inspiring. Scholarly history, of course, is invaluable. Educators, more than anyone, help us understand who we are. But the academic approach often is tedious and technical, particularly in our fast-paced, hectic lives. Our communications, transportation and even our food is prefaced with "fast," and advances in computers and other technology have spawned new and faster ways to collect, process and disseminate information. We're just too busy with work and other responsibilities to absorb lengthy, detailed history and identify with our ancestors' lifestyles.

On the other hand, popular history — or "public" history — takes a more "humanizing" approach to the subject, and it helps us understand the past through concise, personal, identifiable stories. It puts history into perspective, and it recognizes that the experiences of common men and women are as important and as interesting as the exploits of heroes. In this way, it opens up history's support base, makes it more "inclusive," and invites persons of all ages and ethnic backgrounds as constituents. If the people we study were mortals, with human strengths and frailties, why not use these stories to teach history?

There have been, by some estimates, no fewer than 50,000 Civil War-related publications in the past 25 years. They are as diverse as they are voluminous. There are academic texts and fictional novels, broad overviews of the political and social implications, and detailed chronicles on military battles, tactics, and weapons. There are unique collections of war-related letters, diaries, and poems. Still, 50,000 publications represent on average a book a day, every single day, since Appomattox in 1865.

So, why this *Insider's Guide?* This guidebook is for a Mid-Atlantic traveler who is interested in the history of the Civil War's Eastern Theater. This theater covered a vast expanse of land, east of the Appalachian Mountains, from near Harrisburg, PA, south to the Virginia-North Carolina border. Whether you're a serious history student or a Civil War novice, and whether you're making a specific trip or just passing through, you'll likely enjoy and appreciate the material we include.

Our information covers four states in 15 chapters. The region includes southern Pennsylvania, central and western Maryland, the eastern panhandle of West Virginia, and all but the farthest southwestern reaches of Virginia. Each one of the 15 chapters is an individual tour

route. There are four separate tours (chapters) along the Appalachian highlands and great valley from Carlisle, PA, to Lexington, VA; four in the Piedmont from Gettysburg, PA, to Charlottesville, VA; five along the "fall line" from Washington, D.C., to Petersburg, VA; and separate routes of Virginia's Southside and Peninsula. Typically, an individual tour begins in a community, runs in a north-to-south direction, covers about a day's worth of travel, and includes a varied selection of attractions and sites with addresses, telephone numbers and specific mileage and odometer directions. We conclude each tour in a community, and include suggestions for accommodations, dining, and other attractions and points of interest. Each tour also includes a map and a selection of photographs.

The tour routes, of course, are a general guide. You can tailor your visit to fit specific interests. If you have leisure time, you may want to stop at each individual attraction — there are 216 listed in the 15 tours — or stay a day or two longer at places of particular interest. If you're pressed for time, or working on a specific route or schedule, you can pick and choose among the various attractions. For that matter, you can mix and match the individual tours. Try jumping from Tour 6 (which ends in Frederick, MD) to Tour 9 (Washington, D.C.), for example. The overview map will help you plot your course.

If you're the serious Civil War buff, we've added a number of "side trips" in each tour. These side trips — 62 in all — are for military enthusiasts and anyone else interested in traveling a few extra miles to see a little-known site or simple highway marker. If you're interested in little "humanizing" stories as much as battlefield details, we include 88 "personality" sketches: interesting stories that go behind the scenes of the serious action.

Each chapter begins with an overview of the tour's history and geography. And we include a brief description on "getting here" — highway directions and how the tour relates geographically to others listed in the book. Keep in mind that some tour routes are busy interstate highways, while others follow state routes and back country roads. Another travel tip: the interstate highways usually have exit numbers that coincide with milepost markers. So, for example, the distance from milepost 25 to milepost 55 is 30 miles. Anticipate heavy, congested traffic on many of the big highways, particularly in urban areas like Washington, Richmond, or the Peninsula. Likewise, on less traveled roads, like those in the western parts of the Mid-Atlantic, expect the unexpected — anything from school buses to slow-moving tractors. For weather and road conditions, you generally will find a selection of stations on your car radio. For emergencies, remember that state and local police officials monitor citizen band (CB) radios, usually Channel 9 or 19. Except in a few remote areas, all tour routes have adequate mobile telephone services.

At the end of each chapter we list suggested accommodations. These listings are a general guide. Specific

rates and unique features are subject to change. Rate charges for a double room are coded as follows:

ACCOMMODATIONS RATES

$	$30 to $40
$$	$41 to $60
$$$	$61 to $85
$$$$	$86 and up

These rates do not include taxes.

Of course, most cities and communities listed in this book have many other hotels, motels, inns and bed and breakfasts. And, much of the area we cover in this book is also thoroughly covered in one of our sister publications, *The Insiders' Guide to Virginia's Blue Ridge, The Insiders' Guide to Metro Washington, D.C., The Insiders' Guide to Richmond,* or *The Insiders' Guide to Virginia Beach/Norfolk.* So, you may find it helpful to read those publications as well.

In addition, each chapter concludes with a list of suggested places to dine. These listings are a general guide, and specific prices are subject to change. The ratings are for a dinner meal for two persons, and they are coded:

RESTAURANTS RATES

$	Under $20
$$	$21 to $35
$$$	$36 to $50
$$$$	$51 and up.

These prices do not include taxes, tips or alcoholic beverages.

Along with lodging and dining suggestions, each tour offers a list of other travel information that includes annual events, arts, entertainment, historic attractions (not related to the Civil War) and places to shop. All of these suggestions, of course, vary among the tours. Some places, like Sharpsburg, MD, and nearby Shepherdstown, WV, are especially scenic but have little "night life." On the other hand, Washington, D.C., and Williamsburg, VA, to name just two, have quite a bit of evening activities along with a considerable number of motels, restaurants and places to shop.

Our lodging suggestions — 47 in all — are a sample of what's available. So, too, are the 54 dining recommendations. In every case, we list a local visitor center address and telephone number. Travel counselors at each center can help you with detailed planning advice and local street maps.

Remember, it's a good idea to review the entire tour, including lodging, dining, and shopping recommendations at chapter's end, before striking out. Reservations are a must at many of these restaurants, hotels, and bed and breakfast inns, particularly during the summer tourist season.

This is a traveler's "insider's guide" — not a scholarly or technical treatise. We want to lead you through a historic, scenic region with a variety of informative material and individual, personal stories. Hopefully, this will lead you to more serious Civil War studies. As Thomas Jefferson once wrote, "History, by apprizing [students] of the past will enable them to judge of the future." Perhaps he studied Cicero, who wrote, "To know nothing of what happened before you were born is to remain forever a child." Perhaps this *Insiders' Guide* will help you embrace some of yesterday's fellow-citizens, and enjoy it, too.

— Michael P. Gleason
January 1994

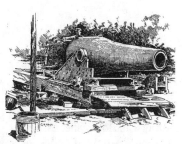

About the Author

Michael P. Gleason has lived or vacationed in almost every part of his native Virginia, including his hometown, Charlottesville, as well as Richmond, Roanoke, the Shenandoah Valley and Northern Virginia. Lately, then, it's not surprising to find him "in my car, somewhere along I-95," as he splits his time between Richmond, where he publishes a monthly newsletter on Virginia history, and McLean, home base of Michael P. Gleason and Co., a consulting firm specializing in communications, government affairs and history-related projects.

Gleason began his career as a Charlottesville newspaper and radio news reporter. His journalism experience led to positions in two successful political campaigns: U.S. Rep. John Marsh's reelection to Congress and state Sen. J. Sargeant Reynolds' election as lieutenant governor. He also worked as a consultant for former Bicentennial Administrator — now U.S. Senator — John Warner. "My love of history, " Gleason says, "can be traced to Jack Marsh, Sarge Reynolds and John Warner, three men who taught me a deep respect for Virginia's rich legacy."

For five years during the 1970s, Gleason was Chairman of the Albemarle-Charlottesville Bicentennial Commission. He helped plan Queen Elizabeth's 1976 visit to Virginia, conceived and wrote an award-winning documentary film, *Mr. Jefferson's Legacy*, lobbied a state tourism strategy before the Virginia General Assembly, and conceived the plan for a Charlottesville-based state visitor center. His extensive, five-year program was cited as one of the top programs in the nation's 200th anniversary commemoration. He was a member of the national Bicentennial Commission's speakers bureau, and he toured Italy in 1977 as part of a "twin community" program sponsored by the U.S. State Department. In 1979, he published *Mr. Jefferson's Upland Virginia*. During this period, he served seven years in the U.S. Army Reserve as a battalion information specialist.

Moving to Northern Virginia in 1980, Gleason worked three years as a special assistant in the U.S. Senate. Then, after a year as production manager with the PBS, Emmy-winning series *Smithsonian World*, he began his own consulting business.

Explore Park, a $147 million visitor destination under construction on the Blue Ridge Parkway, became one of his first clients. He developed the project's history theme, and he devised a legislative strategy that enabled the project to obtain Congressional funding for its parkway entrance road. He was Chairman of Explore's History Advisory Committee, whose membership included U.S. Sen. John Warner and 11 other historians and members of the Congress.

In 1987, Gleason was one of five Virginia delegates at the reconvened Constitutional Convention in Philadelphia as part of the 200th anniversary of the U.S. Constitution. He also served as a consultant for two documentary films, one on the history of the U.S. Supreme Court and the other on Virginia's role in ratifying the U.S. Constitution. And he researched and wrote material for a U.S. Presidential exhibit for the FBI Building in Washington, D.C. Commissioned for the 1989 Presidential Inaugural, it's now a permanent exhibit.

More recently, Gleason directed a Washington-area environmental recycling project that involved 1,900 schools and a million students who collected more than six tons of aluminum in an Earth Day promotional effort. From 1990 to 1992 he wrote a bimonthly history column for the *Richmond Times-Dispatch.* And he was a member of the committee that commissioned the USS *George Washington* nuclear-powered aircraft carrier in Norfolk in 1992.

Last year, he helped produce and write a documentary film on land conservation for the Piedmont Environmental Council, and he produced a promotional video for the Charlottesville/Albemarle Convention and Visitors Bureau.

Mike and his wife, Kendall, are the principals in Gleason Publishing, Inc., which produces *VIRGINIA,* a monthly subscriber newsletter on popular history in the Commonwealth. Mike, who works "on again, off again" on his master's degree in history, writes and edits the newsletter; Kendall, who is finishing work on a master's in business administration, handles marketing and promotions. The two met in 1982 while working in the U.S. Senate. During the past year, they drove more than 10,000 miles, crisscrossing the Mid-Atlantic, gathering material for Mike to write this *Insiders' Guide to the Civil War's Eastern Theater.* Now, they plan a vacation: "somewhere without a car."

Acknowledgments and Dedication

I owe a great deal to Beth P. Storie and Michael McOwen the principals of The Insiders' Guides, Inc. This dynamic, energetic couple share my love of popular history and an interest in the "humanizing" stories that help make history — especially Civil War stories — "come alive." They, and all the staff members at The Insiders' Guides, have been a wonderful source of inspiration and encouragement. I extend special thanks to Albert T. August III. "Tappy" is president and general manager of Richmond Newspapers Inc. (RNI), and he recommended me for this project. RNI's Supplemental Publications Department has been responsible for the marketing and advertising aspects of this book, and I thank Robert Bowerman, Ernie Chenault and Bonnie Widener for their hard work and support.

Special gratitude is reserved for Joseph Whitehorne, a respected military historian who reviewed my chapters for accuracy. Joe served 25 years in the U.S. Army — most of that time as a staff historian at the Pentagon. His last assignment, on the staff of the Secretary of the Army, was devoted mainly to the study and interpretation of battlefield sites throughout the nation. Retired from the military, Joe lives near Front

Royal, VA, and teaches history at Lord Fairfax Community College at nearby Middletown. He has written a number of books and articles on military history topics. His two most recent books deal with the War of 1812 and with Virginia Revolutionary War units.

Of course, I owe so much to my wife, Kendall. She endured much more than she — or I — expected, including endless road trips, late-night research impulses, weekend rewrites, and wrecked vacations. Through it all, with amazing patience, she scurried "one more time" to the library, photocopied hundreds of pages of research materials, read over my drafts — "isn't this the twelfth version of the personality profile?" — and watched endless movie classics on television, alone. During the past 14 months, she went along on most all of the 10,000-plus miles I drove to research this book. We both thank the hundreds of helpful folks we met at battlefields, attractions, national parks, visitor centers, motels, inns, bed and breakfasts, restaurants, stores and shops.

This project inspired me to learn more about my great-grandfather, Robert James Morris, who fought for the Confederacy. I always knew my family boasted a Civil War veteran, but it wasn't until this past year, researching this book, that I dug more deeply in old records to investigate my great-grandfather's experiences.

Born in February 1838 in Louisa County, he married his wife, Amanda, in October 1860. In late July 1861, at the age of 23 — with his wife four months pregnant — he enlisted in Co. H of the 57th Virginia Volunteers (Rivanna Guard) in Charlottesville. His daughter, Sarah, was born in early December; Amanda died less than three weeks later during the Christmas holiday. Unaware of his daughter's birth and his wife's death, Robert took a four-day furlough, returned to Fluvanna and encountered his wife's funeral procession.

He saw considerable action in 1862: Malvern Hill near Richmond on July 1, 2nd Manassas in late August, the Confederate raid on Harpers Ferry in September, Antietam in September, and Fredericksburg in December. (Back home, his daughter died before she was a year old.) The next year, he fought at Suffolk in April, and he was one of the survivors of "Pickett's charge" at Gettysburg in July. In May 1864, he fought at Chester Station, and then he was injured at Drewry's Bluff. He was treated at Chimborazo Hospital in Richmond. A year later, in March 1865, he was on the field at Five Forks.

In April, his company joined Gen. Robert E. Lee's main army at Rice's Station, and fought at Sayler's Creek. He was at Appomattox when Lee surrendered April 9.

Like so many veterans, he returned home after the war to resume a life of quasi-normalcy, took up farming and carpentry, married my great-grandmother, Ella Caroline, and had nine children, including my grandmother, Blanche, in 1890. In 1900, living near Keswick in Albemarle County, VA, he successfully applied for a $15 annual state pension based on his Civil War service. He died in November 1920, at his daughter's home in Richmond. He was 82.

Last year, during a visit to the Gettysburg National Military Park, I saw a photograph of my great-grandfather on the wall of veterans in the visitor center. The picture shows a young Pvt. Morris in uniform, with dark hair, olive complexion, grey eyes and a neatly trimmed beard.

My grandmother, Blanche, died in 1986, and I regret not knowing enough about her father to get any details. But my mother, who was born in 1916 and still lives in Charlottesville, was four-years-old when her grandfather died. She remembers him as "a kind, gentle old man, with a white beard and goatee — like Colonel Sanders." I dedicate this effort to the memory of Confederate Pvt. Robert Morris.

The Eastern Theater

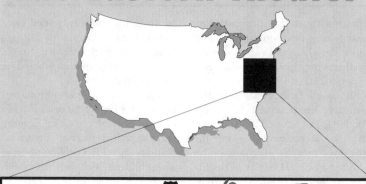

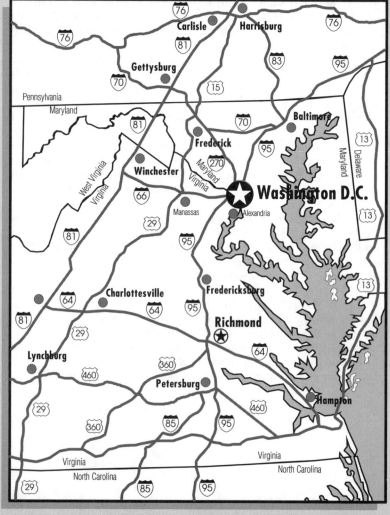

Overview of the Eastern Theater

Opening

A light morning mist fell on Washington, D.C. on Monday, March 4, 1861. It was just enough rain to settle the dust along Pennsylvania Avenue, the inaugural parade route for the nation's sixteenth president, Abraham Lincoln. Just before noon, Lincoln and his wife, Mary, left the Willard Hotel and rode with President James Buchanan in an open, horse-drawn carriage to the U.S. Capitol. There, on the East Portico, the new president took his oath of office. All around, on every visible rooftop, soldiers with fixed bayonets watched — and guarded.

The Capitol dome, sheathed in scaffolding, rose up behind the ceremonial dais. A project to enlarge and resurface the dome was part of an overall effort to expand the Capitol. The work, Lincoln later said, symbolized the nation's union. Indeed, the union was very much on the mind of Lincoln, his audience, and the entire nation. The new president, in his inaugural address, spoke of national survival.

"We are not enemies, but friends," he said. "Though passion may have strained, it must not break the bonds of affection. The mystic chords of memory stretching from every battlefield and patriot grave,

to every living heart and hearthstone, all over this broad land, will yet swell the chorus of union. . . ."

Part One

Lincoln's "broad land" was rather small by today's comparison. There were just over 31 million Americans — about an eighth of today's population — in 34 states. Most Americans — six in ten — lived on farms. Communities were small; they were linked by simple dirt roads. The railroad was a relatively recent phenomenon. Washington, the capital city, was just 72 years old.

The District of Columbia, straddling the Potomac River, was the centerpiece of the Mid-Atlantic, which became the scene of the Civil War's Eastern Theater. One of two principal theaters of operation during the conflict, the Eastern Theater was fought from the Atlantic coast to the Appalachians, from southern Pennsylvania, through Maryland and the present-day West Virginia panhandle, into nearly every part of Virginia.

The Civil War began in the Eastern Theater. Here, John Brown raided Harpers Ferry. The opposing armies tangled in their first major battle, here, on a small creek named Bull Run. The war ended here, too, at a rural Virginia court-house named Appomattox. In be-tween, for four weary years, the con-flict raged here as much as anywhere: in the mountains from Antietam to Winchester to New Market; in the foothills from Gettysburg to Brandy Station to Saylor's Creek; on the edge of the Coastal Plain from Fredericksburg to Richmond to the Virginia's Peninsula.

But looking at the Mid-Atlantic today, imagining the war's extensive death and destruction, simply chal-lenges the imagination. Spend any time at all here and two distinct points become obvious. One is that this region is inarguably the nation's most scenic. Secondly, there is so much early American history here. The region's natural beauty is sur-passed only by its diversity. There are lavender mountains and lush, green valleys. There are rolling fields and farms of rich, fertile loam. Crys-tal clear streams feed mighty rivers that roll east to the sandy flatlands and their marshes and swamps. Not one of these picturesque places es-caped the ravages of the war.

America was born here, at small English settlements in the Tidewater. The Virginia, Maryland, and Pennsyl-vania colonies were instrumental in America's early stages of development and in the ultimate fight for Indepen-dence. The nation's roots run deep in the soil here at Williamsburg and Annapolis, at Valley Forge and Phila-delphia, at Yorktown and Richmond. None of these escaped the war, ei-ther. There are ironies here, too. It's ironic that this land of natural won-der was subjected to so much of the Civil War's ugliness. And it's ironic

that this conflict of "brother against brother" tore at the nation's fabric — a fabric created and nurtured here, more than anywhere else, during the preceding two and half centuries.

History, it seems, is simply a mat-ter of time and place. To appreciate the Civil War in the Eastern The-ater, then, is to understand this region's origins from two inextrica-bly linked viewpoints: time and place. History's time line, from a perspec-tive of "place" — or nature — moves from west to east, from the moun-tains to the ocean. In terms of "time" — of European settlers and pioneers — it runs east to west, from coastal colonies to the upcountry. These histories are not static. Rather, they move back and forth, as if some large, mystical loom was at work here, weaving the stories of characters and events into a tapestry of remarkable history. Strip away the "imaginary" states and community boundaries, and remove the rather recent paths of modern roadways, and it's easier to visualize the three distinct areas of this region: Mountains, Piedmont, and Coastal Plain.

MOUNTAINS

Four years: the time frame of the Civil War. Still, these years are a mere blip in the ageless time line of Appalachian geology. Imagine, pos-sibly, a half billion — that's 500 mil-lion years — ago, when two of the earth's major land masses first met in a series of violent collisions. One continental mass slammed against today's North America. The massive impact folded and buckled the land here into ripples of corrugated ridges, stretching 1,000 miles long and reaching upwards over 2 miles. This was the birth of the Appalachian Mountains. Time, of course, changed the face of these mountains. Rain and various other weather conditions eroded and sculpted these mountains, wearing them down to barely half their height, and creating a fertile loam that eventually accommodated a wide variety of plants and animals.

One of the most distinguishing features here is a grand, open valley running southwest along the mountains' eastern slope. It's a natural funnel. To the northwest it's the Cumberland Valley; farther south it's the Shenandoah; farther south, still, through the watersheds of the James, Roanoke, and New rivers, it's simply the "Great Valley." Native Americans were the first inhabitants of the mountains and along this Great Valley corridor. Here, long before European settlers, they lived and hunted. Their paths crisscrossed the mountains, connecting their villages with those of other tribes. It can be said they were the continent's first "environmentalists," who lived with — rather than off — the land. They left a legacy here in the abundance of place names. "Appalachian" itself ranks among the first words adapted from Indians. It dates to 16th-century Spanish explorers who stumbled on a small Indian village called "Apalchen." Other names survive today: Shenandoah, Allegheny, Catoctin, and Massanutten.

European exploration began here in the mid-18th century, when a flood of Germans and Scotch-Irish migrated overland from Philadelphia and south along the Great Valley. The landscape undoubtedly reminded them of their Old World homelands. Other pioneer paths crossed west from the lower, eastern foothills. Homesteads sprang up all along the valley corridor's path — the Great Wagon Road. These fiercely independent settlers — "mountaineers" — and their succeeding families, took part in a number of significant 18th-century struggles, including both the French and Indian War and the American Revolution. This was Daniel Morgan's home. Andrew Lewis lived here. This was home, too, for the Patton, Preston, and Breckinridge families. The Breckinridges, who settled in the mid-18th century in Augusta County, Virginia, were like so many who eventually migrated west to Kentucky. Ironically, one of the family's descendants, John Cabell Breckinridge, returned a half-century later as the Confederate commander at the Battle of New Market — only 60 miles north of his ancestors' home settlement.

The Civil War was into its first year before major action struck these highlands. Here, in the Spring of 1862, CSA Gen. Jackson led his troops in the Shenandoah Valley Campaign. Later, in September, after the capture of Harpers Ferry, troops fought battles at South Mountain and Antietam. The following year, both sides maneuvered north in this region during the Gettysburg Campaign. In 1864, CSA Gen. Early's Confederates pushed Union troops out of the Shenandoah Valley, moved on Washington, and returned here to meet defeat at the hands of USA Gen. Sheridan.

Today, these mountains are one of the nation's great outdoor playgrounds. Its vast parks are popular retreats, especially during Fall foliage, and its farmland remains one of the nation's major agricultural and poultry centers. U.S. 11 and I-81 run the length of the Great Valley, along the path of the Old Wagon Road, from Pennsylvania, through western Maryland and the West Virginia panhandle, and the entire length of Virginia.

RIVERS AND WATER GAPS

The rivers of the Mid-Atlantic are about as old as the mountains. They've always been the area's lifeline — threads connecting one geographic region to another, from the Appalachians to the Atlantic. They've carried a mighty cargo: mountain sediment. Small streams and rivulets originated in the mountains, and they grew in size and volume over countless centuries of precipitation. The Susquehanna, for example, begins high in Pennsylvania and New York, and flows to the Chesapeake Bay. The Potomac starts in West Virginia; the Shenandoah and Monocacy rivers are among its tributaries. Farther south are the headwaters of the James — Virginia's longest — and the Roanoke. These rivers, rushing from their highest elevations, carved great water gaps through the smallest, easternmost mountain ridges. These gaps were ideal for pioneer settlements: Harrisburg on the Susquehanna, Harpers Ferry on the Potomac. An imaginary line runs parallel to the mountains, and connects the various water gaps. This line is the boundary between two geographic regions, Mountains and Piedmont.

PIEDMONT

Piedmont, in Italian, means "foot of the mountain." This region traces its origins to the same continental collisions that formed the Appalachians. Following a series of violent punches, and as one continental land mass pulled away from North America, the Piedmont was "stretched." This action created rock outcroppings while, simultaneously, rock erupted from the earth's hot, molten core. Erosion and weather eventually smoothed the irregular land, leaving a rich earthen carpet suitable for both woodland growth and farming. The name Piedmont is used throughout Pennsylvania, Maryland, and most of Virginia. In lower Virginia, where the state stretches along much of its border with North Carolina, it's called "Southside." The soil is different here, accommodating the cultivation of tobacco, a plant Native Americans introduced to the colony's earliest settlers.

A number of Indian tribes, especially the Monocans in Central Virginia, lived in the Piedmont, but most left at about the time Anglo pioneers pushed west from Tidewater. But here, too, they left their place names. There's the Rappahannock River in Central Piedmont and the Appomattox River in Southside. The northern Piedmont was settled mainly by Quakers, Scotch-Irish and Germans, most of whom migrated west out of Philadelphia. Settlers in central Piedmont were mainly Anglo pioneers: descendants of early English families in Virginia's Tidewater. Here, the "landed gentry" included Thomas, the Sixth Lord Fairfax, whose vast property stretched from the Chesapeake Bay to the Alleghenys.

Early communities include Lancaster and Gettysburg in Pennsylvania, Frederick in Maryland, and Leesburg and Warrenton in Virginia's Piedmont. Lynchburg and Danville became noted Southside Virginia settlements. Some of the young nation's best known leaders called Piedmont home: James Madison, James Monroe, John Marshall, and Thomas Jefferson. "There is not a better country society in the United States," Jefferson once wrote about his Piedmont homeland. The gentle hills here are evidence of an ancient time, when volcanic lava rolled along the earth's surface.

Great armies rolled along this land, too, during the Civil War. In the first summer of the war, the North and South clashed on the plains of Manassas south of Washington. Throughout 1862, both armies crisscrossed the Piedmont, battling at places like Cedar Mountain and again at Bull Run. Brandy Station and Gettysburg were fought in the Summer of 1863. In the final year of the war, troops led by CSA Gen. Lee and USA Gen. Grant weaved across Southside Virginia from Petersburg, and met at last at Appomattox.

Today, US 15 and US 29 run the length of the Piedmont, from Harrisburg to Danville. US 360 and US 460 cross in Southside. The farms throughout this region, in southern Pennsylvania and central Maryland, and in central Virginia and Southside, remain as evidence of early European settlers. Throughout much of the northern Piedmont the local gentry still practice their adopted English heritage as horse breeders, fox hunters, and steeplechase race enthusiasts. Little homage is paid to the simple, less prominent settlers — families who created the nation's first great farm country. Their trade was grain, which was ground and bagged at any number of mills on the Piedmont's ample streams.

RIVERS AND THE FALL LINE

The streams of the Piedmont feed larger mountain rivers, which increase in size and momentum in their quest for the ocean. Pushing across the hard crust of these foothills, the rivers eventually encountered less resistant rock. This became a distinct geographical place — where they tumble over falls created by great outcroppings of rock. This is the "fall line," which runs parallel to the mountains and the coast, and separates the Piedmont and the Coastal Plain. The fall line was just the place for colonial settlements. Towns grew here, safely upriver as far as water transportation could go. Hinterland goods and crops — mainly tobacco and wheat — were hauled across the Piedmont and loaded on boats headed for ports downriver. In time, a string of communities developed along the line, from Philadelphia to Petersburg. Virginia hamlets along the fall line date to the mid-17th century, and Philadelphia dates to the 1680s. Baltimore was established on the line in

1720, and Washington was situated on the Potomac falls 70 years later.

Some of the Civil War's heaviest fighting took place along this fall line, particularly along the 100-mile stretch between the opposing capitals: Washington and Richmond. Opposing armies tangled at the Battle of Fredericksburg in December 1862, and continued just months later at Chancellorsville. The Battles of the Wilderness and Spotsylvania were fought in May 1864; the Siege of Petersburg lasted throughout the remainder of that year.

Today, this area of the Mid-Atlantic is part of the nation's heavily populated "urban corridor," and US 1 and I-95 follow almost the exact line of the falls. The rivers here continue east, straightening and broadening in a more gentle flow to the Atlantic.

COASTAL PLAIN

Until a few million years ago, the Coastal Plain was submerged by the sea. Originally, the ocean lapped at the fall line, 100 miles upriver. Here, the rivers are estuaries, susceptible to the ebb and flow of the ocean's tides. Mountain sediment is the sand of the beaches of the Chesapeake Bay and the Atlantic.

The rivers here, particularly in Maryland and Virginia, have carved the sandy landscape into webbed "fingers" of land called peninsulas. Many of the river names are of Native American origin: Patuxent, Chickahominy, and Rappahannock. The Rappahannock is the boundary between two of Virginia's historic land "fingers," the Northern Neck and the Middle Peninsula. The Lower Peninsula lies between the York and James rivers. Hampton Roads is the place where the James meets the Atlantic; the region to the south is called Tidewater.

Jamestown, the first permanent English settlement on the continent, was established on Virginia's Lower Peninsula, on the James River. Maryland became a colony in 1632; Pennsylvania in 1681. The Maryland and Virginia colonies were established in a region controlled mainly by Powhatan, a noted Algonquin chief who ruled an area more than 8,500 square miles of the Coastal Plain. Chesapeake became the single, most significant place name settlers inherited from Native Americans here; tobacco, the most significant crop. For a time, colonists made fortunes selling tobacco in England. They built estates along deep tidal rivers. Beginning in 1619, they imported African Americans as a slave labor force for the money crop. But tobacco required the richest loam, and it quickly exhausted the sandy soil. Eventually, planters abandoned their fields. They saw their hope for future wealth in land — land that lay beyond the fall line.

The colonial population of the Coastal Plain grew and pushed west, upriver. In 1694, Maryland moved its capital to the Severn River. Five years later, Virginia moved its capital to Middle Plantation — Williamsburg. Williamsburg and Annapolis were important government centers during the American Revolution, which was fought on soil throughout the Mid-Atlantic. The British surrender, in 1781, took place on the Lower Peninsula, at a small community named Yorktown. A number of prominent Americans traced their roots to the Coastal Plain, not the least of whom was George Washington, the commander of the Continental Army, who was born on the Northern Neck in 1732. Seventy-five years later, and a mere 15 miles down the Potomac, another famous Virginia general was born. His name was Robert E. Lee.

The Civil War came early to the Coastal Plain. In the Spring of 1862, the Union Army attempted a Richmond invasion, shipping troops down the Potomac and the Chesapeake Bay, and advancing up the Lower Peninsula: the Peninsular Campaign. The two ironsides, the *Monitor* and *Merrimack*, fought their battle in Hampton Roads. War action also took place upriver, east of Richmond and Petersburg, just before Confederates evacuated the two cities in 1865.

Today, I-64 and VA 5 run east from Richmond and along the length of the Lower Peninsula. US 17 runs east out of Fredericksburg across the Middle Peninsula to Hampton Roads. Here, fishing is big business. Crabs are a special Maryland delicacy. Peanuts and ham are notable products of the Virginia Tidewater. And there's an array of historical and recreational attractions throughout this area. There is ethnic diversity here, too. There is a rich African American heritage throughout coastal Maryland and Virginia, and in Tidewater and Southside, as well. And Virginia is still home for a number of Native Americans — though, they are much fewer in numbers. Today's Chickahominy, Eastern Chickahominy, Mattaponi, Upper Mattaponi, Nansemond, Pamunkey, and United Rappahannock are descendants of the area's first inhabitants.

RAILROADS

Rivers — and, eventually, their canals — dominated transportation in the Mid-Atlantic for over two centuries. This changed in the 19th century with the advent of the railroad. In many instances, particularly in the mountains, rail lines simply followed the natural course of rivers that meandered through the Appalachians. To the northwest, rail lines originated in Hancock, Martinsburg, and Winchester, funneling through Harpers Ferry and crossing central Maryland to Baltimore. Two rail branches — one in the Shenandoah Valley and another running north through Virginia's central Piedmont — met at Manassas Junction and crossed Northern Virginia to Alexandria. Richmond was a rail center, with trains arriving from every direction. Lines ran to and from Fredericksburg in the north, Gordonsville in the east, Burkeville and Petersburg in Southside, and West Point in the Middle Peninsula. Another line ran southeast from Petersburg to Suffolk.

The railroad played a role in the boundary disputes created with West Virginia's 1863 separation from Virginia — the nation's only map change as a result of the Civil War. West Virginia cut away from Virginia mainly along the Appalachian ridges that form the eastern continental divide. However, the new state took in some land east of the divide, in the Great Valley, forming an eastern panhandle along the Potomac. The panhandle was necessary: it enabled the Baltimore and Ohio Railroad, a Union Army lifeline, to run totally within Northern territory.

Part Two

The Civil War did not just spring up overnight. Nor was there one simple political or social issue. The seeds were sewn in an earlier time in our young nation's history. Its story spans no fewer than three decades, from 1830 to 1860, with events in Washington and throughout the country. This 30-year period was a time of rapid growth. It also was a time of erratic and ever-changing political leadership and allegiances. It was a time in which the nation attempted to define its identity.

The nation's population during these three decades grew from 12.8 million to nearly 31.5 million — an amazing 140 percent increase. The number of states increased from 24 to 34, reflecting the country's intense interest in settling beyond the Ohio and Mississippi river valleys. New states emerged in every region.

There were 10 presidents during these 30 years. Andrew Jackson, the first "modern" Democrat, was inaugurated as the nation's seventh president in 1829. Abraham Lincoln, the first "modern" Republican, was sworn in as the sixteenth chief executive in 1860. In between, there was not a single two-term president.

During the three decades preceding 1860, there were a number of phrases, slogans, legislation and politicians' names that became household words and benchmarks for a nation on a path toward an inevitable Civil War.

"Slavery" was peculiarly Southern, where economics centered on agriculture — tobacco and cotton — and an African American slave labor force. In the North, an area with more advanced manufacturing and industrialization, the sentiment usually was "antislavery." As the nation grew, and new states were admitted into the union, both pro- and anti-slavery proponents became vocal.

The "Missouri Compromise" was a piece of Washington legislation adopted in 1820. It allowed the admission of Missouri as a slave state. Maine was cut from Massachusetts and admitted to balance the U.S. Senate with representatives from both slave and "free" states. This compromise outlawed slavery in the Louisiana Territory, north of Missouri's southern boundary. Even at that early date the issues evoked concern. "We have a wolf by the ears," Thomas Jefferson said, "and we can neither safely hold him, nor safely let him go."

"States' rights" was a term associated with South Carolina and its prominent political leader, John C. Calhoun. This political position suggests a strict interpretation of the U.S. Constitution as it relates to federal government powers and state autonomy. By the time Calhoun became Jackson's vice president, states' rights — "sectionalism" — was a source of heated debate in Washington and elsewhere in the country.

"Nullification" was another word attributed to Calhoun. He, along with fellow South Carolinians and other Southerners, said individual states existed as sovereignities prior to the formation of the United States.

Therefore the states, themselves, could interpret the U.S. Constitution and "nullify" anything they considered "unauthorized" — or unconstitutional. South Carolina put its nullification philosophy into action in 1832, after Congress passed legislation that put protective duties — tariffs — on manufactured goods. Congressmen from the north and west supported the bill; Southerners, who had little manufacturing, disliked it. So, South Carolina enacted an "Ordinance of Nullification," which declared the national law unauthorized.

"Secede" means to withdraw, or break away, from membership in an association. The act of seceding is known as secession. South Carolina, for example, considered its right to nullify a federal law an issue worthy of seceding from the union.

Henry Clay, a Kentucky Senator, helped the nation avoid a serious crisis over the tariff issue. Clay, a native Virginian and former secretary of state, was an unsuccessful presidential candidate against Jackson the previous year. Clay devised a new tariff law designed to lower duties over a period of years. His plan gave South Carolina enough political elbow room to repeal its nullification ordinance. In time, Clay became known as the Great Compromiser.

Massachusetts Senator Daniel Webster gained national fame in 1830, when he spoke out against South Carolina's nullification principles. He served as secretary of state for both Presidents Harrison and Tyler, and he was an unsuccessful Whig candidate for president in 1836. Webster was appointed secretary of state in July 1850, just four months after delivering his stirring speech in the U.S. Senate in support of the "Compromise of 1850." This compromise was designed to prevent a national split over the issue of territorial slavery. In his famous "Seventh of March" speech, Webster said, "I wish to speak today, not as a Massachusetts man, nor as a Northern man, but as an American." He urged his fellow Northerners to accept a stronger fugitive slave law and Southerners to give up all thought of succession.

Illinois Senator Stephen Douglas, at 5'4" and 90 pounds, was known as the "Little Giant." He maneuvered the Clay-inspired "Compromise of 1850" through Congress. The bill tried to determine the fate of the land won in the Mexican War and, again, raised the issue of territorial slavery. California was admitted as a free state; the rest of the Southwest was divided into two sections: one with slavery and one without.

While adopting the 1850 compromise legislation, Congress also passed an act to abolish slave trading in the District of Columbia and help slave owners recover runaways. Known as the "Fugitive Slave Act," it was a new law for an old problem. It furthered ill feelings between sectionalist leaders as well as proponents of both slavery and "abolitionism." "Abolitionism" is the act of abolishing or doing away with something. In this case, the term applied to abolishing slavery.

Uncle Tom's Cabin was written in 1852 by Harriet Beecher Stowe and heralded by abolitionists. It avoided self-righteous accusations, and described slaves as victims of an evil,

Southern system. It had a major impact on Northerner sympathizers. In England, Queen Victoria cried when she read it.

Senator Douglas returned to national prominence in 1854, when he introduce the Kansas-Nebraska Bill to establish a territorial government west of Missouri, to divide the region in both slave and free sections, and repeal the law that banned slavery north of Missouri's southern border.

The Kansas-Nebraska Act, the result of Senator Douglas' bill, prompted thousands of both pro- and anti-slavery supporters to pour into Kansas to take over the government. There were considerable incidences of death and destruction — thus the term "Bleeding Kansas" — including a raid at Pottawatomie led by abolitionist John Brown. Northerners, including Douglas' own supporters, were outraged by the Kansas act. The legislation destroyed the Senator's presidential aspirations, and led the nation further down the road toward an inevitable national conflict.

In the "Panic of 1857," a number of banks collapsed after Americans dropped grain prices, brought on when Russia increased its grain exports. The South generally survived the 1857 panic because of Europe's continued demand for cotton. Southerners, aware of the power of the cotton trade and convinced the North would avoid interfering with their states' rights philosophy, proclaimed "Cotton is King."

In its famous "Dred Scott Decision," the U.S. Supreme Court ruled in 1857 that the Missouri Compromise was unconstitutional because it deprived slave owners the right to take their "property" where they wanted. In this case, slave Scott was taken into the Wisconsin Territory where slavery was barred.

A one-term Illinois Congressman named Abraham Lincoln rose to prominence in 1858, challenging incumbent Senator Douglas. Lincoln, in his famous "House Divided" speech at the senatorial nominating convention, predicted "this government cannot endure permanently half slave and half free." Many, including conservative Northerners, took his speech as a call for abolishing slavery — a position Lincoln never supported prior to the Civil War.

Throughout the campaign, particularly in a notable joint appearance in Freeport, Ill., Lincoln pressed Douglas on two issues: the Senator's Kansas-Nebraska Bill and the Supreme Court's Scott decision. Of Douglas it can be said that he "won the battle but lost the war": he defeated Lincoln in the Illinois senate race, but he lost to Lincoln in the presidential election two years later.

"Dixie" was a song written in 1859 by a Ohio musician, Daniel Emmett. It begins, "I wish I was in the land of cotton." In time, it became the unofficial song of the Confederacy.

Abraham Lincoln was elected president in 1860, and South Carolina seceded a month later. Then, in quick succession prior to the 1861 inaugural, the union lost six more states: Mississippi, Florida, Alabama, Georgia, Louisiana, and Texas. In time, four more states joined the new Confederate States of America: Virginia, Arkansas, Tennessee, and North Carolina.

▼

The Valentine

1015 East Clay Street, Richmond, Virginia 23219 804-649-0711

The Museum of the Life and History of Richmond

History Will Never Be The Same.

Kansas was admitted into the union just five weeks before Lincoln's inaugural. This new state aligned with 18 other Northern, "non-slave" states in the Northeast, north of the Ohio River, and just beyond the Mississippi. The "North" included the states of California, Connecticut, Illinois, Indiana, Iowa, Maine, Massachusetts, Michigan, Minnesota, New Hampshire, New Jersey, New York, Ohio, Pennsylvania, Oregon, Rhode Island, Vermont, and Wisconsin; and the territories of Colorado, Dakota Nebraska, Nevada, and Washington.

Separating the North and South were "border states" — Delaware, Maryland, Kentucky, and Missouri, as well as the District of Columbia and the New Mexico Territory.

Closing

Elizabeth Lindsay Lomax, the widow of an Army officer, lived in Washington and kept a private diary in the 1850s and 1860s. On Inaugu-

ration Day — March 4, 1861 — she wrote: "This dreaded day has at last arrived. Thank Heaven all is peaceful and quiet." Mrs. Lomax's newspaper was printed late that day, in order to carry the new president's inaugural address. "We read it aloud," she wrote in diary, and added, "there was no doubt of its sanity and its excellence."

Lincoln spoke of a nation on the brink of division. "Physically speaking," he said, "we can not separate. We can not remove our respective sections from each other nor build an impassable wall between them." He added, "A husband and wife may be divorced and go out of the presence and beyond the reach of each other, but the different parts of our country can not do this." But the different parts of the country did build an impassable wall. Just ten weeks later, Confederate cannon fired on Fort Sumpter at Charleston, South Carolina. The Civil War was underway.

Officers of The United States Army (USA) and Confederate States of America (CSA)

Throughout the text of this book, for the sake of brevity, most officers are listed by their last name, preceded by their command — USA or CSA. On this page, we list the officers with their full names.

UNION OFFICERS

Averell, Gen. William Woods
Banks, Gen. Nathaniel Prentiss
Buford, Gen. Jonh
Burnside, Gen. Ambrose Everett
Butler, Gen. Benjamin Franklin
Crook, Gen. George
Custer, Gen. George Armstrong
Davis, Col. Benjamin Franklin
Davis, Col. Hasbrouck
Duffie, Gen. Alfred Nattie
Ellsworth, Col. Ephraim Elmer
Fremont, Gen. John Charles
French, Gen. William Henry
Grant, Gen. Ulysses Simpson
Halleck, Gen. Henry Wager
Hancock, Gen. Winfield Scott
Hartsuff, Gen. George Lucus
Hooker, Gen. Joseph ("Fighting Joe")
Hunter, Gen. David
Kearny, Gen. Philip
Kilpatrick, Gen. Hugh Judson
McClellan, Gen. George Brinton ("Young Napoleon")
McPherson, Gen. James Birdseye
Meigs, Quartermaster Gen. Montgomery Cunningham
Miles, Col. Dixon S.
Milroy, Gen. Robert Huston
Pleasants, Lt. Col. Henry
Pope, Gen. John
Porter, Adm. David D.
Rathbone, Maj. Henry
Reno, Gen. Jesse Lee
Scott, Gen. Winfield
Sedgwick, Gen. John
Shields, Gen. James
Sheridan, Gen. Phillip Henry ("Little Phil")
Sherman, Gen. William Tecumseh
Sigel, Gen. Franz
Stoneman, Gen. George
Stoughton, Gen. Edwin Henry
Thomas, Gen. George Henry
Torbert, Gen. Alfred Thomas Archimedes
Wallace, Gen. Lewis

CONFEDERATE OFFICERS

Anderson, Gen. Richard Heron
Ashby, Gen. Turner
Beauregard, Gen. Pierre Gustave Toutant (P.G.T.)
Breckinridge, Gen. John Cabell
Early, Gen. Jubal Anderson ("Old Jube")
Ewell, Gen. Richard Stoddert
Hampton, Gen. Wade
Hill, Gen. Ambrose Powell (A.P.)
Hunton, Gen. Eppa
Jackson, Gen. Thomas Jonathan ("Stonewall")
Jenkins, Gen. Albert Gallatin
Johnston, Gen. Joseph Eggleston
Jones, Gen. William Edmonson
Lee, Gen. Fitzhugh ("Fitz")
Lee, Gen. Robert Edward
Lomax, Gen. Lunsford Lindsay
Longstreet, Gen. James ("Pete")
Magruder, Gen. John Bankhead
Marr, Lt. John Q.
McCausland, Gen. John
Mosby, Col. John Singleton
Paxton, Gen. Elisha Franklin
Pettigrew, Gen. James Johnston
Pickett, Gen. George Edward
Rosser, Gen. Thomas Lafayette
Stuart, Gen. James Ewell Brown (J.E.B., "Jeb")
Withers, Col. R.E.

Photo: Richmond Newspapers

Julia Ward Howe wrote "The Battle Hymn of the Republic."

TOUR 1
Carlisle, PA to Sharpsburg, MD

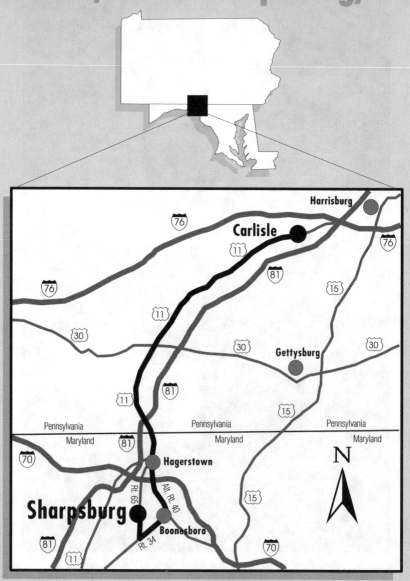

Tour 1
Cumberland Valley

About This Tour

This first tour route covers the Cumberland Valley of Pennsylvania and Maryland, from Carlisle, PA, to Sharpsburg, MD. This route is the first of four in succession — along with Tour routes 2, 3 and 4, Middle Valley, Shenandoah Valley and Southern Valley — that covers the long stretch of the Great Valley that runs through Pennsylvania, Maryland, West Virginia and Virginia. This tour route ends at Sharpsburg, MD, near Shepherdstown, WV, two localities where you can plan evening dining and lodging.

Travel Tips

I-81 is a heavily traveled interstate highway. There are two words to describe this major thoroughfare: trucks and construction. The various lane changes and narrow-lane construction sites create potential for congestion and accidents. As a result, this tour — and the succeeding two in the Great Valley — leads you south mainly along US 11. And that's just as well, because US 11 is a more historic route, following the path of the old Great Wagon Road, and it leads through the heart of a number of quaint, attractive Cumberland Valley communities.

Generally, US 11 is a dual-lane, divided highway. Remember, though, this is great farming country, so be alert to slow-moving farm vehicles.

History, Geography

The Tuscarora and Kittatinny mountains, parts of the Appalachians, rise up to the west of the Cumberland Valley — the northern part of a vast trough that stretches into Maryland and Virginia to the southwest. The Catoctin Mountains form the valley's eastern boundary. The Susquehanna River, originating high in the Appalachians, cuts through the highlands at Blue Mountain. Harrisburg, the Pennsylvania state capital, is located on the fringe of the valley, at the Susquehanna water gap.

The Cumberland Valley stretches from Harrisburg south to the Potomac River. The name "Cumberland" was first used in this region in 1754, with the construction of a fort that served as the headquarters for George Washington and British Gen. Edward Braddock during the French and Indian War. The fort was named for William Augustus, the Duke of Cumberland, who was the son of England's George II. Cumberland is also the name of the Pennsylvania county located just across the Susquehanna from Harrisburg.

The Cumberland Valley was once the home of various Native American tribes. The Great Wagon Road through the valley followed an old buffalo trail used by Indians to travel north and south from the Southern highlands to the Great Lakes. German farmers began settling in this region in the early 1700s, followed almost immediately by Scotch-Irish pioneers. The fertile valley was a haven for German farmers, and their culture and lifestyle remain in evidence to this day.

This region of Pennsylvania and Maryland was a haven for runaway African-Americans during the Civil War. Quakers ran the Underground Railroad in this area, just north of the Mason-Dixon Line. Civil War action took place throughout the valley, beginning in 1862, and continuing through the next two years — both before and after the Battle of Antietam and the Battle of Gettysburg. CSA Gen. Early was back in this region in 1864 on an attempt to invade Washington, D.C.

Getting Here

This tour route begins south of Harrisburg, PA, and directions are given from I-81 as well as the Pennsylvania Turnpike (I-76), which both converge with US 11.

DIRECTIONS

Harrisburg to Carlisle, PA
Leave the Harrisburg, PA, vicinity on either US 11, I-81 or the Pennsylvania Turnpike (I-76).

Note that this Pennsylvania city is located at the Susquehanna River water gap, where Englishman John Harris established a trading post in the early 18th century. By the mid-1700s, John's son — John Jr. — operated a ferry across the Susquehanna: thus, Harris' Ferry. John Jr. laid out a town in 1785. Then, questions arose over what to name the village. The town is located in Dauphin County — a name of French origin — so state legislators thought it should be named Louisburg, for France's Louis XVI. But the community remembered its founder, and Harrisburg was the choice. John Harris Jr. died in 1791. Harrisburg became the state capital in 1810, and it was incorporated as a city in 1860, just a year before the outbreak of the Civil War. Harrisburg escaped major war action, although there was a bit of action just across the Susquehanna at Lemoyne (see Tour 5: Gettysburg).

DIRECTIONS

Continue south on US 11 from Harrisburg for 18 miles to Middlesex, PA. Here, US 11 intersects with I-81 (Exit 11). Continue south on US 11 from this
— continued on page 3

Governor Andrew G. Curtin
Pennsylvania Gov. Andrew Gregg Curtin served throughout the Civil War, and actively supported the Union cause. He was considered a possible candidate for vice president in 1868. He lost the bid, but he was named minister to Russia by President Grant. Camp Curtin, a Union training (rendezvous) camp south of Harrisburg, was named in his honor.

— continued from page 2
junction, and go south 3.2 miles to the entrance to the U.S. Army military post, Carlisle Barracks, north of the community of Carlisle, PA. Turn left into the post; a guard will direct you to park on the right just inside the post.

U.S. Army Military History Institute and Museum

Carlisle Barracks, Building 22
Carlisle, PA 17012-5008   717-245-3611

Carlisle Barracks, home of the U.S. Army's War College, has been the site of a military installation since the French and Indian War in the 1750s. Later, George Washington reviewed troops here during the Whiskey Rebellion. In July 1863, CSA Gen. Stuart's men skirmished with a Union force and burned some of the old barracks. Carlisle Indian School, the first non-reservation school for Native Americans, opened in 1879 at Carlisle Barracks; Olympian Jim Thorpe was a student.

The U.S. Army Military History Institute, located on the military installation grounds, has a military library and a display of some Civil War artifacts. The library and display justify a visit to the grounds of this attractive, serene open military post. The institute has a vast collection of Civil War books, papers and photographs, and it possesses a voluminous record of Civil War regiments — both Union and Confederate. It is open (no charge) Monday through Friday from 8 AM to 4:30 PM. It is open on weekends during the summer but is closed on all federal holidays.

DIRECTIONS

Carlisle Barracks to Shippensburg, PA

Return to U.S. 11, turn left, and continue a mile to the heart of Carlisle, PA.

Frenchman James Le Tort, who traded with the Native Americans, built a cabin in this region. By the mid-1750s, the settlement was called Carlisle — named for an English town. This was the home of two signers of the Declaration of Independence, James Wilson and George Ross. It was also the home of Mary Ludwig Hays, the Revolutionary War heroine also known as "Molly Pitcher." Dickinson College, one of Pennsylvania's oldest schools of higher education, was chartered here in 1783, and one of its graduates was President James Buchanan, who was born just to the south near McConnellsburg, PA. CSA Gen. Ewell's troops camped at the college in June 1863, just before Gettysburg. On another occasion, Confederates camped in Carlisle planned to move on Harrisburg, but were ordered to nearby Cashtown instead.

DIRECTIONS

In Carlisle, follow signs for US 11 south, and continue south 11 miles to downtown Shippensburg, PA.

Shippensburg, PA

Settled in the 1730s by Edward Shippen, this is the second oldest Pennsylvania town west of the Susquehanna. One of Shippen's relatives, Peggy Shippen, married Benedict Arnold. The Cumberland-Franklin county line runs through Shippensburg. From here, USA cavalry monitored CSA Gen. Robert E. Lee's movements into Chambersburg.

DIRECTIONS

Shippensburg to Chambersburg, PA

Follow signs for US 11 south, and continue 11 miles to downtown Chambersburg, PA.

CHAMBERSBURG, PA

This Pennsylvania county suffered more military activity during the Civil War than any comparable area in the "North." Strategically located in the heart of the Cumberland Valley, this county was the target of three major Confederate cavalry raids. CSA Gen. Stuart raided here in October 1862. CSA Gen. Jenkins arrived in 1863. CSA Gen. McCausland fought here in 1864. Confederate plans for Gettysburg were formed here, as well. The 1864 Confederate raid left Chambersburg, the county seat, in smoldering ruin. It was the only northern town so burned during the Civil War. US 11 becomes Philadelphia Avenue and then Main Street through Chambersburg.

Benjamin Chambers settled here in the 1730s, built a sawmill and a gristmill, and laid out the town in 1764. Chambersburg was John Brown's base of operations prior to his raid on Harpers Ferry in 1859. Brown posed as a prospector while collecting arms; his headquarters was located at 225 E. King Street, a street that intersects US 11 near the heart of downtown.

Following the 1862 Battle of Antietam, Chambersburg served as a supply and hospital center for the Union Army. CSA Gen. Lee camped here in June 1863, just before Gettysburg, with an estimated 65,000 Confederate soldiers. Two-thirds of Chambersburg was destroyed by fire in July 1864. CSA Gen. McCausland demanded $100,000 in gold or $500,000 in U.S. greenbacks from townspeople to repay Virginia for USA Gen. Hunter's Shenandoah

Photo: Antoinette W. Roades

The graceful arch of Burnside's Bridge at Antietam serves as a reminder of one of the bloodiest battles between Union and Confederate forces in the Civil War. (See page 11)

Valley destruction. The Confederates made their demand at daybreak; at 9 AM, despite objections from some Southern troops, the town was torched. More than 500 structures were ruined.

DIRECTIONS

Chambersburg to Memorial Square

Continue on US 11 — Main Street — to the downtown main intersection, where US 11 (Main Street) and US 30 (Lincoln Way) meet.

MEMORIAL SQUARE

Memorial Square, with a fountain, was known as "The Diamond" in the 19th century. On June 26, 1863, CSA Gens. Robert E. Lee and A.P. Hill held council at this spot. There is a star on the pavement just south of the fountain to mark the place. The memorial fountain and statue were erected in 1878 to honor soldiers from Franklin County.

DIRECTIONS

Memorial Square to Franklin County Courthouse

The county courthouse is located on the northeast corner of Memorial Square.

FRANKLIN COUNTY COURTHOUSE

The Franklin County Courthouse served as the 1863 headquarters of the provost marshall of CSA Gen. Ewell's Corps. As a result, a Confederate flag flew from the top of this building for a time.

DIRECTIONS

Chambersburg to Greencastle, PA

Continue south on US 11 for 11 miles to Greencastle.

GREENCASTLE, PA

A Union cavalry unit arrived in Greencastle after escaping from CSA Gen. Stonewall Jackson's rout of Harpers Ferry in September 1862 (see Tour 2: Middle Valley).

MCCONNELLSBURG, PA

Just west of Chambersburg is McConnellsburg, a community that avid Civil War buffs might want to visit — if only for a drive through town. McConnellsburg was incorporated in 1814 and laid out by Daniel and William McConnell. Two brief fights occurred in here on June 24 and 29, 1863, just before Gettysburg. This is where CSA Gen. Bradley Johnson camped after his Chambersburg raid in 1864. There is a monument, south of town on US 522, that notes the campsite. James Buchanan — the only Pennsylvanian elected president — was born near McConnellsburg in Cove Gap. The site is in the Buchanan Birthplace Historical State Park at Cove Mountain. Buchanan, elected president in 1857, tried to keep peace between the North and South. Still, he remained passive when South Carolina seceded in 1860.

Chambersburg
Side Trip

And there were 20 Confederate casualties here in a brief fight June 20, 1863, just before Gettysburg. USA Corp. William Rihl, a member of the First New York Cavalry, was killed north of Greencastle on June 20, 1863, just before Gettysburg, and became the first Union casualty north of the Mason-Dixon Line. (A marker notes the site, on US 11 about a mile north of Greencastle's downtown.) Confederates controlled this town for nearly three weeks prior to Gettysburg.

DIRECTIONS

Greencastle to Town Square
US 11 through Greencastle becomes Carlisle Street. The town square is at the Carlisle Street intersection with PA 16, or Baltimore Street.

TOWN SQUARE

Union Hotel, the large red brick building on the southwest corner of Town Square, is thought to be the place where John Brown stayed in 1859. On the northeast corner of the square, across from the bank, is a

---

Greencastle Side Trip

Mercersburg, PA

Just west of Greencastle is Mercersburg, PA. This is another place that an avid Civil War historian might want to see. This town was named for Virginian Hugh Mercer, who was killed at the Battle of Princeton in the American Revolution. President Buchanan's log cabin birthplace is located at Mercersburg Academy. Harriet Lane, Buchanan's niece and his White House hostess, was born in Mercersburg. The community, 6 miles north of the Mason-Dixon Line, was a haven for abolitionist activity during the two decades that preceded the war. Fugitive slave hunters claimed the ground here "swallowed up" their prey. They said "there must be an underground road somewhere." Thus, the origin of the term "Underground Railroad."

Greencastle Side Trip

Waynesboro, PA

Just east of Greencastle is Waynesboro, PA, a place for Civil War enthusiasts. Waynesboro was settled in the mid-18th century and laid out in 1797. Founder James Wallace Jr, who served Gen. "Mad" Anthony Wayne in the American Revolution, named the town for his former commander. The Mason-Dixon Line's 105th milestone, a Crown-Stone marker that bears the crest of Lord Baltimore of Maryland and William Penn of Pennsylvania, is located just south of town (See State Line, PA, later in the tour.) John Brown taught Sunday School in town. In July 1863, CSA Gen. Early's troops raided the town and demanded the townspeople bake them bread. At Mont Alto, north of Waynesboro, the Episcopal chapel on the Penn State campus was the final refuge for some of John Brown's men. When Brown's raid at Harpers Ferry collapsed, his men sought sanctuary in the church.

VIRGINIA

A MONTHLY NEWSLETTER
DEVOTED TO POPULAR VIRGINIA HISTORY

Virginia is a new and informative newsletter on popular history, published by Michael P. Gleason, author of the Insiders' Guide to The Civil War.

The Commonwealth's rich history comes to life each month in the colorful eight page issue.

For a one year subscription rate of $29.95, you'll recieve 12 colorful issues and a bounty of up-to-date information about atractions, events and news about the people and places of Virginia.

A perfect gift for the history buff.

shoe store that was once the location of Ziegler General Store. Ziegler's was a busy place in June 1863, when Confederates marched through town. A week later, after Gettysburg, a 17-mile Confederate wagon train passed though this vicinity.

DIRECTIONS

Greencastle to State Line, PA
Continue 5 miles south of Greencastle to State Line, PA.

STATE LINE, PA - PENNSYLVANIA-MARYLAND BOUNDARY

The Mason-Dixon Line — the border between Pennsylvania and Maryland — crosses here. The line was surveyed by Charles Mason and Jeremiah Dixon in 1765 to align the border between the Pennsylvania and Maryland colonies. During the Civil War, the Mason-Dixon Line became an artificial "boundary" between the North and the South. The Potomac River, however, is a more realistic boundary between the two sections.

DIRECTIONS

State Line to Hagerstown, MD
US 11 crosses into Washington County, MD. US 11 continues 4 miles to the Hagerstown town limits. Follow US 11 signs — just inside the town limits, US 11 becomes South Burhams Boulevard, a route that weaves its way through town but avoids the downtown business.

HAGERSTOWN, MD

Here, both US 11 and I-81 cross the historic, east-west National Road. An extension of old Highway 40 across Maryland, the National Road — or Cumberland Trail — was the nation's first federally-funded highway. The National Road runs west to Cumberland, the site of western Maryland's historic fort and, later, the end of the line for the C&O Canal.

Jonathan Hager settled here in the mid-18th century, and named his new community Elizabeth Town — for his wife, Elizabeth Kershner Hager. But new settlers called it Hager's Town, which became a one-word name in 1814.

Because a number of roads converged on Hagerstown, the community was a busy place during the war. Troops of both armies frequently passed through Hagerstown, particularly before and after the Antietam and Gettysburg campaigns in 1862 and 1863. More than 2,000 Confederates, victims of battles at South Mountain and Antietam, are buried at Rose Hill Cemetery in Hagerstown. In 1864, CSA Gen. Early's troops demanded $20,000 ransom from Hagerstown's residents or they would burn the town down.

DIRECTIONS

Hagerstown to Boonsboro, MD
Continue following South Burhams Boulevard southeast through Hagerstown. Crossing Virginia Avenue, Burhams Boulevard becomes Wilson Boulevard. Take Wilson 1.5 miles to where Wilson Boulevard ends at Frederick Street (US 40 ALT). Turn right on US 40 ALT. Note historical markers along US 40 ALT. Along this route, CSA Gen. Longstreet entered Hagerstown on his way north to establish a base of operations in Pennsylvania. From this area, Confederate and Union
— continued on page 9

Oliver Wendall Holmes

In 1862, after the Battle of Antietam, two women — Mrs. Howard Kennedy and her daughter, Annie — found a wounded Union soldier lying in a Hagerstown road. The pair cared for the officer at their home, Mount Prospect. The captain was Oliver Wendall Holmes Jr. Oliver's father went looking for the young soldier, and his travels inspired the poem, "My Search for the Captain." Oliver Jr. graduated from Harvard in 1861 at the age of 20. After the war, in 1866, he graduated from Harvard Law School. Later, he became an Associate Justice of the U.S. Supreme Court. The Kennedy home, where he was nursed to health, is located on W. Washington Street in Hagerstown.

Hagerstown Personalities

Hagerstown Side Trip: Williamsport, MD

South of Hagerstown, on the Potomac River, is Williamsport, MD, just across from Falling Waters, WV. CSA Gen. Jackson was nearly killed while sitting under an oak tree at Falling Waters on July 2, 1861. A Union cannonball struck a tree limb; the falling limb missed Jackson and he escaped unharmed. Then, in July 1863, CSA Gen. Lee's troops — retreating from Gettysburg — were attacked by Union forces at the Battle of Falling Waters. The Confederates escaped to the south after tearing down nearby buildings for lumber to make a bridge to ford the swollen Potomac. CSA Gen. Pettigrew of North Carolina was killed in the battle.

Hagerstown Side Trip

— continued from page 8
forces went into battle at South Mountain and Antietam.

Continue south on US 40 ALT and continue through Funkstown on Baltimore Street to the National Pike (all US 40 ALT signs). Continue on US 40 ALT for 7 miles to Boonsboro. In Boonsboro, US 40 ALT becomes Main Street.

BOONSBORO, MD

CSA Gen. Stonewall Jackson was nearly captured at Boonsboro in September 1862. Camped a mile east of town, on the road from Turner's Gap, he walked his horse and barely slipped from a group of Union cavalry. There was action in the streets of Boonsboro, just before Antietam in September 1862, when CSA Gen. Fitzhugh Lee's cavalry fought Union soldiers. Churches and homes were used as hospitals after Antietam, and troops fought here the next year, in July 1863, after Gettysburg.

BOONSBOROUGH MUSEUM

113 N. Main St.
Boonsboro, MD   301-432-5151

Located on Boonsboro's Main Street, on the left side of the street at Brining Lane, this little building is within a block of the downtown's main intersection. This museum has an extensive Civil War exhibit. It is open on Sundays from 1:00 to 5:00 PM from May through September.

Photo: AP

U.S. Supreme Court Justice Oliver Wendell Holmes (right) is shown here in 1922 as he attended a White House reception with Chief Justice William Taft, former president.

DIRECTIONS

Boonsboro to Sharpsburg, MD
A block beyond the Boonsborough Museum, at the traffic signal, turn right onto MD 34, and proceed west 6.3 miles to Sharpsburg.

SHARPSBURG, MD

Enter Sharpsburg on MD 34, which becomes Main Street. In 1763, at the end of the French and Indian War, a real estate investor laid out a town here on Antietam Creek, where it flows into the Potomac River. The settlement was named for Horatio Sharpe, governor of Maryland at the time. Antietam is an Algonquian word that means "swift water."

Sharpsburg to Antietam National Battlefield Visitor Center
Continue on MD 34 (Main Street) just beyond National Cemetery (on the left), to MD 65. Turn right on MD 65 (Church Street, Hagerstown Pike) and go 0.8 miles to the Antietam National Battlefield Visitor Center.

ANTIETAM NATIONAL BATTLEFIELD VISITOR CENTER

Box 158
Sharpsburg, MD 21782   301-432-5124

This fine National Park Service (NPS) facility is open from 8:30 AM to 5:00 PM daily except New Years Day, Thanksgiving Day and Christmas Day. There is a fee: $4.00 per family; $2.00 for persons ages 17-61. All visitor center facilities are wheelchair accessible. The visitor center features exhibits and audiovisual programs. The center provides an extensive, informative brochure, which outlines all important information on the Battle of Antietam. The brochure includes a motor tour route that outlines all significant sights in the area.

Antietam — Sharpsburg — was fought on Sept. 17, 1862. It has been described as the bloodiest day of the Civil War. More soldiers were killed or wounded here than on any other single day. There were more than 25,000 casualties, equally divided between the North and South.

The battle climaxed the first of two attempts by CSA Gen. Robert E. Lee to take the war above the Potomac: to encourage anti-war sentiments in the North, gain support from this border state, solicit European interest in the Confederacy, and draw Union troops from Virginia. The course of the war was greatly altered on this summer day, when 40,000-plus CSA troops faced a Union force over double in size. While the battle was not a tactical victory for the Federals, it was just what President Lincoln needed to announced his Emancipation Proclamation, which

USA Gen. Jesse Reno
Union Gen. Jesse L. Reno was killed at South Mountain in 1862. The town of Reno, in western Pennsylvania's oil country, is named for General Reno.

South Mountain Personality

Photo: AP

The Sherrick Farmhouse with a Civil War soldier statue in the foreground on the grounds of the Antietam National Battleground.

shifted the war from a political issue to a struggle to free slaves.

The stage for Antietam was set after CSA Gen. Lee pushed north into Maryland after his August victory at Manassas (Bull Run). He was followed closely by USA Gen. McClellan (see Tour 6: Northern Piedmont). Lee sent CSA Gen. Jackson to capture Harpers Ferry. Lee stayed on the western side of Antietam Creek to delay the approaching Union army, crossing west into the valley through the gaps in South Mountain (see Tour 7: Middle Piedmont). When Jackson returned from Harpers Ferry, the Southern troops consolidated for battle at Sharpsburg.

Antietam was fought in a 12-square-mile area — in three phases: morning, midday and afternoon. At dawn, USA Gen. Hooker's artillery struck at Jackson's troops in a cornfield just north of town. Hooker's men rushed the Confederates, who drove back the Union forces by 7 AM. An hour later, the Northerners counterat-

tacked and regained some of Hooker's lost ground. Later, the opposing armies fought in an area now called the West Woods near the Dunkard Church. Forces under USA Gen. Sedgwick suffered numerous casualties. USA Gen. French's men moved to support Sedgwick, resulting in a four-hour battle that became known as Bloody Lane. In mid-afternoon, USA Gen. Burnside succeeded in crossing a stone bridge — it now bears his name — over Antietam Creek. He advanced on the Confederate's right flank, just south of Sharpsburg. The Southerners were saved when CSA Gen. Hill's troops, on a forced march from Harpers Ferry, arrived in time to stop the advancing Federals.

"War is a dreadful thing, " said Clara Barton, who treated the wounded during and after Antietam. "Oh, my God, can't this civil strife be brought to and end."

Ask NPS counselors about side trips to the gaps in South Mountain, scenes of other Civil War action.

DIRECTIONS

Sharpsburg to Shepherdstown, WV

Return on Church Street (MD 35) to Main Street. Make a right on Main Street and go 3.4 miles — across the Potomac River — into Shepherdstown.

The Potomac River forms the border between Maryland and West Virginia. This area of West Virginia was settled as part of the western region of Virginia. West Virginia broke away from Virginia and obtained separate statehood in June 1863 — just before Gettysburg. Here in the panhandle, as in the rest of the Cumberland and Shenandoah valleys, loyalties were mixed.

West Virginians

West Virginia, it can be said, was a child of war. The Civil War pitted "brother against brother" and — in Virginia — "county against county." Prior to the war there already existed in Virginia a difference in social life between the eastern and western regions. These, in turn, led to political feuds. There were other differences, too: the distance between the two regions, the mountain barriers, the diverse physical settings, the separate commercial alliances and various misunderstandings and jealousies.

In early 1861, following President Lincoln's inaugural in Washington, crowds assembled in unorganized meetings throughout the western counties to debate the likelihood that Virginia might follow South Carolina's secession from the nation.

The first organized meeting, a mass convention, was held at Clarksburg, VA — now in West Virginia — on April 22, only five days after Virginia approved an Ordinance of Secession. This group adopted a resolution that proposed a representative convention at Wheeling in May. Representatives of 24 Virginia counties sent delegates to the May 13 meeting that became known as the First Wheeling Convention. Delegates at the three-day meeting decided to hold a more widely representative session in June.

The Second Wheeling Convention met in Wheeling on June 11. This time, 35 counties were represented. This second convention reorganized the state's western counties into a separate state government, which it called the Restored Government of Virginia. It was this "restored government" in Virginia that made West Virginia's creation possible. The new legislature approved West Virginia's creation and that technically satisfied a U.S. constitutional requirement that new states can be created only with the consent of the state whose territory is involved. Francis H. Pierpoint, a forceful orator from Marion County, was elected governor of West Virginia.

A convention met again in August 1861. It approved a state name — Kanawha — and passed an ordinance to select delegates to a constitutional convention. In November 1861, delegates approved a new name — West Virginia — and adopted a constitution, which received voter approval in April 1862. This first West Virginia constitution was silent on the question of slavery, however, and the U.S. Congress refused to admit the new state until it adopted an amendment providing for the emancipation of slaves.

The bill for admitting West Virginia into the Union passed the U.S. Senate on July 14, 1862. It was approved by the U.S. House on December 30, and President Lincoln signed the legislation at midnight on December 31, 1862. On April 20, 1863, after receiving word that West Virginians ratified their constitutional amendment, President Lincoln issued a proclamation that provided statehood for the territory 60 days later. Thus, West Virginia entered the Union as the 35th state on June 20, 1863.

The northern and western boundaries of West Virginia, of course, were fixed because they were the Virginia borders with Maryland, Pennsylvania, Ohio, and Kentucky. The eastern boundary, along the Appalachian Mountains, bordered Virginia. This line holds a unique place in history: it is the only dual-state boundary created without a formal survey. Thus, the boundary was created with the county lines that existed at the time.

It is clear that the earliest conventions in Wheeling were uncertain which counties to include in the new state. There were numerous proposals on what territory to claim. One included Buchanan and Wise counties in southwest Virginia, which would have given West Virginia a panhandle on the south, similar to the panhandle along the Ohio River west of Pittsburgh, PA. Another proposal would have placed the eastern boundary along the Blue Ridge Mountains, taking in all of Virginia's Great Valley region from Winchester to Abingdon.

The matter was finally resolved when West Virginia included McDowell, Mercer, Monroe, Greenbrier, and Pocahontas counties. It allowed Pendleton, Hardy, Hampshire, Morgan, Berkeley, Jefferson and Frederick counties to vote on which state they wanted to join.

Only Frederick refrained from voting on the question. All the others joined West Virginia. Thus, in 1863 the number of Virginia counties dropped from an all-time high of 149 to 101— a total loss of 48.

Berkeley and Jefferson counties were important additions to West Virginia. These "eastern panhandle" counties, east of the Allegheny Mountains, were purposefully tacked on so the Baltimore and Ohio Railroad, a Union lifeline, could be wholly within Northern territory. The new state sent over 30,000 men to the Union army, and another 10,000 to the South. Over a dozen Union generals, and nearly as many Southern generals, were from West Virginia.

After the Civil War, Jefferson and Berkeley county leaders changed their minds. They wanted to return to Virginia. Virginia ultimately sued West Virginia to recover the two counties, but lost the battle in the U.S. Supreme Court. The loss of Berkeley and Jefferson in 1866 reduced the number of counties in Virginia to 99 and increased West Virginia's number to 50.

Following West Virginia's admission into the Union, Governor Pierpoint's administration moved from Wheeling to Alexandria— south of Washington — to govern the Virginia area under federal control. Pierpoint, known as the "Father of West Virginia," was named by President Lincoln as the

— continued on next page

— continued from previous page

Sheperdstown Personalities

provisional governor of Virginia after the Civil War. He moved to Richmond and served in that capacity until April 1868.

Another legal battle resulted after Virginia asked West Virginia to reunite after the Civil War's end. West Virginia refused. Virginia then asked West Virginia to pay part of the state debt at the time of separation. Legal battles continued over the debt issue until 1915, when the U.S. Supreme Court ruled that West Virginia owed Virginia $12,393,929.50. West Virginia made its final payment in 1939.

West Virginia's creation became the only permanent change in the nation's map as a result of the Civil War.

SHEPHERDSTOWN, WV

Imagine Shepherdstown — not Washington, D.C. — as the nation's capital. George Washington considered locating the capital here in 1790, but chose a place farther down the Potomac. Shepherdstown was settled by Thomas Shepherd, who received a land grant in the early 1730s. During the French and Indian War, in the early 1760s, the community was known as Mecklenburg. After the American Revolution, in 1787, James Rumsey demonstrated the first successful steamboat on the Potomac. A few years later, residents honored the founder and changed the town name to Shepherdstown. It is considered West Virginia's oldest municipality.

There was a skirmish at Blackford's Ford, downriver from Shepherdstown, on Sept. 20, 1862. CSA Gen. Lee, withdrawing from Antietam, was awakened just after midnight with news that Union forces captured his entire reserve artillery. The stories were exaggerated, but the Union did cross the Potomac and take four Confederate guns. The Northerners suffered heavy casualties when CSA Gen. Hill mounted a

vigorous counterattack. Earlier, in 1862, in this vicinity, CSA Gens. Jackson and Hill used the river ford on their way to the Battle of Antietam.

Sharpsburg, MD/ Shepherdstown, WV Accommodations

Refer to the Foreward for an explanation of the rating system for both the accommodations and restaurants.

PIPER HOUSE BED AND BREAKFAST
Antietam National Battlefield
P. O. Box 100
Sharpsburg, MD 21782   301-797-1862
$$$

This quaint, comfortable bed and breakfast is located right in the middle of the Antietam National Battlefield. The location is on hallowed ground, and the site is quiet and serene. Paula and Doug Reed lease the farmhouse as Heritage House Inns, Inc. They have just four rooms, each with a private bath, and you need to call at least eight weeks in advance during the tourist season to get in. Each room costs $79 nightly. The farmhouse offers period decor and a continental breakfast with muffins and fresh fruit. Piper House accepts younger guests, but request that youths be well-behaved. Confederate Gen. Longstreet used the house as a battlefield headquarters during the Battle of Antietam. The house has no affiliation with the National Park Service, which operates the national battlefield.

INN AT ANTIETAM
BED AND BREAKFAST

220 E. Main St.
Sharpsburg, MD 21782   301-432-6601
$$$

This gorgeous, white Victorian farm house is located on Main Street just south of the Antietam National Battlefield. Innkeepers Betty and Cal Fairbourn have turned this bed and breakfast into one of the finest lodging experiences in the region. This inn, bordering on the national battlefield parkland, has been featured in numerous regional and national magazines. The Fairbourns offer four suites. They welcome well-behaved children over six years of age. Pets are not accommodated, and smoking is prohibited throughout the house. Contact the inn at least a month in advance for reservations.

BAVARIAN INN AND LODGE

Route I, Box 30
Shepherdstown, WV 25443 304-876-2551
$$$-$$$$ 304-876-9355 (fax)

This elegant, 11-acre resort-style facility is a gem sitting on a bluff that overlooks the historic Potomac River. Established in the 1930s, the inn has been owned and managed the past 17 years by the Asam family — Carol, an Englishwoman, and her

husband, Erwin, a native of Munich, Germany. Erwin recently was chosen West Virginia's businessman of the year, which serves as fine a reference for the Bavarian Inn as anything. There are three rooms in the old inn, and 39 chalet rooms, many that feature a fireplace or a Jacuzzi. There is a tennis court and outdoor pool as well as a jogging path along the historic river canal. Expansion and additions are planned for 1994. Some rooms are non-smoking, and package rates are available. The dining experience here is equally divine (see Restaurants listing below).

There are other motels, inns and bed and breakfast facilities in the Sharpsburg, MD/Shepherdstown, WV area. If you have questions, or if you need a complete list of area accommodations, see a travel counselor at the Antietam National Battlefield Visitor Center (see listing in this tour). The National Park Service counselors are prohibited from making specific recommendations, but they have lists of addresses and telephone numbers that can be most helpful.

Sharpsburg, MD/ Shepherdstown, WV Restaurants

BAVARIAN INN AND LODGE

Route I, Box 30
Shepherdstown, WV 25443 304-876-2551
$$-$$$ 304-876-9355 (fax)

Like the inn and lodge (see listing above), the restaurants here are superb. Owner Erwin Asam is a native of Germany, so you might expect to find some of the finest German dining this side of — Munich. Actually, the cuisine here is known throughout the region; travelers from Washington, D.C., and Baltimore, MD, make the trek to the mountain village here just to sample Asam's award-winning menu. Two musts: Bavarian Sauerbraten ($13.75, complete with potato dumpling, red cabbage and a house salad), and Wiener Schnitzel ($15.50, and served with two vegetables and a house salad). And there's more: everything from venison and daily baked bread to a "game festival" each Spring that features rabbit, roast venison, pheasant and roast wild boar. Fireplaces provide a romantic European atmosphere, and the Rathskeller downstairs is a place for casual and weekend dining. The restaurants here are worth the visit to Shepherdstown. Breakfast is served from 7:30 to 11:00 AM; lunch is from 11:30 AM to 2:30 PM; dinner is served from 5:00 to 10 PM.

RED BYRD RESTAURANT
MD 34
Keedysville, MD   *301-791-5915*
$

Located on MD 34, back toward Boonsboro from Antietam, and just beyond Antietam Creek. This restaurant — like the adjacent Red Byrd Motel — is right out of the 1950s or 1960s. In fact, the restaurant was opened 35 years ago, and the food and service is strictly family style. Nothing fancy — just real good. Dinner platters, for example, range from country ham and rib steaks to grilled liver and Maryland crab cakes. Each dinner meal is in the $7 to $9 range (that's right!). This is a welcome site for families with lots of mouths to feed. There is even a section for non-smokers. Enjoy the local clientele with your meal.

AL'S PIZZA AND SUB SHOP
120 W. German St.
Shepherdstown, WV   *304-876-2720*
$

This is just what its name implies — a pizza and sub shop. And this just might be what you need for a quick snack that's reasonably priced. Kids will enjoy the choices here.

Other Sharpsburg, MD/ Shepherdstown, WV Attractions

This tour affords the opportunity to browse the streets of Shepherdstown, WV, a cozy town on the banks of the Potomac River. There are plenty of cute shops and stores.

Shepherdstown and Sharpsburg have little "night life" to offer. Forget about bustling shopping centers and movie theaters. This area is among the more rural locations listed in this book. As a result, the traveler has fewer choices for amenities and attractions — but the serenity is unequaled. Try to stay several days here. This area grows on you. Considering the number of attractions and points of interest in other communities listed throughout this book, the tranquility in this area is a blessing in disguise.

YE OLD SWEET SHOPPE
100 W. German St.
Shepherdstown, WV   *800-876-2432*

This is a cute bakery that offers European breads, pastries and an assortment of gift items.

Photo: Cumberland County Historical Society

Confederate troops deployed around Peace Church, near Camp Hill, Pennsylvania, during their 1863 invasion.

DIRECTIONS

Back across the Potomac River in Maryland, the National Park Service operates the C&O Canal National Historical Park.

C&O CANAL NATIONAL HISTORICAL PARK

P.O. Box 4
Sharpsburg, MD 21782   301-739-4200

This facility is on the banks of the Potomac River. It is located on the site of Ferry Mill, once the home of Henry Douglas, one of CSA Gen. Jasckson's aides. The entrance is from MD 35. The C&O Canal runs 184 miles along the Potomac from Cumberland, MD, to Georgetown in Washington, D.C. There are places to view the canal all along its route. This site — between Sharpsburg and Shepherdstown — is a convenient one.

TOUR 2

Shepherdstown to Winchester

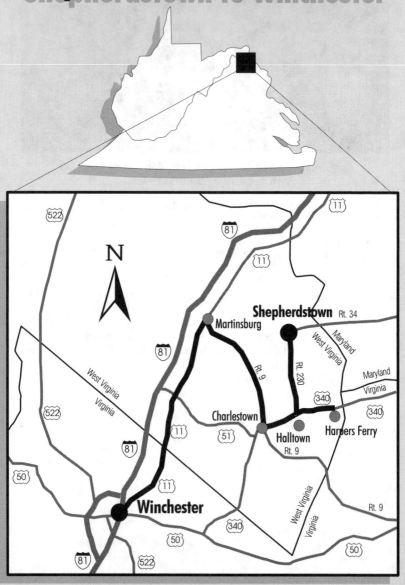

Tour 2
Middle Valley

About This Tour

This tour route covers the lower portion of the Cumberland Valley, including the West Virginia panhandle, and the northern portion of the Shenandoah Valley. This route is the second of four in succession — along with Tour routes 1, 3 and 4, Cumberland Valley, Shenandoah Valley and Southern Valley — that cover the long stretch of the Great Valley that runs through Pennsylvania, Maryland, West Virginia and Virginia. This tour route begins at Shepherdstown, WV, and ends in Winchester, VA.

Travel Tips

The preceding tour — Chapter 1: Cumberland Valley — follows US 11, which runs parallel to I-81. This tour utilizes more rural routes just to the east of US 11, before winding its way westward to Martinsburg, WV, and Winchester, VA, two communities back on US 11. The rural roadways in the early phase of this route, as well as US 11, weave their way through the heart of a number of quaint, attractive valley communities. Generally, US 340 and US 11 are dual-lane, divided highways. This is great farming country, so be alert to slow-moving farm vehicles.

History, Geography

This route, south of the Potomac River, follows the great north-south trough through the mountains and takes the traveler from the Cumberland Valley to the Shenandoah Valley. This area is all a part of the Great Valley, once used by Native Americans. The Great Wagon Road through the valley followed an old buffalo trail used by Indians to travel from the Southern highlands to the Great Lakes. This route was inundated by European pioneers, mainly Germans and Scotch-Irish, who landed at Philadelphia in the early 18th century and settled the region's mountain highlands.

As was the case in the Cumberland Valley, German farmers settled in this region in the early 1700s, quickly followed by Scotch-Irish pioneers. The influence of these German farmers is evident today in the culture and lifestyle in the fertile valley.

Civil War action took place throughout this region. In 1859, two years prior to the outbreak of war, John Brown staged a raid on Harpers Ferry. He was captured and stood trial in Charles Town, WV, where he was hanged (see the separate listings below for more information on John Brown).

This area was included in CSA Gen. Jackson's famous Shenandoah Valley Campaign of 1862, and there was significant action at Harpers Ferry, and nearby Antietam and South Mountain that year. In 1863, CSA Gen. Robert E. Lee led his Confederate troops on a sweep through Winchester, VA, and Martinsburg, WV, on their way north to the Battle of Gettysburg. In 1864, CSA Gen. Early was back in this region, pushing north and east on an attempted invasion of Washington, D.C.

Getting Here

This tour route begins at Shepherdstown, WV, just across the Potomac River from Sharpsburg, MD. It is a natural continuation of Chapter 1: Cumberland Valley.

DIRECTIONS

Shepherdstown to Halltown, WV

Leaving Shepherdstown, follow signs for WV 230 south. Through the town the route changes street names: use German, Princes and Washington streets. Returning to the rural countryside south of Shepherdstown, this single lane country road is 9 miles to Halltown, and a stop sign at Halltown Road.

HALLTOWN, WV

Col. Lewis Washington, George Washington's great-grandnephew, lived in the vicinity of Halltown. John Brown, on the night of his Harpers Ferry raid, captured Col. Washington in his home and held him hostage. Brown demanded that Col. Washington give him the sword that

Prussia's Frederick the Great gave George Washington. The sword was inscribed, "The oldest general in the world to the greatest." Brown was wearing the sword when he was captured in Harpers Ferry.

DIRECTIONS

Halltown to Harpers Ferry National Historical Park, WV

From the stop sign at Halltown Road, turn left and then right to the intersection with US 340. Turn left (north) on US 340 and go 1.7 miles to Harpers Ferry National Historical Park.

HARPERS FERRY NATIONAL HISTORICAL PARK, WV

P.O. Box 65
Harpers Ferry, WV 24525

The National Park Service (NPS) operates Harpers Ferry National Historical Park. The visitor center provides a panoramic view of the park's 2,500 acres in three states — Maryland, West Virginia and Virginia. The visitor center is open every day except Thanksgiving, Christmas and New Years Day.

The NPS offers a brochure that outlines the extensive park sites in and around the lower town of Harpers Ferry. Park buildings are shown in red on the brochure map, and the sites are keyed to numbered descriptions of important locations — more than two dozen in all — including Bolivar Heights, Camp Hill, Virginius Island, Maryland Heights, and Loudoun Heights. Automobiles are restricted to only a few specific streets in Harpers Ferry, and it is best to use one of several NPS buses from the visitor center to get downtown. There is a nice picnic area at the visitor center. During the winter months, the NPS restricts much of its historical interpretation to the weekends.

The town of Harpers Ferry, originally called The Hole, is located in the water gap of the Blue Ridge Mountains where the Shenandoah and Potomac rivers meet. Robert Harper arrived here in the 1730s, and operated a ferry across the Potomac. It was established as a town in the late 1700s, and there were about 3,000 residents when the town incorporated in the mid-1800s. President Washington suggested Harpers Ferry as the site for a federal arsenal and armory. Work began in 1796, and the armory produced its first weapons in 1801. Meriwether Lewis, on his way to Pittsburgh, PA, stopped in Harpers Ferry to load rifles from the armory for his famous Lewis and Clark Expedition. In 1803, Henry Dearborn, President Jefferson's secretary of war, issued a requisition for production of the Model 1803 rifle. By 1810, more than 10,000 rifles were produced a year.

The Harpers Ferry armory and arsenal helped the economy of the surrounding Virginia countryside. Small industries sprang up on adjacent Virginius Island. Business continued growing in the 19th century with the arrival of the C&O Canal and the B&O Railroad.

In 1859, this peaceful, prosperous town received a jolt. After months of plotting, a man named Isaac Smith raided the town on Oct. 16. Smith — really John Brown — chose Harpers Ferry because it was "the safest natural entrance to the Great Black Way. . . . Here, amid the mighty protection of overwhelming numbers, lay a path from slavery to freedom." A free African-American, Heywood Shepherd, was the first casualty of the raid. He was shot after disobeying an order from Brown's men to halt. A self-described "instrument of God sent to liberate all slaves," Brown captured the federal arsenal and refused to surrender. He was captured two mornings later when federal troops stormed the arsenal firehouse where Brown was ensconced. The rebel was indicted and tried for treason in nearby Charles Town (see separate listing below).

Harpers Ferry was a strategic location during the Civil War. The arsenal and armory were destroyed by federal authorities, who set the buildings — with 17,000 stored muskets — ablaze to keep them out of Confederate hands. In September 1862, just days before Antietam, CSA Gen. Jackson captured a 12,500-man Union garrison at this river town. It was considered the largest surrender of Union troops during the war. USA Col. Miles, the Union commander, was accidentally killed just after the white flags of surrender were flown.

A Union cavalry group was able to avoid capture in an event known as the "Davis and Davis Escape," developed by USA Col. B.F. Davis of Mississippi and USA Lt. Col. Hasbrouck Davis of Illinois. The two Davises rode together at the head of the column of escapees. The Union soldiers reached the rear of their line at Greencastle, PA, without losing a soldier. Along the way, the Union force captured a number of Confederate ammunition wagons and their 600-man escort. Harpers ferry was frequently occupied by troops of both armies throughout the war.

After Appomattox, the town established a normal school for the education of freed African Americans. The school became Storer College — the sole bright hope for the postwar community. The federal arsenal never reopened, and the town was hit by several Potomac floods. Later, the Potomac bridge — the tollgate keeper was a retired minister — became a favorite spot for eloping couples.

DIRECTIONS

Harpers Ferry to Charles Town, WV

From the NPS visitor center, return to US 340 and turn left (south) for Charles Town, WV. Continue on US 340 for 7.4 miles, then follow signs for WV 51. Continue west on WV 51 for 4.7 miles to the Charles Town city limits. WV 51 becomes Washington Street in downtown Charles Town; from the city limits continue 0.3 miles to Samuel Street.

Harpers Ferry Personality

This portrait of John Brown is based on a photograph taken in May 1859.

Photo: RNI

John Brown

John Brown, a Connecticut native, was an abolitionist all of his life. A religious fanatic, he led a siege of bloody murder in Kansas in 1856. He began developing plans in 1857 for an invasion of the South to free African American slaves. Brown planned a free-Negro stronghold in the western Virginia mountains. He considered Harpers Ferry a perfect location: the community, near the Mason-Dixon Line, had an arsenal with thousands of arms to outfit his guerilla force. His "army of liberation" struck on the night of Oct. 16. Barricaded in the armory's guard house, Brown and his men were captured when federal Marines stormed the building. The troops were led by Brevet Col. Robert E. Lee and Lt. J.E.B. Stuart. The militia included a 21-year-old aspiring actor named John Wilkes Booth. Brown was tried and convicted of murder, treason, and conspiracy. He was hanged Dec. 2, 1859 (See Charles Town, WV, listing in this chapter). A Northern martyr, Brown was immortalized in the marching song, "John Brown's Body."

CHARLES TOWN, WV

Charles Town, WV, is the county seat of Jefferson County, WV. George Washington's youngest brother, Charles, laid out this community in the 1780s — and it bears his name. Most of Charles Town's streets honor the Washington family. James and Dolley Madison were married in 1794 near Charles Town at an estate, Harewood. Dolley Madison's sister, Lucy Payne Washington, was the mistress of Harewood.

Harewood was one of many fine old estates that suffered the impact of the Civil War in the Charles Town area. In August 1864, USA Gen. Sheridan's troops were defeated by CSA Gen. Early's men, and the fighting swept over Harewood's neighboring farms, including Sulgrave, Tuscawillow, Cedar Lawn and Locust Hill. A number of Jefferson County residents supported the Confederacy, and the town paid a heavy price at the hands of Union soldiers. Just prior to the war, John Brown was put on trial at the Jefferson County Courthouse for his ill-fated raid on Harpers Ferry. Brown was found guilty and later hanged in Charles Town.

Charles Town was the home of W.L. Wilson, U.S. Postmaster-General in the late 1800s, who is credited with beginning in Jefferson County the nation's first rural free mail delivery. Today, Charles Town's two-word name keeps it from being confused with Charleston — the capital city of West Virginia.

DIRECTIONS

Charles Town to John Brown's Gallows' Site

From the intersection of Washington and Samuels streets, turn left (south) onto Samuels Street and go five city blocks to a historical marker on the left.

JOHN BROWN'S GALLOWS' SITE

After the trial at the county courthouse, John Brown was brought to this site to be hanged. Major Thomas — later "Stonewall" — Jackson commanded a howitzer unit at the Brown hanging. John Wilkes Booth (see Chapter 9: Washington) was a member of the militia.

DIRECTIONS

John Brown's Gallows to Jefferson County Courthouse

Return north on Samuel Street toward Washington Street. A block prior to Washington Street, Samuel Street becomes one-way south. So, go east or west a block and get back to Washington Street. Here, turn left (west) and go a block past Samuel Street to George Street.

JEFFERSON COUNTY COURTHOUSE
George and Washington Sts.
Charles Town, WV

The restored 1836 courthouse, at the corner of George and Washington streets, includes the room where John Brown was tried and found guilty after his Harpers Ferry raid.

DIRECTIONS

Charles Town to Martinsburg, WV

From the Jefferson County Court-house, leave downtown Charles Town headed west on George Street (WV 9) and go 3 miles. Turn left, still on WV 9, and go 11.3 miles to the Queen Street exit in Martinsburg, WV.

MARTINSBURG, WV

Martinsburg is the seat of Berkeley County. Col. Bryan Martin, a wealthy landowner, established a Berkeley County community here in 1778. The town's father is Gen. Adam Stephen, George Washington's second-in-command in the French and Indian War and a veteran of the American Revolution. His home, built of native limestone, is located on E. John Street.

The B&O (Baltimore and Ohio) railroad reached Martinsburg in 1842. Seven years later, a roundhouse and shops were built in the town. With the railroad, Martinsburg became a major valley supply and shipping center. Martinsburg, another town of split loyalties during the Civil War, was raided in 1861 by CSA Gen. Jackson, who burned the old roundhouse and rail shops. During the raid, Jackson captured a number of railroad locomotives and had them drawn south by horse to Winchester. There were three other assaults on Martinsburg: CSA Gen. Jackson in 1862 on his way to Harpers Ferry; in mid-June 1863 as part of the Gettysburg Campaign; and in August 1864 as part of CSA Gen. Early's Shenandoah Valley Campaign.

After the war, Martinsburg's present west roundhouse and two

Photo: Richmond Newspapers

The National Armory at Harpers Ferry before it was burned during the Civil War.

shops were built by the B&O. The east roundhouse was built in 1872. These buildings are some of the last remaining examples of American industrial railroad architecture still in use.

BOYDVILLE HOUSE

From the Queen Street exit on WV 9, take the exit ramp to the stop sign and turn left on Queen Street toward downtown Martinsburg. About a half-mile down Queen Street is Boydville, a large house on the left (historical marker in front). This home site was saved from destruction during the Civil War following a presidential order signed by President Lincoln.

DIRECTIONS

Boydville House to Berkeley County Courthouse

Continue farther into downtown on Queen Street another half-mile toward the Berkeley County Courthouse. Along the way, note the historical woolen mill on the right side of Queen Street — now the site of several shopping outlets. The courthouse is at the corner of King and Queen streets.

BERKELEY COUNTY COURTHOUSE
King and Queen Sts.
Martinsburg, WV

Author Porte Crayon — Union Gen. David Hunter Strother's pen

Belle Boyd was a Confederate spy.

Belle Boyd

Belle Boyd, the noted Confederate spy, was born in Martinsburg in 1843. She was just 17 when she began running information on Union troop movements to CSA Gen. Stonewall Jackson during his 1861 Valley Campaign. Boyd knew the terrain well. Besides Martinsburg, she lived in West Virginia and at Front Royal, Virginia. She was arrested twice — and twice released. Often, she was imprisoned at the courthouse in Martinsburg. She escaped the country in 1863 and sailed to England, where she became a stage performer. Boyd returned to America after the war and went on tour, where she died, at Kibourne, Wisconsin, in 1900.

Photo: Richmond Newspapers

Martinsburg Personality

name — lived in Martinsburg. Writing his *Personal Recollection of the War*, Crayon said the Martinsburg townspeople "kept their headquarters at the courthouse, sat up nights, arrested each other and everybody else they found prowling about." The courthouse was used as a prison for Confederate spy Belle Boyd, a Martinsburg native.

CSA Gen. Jackson made his headquarters at a house once located at the nearby intersection of Queen and Burke streets. USA Gen. Sheridan later headquartered at the same location. St. John's Lutheran Church, at Queen and Martin streets, was used as a Union hospital during the war.

DIRECTIONS

Martinsburg to Winchester, VA

From the Berkeley County Courthouse, take King Street (US 11) south toward Winchester, VA. Follow signs for 0.3 miles to Winchester Street, turn left onto Winchester Street, and continue 20 miles on US 11 to Winchester. Along the way, this route crosses from West Virginia into Frederick County, VA. Frederick County was formed in 1738 and named for Frederick, England's Prince of Wales and the father of King George III.

Six miles south of the Virginia border, US 11 intersects with I-81 (exit 317). At this point, it is best to get on the interstate — it's the easiest, most convenient way to the Winchester-Frederick County Visitor Center. So, take the entrance ramp onto I-81 south, and go 4.1 miles south to mile marker

— continued

314 and exit 313-B. This is the intersection of US 50. Take the exit ramp off to the right, and go west on US 50 (Millwood Avenue) for 0.4 miles to the intersection of Pleasant Valley Road. At the traffic signal, turn right on Pleasant Valley Road and go 0.1 mile to the entrance to the Winchester-Frederick County Visitor Center (and Abram's Delight) on the right.

WINCHESTER-FREDERICK COUNTY VISITOR CENTER

1360 S. Pleasant Valley Rd.
Winchester, VA 22601   *703-662-4135*
                  800-662-1360

The Winchester-Frederick County Visitor Center is operated by the City of Winchester, the County of Frederick, and the city-county Chamber of Commerce. The center has a slogan: "The Top of Virginia," a nice play on words that describes Frederick's location in the northwestern-most part of Virginia. The center has an 18-minute video on the city and county, and it offers brochures and travel information on all the places to see in and around the Winchester area. In addition, the Chamber of Commerce sells booklets, maps, a calendar of events, community profiles, and a membership directory. The center is open seven days a week from 9:00 AM to 5:00 PM. It closes six days a year: New Year's Eve and New Year's Day, Easter Sunday, Thanksgiving Day, Christmas Eve and Christmas Day.

Winchester is one of the oldest communities in Western Virginia. Originally known as Frederick Town, the town name was changed in 1752 in honor of Winchester, the old

English capital. Soon, Winchester, VA, became an important colonial transportation and commercial center, mainly because of the Great Wagon Road than spanned the length of the Great Valley.

The Winchester area is rich in colonial history. The French and Indian War brought a number of prominent military leaders—mainly Virginian George Washington and British Gen. Edward Braddock—to this frontier community. Daniel Morgan, a wagoner who served in both the French and Indian War and the Revolutionary War, was a native of the area. He is buried here. George Washington spent a great deal of time in the Winchester area, and Frederick County voters showed their affection for Washington by electing him their representative in the Virginia House of Burgesses.

Winchester's vital location and prominence made it a prize control center during the Civil War. From the Spring of 1862 to the Fall of 1864, Winchester changed flags no fewer than 70 times. Six major battles, including three in the immediate Winchester vicinity, were fought around the Frederick County area: the First, Second and Third Battles of Winchester, the First and Second Battles of Kernstown (just south of Winchester) and Cedar Creek (still farther south, near Strasburg, VA). Principal Civil War action in this region included CSA Gen. Jackson's 1862 Shenandoah Valley Campaign, and CSA Gen. Early's Washington Campaign and USA Gen. Sheridan's Shenandoah Valley Campaign, both in 1864. During the Civil War, Winchester's citizenry generally remained loyal to the Confederacy; some remained neutral as the community frequently adjusted to changing occupation.

This tour route concludes here in Winchester. At this point, you have two options. If time permits, you might want to scout out some of the Civil War attractions in and around downtown Winchester. Or, if you arrive in the Winchester area late in the day, you can arrange for lodging and dining for the evening, and then start your tour of Winchester another day. In either instance, please refer to the next tour: Chapter 3: Shenandoah Valley, which begins with the significant, individual Winchester stops that relate to Civil War history.

Winchester Accommodations

There are no bed and breakfast facilities in the immediate Winchester vicinity.

BEST WESTERN LEE-JACKSON MOTOR INN

711 Millwood Ave.
Winchester, VA 22601   703-662-4154
$$

The Lee-Jackson is now a Best Western, but it dates to the 1930s — one of the Winchester area's oldest lodging facilities. Owner Donald Vaden remembers when travelers used oil-fired space heaters to keep rooms warm. The Lee-Jackson is much more modern today. Vaden arrived on the scene in the 1960s; he's been the owner for the past two decades. The motel has 140 rooms, and they are among Winchester's most comfortable. Non-smoking rooms are available. Some rooms have microwaves and refrigerators.

HAMPTON INN
643 Millwood Ave.
Winchester, VA 22601   703-667-8011
$$ ·   800-426-7866

This is a reliable sign among a host of motels at this interchange. The Hampton Inn offers 103 rooms, and children under 18 stay free when accompanied by a parent. This motel has smoking and non-smoking rooms, and a swimming pool. A continental breakfast is served in the lobby from 6:00 to 10 AM daily.

There are other motels and inns in the Winchester, VA, area. If you have questions, or if you need a complete list of area accommodations, see a travel counselor at the Winchester-Frederick County Visitor Center (see listing). The counselors refrain from making specific recommendations, but they have lists of addresses and telephone numbers that are helpful.

It would also serve you well to read a copy of our sister publication, *The Insiders' Guide to Virginia's Blue Ridge*, as it provides "insiders information" on shopping, dining, accommodations, and attractions in this area.

Winchester Restaurants

CORK STREET TAVERN
8 W. Cork St.
Winchester, VA 22601   703-667-3777
$$

Located in historic Old Town Winchester, the Cork Street Tavern repeatedly wins the community award for the "best ribs in the Valley." Besides ribs, the tavern offers chicken, steaks and hamburgers in a casual atmosphere. This is the place for a hearty appetite. Open Monday through Saturday from 11:00 AM to 1:00 AM; Sunday from noon to 10:00 PM.

T. JEFREY'S
168 N. Loudoun St.
Winchester, VA 22601   703-667-0429
$$

T. Jefrey's has a unique dining arrangement that suits both the casual and the more serious diner. Deli sandwiches are available for drop-in traffic. For those with more time, T. Jefrey's has a nice menu that includes steak, lamb, soups and salads. Located on the downtown mall, T. Jefrey's is open for lunch and dinner Monday through Saturday from 11:00 AM to 10:00 PM; Sunday from 4:00 to 10:00 PM.

THE OLD POST OFFICE RESTAURANT
200 N. Braddock St.
Winchester, VA 22601   703-722-9881
$$

The Old Post Office Restaurant is one of the fancier places in Winchester. Yes, it is located in the community's elegant, old post office building. The menu here is "uptown" — including fresh veal, pasta and seafood, along with beef and chicken. This restaurant also offers banquet rooms for special occasions. And the restaurant caters. They're open for lunch and dinner. Lunch is served Monday through Friday from 11:30 AM to 2:30 PM. Dinner is served Monday through Thursday from 5:00 to 9:00 PM; Friday and Saturday from 5:00 to 10:00 PM; and Sunday brunch from 11:00 AM to 2:00 PM.

Other Winchester Attractions

There is much to do in the Winchester area — Civil War-oriented and otherwise. For questions and assistance, ask for help at the Winchester-Frederick County Visitor Center (see listing).

Annual Events: Winchester is apple country, and the biggest event of the year is the Shenandoah Apple Blossom Festival, a four-day event in April that dates to the late 1920s. Apples are the center of attention again in August each year, when the annual Apple Harvest Arts and Craft Festival is held in September. Other significant events include the George Washington's Birthday Cel-

ebration (February), the annual Spring opening of Belle Grove Plantation (March), the Frederick County Fair (August), a Civil War skirmish sponsored by the North-South Skirmish Association (October), and historic holiday tours of museums and private homes (December).

Arts: The Eugene B. Smith Gallery is located on the mall in downtown Winchester. It offers a nice selection of original art of scenes from the Frederick County area. The Winchester Little Theatre (315 W. Boscawen Street, Winchester 22601, 703-6621-3331) presents at least four performances during the year. The organization is 65 years old, and the past two decades it has presented programs in the town's old train station. The Shenandoah College and Conservatory of Music offers more than 300 performing arts programs during the year, and many are free. Local galleries at the school show a variety of visual arts.

Historical Sites: Abram's Delight Museum (located adjacent to the Winchester-Frederick County Visitor Center on Pleasant Valley Road) was built in 1754 of native limestone. It is operated by the local historical society. The historic home gets its name from Abraham Hollingsworth, a Quaker, who arrived in Winchester in the early 18th century. Finding a suitable home site, complete with rich land and a clear, clean spring, he declared it "A delight to behold." Abraham's son, Isaac, built the current house. In later days, the name was shortened from

"Abraham's Delight." The house is open daily from 9:00 AM to 5:00 PM. For information, call 703-662-6519. George Washington's Office Museum (corner of Braddock and Cork streets) is a registered state landmark. It, too, is operated by the historical society. Washington is said to have used the little log building during the mid-1750s while serving in the Virginia militia. The museum is open daily from 9:00 AM to 5:00 PM. For information, call 703-662-4412.

Shopping: Try the downtown mall in Winchester for a variety of specialty shops and unique stores. Wisteria Manor (703-722-0145) has a wide selection of decorative and gift items. The Stone Soap Gallery and Studio (107 N. Loudoun Street, 703-722-3976) offers country specialties, including food and crafts and is open Monday through Saturday from 10 AM to 5 PM; and Sunday from 1:00 to 5:00 PM. It stays open an hour later on Fridays. Handcrafts are available at Handworks Gallery (150 N. Loudoun Street, 703-662-3927). The downtown mall also has a 5 & 10 store and a drug store. Over at Sheridan's Headquarters you will find Kimberly's Antiques and Linens (135 N. Braddock Street, 703-662-2195). Among the more prominent shopping areas is Apple Blossom Mall just off US 50 near I-81. A tour of the Winchester area, particularly in the Spring and Fall, is unforgettable. There are few greater enjoyments than a visit to the Frederick County countryside and picking apples from the abundant orchards and local farm markets.

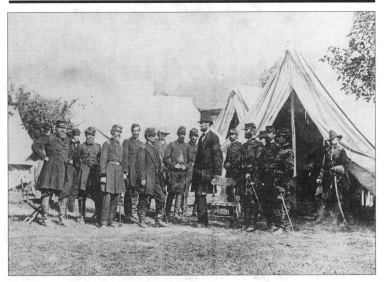

President Lincoln met regularly with many of his generals.

Detail of "Lee and His Generals," a painting by George B. Matthews, which depicted a gathering of Confederate generals that never occurred.

TOUR 3
Winchester to Harrisonburg

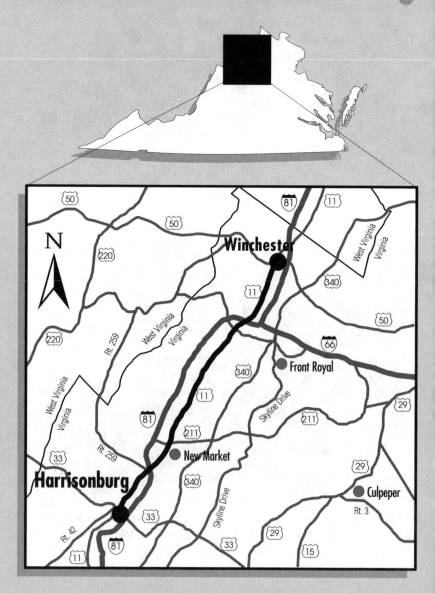

Tour 3
Shenandoah Valley

About This Tour

This tour route begins at Winchester, VA, and runs through the Shenandoah Valley of Virginia as far south as Harrisonburg, VA, and its environs. This route is the third of four in succession — along with Tour routes 1, 2 and 4, Cumberland Valley, Middle Valley and Southern Valley — that cover the long stretch of the Great Valley that runs through Pennsylvania, Maryland, West Virginia and Virginia. This route ends in Harrisonburg, and accommodations and dining suggestions are listed at the end of the chapter.

Travel Tips

The preceding two tours — Chapter 1: Cumberland Valley and Chapter 2: Middle Valley — generally followed US 11, which runs parallel to I-81. There were some side, country roads in the Middle Valley that veered east of US 11. This tour utilizes US 11 exclusively. Be alert to slow-moving farm vehicles.

History, Geography

This area is the popular and renowned Shenandoah Valley, part of the Great Valley — once a north-south route of Native Americans.

The Great Wagon Road through the valley followed an old buffalo trail used by Indians to travel north and south from the Southern highlands to the Great Lakes. This route was inundated by European pioneers, mainly Germans and Scotch-Irish, who landed at Philadelphia in the early 18th century and settled the region's mountain highlands. Evidence of this heritage remains today in the culture and lifestyle.

A word about the geography of the Shenandoah Valley: the trough through the Great Valley is at the highest elevation farther south, near Roanoke, VA. This means that your travels will take you "up" — in elevation — as you go "down" — or south.

Civil War action took place throughout the Shenandoah Valley, beginning in June 1861 and continuing through the next three years.

Getting Here

This tour route begins at Winchester, VA, and it is a natural continuation of Chapter 2: Middle Valley. Winchester, located in the northwestern corner of Virginia, is accessible via I-81 or US 11.

DIRECTIONS

We ended Tour 2 in Winchester at the Visitor Center. This tour begins at the center, so return to that point.

WINCHESTER-FREDERICK COUNTY VISITOR CENTER

1360 S. Pleasant Valley Rd.
Winchester, VA 22601   703-662-4135
                              800-662-1360

For complete information on this Visitor Center, see the conclusion of the previous tour to the Middle Valley. In preparation for this tour, check with counselors at the Visitor Center for detailed Civil War booklets and self-guided tours.

A brief look at a Virginia map reveals Winchester's important location in the middle of the Great Valley, along the path of the Great Wagon Road. To the north, the Potomac River flows east — cutting through the Blue Ridge at Harpers Ferry on its way to Washington, D.C., and beyond. An important rail line follows the Potomac from upland West Virginia to eastern stations.

Winchester was a prize for Union and Confederate armies alike. The community lay in the path of a major route, the Valley Pike, often laden with grain and supply wagons. This path also was a major roadway for Confederates moving north and Federals moving south. As noted in the previous chapter, Winchester's vital location and prominence made it a prize control center during the Civil War. From the Spring of 1862 to the Fall of 1864, the town changed flags no fewer than 70 times.

Winchester was the scene of three significant Civil War battles: the First, Second and Third Battles of Winchester, in 1862, 1863, and 1864, respectively. All three engagements were strategically significant to the Confederacy, as they lured Union military might away from Richmond, the South's capital city.

The First Battle of Winchester was fought May 25, 1862. The action took place around Winchester's southern perimeter, just north of Abram's Creek. CSA Gen. Jackson, as part of his famed 1862 Shenandoah Valley Campaign, defeated USA Gen. Banks, who was retreating north along the Valley Pike. Jackson's force of 17,000 Confederates outnumbered Banks' force by two-to-one, and drove the Union troops north (along present-day US 11) and across the Potomac River.

The Second Battle of Winchester was fought June 14 and 15, 1863. This two-day battle took place around Winchester's northwestern area, and included a battle at Stephenson's Depot. CSA Gen. Robert E. Lee, following action at Chancellorsville — and the loss of Gen. Jackson — moved northwest across Virginia on the way to an invasion of Maryland and Pennsylvania. CSA Gen. Ewell, one of Lee's top commanders, defeated Federals under the command of USA Gen. Milroy. Milroy withdrew to the north, and suffered losses on the way to the Potomac River. Following this engagement, Lee's army pushed north toward Gettysburg.

The Third Battle of Winchester was fought September 19, 1864. This battle took place along the northeastern section of Winchester, and is also known as the Battle of Opequon, for

This photo of Gen. George Armstrong Custer was taken by Matthew Brady. (See page 49)

the nearby Opequon Creek. USA Gen. Sheridan put a stop to CSA Gen. Early's Shenandoah Valley Campaign and the Confederate dominance in the region. Sheridan pushed toward Winchester along the Berryville Pike (present-day VA 7), and struck Early in an engagement that lasted all day. Early retreated south, along the Valley Pike (present-day US 11), and the opposing generals met again two days later at Fisher's Hill south of Strasburg.

DIRECTIONS

Winchester Visitors Center to Jackson's Headquarters

From the Visitors Center, turn right (north) on Pleasant Valley Road, and go to the first traffic signal at Cork Street. Turn left (west) on Cork Street and follow Cork into the Winchester historical district to S. Braddock Street (S. Braddock Street is one-way south). At this corner is George Washington's Office Museum (see listing at end of chapter under Attractions). Continue west on Cork Street a block to Washington Street (US 11). Turn right (north) on Washington Street and go two blocks to the corner of Washington and Boscowen streets. At this intersection is Christ Episcopal Church and the tomb of Lord Fairfax (see Attractions) Continue north on Washington Street two more blocks to Piccadilly Street and turn left (west). The road immediately curves to the right (north) as Fairmont Street. Continue north two blocks on Fairmont Street to North Avenue. Turn right (east) on North Avenue, go a block, and turn right (south) on N. Braddock Street. Go a half-block south on N. Braddock Street to Jackson's Headquarters on the right. There is street parking and you'll see the signs.

Hunter Holmes McGuire

According to historian Joseph Whitehorne, Winchester was filled with wounded soldiers following CSA Gen. Jackson's famous 1862 Shenandoah Valley Campaign. The wounded were hospitalized in various public buildings, including — suitably enough — the old Union Hotel. They were treated by a group of Federal medical officers who volunteered to remain behind after their own forces withdrew. Up until this time, all enemy personnel were treated the same, regardless of their function. So, those who remained in Winchester faced capture and the prospect of months in grim Confederate prisons.

Winchester native Hunter Holmes McGuire, Jackson's 26-year-old surgeon, urged his commander to let the Federal doctors continue caring for their patients. Jackson agreed, so long as the doctors struck to their medical business and performed no hostile acts. Jackson instructed McGuire to formalize the understanding by reaching an accord with the Federal doctors. The Union physicians were given their unconditional freedom. In exchange, they agreed to work for the freedom of Confederate doctors when they got back to their own lines. This sensible and merciful

Winchester Personality

approach assured better patient care during the war, and it made an impression on the senior leaders of both the North and South.

Within a month, both sides agreed that, in the words of USA Gen. McClellan, their medical officers should "be viewed as non-combatants." This policy later was extended to include chaplains and any others assigned to medical work. Thus, McGuire's practical suggestion in the name of mercy established a practice that since has become global — its violation contemptible.

McGuire himself benefited directly from the policy when he was captured at Waynesboro in March 1865, and then released on orders of USA Gen. Sheridan. After the war, McGuire enjoyed a distinguished medical career in Richmond (see Chapter 12: Richmond), where he taught at the Medical College of Virginia. He founded St. Luke's Hospital and a nurses' training school. Later, he served as president of the American Medical Association. When he died in March 1900, he was one of the best loved and most well known figures in the state.

A statue of McGuire was erected in Capital Square in Richmond in 1904. Few of his distinguished contributions have had a more lasting effect on more people than his wartime establishment of medical non-combatant status. Whitehorne writes that we know what one grateful Federal meant when he said McGuire "humanized war."

Winchester Personality

"STONEWALL" JACKSON'S HEADQUARTERS

415 N. Braddock St.
Winchester, VA 22601   703-667-3242

This was the home of Lt. Col. Lewis T. Moore, who invited CSA Gen. Jackson to use the house as his headquarters prior to Jackson's Shenandoah Valley Campaign of 1862. Jackson spent the winter of 1861 in Winchester. A registered state and national landmark, this Gothic Revival-style house is open daily, April through October, from 9 AM to 5 PM. The last tour of the day begins at 4:15 PM. The admission fee is $3.50, with a discount for seniors and children. The Winchester-Frederick County Historical Society, which administers the building, has special functions during the off-season, particularly on weekends and holidays.

DIRECTIONS

Jackson's Headquarters to Handley Library

From Jackson's Headquarters, continue south on one-way N. Braddock Street to the next intersection, at Braddock and Piccadilly streets.

HANDLEY LIBRARY

Braddock and Piccadilly Sts.
Winchester, VA 22601   703-662-9041

The Archives Room of the Handley Library contains volumes of newspapers, diaries, maps, correspondence, photographs, census records, books and original manuscripts related to the histories of Winchester and Frederick counties, particularly the Civil War period. Some of the materials date to the early 1700s. The Archives Room is open to the public every day except Sunday. The archives are handled by the library and the Winchester-Frederick County Historical Society. Across the street from the library is the house that USA Gen. Sheridan used for his headquarters after the Third Battle of Winchester in 1864. Sheridan left this house on the morning of Oct. 19, 1864, and rode south along the valley pike to rally his faltering troops at the Battle of Cedar Creek. This house now displays a big red apple in the front yard.

DIRECTIONS

Handley Library to Kurtz Cultural Center

Continue south on one-way Braddock Street two blocks to Boscowen Street. Turn left (east) on Boscowen Street and cross over downtown Winchester's attractive Old Town pedestrian mall, which incorporates store fronts along the former Loudoun Street. Another block east on Boscowen Street, at the corner of Boscowen and Cameron streets, is the old Winchester City Hall. Park in this vicinity — there are a number of street and garage spaces available near this intersection. The Kurtz Cultural Center is located across the street from City Hall, at 2 N. Cameron Street.

KURTZ CULTURAL CENTER
2 N. Cameron St.
Winchester, VA 22601   703-722-6367

This center, home of the Old Town Welcome Center, boasts the Civil War Center that includes a permanent exhibit, "Shenandoah: Crossroads of the Civil War." This visit provides a thorough, interesting introduction to the Shenandoah Valley's important role during the four-year war. The Civil War Center provides an overview of 15 military engagements, and it includes a summary of valley campaigns conducted by CSA Gen. Jackson and other leaders. Take advantage of the center's literature on Civil War attractions and sites, as well as walking and driving tours. There is no admission charge. The center is open Monday through Saturday, from 10:00 AM to 5:00 PM, and Sunday from noon to 5:00 PM.

Winchester Side Trip

Stonewall Cemetery, National Cemetery

Two blocks east of the Kurtz Cultural Center is Mt. Hebron Cemetery, which includes the Stonewall Cemetery. Just to the north, on National Avenue, is the National Cemetery. There are 3,000 Confederate graves in Stonewall Cemetery, and a shaft honors more than 800 unknown Confederates who were killed in battles in the vicinity. CSA Gen. Turner Ashby (see Chapter 4: Southern Valley) is among the more prominent individuals buried in the cemetery. National Cemetery is one of the largest national cemeteries in Virginia, and it includes the bodies of more than 4,000 Union soldiers — half of them unidentified. Some of the action of the Third Battle of Winchester in 1864 was fought in this vicinity, and along present-day Berryville Avenue (VA 7) northeast of Winchester.

DIRECTIONS

Winchester to Kernstown, VA
Return to your vehicle, and follow any Old Town street west to Braddock Street, which is one-way south. Turn right and go south on Braddock Street, which is US 11.

Some of the fighting of the First Battle of Winchester in 1862 took place along the valley road, along Abram's Creek just south of the downtown historic district. On the morning of May 25, 1862, New England soldiers serving under USA Gen. Banks held a position along the valley road in this vicinity. They faced CSA Gen. Jackson, who led his troops on an advance from the south. Later than morning, Jackson halted his advance guard in this area to observe the Union position. Interestingly, in this same area a year later — June of 1863 — CSA Gen. Ewell instructed fellow-general Early to move around USA Gen. Milroy's flank to attack a Union position west of town, a little to the south in Kernstown.

KERNSTOWN, VA

Just to the west of this community, in March 1862, CSA Gen. Jackson struck a Union force under USA Gen. Shields. This action became known as the first Battle of Kernstown. Jackson held Winchester early in the war. Then, when USA Gen. Banks moved south toward Winchester from the Potomac River, Jackson moved south 40 miles to Mt. Jackson. Twelve days later, Jackson moved on Winchester against the Union forces, and the opposing troops met at Kernstown on March 23. Jackson was forced back; the Union troops fell back to Winchester. The enemy forces met again two months later in the First Battle of Winchester.

A Second Battle of Kernstown was fought in July 1864. CSA Gen. Early pushed north through the Shenandoah Valley, into Winchester and Frederick, MD, and farther northeast in an attempted invasion of Washington, D.C. Meeting resistance in the nation's capital, Early fell back to south of Winchester, then attacked USA Gen. Crook on July 24. The Union troops, defeated after a serious battle, retreated across the Potomac River.

DIRECTIONS

Kernstown to Stephens City, VA
Continue south on US 11 for 3.6 miles to the community of Stephens City.

STEPHENS CITY, VA

CSA Gen. Jackson's troops rested in this vicinity in May 1862 on their way to the First Battle of Winchester. In May 1864, USA Gen. Hunter ordered Stephens City burned to the ground, but USA Maj. Sterns of the 1st New York cavalry prevented the destruction. USA Gen. Sheridan passed this way from Winchester in October 1864 to join his troops at the Battle of Cedar Creek.

DIRECTIONS

Stephens City to Middletown, VA
Continue south on US 11 for 5.2 miles to Middletown.

MIDDLETOWN, VA

CSA Gen. Jackson attacked USA Gen. Banks here on May 24, 1862. Jackson's action forced Banks to go on the defensive at Winchester.

DIRECTIONS

Middletown to Cedar Creek Battlefield

Continue south on US 11 for 1.5 miles. See signs on the right for Cedar Creek Battlefield.

CEDAR CREEK BATTLEFIELD

This site is the central area of the Battle of Cedar Creek, which was fought in October 1864. USA Gen. Sheridan's army pushed south toward Harrisonburg, then reversed and marched north toward Winchester. His troops were followed closely by a force under CSA Gen. Early. Along Cedar Creek, Early decided to attack Sheridan's men — Sheridan, himself, was in a conference in Washington, D.C. Early moved out on the night of Oct. 18, and his attack was successful during the hours between sunrise and mid-morning: The Confederates routed Union troops from their campsites and captured 1,300 prisoners and a number of guns. But Early's efforts evaporated when he failed to continue his push against the enemy.

The head count of the battle was awesome: the Union suffered 3,994 killed and wounded and 1,770 missing in action; the Confederates suffered 1,860 killed and wounded. The Confederates, with the defeat, essentially lost control of the Shenandoah Valley. The Union success helped bring an end to the war. A Union infantryman, Cpt. S.E. Howard, wrote of the battle: "Never since the world was created was such a crushing defeat turned into such a splendid victory as at Cedar Creek."

The Cedar Creek Battlefield Foundation (see personality below) and the National Trust own small parcels of land that sit along US 11 just south of the town of Middleburg.

Cedar Creek Personality

USA Gen. Philip Sheridan, President Abraham Lincoln

USA Gen. Philip Sheridan was not at his headquarters at Belle Grove Planation, as the Confederates thought, when the Battle of Cedar Creek began. He was off in Washington, D.C., at a War Department strategy meeting. Finishing his meeting, he rode back to Winchester, VA, to spend the night. Early the next morning, Sheridan was roused from his bed by the sound of cannon fire. His troops, he soon learned, were engaged in a fierce struggle at Cedar Creek against troops led by Confederate Gen. Jubal Early. The general sped off down the Valley Pike, arriving in time to urge his men on and turn the tide against early Confederate advances. Sheridan eventually was victorious. A short time later, Sheridan received a note, dated Oct. 22, from the Executive Mansion in Washington. President Lincoln wrote the Union general: "With great pleasure I tender to you and your brave army, the thanks of the nation, and my own personal admiration and gratitude, for the months' operation in the Shenandoah Valley, and especially for the splendid work of Oct. 19, 1864."

The Cedar Creek Battlefield Foundation

A nonprofit organization, the Cedar Creek Battlefield Foundation attempts to preserve land and promote the valor displayed at the Battle of Cedar Creek. Each year in October, the foundation conducts one of the largest battle reenactments in the nation. The foundation has purchased 158 acres of the battlefield site, and proceeds from the reenactment go to pay off the foundation's mortgage. Infantry, cavalry and artillery units participate in the event. In 1991, in an effort to increase support for the Cedar Creek preservation effort, the Association for the Preservation of Civil War Sites challenged the Cedar Creek Battlefield Foundation to raise $25,000 a year for four years. Since 1991, the foundation has sponsored a fundraising program that sells a one square foot plat of the battlefield's acreage for $25. Purchasers receive a certificate. The foundation also operates a visitors center on the grounds of Belle Grove Plantation (see listing below). The foundation can be contacted at P.O. Box 229, Middletown, VA 22645 (703-869-2064).

DIRECTIONS

Cedar Creek Battlefield to Belle Grove Plantation
Continue south on US 11 for 0.5 miles to the Belle Grove Plantation entrance road on the right.

BELLE GROVE PLANTATION
P.O. Box 137
Middletown, VA 22645   703-869-2028

This fine old plantation, built in the 1790s, was the home of Major Isaac Hite Jr. and his family for close to 75 years. Hite was a grandson of Joist Hite, one of the first settlers in the Shenandoah Valley. The younger Hite married Nelly Conway Madison, the sister of President James Madison. Madison reportedly enlisted the help of Thomas Jefferson in helping his brother-in-law design Belle Grove, an attractive architectural prize of the Shenandoah. Madison and his wife, the former Dolley Payne Todd, reportedly spent part of their honeymoon at the estate. The building includes a limestone dressed south facade.

A sketch of the Battle of Cedar Creek.

Richmond Newspapers

During the Battle of Cedar Creek, Union troops camped on the grounds of Belle Grove. Today, the estate is operated by the National Trust for Historic Preservation. Tours are available from mid-March through mid-November, on Monday through Saturday from 10:00 AM to 4:00 PM, and Sunday from 1:00 to 5:00 PM. There is a $3.50 admission charge, but seniors and children get reduced rates. Special events are scheduled during the off-season, and gift and quilt shops are open year round.

DIRECTIONS

Belle Grove to Hupp's Hill Battlefield Park

Return to US 11, turn right (south) and continue south on the Valley Pike for 3.0 miles to the entrance on the right to Hupp's Hill Battlefield Park. Along this route make two notes. First, just south of Belle Grove, US 11 crosses over Cedar Creek, a significant river crossing during the Battle of Cedar Creek. Also, in the distance to the southeast, the imposing Signal Knob first becomes evident. The knob is the northern face of the Massanutten Mountain range. It was used at one time or another by both the Union and Confederacy as a signal station to relay information on troop movements.

Hupp's Hill Battlefield Park

Route 11 North, P.O. Box 31
Strasburg, VA 22657   703-465-5884

Hupp's Hill gets its name from the locally prominent Hupp family, whose members homesteaded in the Strasburg, VA, in the mid-1750s. This battlefield park and study center

features "hands-on" exhibits. Visitors, particularly youths, can see and feel Civil War uniforms and weaponry. Younger visitors are encouraged to try on uniforms and civilian clothing patterned after those of the Civil War era. A topographic map shows the scope of the Battle of Cedar Creek. On the grounds are trenches and gun placements built during the Cedar Creek conflict. The park and study center are open Monday through Friday from 10:00 AM to 4:00 PM, and Saturday and Sunday from 11:00 AM to 5:00 PM. The facility is closed on Tuesdays during the off-season. It also is closed on Thanksgiving and Christmas. A fee of $3.50 for adults and $2.50 for children is charged. Group tours of the study center and guided tours of the nearby Cedar Creek battlefield are available.

DIRECTIONS

Hupp's Hill to Strasburg, VA

Return to US 11, turn right, and follow US 11 0.5 miles into downtown Strasburg.

STRASBURG, VA

Earthworks just west of town were built by USA Gen. Banks during CSA Gen. Jackson's Shenandoah Valley Campaign of 1862. Going through Strasburg, cross over the little creek just south of town. This bridge was destroyed by the weight of retreating Confederate troops following the Battle of Cedar Creek. This delay enabled USA Gen. Sheridan to recapture his wagons and cannon taken by the Southerners.

DIRECTIONS

Strasburg to Tom's Brook
Continue south on US 11 for 5.5 miles to Tom's Brook. Along the way, this route passes through Fisher's Hill, the site of a battle on Sept. 22, 1864. CSA Gen. Early took a position here after the Third Battle of Winchester. He was attacked and defeated by USA Gen. Sheridan. Early's adjutant-general, A.S. Pendleton, was killed during the conflict.

TOM'S BROOK, VA

Two weeks after Fisher's Hill, on Oct. 9, 1864, CSA Gens. Rosser and Lomax lost a cavalry battle to USA Gen. Torbert. Prior to the battle, USA Gen. Sheridan, unhappy with his cavalry's performance, told Torbert to "either whip the enemy or get whipped yourself." Nine Union soldiers were killed, but the Confederates suffered 400 killed. The Southerners were pushed back so fiercely and so quickly that the Federals called the victory the "Woodstock Races," referring to the Valley Pike route south to Woodstock, VA.

DIRECTIONS

Tom's Brook to Edinburg, VA
Continue south on US 11, through Woodstock, for 11 miles to Edinburg.

EDINBURG, VA (TG-286)

Although this region was settled by Scotch-Irish — as well as German — pioneers, this town's name is not of Scottish origin. Rather, early townspeople considered this attractive area like the Garden of Eden — but they ended up spelling it incorrectly. This was the "Graniary of the Confederacy," although a prominent mill, Edinburg Mills, was among the few buildings saved from the torches of USA Gen. Sheridan. A local legend says two local girls appealed to Sheridan's men to save the mill.

DIRECTIONS

Edinburg to Mount Jackson
Continue south on US 11 for 7.4 miles to Mount Jackson.

MOUNT JACKSON, VA (TG-292)

No, this town is not named for the immortal Stonewall Jackson. Legend says Gen. — later President — Andrew Jackson was a frequent visitor to the area, and thus the community name was changed in the 1820s from Mount Pleasant to Mount Jackson.

The Confederate cemetery on the north of town, along US 11, is the last vestige of a large Southern hospital created here.

DIRECTIONS

Mount Jackson to New Market
Continue south on US 11 for 6.9 miles to New Market. A mile south of town, enemy cavalry units fought a battle in the vicinity of the Valley Pike. A bridge over the Shenandoah River in this vicinity was burned by Union troops retreating from the Battle of New Market in May 1864.

NEW MARKET, VA

This tranquil valley community was struck by warfare in May 1864, when the Battle of New Market raged in and around the town. A Confederate force under Gen. Breckinridge arrived from Staunton and Lacey Spring (just to the south) and faced Union troops under the command of Gen. Sigel.

DIRECTIONS

New Market to New Market Battlefield Historical Park

In downtown New Market, look for the traffic signal at the intersection of US 11 and US 211. Turn right (west) on US 211 and go 0.3 miles — beyond the I-81 interchange — to the New Market Historical Battlefield Park entrance on the right. Turn right onto VA 305 (George Collins Parkway) and go one mile to the park and visitor center.

NEW MARKET BATTLEFIELD PARK AND HALL OF VALOR MUSEUM

Box 1864
George Collins Parkway, VA 305
New Market, VA 22844   703-740-3101

This museum and visitor center is operated by Virginia Military Institute (VMI) and listed in the national register of historic places. The facility is open daily from 9:00 AM to 5:00 PM except on New Years Day, Thanksgiving and Christmas. The museum is wheelchair accessible. Adults are charged a $5.00 fee for the museum; children under 16 are charged $2.00.

The museum features artifacts, murals, life-size models and films to relate the story of the Battle of New Market. Here, on May 15, 1864, Union Gen. Sigel pushed south with 6,500 troops on the way to destroy the railroad at Staunton, VA. He was met by Confederate Gen. Breckinridge. A day-long battle took

---

New Market Personality

Franz Sigel

Franz Sigel — born in Germany — was a graduate of Baden Military Academy. He fled Germany in the 1840s, traveled to Switzerland and England, and immigrated to the U.S. and became a school administrator in New York and St. Louis.

Early in the Civil War, Sigel served in the Western Theater before leading a Union division against CSA Gen. Jackson in the Shenandoah Valley Campaign of 1862. Sigel was defeated at the Battle of New Market in May 1864, after which he moved north to defend Harpers Ferry against CSA Gen. Early.

Sigel, according to Union military leaders, lacked aggression, thus was dismissed from his command. Still, he didn't resign from the Union army until May 1865 — a year after New Market and a month after the Confederate surrender at Appomattox. He moved to Baltimore, MD, and then to New York, where he became known as a publisher, political activist and lecturer. He died in 1902, more than three decades after the end of the war. He was 86.

Richmond Newspapers

John C. Breckinridge

There is irony that General Breckinridge, a Kentucky native, saw Civil War action in the Great Valley of Virginia. His family roots were in the valley. The general's great-grandfather was Robert Breckinridge, who married Lettice Preston near Staunton, VA, in 1758. Both Robert and Lettice were natives of Ireland, and both were members of families that were among the numerous Scotch-Irish who immigrated to the colonies in the 1730s and settled in the Valley of Virginia.

Robert and Lettice had six children, including two sons, John and James Breckinridge. James, the younger of the two, was born and raised in the newly created Botetourt County, which he represented in the legislature. He ran for governor of Virginia in 1799 but lost to James Monroe. John Breckinridge was born near Staunton in 1760. He, too, represented Botetourt County in the Virginia legislature, a service he provided while also attending the College of William and Mary. Once, he was refused a seat in the General Assembly because he was underage.

In 1785, John married Mary Hopkins Cabell, the daughter of Joseph and Mary Cabell of Buckingham County, VA. John and his wife lived in Albemarle County, VA, and had two of their nine children there. John was elected to the U.S. Senate from Albemarle County in 1792, but he failed to take the seat. Instead, he and his family — along with his mother, aunts, and uncles — moved to the newly established Kentucky.

John was active in Kentucky politics, serving as the new state's attorney general, and in the legislature as a U.S. Senator, and eventually as President Jefferson's attorney general. His oldest son, Joseph Cabell Breckinridge, also took an active part in Kentucky politics. Joseph became speaker of the Kentucky house and secretary of state. He married Mary Clay Smith in Kentucky in 1811.

Joseph and Mary had only one child, John Cabell Breckinridge, who was born in Lexington, KY, in 1821. John carried on his family's political tradition, serving in the Kentucky legislature and as a Congressman. In 1856, John was elected vice president on the ticket with President James Buchanan. In the U.S. presidential election four years later, John Breckinridge unsuccessfully opposed Abraham Lincoln. He then served as U.S. Senator from Kentucky.

In the Civil War he saw action at Shiloh, Baton Rouge, Vicksburg, Chickamauga and Missionary Ridge. After serving in the Shenandoah Valley, he commanded his division at Cold Harbor and fought at the

— continued on page 48

New Market Personality

— continued from page 47

Battle of the Monocacy in Maryland. He was named the Confederate secretary of war just two months before the surrender at Appomattox.

Following the Civil War, Breckinridge went to Cuba, Europe and Canada before being allowed to return to his native Kentucky. The Breckinridge family was seriously divided during the Civil War. The general and his three sons fought for the Confederacy, but two Breckinridge cousins supported the Union. One of the cousins, in fact, had two sons that fought for the South and two that fought for the North. One of the general's cousins, Margaret Elizabeth Breckinridge, ministered to Northern soldiers in camps along the Mississippi River. She ran a relief boat between St. Louis and Vicksburg, but she contracted typhoid fever and died in 1864, just as she prepared to return to the battlefield — in Virginia.

place, sometimes in chilling Spring thunderstorms. The Southerners overran the Federals; one Pennsylvania regiment suffered 45 percent casualties.

The battle story is enhanced by the fact that more than 200 cadets from Virginia Military Institute (VMI) were part of Breckinridges's troop strength. The youngsters were not the principal part of the Confederate offensive, but they did take part in a portion of the battle, and they captured a Union gun. Sigel retreated north as far as Strasburg.

DIRECTIONS

New Market Battlefield Park to New Market Battlefield Military Museum

From the New Market Battlefield Park, backtrack on George Collins Parkway (VA 305) halfway to US 522, to the New Market Battlefield Military Museum.

NEW MARKET BATTLEFIELD MILITARY MUSEUM

George Collins Parkway, VA 305
New Market, VA 22844 703-740-8065

This is a private museum. It includes a number of artifacts — many military oriented and many from the Civil War. The museum is open from 9:00 AM to 5:00 PM. There is an abbreviated schedule during the off-season.

DIRECTIONS

New Market Battlefield Military Museum to the Museum of American Cavalry

Continue to backtrack on George Collins Parkway (VA 305) to US 522, to the Museum of American Cavalry.

MUSEUM OF AMERICAN CAVALRY

George Collins Parkway, VA 305
New Market, VA 22844   703-740-3959

This cavalry museum is a relatively new facility, taking in 3,000 square feet and incorporating exhibits on the history of the American cavalry from Jamestown, VA, to World War II. There are three galleries, one of which covers the period from 1860 to 1865 and includes a fully mounted Confederate cavalryman of the 1st Va. Cavalry. The museum is open daily, April through November, from 10:00 AM to 4:30 PM. An admission fee is charged.

Civil War, Rosser went into railroading and was the chief engineer in the Indian Territory. He and Custer, his old adversary, again became friends when Custer's Army unit was deployed to protect Rosser's railroad construction. Rosser later became a gentleman farmer in Albemarle County, VA, and died in 1910. Custer was killed at the Battle of Little big Horn in South Dakota in June of 1876.

DIRECTIONS

Museum of American Cavalry to Lacey Spring, VA

From the Museum of American Cavalry, backtrack on George Collins Parkway (VA 305) to US 522. Turn left (east) on US 522 and go 0.3 miles to US 11 in New Market. Turn right (south) on US 11, and go 8.8 miles to Lacey Spring, VA.

LACEY SPRING, VA

On Dec. 20, 1864, a significant cavalry battle was fought here between USA Gen. Custer and CSA Gen. Rosser. Ironically, Rosser and Custer were roommates at West Point. After the

---

DIRECTIONS

Lacey Spring to Harrisonburg Rockingham Convention and Visitors Bureau

Continue south on US 11 for 5.1 miles to the entrance road to I-81. Turn left at the entrance road and go 0.2 miles to the entrance ramp to I-81 south. Take I-81 south for 3.5 miles to the next exit (exit 247-A, US 33 west). Take the right exit ramp off the interstate and go west on US 33 (E. Market Street) for 0.4 miles to Vine Street. Turn right on Vine Street and go a quarter-block to the Visitors Bureau — at the intersection of Vine Street and Country Club Road.

Lincoln Family

On Feb. 12, 1809, Nancy Hanks Lincoln gave birth to a son in her Hardin County, KY, cabin. She and her carpenter husband, Thomas, named the new child Abraham. Young Abraham traced his family roots to Virginia. John Lincoln — "Virginia John" — settled on 600 acres on Linville Creek in Rockingham County, VA — here at Lacey Spring. Virginia John's son, Abraham L. Lincoln, was an officer in the American Revolution. Capt. Abraham and his son, Thomas, moved to Kentucky in 1782, a decade before the region was cut from Virginia for the creation of the new state. Virginia John remained in Rockingham County, near Lacey Spring, with a younger son, Jacob. On Feb. 24, 1829, exactly two decades after the future President Lincoln was born, Jacob's grandson, Franklin, carved his name and the date on the wall of Melrose Caverns, or Harrison's Cave, in this vicinity just north of Harrisonburg, VA. Franklin Lincoln, President Lincoln's distant cousin, went on to serve in the Civil War as a soldier in — ironically — the Confederacy.

Lacey Spring Personalities

HARRISONBURG ROCKINGHAM CONVENTION AND VISITORS BUREAU
800 Country Club Rd., P.O. Box 1
Harrisonburg, VA 22801   703-434-2319
703-434-4508 (fax)

This convention bureau and visitors center is operated by the Chamber of Commerce of Harrisonburg and Rockingham counties. Travel counselors have information packets on area attractions. They can also help with planning accommodations and dining. This center is open Monday through Friday, from 8:30 AM to 5:00 PM. It is closed on weekends and during holidays.

This tour route concludes here in Harrisonburg. At this point, you have two options. If time permits, you might want to scout out some of the Civil War attractions just outside Harrisonburg. Or, if you arrive in Harrisonburg late in the day, you can arrange for lodging and dining for the evening, and then start your tour of Harrisonburg another day. In either instance, please refer to the next tour: Chapter 4: Southern

Valley, which begins with the significant, individual Harrisonburg-area stops that relate to Civil War history.

Harrisonburg Accommodations

Refer to the Foreward for an explanation of the rating system for both the accommodations and restaurants.

JOSHUA WILTON HOUSE
412 S. Main St.
Harrisonburg, VA 22801   703-434-4464
$$$

The Joshua Wilton House is an elegant Victorian home, located in the vicinity of James Madison University. It is one of the finest inns in the Shenandoah Valley. Each room is furnished with period antiques. All five bedrooms have private baths. Roberta and Craig Moore are the owners and, as their brochure suggests, they will spoil you. Expect complimentary wine or beer, and a gourmet breakfast that includes homemade pastries, fresh fruits, and a steaming pot of coffee.

SHERATON INN

1400 E. Market St.
Harrisonburg, VA 22801   703-433-2521
$$ 703-434-0253 (fax)

This Sheraton is located at the intersection of I-81 (milepost 247) and US 33. The inn has 138 rooms, many non-smoking, and three suites. Also featured are a restaurant, lounge, indoor pool, outdoor pool, whirlpool and sauna.

COMFORT INN

1440 E. Market St.
Harrisonburg, VA 22801   703-433-6066
$$ 800-228-5150

There are 60 rooms at this Comfort Inn, located at the intersection of I-81 and US 33. This inn has no restaurant, but it offers a continental breakfast. A quarter of its rooms are non-smoking. It offers an outdoor heated pool.

There are other motels, inns and bed and breakfast facilities in the Harrisonburg, VA, area. If you have questions, or if you need a list of area accommodations, see a travel counselor at the Harrisonburg Rockingham Convention and Visitors Bureau (see listing). The counselors refrain from making specific recommendations, but they have lists of addresses and telephone numbers that are helpful. See, also, *The Insiders' Guide to Virginia's Blue Ridge*, which provides details on all the area has to offer.

Harrisonburg Restaurants

THE BLUE STONE INN RESTAURANT

US 11
Lacey Spring, VA   703-434-0535
$$

This restaurant has become a landmark on US 11. Located at historic Lacey Spring (see listing above), 9 miles north of Harrisonburg, the Blue Stone Inn was started in 1949 — that's 45 years ago! — by Karl Olschofka's parents. Karl, himself, ran this restaurant until just recently, and then turned over the operation to his son and

daughter-in-law, Mike and Janet. The Olschofka family takes advantage of a trout hatchery located near the restaurant and offers some of the finest baked and stuffed trout anywhere. The Blue Stone is also known for its fine steaks. The restaurant is open Tuesday through Saturday from 4:30 to 9:30 PM. Reservations are required for groups of six or more. Smaller groups can only take their chances at the door — and it's usually a few minutes wait, especially in the summer months. But any wait is worth it.

JOSHUA WILTON HOUSE
412 S. Main St.
Harrisonburg, VA 22801   703-434-4464
$$$-$$$$

See the accommodations listing above for information on the Joshua Wilton House. The elegant restaurant at this historic house offers one of Harrisonburg's finest dining experiences. Among the many specialties are a fresh, pan-seared Norwegian salmon (served on a bed of couscous and topped with curry sauce and toasted almonds), and grilled lamb chops. The entire restaurant, which seats 26, is non-smoking. Advance reservations are necessary. The restaurant is open Monday through Saturday from 5:00 PM to closing — usually about 10:00 PM.

BAR B-Q RANCH DRIVE INN
US 11 North
Harrisonburg, VA 22801
$

This old drive-in restaurant dates to the 1950s — the "Elvis era," as locals say. Four decades later, you can still drive up, check the menu — mainly hot dogs, hamburgers and

french fries — and have a "car hop" come get your order. Truly a time-honored relic and a real treat. We met one waitress who has worked here since it opened in the mid-1950s. Located three miles north of town on US 11, the Bar B-Q Ranch is open Monday through Thursday from 11:00 AM to 8:00 PM; Friday and Saturday from 11:00 AM to 10:30 PM; and Sunday from 11:00 AM to 9:00 PM. Having gone "upscale" in recent years, the Bar B-Q Ranch now offers, in addition to the usual roadside menu, a variety of sauces, mugs and t-shirts.

SISSON'S STEAKS, ETC.
20 W. Mosby Road
Harrisonburg, VA 22801   703-564-1909
$$

Gene and Lynn Sisson ran a restaurant near New Market, VA, for years before Gene, an artist, took time off a decade ago to paint. Three years ago, the couple, along with son Ken and daughter-in-law Katie, opened this steak house, located south of Harrisonburg, just off US 11. Gene and Ken cook the steaks; Lynn greets diners and handles the cash register. (Gene's art work is part of the decor.) The Sissons hand-cut their beef in their kitchen daily. Every kind of beef entree is available: T-bones, sirloins, New York strips, prime roast — even shish ka-bob. Other popular items include a "surf and turf." Prices are reasonable. A 24-ounce chopped sirloin steak dinner, complete with salad, potato and vegetable, is $8.50. The restaurant seats 110, and a non-smoking section is available. It's open Tuesday through Thursday from

5:00 AM to 9:00 PM; Friday from 5:00 AM to 10:00 PM; Saturday from 4:00 AM to 10:00 PM; and Sunday from 4:00 AM to 10:00 PM.

Other Harrisonburg Attractions

Annual Events: The Harrisonburg region offers a number of annual events including the Rockingham County Fair, Chamber of Commerce Horse Show, Shenandoah Valley Bike Festival, Jousting Tournament, Bluegrass Festival, and activities related to fall foliage. For a detailed calendar, contact the Harrisonburg Rockingham Convention and Visitors Bureau (see listing).

Arts: Local educational institutions provide a wealth of entertainment. Bridgewater College, Eastern Mennonite College and James Madison University offer theater productions, museums, and visiting scholar presentations.

Historical and Natural Sites: Natural scenery is this region's most popular commodity. Nature lovers will enjoy the fine parks located in the Shenandoah Valley region, including the Shenandoah National Park and the George Washington National Forest. Of course, there are the famous Skyline Drive and Blue Ridge Parkway that skirt across the tops of the Blue Ridge Mountain range. Don't miss the famous and gorgeous Shenandoah River, fly fishing and various wildflower exhibitions in the Shenandoah National Park.

Among the most popular area attractions are natural caverns, including Endless Caverns near New Market, VA, and Shenandoah Caverns near Mt. Jackson, VA, both just north of Harrisonburg, and Luray Caverns at Luray, VA. Also, see the Natural Chimneys — several natural limestone towers that rise more than 100 feet above the Shenandoah Valley floor.

There are several vineyards — complete with tours and wine tastings — in the vicinity. Among them: Shenandoah Vineyards, off US 11 near Edinburg (see listing). This vineyard is open every day except major holidays from 10:00 AM to 6:00 PM (call 703-984-8699).

During the colder months, try skiing at Massanutten, located 10 miles east of Harrisonburg on US 33. For Massanutten ski information call 703-289-9441; for snow conditions call 703-432-7000.

The Daniel Harrison House, just north of the town of Dayton, is the site of a home built in the 1740s. Daniel Harrison's brother, Thomas, was the founder of Harrisonburg. The front porch of the original structure is incorporated in the present-day historical site. The Harrison house is open on Saturdays and Sundays from late May to late October. The property is operated by Fort Harrison Inc. For more information call 703-879-2280.

Shopping: The Dayton Farmers Market — located in the town of Dayton, three miles south of

Virginia Historical Society

USA General Sheridan assumed the command of the Army of the Shenandoah at the day-long battle at Winchester.

Harrisonburg on Va. Rte. 42 — has 21 specialty shops open year round. The shops offer local produce, bulk food, country hams, handcrafted furniture, jewelry, collectibles, art work, books and antiques. The shops are open Thursday from 9:00 AM to 6:00 PM; Friday from 9:00 AM to 8:00 PM; and Saturday from 9:00 AM to 5 PM. Small antique shops are located throughout the Harrisonburg vicinity, and a large, convenient shopping mall is located at the intersection of I-81 and US 33 (Market Street).

Mid-way along this tour route, in New Market, VA, are two motels of note: Blue Ridge Motor Lodge on US 11 north (800-545-8776) and the Days Inn-New Market, at 9360 George Collins Parkway (703-740-4100). Also in New Market, the John Sevier Gallery (9391 Congress Street, 703-740-3911) offers original art by local artists, and the River Farm Shop (Main Street, 703-740-3314) specializes in knitting and weaving items. The Ming Dynasty Restaurant is also located in New Market, on (185 Lee Highway, 703-740-4321).

The Sky Chalet County Inn and Restaurant is just the place for a "great escape." Located at Bayse, ten miles west of New Market atop of the Supinlick Ridge mountain chain, this facility offers a 90-seat restaurant — complete with cozy fireplace— and an eight-room inn. The Sky Chalet was built in 1937, and the decor reflects Bayse's principal draw: skiing. The restaurant offers "country gourmet" dining. Reservations are suggested, but not required; the entire dining area is open to smokers. Rooms in the inn range from $49 to $75. The higher price range includes a fireplace and sitting room. To reach the Sky Chalet, take exit 273 (Mt. Jackson) off I-81, go into downtown Mt. Jackson on US 11. From US 11, turn west on VA 263 and go 10 miles to the Sky Chalet on the right, at the top of the mountain. (For more information, telephone 703-856-2147).

TOUR 4

Harrisonburg to Lexington

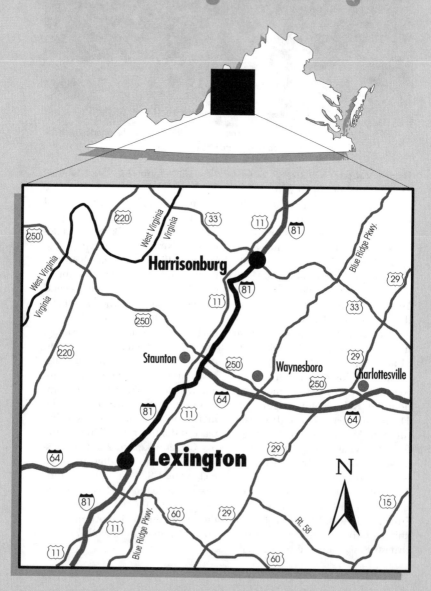

Tour 4
Southern Valley

About This Tour

This tour route begins at Harrisonburg, VA, and runs south through the Great Valley of Virginia to Lexington, VA. This route is the fourth of four in succession — along with Tour routes 1, 2 and 3, Cumberland Valley, Middle Valley and Shenandoah Valley — that cover the long valley stretch through Pennsylvania, Maryland, West Virginia and Virginia. This route ends in Lexington, and accommodations and dining suggestions are listed at the end of the chapter.

Travel Tips

The preceding valley tours generally followed US 11, which runs parallel to I-81. There were some side, country roads in the Middle Valley that veered east of US 11. This tour utilizes both US 11 and I-81. There is a long stretch of highway between Harrisonburg and Lexington — with a stop in Staunton — and it is best to stay with I-81 to save time. Be alert to slow-moving farm vehicles when you travel off the interstate.

History, Geography

As noted in previous chapters, this valley region is part of the Great Valley — once a north-south route of Native Americans. This route, an old buffalo trail and Native American route, became known as the Great Wagon Road that was inundated by German and Scotch-Irish pioneers who settled here in the early 18th century. A word about the geography, which is worth repeating. The trough through the Great Valley is at the highest elevation farther south, near Roanoke, VA. This means that your travels will take you "up" — in elevation — as you go "down" — or south. This portion of Virginia's "Great Valley" stretches to the southwest to the Virginia border with Tennessee. The Appalachians rise up dramatically to the west; the Blue Ridge Mountains form the valley's eastern side. Two major Virginia rivers, the James and the Roanoke, begin high in the Allegheny Mountains and cross this great valley trough on their way to the eastern seacoast. Another, the New River, begins in North Carolina, flows north to near Radford, and flows west — not east — to become a part of the watershed of the Ohio River.

Civil War action took place in the Great Valley, beginning in June 1861 and continuing throughout the war. A number of communities in this southern valley section felt the impact of the Civil War. Lexington remains the one valley town that reflects considerable Civil War history. Lexington was the home of two Confederate heroes, Robert E. Lee and Stonewall Jackson, and both are buried in the town.

Getting Here

This tour route begins at Harrisonburg, VA, where Tour 3 left off, and it is a natural continuation of Chapter 3: Shenandoah Valley. Harrisonburg, located in the middle of Virginia's Great Valley, is accessible via I-81 or US 11.

DIRECTIONS

The Harrisonburg Rockingham Convention and Visitors Bureau is located on Country Club Road. From I-81, take exit 247-A (US 33 west) and go west on US 33 (E. Market Street) for 0.4 miles to Vine Street. Turn right on Vine Street and go a quarter-block to the Visitors Bureau — at the intersection of Vine Street and Country Club Road.

HARRISONBURG ROCKINGHAM CONVENTION AND VISITORS BUREAU
800 Country Club Rd., P.O. Box 1
Harrisonburg, VA 22801   703-434-2319
703-434-4508 (fax)

For complete information on this Visitor Center, see the conclusion of the previous tour to the Shenandoah Valley. This convention bureau and visitors center is operated by the Chamber of Commerce of Harrisonburg and Rockingham counties. Travel counselors have information packets on area attractions. They can also help with planning accommodations and dining. This center is open Monday through Friday, from 8:30 AM to 5:00 PM. It is closed on weekends and during holidays. In preparation for this tour, check with counselors at the Visitor Center for detailed Civil War booklets and self-guided tours.

Rockingham County was established in 1778 and named for Charles Watson-Wentworth, the second marquess of Rockingham, who enthusiastically supported the American colonists in their struggle for independence from Great Britain. Harrisonburg, the county seat, was established the next year, when farmer Thomas Harrison donated two acres of land for a county courthouse. Rockingham has been — and remains — largely agricultural. Farms in this region helped feed the Confederate Army. Today, Rockingham boasts more than 2,000 farms, with an average size of nearly 130 acres. The county, which ranks among the nation's top ten turkey producers, leads the state in income from dairy, lamb, veal, beef and pork production.

Much of the Rockingham County area suffered the impact of CSA Gen. Jackson's famous Valley Campaign of 1862. Jackson's campaign served as a diversionary tactic to prevent USA Gen. McDowell from pushing east toward Richmond and reinforcing the troops under USA Gen. McClellan. From April to June 1862, Jackson and his 17,000 Confederate troops used their knowledge of the valley to outmaneuver and confuse

Union forces. Significant battles were fought at Harrisonburg, Port Republic and Cross Keys.

Later, in 1864, CSA Gen. Early was in the valley after an unsuccessful raid on Washington, D.C. Early and Sheridan fought a series of battles (see Tour 3: Shenandoah Valley), including a final conflict in Augusta County near Waynesboro, VA.

DIRECTIONS

Harrisonburg Visitors Bureau to Rockingham County Courthouse

From the visitors bureau, take US 33 (Market Street) west one mile into downtown Harrisonburg, to the Rockingham County Courthouse.

ROCKINGHAM COUNTY COURTHOUSE
Main St.
Harrisonburg, VA

This dominant building was built in 1896. It is the fifth courthouse to occupy the 1.5-acre "public square" that was donated by the county's founder, Thomas Harrison, and his wife, Sarah.

DIRECTIONS

Rockingham County Courthouse to Dayton, VA

Continue west on Market Street (US 33) around court square to VA 42 (High Street). Turn left on High Street and take VA 42 for 4 miles to Dayton.

DAYTON, VA

This small valley community barely escaped being burned to the ground during the Civil War. In 1865, USA Gen. Sheridan decided

to seek revenge for the death of his staff officer, USA Lt. Meigs, the apparent victim of a Confederate guerrilla attack a few months earlier. Sheridan ordered the burning of all houses within 5 miles of Dayton. USA Gen. Custer assumed the task with enthusiasm. But Sheridan had a last-minute change of heart. Instead, he ordered all local able-bodied men be taken prisoner.

DIRECTIONS

Dayton to Shenandoah Valley Heritage Museum

From VA 42 in Dayton, turn right on VA 732, go 0.2 miles and follow signs across Cooks Creek to the Shenandoah Valley Heritage Museum at 382 High Street.

SHENANDOAH VALLEY HERITAGE MUSEUM
382 High St.
Dayton, VA 22821   *703-879-2681*

This attractive brick museum offers exhibits on the history of the Rockingham County and Shenandoah Valley regions, particularly an electronic map of Civil War action in the valley. The museum also features seasonal exhibits and lecture programs, as well as a gift shop and a book store. Its hours vary: from early May to late October it is open Monday through Saturday from 9:00 AM to 4:00 PM, and Sunday from 1:00 PM to 4:00 PM. During the winter it is open Thursday through Saturday from 10 AM to 4:00 PM. Admission is free.

DIRECTIONS

Dayton to Turner Ashby's Monument

Return on VA 42 to Harrisonburg, jog from VA 42 (High Street) to Main Street (US 11). Go south on Main Street beyond James Madison University to Port Republic Road (VA 659). Turn left (southeast) on Port Republic Road, cross over I-81, and continue southeast for 1.1 miles. Look for a brown directional sign for the Ashby monument. At the sign, turn left on a single-lane state route and go 0.3 miles to the monument.

TURNER ASHBY'S MONUMENT, BATTLE OF HARRISONBURG

CSA Gen. Ashby took a delaying position against Union forces here, at Chestnut Ridge, on June 5, 1862, as part of CSA Gen. Jackson's withdrawal after 2nd Winchester. The next day, the Battle of Harrisonburg involved Ashby's cavalrymen — reinforced by the 48th Va. Cavalry — against a force led by USA Col. Wyndham. USA Gen. Fremont sent a group of sharpshooters, known as the Pennsylvania Bucktails, to attack the Confederate rear guard. To encourage his Southern troops, Ashby

Cross Keys, Port Republic

Return to VA 659 (Port Republic Road), turn left, and continue southeast for 4.5 miles to VA 276. Here, two days after the Battle of Harrisonburg, on June 8, 1862, Union and Confederate troops fought the battle in the shadow of the Blue Ridge Mountains. CSA Gen. Ewell's men were outnumbered by USA Gen. Fremont's troops by nearly two-to-one. Still, CSA Gen. Jackson ordered Ewell to attack Fremont in a timely battle to prevent Fremont from shifting north to Port Republic and uniting with force up the other side of the Massanutten Mountains. During the morning battle, Union troops were forced to retreat, suffering the majority of the battle's casualties. The farms and fields in this vicinity look much as they did over 130 years ago.

Continue southeast on Port Republic Road (VA 659) for 5.3 miles to the community of Port Republic. The day after the Battle of Cross Keys, June 9, fighting shifted to Port Republic, a community located on the South Fork of the Shenandoah River. This battle, a Confederate victory, marked the end of CSA Gen. Jackson's Valley Campaign of 1862. After this series of battles, Confederate troops rested a week in Brown's Gap in Albemarle County's Blue Ridge Mountains before marching to Mechum's River Station and boarding the Virginia Central Railroad for Richmond. In the Confederate capital city, Jackson's men helped stem the tide of USA Gen. McClellan's Peninsular Campaign.

Cross Keys and Port Republic are two of the three least-altered battle sites of the Jackson's famous Valley Campaign (the other is McDowell — see listing below). Return on VA 659 (Port Republic Road), beyond the Turner Ashby Monument, to I-81. If you've taken this side trip, there is an alternate way back to I-81. East of Port Republic, turn right (south) on US 340 and go 2 miles to Grottoes, turn right (west) on VA 256 and go 6 miles to I-81.

Turner Ashby

Turner Ashby was a dashing, colorful horseman who traced his roots to a long line of Virginia country gentlemen. His great-grandfather served with George Washington in the French and Indian War, and his father was a colonel in the War of 1812. Ashby was only 6 when his father died in 1834, and his mother, Elizabeth, made sure he was properly educated by private tutors. Ashby entered adulthood as an enviable gentleman whose days were filled with horse riding and hunting. A handsome man, with dark hair, he never married.

In 1855, at the age of 27, he formed a cavalry group to police the workers building the Manassas Gap Railroad. Four years later, when John Brown raided Harpers Ferry, Ashby's cavalrymen were among the first militia on the scene. With the outbreak of the Civil War, Ashby became a daring Southern cavalry officer — some say he was as colorful as his fellow Confederate, Stonewall Jackson. Ashby became a part of Jackson's famous Valley Campaign of 1862.

According to Civil War legend, Ashby once disguised himself as an old horse doctor and rode a nag into Pennsylvania to spy on Union Army activities. Ashby's bravery was renowned. During the retreat from Winchester in March 1862, Ashby apparently was the last Confederate to leave town. But his lack of military discipline led him to a confrontation with Jackson, who stripped the cavalry officer of his command. Ashby, angered by Jackson's decision, said he would have challenged Jackson to a duel if the two were the same rank. Instead, Ashby threatened to resign his commission and remove his cavalry command from Jackson's army. Jackson, in a rare move, backed down and reinstated Ashby.

The reckless cavalier met his doom at the Battle of Harrisonburg, performing the expected: leading a charge against Union soldiers. Jackson reacted to Ashby's death, saying "as a partisan officer I never knew his superior; his daring was proverbial; his powers of endurance almost incredible; his character heroic. . . ."

charged the front of the Union advance. When his horse was shot out from under him, Ashby continued on foot until he was struck in the chest by a Union bullet. He died on the spot. His death seemed to rally the Confederates, who eventually defeated the Northerners — including the Bucktails. The Ashby monument reads, "General Turner Ashby, C.S.A. was killed on this spot, June 6, 1862, gallantly leading a charge."

DIRECTIONS

Harrisonburg to Staunton, VA

From I-81, go south to Staunton. Along the route is the community of Mount Crawford. A cavalry engagement was fought in this vicinity on March 1, 1865. Continue south on I-81 to Staunton.

STAUNTON, VA

This community was settled in the 1730s by a group of Scotch-Irish pioneers, led by John Lewis. Other prominent Scotch-Irish families included the Pattons, Prestons, and Breckenridges (see the Breckenridge story in Tour 3). Staunton is the seat of Augusta County, which was formed in 1738 along with Frederick County to the north. These two valley counties were named in honor of Princess Augusta of Saxe-Gotha, and her husband, Frederick Louis, England's Prince of Wales. These two were the parents of King George III.

Staunton Side Trip

McDowell, VA

McDowell is located high in the Appalachian Mountains, 30 miles west of Staunton. This trip is only for the avid Civil War buff — it takes 45 minutes to an hour to reach McDowell over the twisting, curvy US 250. Here, just 10 miles east of Monterey, the seat of Highland County, the Bullpasture and Cowpasture rivers begin their tumble south and east as the origins of the historic James River. McDowell, the oldest village in Highland County, was named for former Virginia Governor James McDowell, who was born in nearby Rockbridge County and served as governor from 1843 to 1846.

CSA Gen. Jackson, during his 1862 Valley Campaign, held back an advance by troops here under USA Gen. Fremont. As part of this battle, on May 8, Jackson undertook what some historians consider one of the most difficult marches of the war.

To deceive his enemy, Jackson took a round-about route, starting from Port Republic east of Harrisonburg, crossing the muddy Blue Ridge Mountains at Brown's Gap, marching to Mechum's River Station in nearby Albemarle County, and boarding the Virginia Central Railroad for a west-bound ride to Staunton. Near Staunton, Jackson met with reinforcements and moved on McDowell. In all, Jackson's men marched 92 miles in four days, not including the brief 25-mile train ride. During the battle at McDowell, the Confederates suffered more casualties than the Federals, but Jackson successfully held the Union force, allowing him to implement an advance down the valley — thus opening his 1862 Valley Campaign. The McDowell Presbyterian Church in town was used as a hospital after the fighting.

Waynesboro, VA

Here's another side trip for history buffs only. From Staunton, take US 250 east to this Augusta County community named for Gen. "Mad" Anthony Wayne, a Revolutionary War veteran. From 1847 until the outbreak of the Civil War, R. L. Dabney was the minister at Tinkling Spring church, just west of town. Dabney went on to become a member of CSA Gen. Jackson's staff. On March 2, 1865, in what was considered the last important struggle in the valley, "Early's Last Battle" was fought on the western side of town. CSA Gen. Early was driven from a ridge during Sheridan's Valley Campaign. USA Gen. Custer's cavalry division led the Union attack and completely enveloped the enemy. Early escaped, but Custer caught some 1,600 men and claimed 17 flags, 11 guns, and all of Early's supplies. Riverview Cemetery, at the intersection of US 250 and US 340, features a marker honoring Southern soldiers from four states who were killed in the Waynesboro battle.

Staunton was the headquarters for the Stonewall Brigade Band, which served the revered Stonewall Jackson. USA Gen. Grant, following the Confederate surrender at Appomattox, allowed unit members to take home their musical instruments. Later, ironically, the band played at Grant's funeral in July 1885 in New York. Staunton is the birthplace of President Woodrow Wilson.

DIRECTIONS

Staunton to Steele's Tavern, VA

From Staunton (milepost 225), continue south on I-81 to Steele's Tavern (milepost 205), on the Augusta-Rockbridge county line. The settlement was named for Daniel Steele, a Revolutionary War veteran who operated a tavern on the Great Wagon Road.

McCormick Farm and Workshop

Cyrus McCormick was born here in 1809. Cyrus' father, Robert McCormick, spent more than two decades experimenting with a grain reaping machine. Picking up on his father's efforts, Cyrus successfully demonstrated a reaper in 1831. The invention revolutionized agriculture because it enabled farmers to reap as much grain as they could sew. Cyrus patented the machine in 1834 and began commercial manufacture in the valley in the 1840s. In 1847, the valley inventor moved to Chicago and founded the McCormick Harvesting and Machine Company, the forerunner of International Harvester. In 1851, McCormick's "Virginia Reaper" won a gold medal at London's Crystal Place Exhibition. It was the highest award of the day, and it made McCormick a world celebrity. Ironically, during the Civil War, McCormick's invention had a profound impact on American manufacturing. His machine enabled Midwestern farmers to provide the grain necessary to feed the Union Army. McCormick died in 1884 after

— continued on next page

— continued from previous page

Steele's Tavern Side Trip

becoming one of the most successful manufacturers in the nation's industrial age. Today, the McCormick Farm is a National Historic Landmark. Operated as part of the Shenandoah Valley Agricultural Experiment Station, a network managed by Virginia Polytechnic Institute and State University, the site is open free from 8:30 AM to 5:00 PM daily. From I-81 take VA 606 east.

DIRECTIONS

Steele's Tavern to Lexington Visitor Center

From Steele's Tavern (milepost 205), continue south on I-81 to Lexington (milepost 189) at exit 188-B. Take the exit ramp and head west on US 60 toward Lexington. After 2.4 miles, take a right onto Lewis Street (follow signs for visitor center). Go a block and shift left onto Washington Street, and continue west another 0.2 miles to the visitor center parking lot on the right.

LEXINGTON VISITOR CENTER

102 E. Washington St.
Lexington, VA 24450   *703-463-3777*
                           703-463-1105 (fax)

History comes alive during a stroll through Lexington amid authentic 18th- and 19th-century buildings. This community, founded by Scotch-Irish pioneers in the 1770s, was named not long after the famous Battle of Lexington — in Massachusetts — during the American Revolution. Lexington's historic claim is based in part on Civil War greats Robert E. Lee and Thomas "Stonewall" Jackson. Both were native Virginians, graduates of West Point, distinguished veterans of the Mexican War, and college educators in this valley town. Their homes, colleges, churches and burial sites are here. Today, their birthdays — both in January — are celebrated by a joint observance in Virginia.

During the Civil War, Virginia Military Institute, located here in Lexington, was damaged by fire set in June 1864 by USA Gen. Hunter. CSA Gen. E. F. Paxton, one of commanders of the Stonewall Brigade and a victim of the 1863 Battle of Chancellorsville, lived nearby before the Civil War began. And Lexington was the home of Virginia's wartime governor, John Letcher.

This Lexington Visitor Center is one of the nicest facilities of its kind anywhere in the Mid-Atlantic — or anywhere! Here, travel counselors greet you in a living room atmosphere. There's no counter — barrier — between the hosts and guests. Rather, easy chairs, couches, exhibits and displays provide a cozy, comfortable setting. Still, the center is full of the usual, informative brochures, packets, tour maps and other travel information. The center offers restroom facilities, water fountain and vending machines. An Accommodations Gallery has plenty of information on where to stay in the Lexington area, and it features a direct dial telephone to some accommodations. The center is open daily from 8:30 AM to 6:00 PM dur-

Historic Lexington

STONEWALL JACKSON HOUSE

Guided tours on the hour and half hour

HISTORIC HOUSE, GARDEN AND MUSEUM SHOP
8 E. Washington St. • Lexington, VA 24450
703-463-2552

Visit Historic Lee Chapel on the
Campus of Washington and Lee University.

General Lee's final resting place.
Lexington, Virginia

Llewellyn Lodge at Lexington

- Full Gourmet Breakfast
- Walking distance to downtown
- Unique packages available

- Nearby Hiking, horseback riding, & cycling
- 11 miles from Blue Ridge Parkway
- Gift certificates

A B&B as a B&B should be.

603 S. Main Street Lexington, VA 24450 1-800-882-1145

| Theatre at Lime Kiln | Memorial-Labor Day Plays Tues.-Sat. Concerts Sun. (703) 463-3074 |

STONEWALL COUNTRY

Exciting battle scenes, vivid portraits of Civil War heroes, and Robin & Linda Williams' unforgettable music have been bringing audiences to their feet since 1985.

Virginia BORN & BRED, INC.

Uncommon Gifts From The Commonwealth
16 W. Washington St.
(800) 437-2452

Civil War
autographs, documents, maps & prints
ORIGINAL FRAMEWORKS
4 E. Washington St.
Lexington, VA
(703) 464-6464
HRS: M-Sat 10-5:30

LEXINGTON HISTORICAL SHOP

Rare & Used Books, Prints
9 E. Washington St.
(703) 463-2615

The WILLSON-WALKER HOUSE *Restaurant*

Fine Dining
30 N. Main St.
(703) 463-3020

Artists in Cahoots

A dazzling display of beautiful things made by local artists and crafters.

1 West Washington St.
(703) 464-1147

★★★ FOR MORE INFORMATION, CALL OR STOP BY ★★★
Historic Lexington Visitor Center   102 E. Washington Street • (703) 463-3777

ing June, July and August, otherwise from 9:00 AM to 5:00 PM. It is closed New Year's Day, Thanksgiving Day and Christmas Day.

DIRECTIONS

Lexington Visitor Center to Stonewall Jackson House
Walk one block west on Washington Street to the intersection of Washington and Main streets, and the Stonewall Jackson House at 8 E. Washington Street.

STONEWALL JACKSON HOUSE
8 E. Washington St.
Lexington, VA 24450   *703-463-2552*

Stonewall Jackson, one of Lexington's most celebrated former residents, lived in this community for ten years before going off to the Civil War. Jackson taught at Virginia Military Institute. His home, made of brick and stone, was the only house he owned. He married, suffered from his wife's death, traveled abroad, engaged in business, joined a debating society, and worshiped at Lexington Presbyterian Church. He married a second time, to Mary Anna Morrison, and the couple moved into the house in 1859. Two years later, Jackson rode off to war. The structure was used as a hospital for a number of years before being re-

stored and opened to visitors. A Registered National Landmark, it includes a number of Jackson's personal effects. It is open Monday through Saturday from 9:00 AM to 5:00 PM, and Sunday from 1:00 to 5:00 PM. In the summer, the museum stays open until 6:00 PM. An admission fee of $4 for adults and $2 for children is charged. Tours begin on the hour and half-hour, with the last tour beginning at 4:30 PM (in the summer, the last tour begins at 5:30 PM). To keep young visitors involved, Stonewall Jackson House guides provide children with slates listing items on the house tour. Youngsters circle items on the slates when they see the objects.

DIRECTIONS

Stonewall Jackson House to Lexington Presbyterian Church
Walk one block south along Main Street to the intersection of Nelson Street.

LEXINGTON PRESBYTERIAN CHURCH
Main and Nelson Sts.
Lexington, VA 24450

This building, constructed in 1845, is where Stonewall Jackson worshipped, taught Sunday School, and served as a deacon.

Lexington Personality

Mary Anna Jackson
Of her husband's home, Mary Anna Jackson wrote: ". . . it was genuine happiness to him to have a home of his own: it was the first one he had ever possessed, and it was truly his castle. He lost no time in going to work to repair it and make it comfortable and attractive. His tastes were simple, but he liked to have everything in perfect order — every door 'on golden hinges softly turning,' as he expressed it; 'a place for everything, and everything in its place. . . .'"

Photo: Richmond Newspapers

A photo of General Lee astride Traveller, taken while Lee was president of Washington College.

DIRECTIONS

Lexington Presbyterian Church to Stonewall Jackson Memorial Cemetery

Walk two blocks farther south along Main Street, beyond the intersection with McDowell Street.

STONEWALL JACKSON MEMORIAL CEMETERY

S. Main St.
Lexington, VA 24450

Stonewall Jackson is buried in this cemetery, along with a number of other Confederate veterans. Jackson's statue, sculpted by Richmond's Edward Valentine, was dedicated in 1891, 23 years after Jackson's death during the Battle of Chancellorsville. The setting here — the town in general and the cemetery in particular — fulfill Jackson's dying wish: "Let us pass over the river, and rest under the shade of the trees." Visit the cemetery free from dawn to dusk.

DIRECTIONS

Stonewall Jackson Memorial Cemetery to Washington and Lee University

Return north on Main Street to Washington Street. Turn left and head west one block on Washington Street, beyond Jefferson Street to the campus of Washington and Lee University (W&L).

WASHINGTON AND LEE UNIVERSITY

Lexington, VA 24450   703-463-8400

W&L was founded by Scotch-Irish pioneers in the 1740s as Augusta Academy. Later, it was called Liberty Hall Academy and located just north of Lexington. It was saved from bankruptcy when former President George Washington bequeathed $50,000 and became the school's namesake. After the Civil War, Robert E. Lee accepted the school's presidency and infused new vitality into this early American academy of learning. After Lee died in 1870, the school name was changed to Washington and Lee to honor the two most prominent men in its history. The 55-acre campus has 30 principal buildings, including the historic Washington College group that forms the colonnade facing Lee Chapel. A four-building cluster is worth noting:

R.E. LEE MEMORIAL EPISCOPAL CHURCH

This church was founded in 1840, mainly through the efforts of Gen. Francis H. Smith, the first superintendent of Virginia Military Institute and a colleague and friend of Robert E. Lee. Lee was a senior warden of Grace Episcopal Church. In 1870, a few days before his death, Lee approved plans for a new church building. This church was completed in 1883.

LEE HOUSE

This is the college president's house, so it's not open to the public. It was built for Robert E. Lee while he was president of W&L. Lee died in a room on the first floor. The large porch was included for Mrs. Lee, who was confined to a wheelchair, and the garage was formerly used as a stable for Lee's famous horse, Traveller.

LEE-JACKSON HOUSE

This house also is closed to the public. Stonewall Jackson married W&L President George Junkin's daughter, Elinor, in this house in 1853. Jackson and his wife lived in the north wing for a number of years. Robert E. Lee and his wife lived in the house after he became president of the college and before the adjacent Lee House was constructed.

LEE CHAPEL

Lee Chapel is a memorial to the Confederate general and his family. The general, and his father, Revolutionary patriot Henry "Lighthorse" Harry Lee, are among several family members interred in a crypt beneath the chapel. "The Recumbent Statue of R. E. Lee," by Edward Valentine, the centerpiece of the chapel, portrays Lee sleeping — not dead — on the field of battle. A plaque honors the Liberty Hall Volunteers of the Stonewall Brigade, a Confederate unit during the Civil War. The chapel is open free of charge. From April to October it is open Monday through Saturday from 9:00 AM to 5:00 PM, and on Sunday from 2:00 to 5:00 PM. During the winter it is open until 4:00 PM. In the chapel is Lee's Office, preserved as he left it in 1870. It is open (same hours) free of charge. The annual Lee Memorial Service is held here in October. Lee's famous horse, Traveller, is buried outside the chapel. For more information, call 703-463-8768.

DIRECTIONS

**Lee Chapel to
Virginia Military Institute**
Just to the north of the W&L campus, along Letcher Avenue, is Virginia Military Institute (VMI).

VIRGINIA MILITARY INSTITUTE

Letcher Avenue   703-464-7000
Lexington, VA 24450

Founded in 1839, on the site of an arsenal, VMI is known as the "West Point of the South." It is the nation's oldest state-supported military school, and it has sent graduates to every American conflict since the Mexican War. Stonewall Jackson, a graduate of West Point, is the big hero at VMI, where he taught natural philosophy and artillery tactics. He was austere, and he chose to prepare all his school lessons while standing. He also ate while standing, believing it was better for digestion. His cadets thought he was crazy; they called him "Tom Fool." A plain, silent, polite man, he was shabbily dressed, sucked on lemons, and believed passionately in the sternest aspects of Presbyterianism and predestination. John Mercer Brooke, the chief of naval ordnance for the Confederacy, also taught at VMI, as did Matthew Fontaine Maury, the "Pathfinder of the Sea" (see listing below). In May 1864, VMI cadets fought as a corps in the Battle of New Market, north of Harrisonburg (see Tour 3: Shenandoah Valley). There are several buildings clustered around the parade field at VMI, including:

COMMANDANT'S QUARTERS

Built in 1852, this served as the home of VMI professor Matthew Fontaine Maury from 1868 to 1872. This building is not open to the public.

THE BARRACKS

VMI cadets live here. One arch is named in honor of Stonewall Jackson, and the statue in front of the arch depicts the general surveying the field at Chancellorsville. The cannons beside the statue were cast in 1848 and used by Jackson to teach artillery at VMI.

JACKSON MEMORIAL HALL, VMI MUSEUM

This is the assembly hall for VMI cadets, and named in honor of Stonewall Jackson. The prominent oil painting depicts the VMI cadets who fought in the Battle of New Market in the Shenandoah Valley in 1864. The painting is the work of Benjamin West Clinedinst, an 1880 VMI graduate.

The VMI Museum, downstairs in Jackson Memorial Hall, displays Stonewall Jackson memorabilia, including his uniform coat, the handkerchief used to stop the blood of his mortal wound at Chancellorsville, and a flag that was designed to mourn his death. The remains of Jackson's Civil War horse, Little Sorrel, are preserved and displayed at the museum, too. There is a special display of a typical VMI cadet's room, usually a big hit with children. The museum is open free of charge, Monday through Saturday from 9:00 AM to 5:00 PM, and Sunday from 2:00 to 5:00 PM.

Adjacent to Jackson Memorial Hall is a statue, "Virginia Mourning Her Dead," which honors the VMI cadets who fought at the Battle of New Market. Six of the 10 cadets killed in the Civil War battle are buried behind the monument.

Matthew Fontaine Maury

In the decade prior to the Civil War, Matthew Fontaine Maury was one of the most famous men in the world. A Virginia native, Maury was a pioneer in oceanography, earning him dozens of international medals, honorary degrees, and diplomas. Today, ironically, Maury's name is an enigma, even in his home state. He has been described as one of the most neglected figures in the history of America and science.

Born in Spotsylvania County, VA, young "Matt" Maury was only four when his family moved west to

Photo: Richmond Newspapers

Franklin, Tennessee. In 1825, at the age of 19, he turned down a future in farming, opting instead for a midshipman's warrant in the U. S. Navy. Maury was determined to learn about the sea, and ships, and sailing. And for nearly a decade of cruises he conducted a detailed and exhaustive study of navigation. Taking a leave of absence in 1834, he married his cousin, Ann Herndon of Fredericksburg, VA. There, where the couple made their home, he published his studies: *A New Theoretical and Practical Treatise on Navigation*.

In 1836, the newly promoted Lt. Maury was assigned to survey the harbors of towns along the southeast. Two years later he became a strong advocate of a naval academy, which the nation eventually established at Annapolis. Maury's break came when he was assigned to the Depot of Charts and Instruments in Washington, D.C., and named superintendent of the new Naval Observatory. By 1847 he released his *Winds and Currents Chart of the North Atlantic*, which cut two weeks off a ship's travel from New York to Rio de Janeiro. Maury conceived a universal system of oceanography, prompting an international congress in Brussels in 1853. He was the U. S. representative at the meeting, which adopted a uniform world oceanography system. Two years later, during the Gold Rush, Maury's updated information cut the average travel time for a ship from New York to San Francisco from 180 to 133 days. That same year he prepared a report that proved the practicality — and assured the success — of the first trans-Atlantic cable between the United States and Europe.

In April 1861, after Virginia's secession from the Union, Maury joined the Confederate Navy. He tinkered with the concept of electric mines, and was sent to England the next year on "special service" for the Southern cause, testing his new idea. At war's end he was among Confederate representatives abroad who were excluded from the pardon of the amnesty. "Exiled" in Mexico, he was named imperial commissioner of immigration in an unsuccessful scheme to colonize former Confederates.

— continued on next page

— continued from previous page

Then, he spent two years back in England, writing geography school books.

Maury returned in 1868 to become professor of meteorology at Virginia Military Institute in Lexington. Ever the scientist, he published his *Physical Survey of Virginia* and lectured on how farming could benefit from weather observations.

Maury died in Lexington in February 1873. His remains were removed to Richmond seven months later. VMI cadets escorted the cortege north out of Lexington along the North River. At Goshen Pass, his favorite retreat, his casket was covered with mountain laurel and rhododendron. Upriver, at Goshen, his body was put on the train for Richmond and a burial in Hollywood Cemetery.

Today, Maury's name is honored. The North River was renamed Maury; a VMI building bears his name. VA 39 out of Goshen was named the Maury Highway in 1923, the same year a monument was dedicated at Goshen Pass. In 1929, a sculpture was unveiled on Monument Avenue in Richmond (see Tour 12: Richmond) to honor the Virginian once known around the world as the "Pathfinder of the Seas."

Sam Houston

Sam Houston, a hero of Texas independence, was the Lone Star State governor who resigned rather than sign a Confederate oath of allegiance. Houston was born in a log cabin just north of Lexington in Rockbridge County in March 1793. Young Sam moved with his family to Tennessee after his father died. He spent much of his youth with Cherokee Indians. After a career in Tennessee politics, during which time he was a governor and congressman,

Source: Richmond Newspapers

Houston moved to Texas. In 1835 he assumed command of a 400-man army, and defeated Mexican Gen. Santa Anna at Buffalo Bayou in April 1836 to gain independence for Texas. Two months later he was chosen over another Texas hero, Stephen Austin, as president of the new Republic of Texas. Ironically, Austin also was born in western Virginia — 125 miles away from present-day Wytheville — only eight months after Houston. Houston went to the U.S. Senate from the new state of Texas and served from 1846 to 1849. Elected governor in 1859, Houston served from 1860 to 1861, when he resigned in order to avoid signing a Confederate oath of allegiance. He died in Huntsville, Texas in 1863, during the Civil War, at the age of 70.

Natural Bridge and Points South

Continuing south, down US 11 or I-81, are a string of attractive locations:

Natural Bridge: The "Bridge of God," as the Monocan Indians called it, this is considered one of the seven natural wonders of the world. Thomas Jefferson once owned it. Today, U.S. 11 runs over the top of the natural bridge, a tourist attraction complete with accommodations, a restaurant, a gift shop, a wax museum, tennis and swimming, and an indoor golf course. An admission fee of $7 per adult and $3.50 per child is charged (I-81, milepost 175).

Buchanan: This community, a water gap of the James River, is named for John B. Buchanan, the son-in-law of prominent local landowner, Col. James Patton. Construction on the noted James River and Kanawha Canal, originating in Richmond and slated to cross the eastern continental divide to the Kanawha River, ended here in 1851. USA Gen. Hunter, on his way to Lynchburg, passed through Buchanan in June 1864 (I-81, milepost 167).

Troutville: Here, in colonial times, the Great Wagon Road split, with one route heading south to the Carolinas and the other shifting west over the Catawba Mountains toward the Cumberland Gap (I-81, mileposts 156, 150).

Roanoke: Originally called Big Lick, for the salt licks used by native fauna, this community was named Roanoke for the river of the same name. Roanoke is a word of Native American origin, and is among the first Indian words used by Anglo pioneers in the late 16th century (I-81, mileposts 146, 143).

Salem: USA Gen. Hunter, retreating from Lynchburg, traveled through Roanoke County in the vicinity of Salem in June 1864. He was pursued by CSA Gen. Early. Hanging Rock, south of Salem, is where USA Gen. Hunter and CSA Gen. Early fought a significant battle in June 1864 (I-81, mileposts 141, 140, 137).

Christiansburg: This town was named for Col. William Christian, a veteran of the American Revolution. It was raided by USA Gen. Averell in May 1864, and again by USA Gen. Stoneman in April 1865 (I-81, mileposts 118, 114).

Radford: Named for Dr. John B. Radford, a local citizen, this community was often raided by troops from both the North and South. The New River, one of the oldest rivers in the world, flows west — not east — and is part of the watershed of the Ohio River. Confederate troops once burned the New River bridge to deter approaching Federals (I-81, mileposts 109, 105).

— continued on next page

— continued from previous page

Dublin: Despite a large influx of Scotch-Irish settlers in the Great Valley of Virginia, this town apparently is the only one in the state named for a place in Ireland. CSA Gen. Jenkins, captured in Pennsylvania during the Gettysburg Campaign and wounded at the Gettysburg battle, was killed just north of Dublin in May 1864. During the Battle of Cloyd's Mountain, USA Gen. Crook pushed back CSA Gen. Jenkins during a raid to destroy the Virginia and Tennessee Railroad. Jenkins, who served as both a U.S. and Confederate congressman, was a Harvard graduate (I-81, milepost 98).

Wytheville: This town is the Wythe county seat. Both the town and county names honor George Wythe, a Virginia signer of the Declaration of Independence. This area is known for the lead deposits located in the nearby mountains. Lead was essential to ammunition production. Molten lead was dropped from the top of a "shot tower," into a water tank at the bottom. The nearby Austinville mine was begun by Moses Austin, the father of Texas hero, Stephen Austin, a Wythe County native. Today, the Shot Tower Historic State Park (closed in the winter) is located 10 miles south of Wytheville on the New River. The Wythe Union Lead Mine Company was the chief domestic supplier of lead to the Confederacy. Because of the lead, the North and South fought over this community on a number of occasions, in July 1863, May and December 1864, and April 1865. According to local legend, young Molly Tynes rode 40 miles over the mountains to alert local riflemen of a Union raid, and the town was saved because of her bravery. Col. R. E. Withers, a Confederate officer, a lieutenant governor of Virginia, U.S. senator and consul at Hong Kong, lived at Ingleside just east of town (I-81, mileposts 73, 72, 70).

Lexington Accommodations

MAPLE HALL

Route 5, Box 223
Lexington, VA 24450   703-463-6693
$$$-$$$$

Maple Hall is located on 56 rolling acres just 6 miles north of Lexington. It is owned by Historic Country Inns, which offers two other inns in the Lexington area: the Alexander-Withrow House and the McCampbell Inn, both downtown. All three offer antiques, private baths, and some working fireplaces. Maple Hall is a fully restored, 1850 ante-bellum plantation home. The fine old, three-story brick structure features an elegant white-columned front portico. The inn has 21 rooms, and it features a three-bedroom guest house, three separate dining rooms, a swimming pool, a tennis court and walking trails.

LLEWELLYN LODGE

603 S. Main St.
Lexington, VA 24450   703-463-3235
$$$ 800-882-1145

John Roberts is a Lexingtonian. His wife, Ellen, is a gourmet cook with extensive experience in the travel and hospitality business. Together, they've run their 53-year-old, brick colonial, six-bedroom inn since 1985.

Rooms feature air conditioning and private baths. Well-behaved children over the age of 10 are welcomed. The hosts serve a full gourmet breakfast from 8:00 to 9:30 AM.

COMFORT INN

US 11 South, P.O. Box 905
Lexington, VA 24450   703-463-7311
$$

This Comfort Inn, located just north of town at the intersection of I-64 and US 11, has 80 units. The inn offers a complimentary continental breakfast, an indoor heated pool, and color television in each room. Some non-smoking rooms are available.

There are other motels, inns and bed and breakfast facilities in the Lexington, VA, area. If you have questions, or if you need a list of area accommodations, see a travel counselor at the Lexington Visitor Center (see listing).

Or, pick up a copy of *The Insiders' Guide to Virginia's Blue Ridge* for comprehensive, "insider's" information on the area and all it has to offer.

Lexington Restaurants

WILLSON-WALKER HOUSE RESTAURANT

30 N. Main St.
Lexington, VA 24450   703-463-3020
$$

Located in historic downtown Lexington, this 1820 classic revival home was built by William Willson, postmaster, merchant and treasurer of Washington College. In 1911, Harry Walker converted the fine home into a grocery store. Now a registered Virginia landmark, the Willson-Walker House is a restaurant that's been featured in

Colonial Homes magazine. Lunch and dinner are served Tuesday to Saturday from 11:30 AM to 2:30 PM, and from 5:30 to 9:00 PM. The menu offers American cuisine. Reservations are recommended.

SOUTHERN INN

37 S. Main St.
Lexington, VA 24450   703-463-3612
$

Locals and alumni from W&L and VMI sing the praises of the Southern Inn — and travelers do too after they've sampled the southern home cooking. A downtown Lexington fixture since 1932, everybody eventually ends up dining at the Southern Inn. Lunches feature homemade soups and sandwiches. There are full dinners with such staples as chicken and beef, as well as Greek and Italian dishes. Nothing fancy here, just exceptionally good food. Open Monday through Friday from 10:30 AM to 11:00 PM, and Saturday and Sunday from 9:00 AM to 11:00 PM.

Other Lexington Attractions

Annual Events: The birthdays of both Robert E. Lee and Stonewall Jackson (the two are honored by a Virginia state holiday) are celebrated annually in January. Special functions honoring the two Confederate heroes are conducted at Stonewall Jackson House, Washington and Lee University, and Virginia Military Institute. Sunrise Easter services are conducted at nearby Natural Bridge (see listing). The Rockbridge Community Festival is held in August each year. "Holiday in Lexington" is an annual event in December.

Arts: The Theater at Lime Kiln has been called "the most unusual theater setting in the United States." The summer outdoor theater is part of Lime Kiln Arts Inc., a not-for-profit organization in Lexington. The site itself is historic. A.T. Barclay, a Confederate veteran who served with Stonewall Jackson, began the kiln in 1896 to make lime. A highlight of each year's performances is "Stonewall Country," a musical about the Confederate general. Play-goers dress casually and have a chance to sit on the lawn in the Bowl, one of the three performance spaces at the 12-acre site. Plays are presented Tuesday through Saturday. Musical performances are featured each Sunday. Gates open at 6:00 PM and performances begin at 8:00 PM. For information contact Theater at Lime Kiln, P.O. Box 663, Lexington, VA 24450, or call 703-463-3074. From downtown Lexington, take Nelson Street (US 60) west a mile to Borden Street on the left. The Henry Street Playhouse presents musicals, comedies and historical plays during the summer months.

Historical Sites: Lexington Carriage Company offers tours of historic downtown Lexington. The 40-minute, narrated tours begin at the Lexington Visitor Center. For schedule and rate information, contact Lexington Carriage Company at P.O. Box 1242, Lexington, VA 24450, or telephone 703-463-5647.

The George C. Marshall Museum at VMI highlights the life of the famous World War II general, a 1901 graduate of VMI. The museum details the course of World War II and includes an electronic map. It also has a treasure hunt for children, displays the general's Nobel Peace Prize, and features a museum shop. The museum is open free, March to October, from 9:00 AM to 5:00 PM. It closes at 4:00 PM during winter months. For more information, contact the George C. Marshall Library and Museum, Drawer 1600, Lexington, VA 24450, or telephone 703-463-7103.

Goshen Pass, a 3-mile mountain gorge, provides the setting for canoeing, fishing, trail walking and picnicking. The gorge is located on VA 39, northwest of Lexington.

The Virginia Horse Center offers horse shows, educational seminars, and horse sales. The center is located on 400 rolling Rockbridge County acres, just north of Lexington. For information contact the Virginia Horse Center, P.O. Box 1051, Lexington, VA 24450, or telephone 703-463-2194.

Two attractions in Staunton (during the earlier part of this tour route) are worth noting. The Woodrow Wilson Birthplace and Museum is located at 18-24 N. Coulter Street. The Wilson birthplace is a stately Greek Revival manse and is listed as a National Historic Landmark. It includes free parking, handicap parking, and a gift shop with period reproductions. It is open daily from 9:00 AM to 5:00 PM, but closes on Sundays during the winter. It is closed New Year's Day, Thanksgiving Day and Christmas Day. A fee of $5 for adults and $1 for children is charged. For more information, telephone the museum at 703-885-0897, or fax 703-886-9874. Also, the Museum of American Frontier Culture in Staunton is worth seeing. See four authentic working farms that illustrate the European influence on American — particularly Shenandoah Valley — lifestyles. The museum is open daily in the summer from 9:00 AM to 5:00 PM. During the winter it is open daily from 10:00 AM to 4:00 PM. It is closed New Year's Day, Thanksgiving Day and Christmas Day. A fee of $5 for adults and $2.50 for children is charged. For more information, telephone 703-332-7850.

Shopping: Take a visit to the historic downtown Lexington area for a variety of specialty shops and unique stores. Bob Lurate at

Lexington Historical Shop offers a wide variety of used and rare books, local history items, and Civil War memorabilia, including first edition materials, artifacts, prints and documents. This store boasts one of the largest collections of historical materials in the state. It is open Monday through Saturday from 11:00 AM to 6:00 PM, and any other time by appointment. For more information, contact Lexington Historical Shop, 9 E. Washington Street, Lexington, VA 24450, or telephone 703-463-2615.

Virginia Born and Bred is a gift shop that offers a variety of Virginia-made products. It is located in historic downtown Lexington at 16 W. Washington Street (800-437-2452).

Downtown Lexington also includes clothing stores, a coffee roaster, local artisans — even a parlor that serves up homemade ice cream.

This rare profile view of General Lee was taken by Matthew Brady in 1865.

Photo: Library of Congress

TOUR 5

Harrisburg, PA to Gettysburg

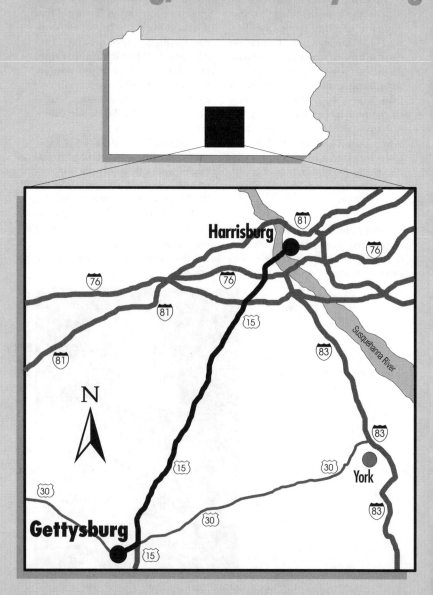

Tour 5
Gettysburg

About This Tour

This tour route covers the community of Gettysburg, PA, and its environs. Tour routes 1, 2, 3 and 4 — Cumberland Valley, Middle Valley, Shenandoah Valley and Southern Valley — cover the long stretch of the Great Valley that runs through Pennsylvania, Maryland, West Virginia and Virginia, from Harrisburg, PA, to Lexington, VA. This tour route on Gettysburg is the first of four in succession that cover a separate, distinct geographic feature of the Mid-Atlantic: the Piedmont, which runs north-to-south along the eastern slopes of the Appalachian Mountains. The other tour routes in this Piedmont series are Tour 6: Northern Piedmont; Tour 7: Middle Piedmont; and Tour 8: Southern Piedmont.

This tour route concludes in Gettysburg, where we suggest you plan evening dining and lodging.

Travel Tips

US 15 is a dual-lane, divided highway in this section of southern Pennsylvania. This is farming country, as the scenery attests. Be on the lookout for slow-moving tractors and other farm vehicles.

History, Geography

This area, the Piedmont of southern Pennsylvania, runs north-to-south along the eastern slopes of South Mountain and the Catoctin Mountains. To the north of Gettysburg, the rolling Pennsylvania farmland is part of the watershed for the great Susquehanna River. Native Americans lived and traveled in this scenic region long before Anglo pioneers arrived in the mid-18th century. Europeans, mainly Germans and Scotch-Irish, settled in the Pennsylvania Piedmont in the 1730s and 1740s. Most of these early pioneers, lured to the colonies by pacifist William Penn's advertisements, landed at Philadelphia and began a search for land to build their homes and take up farming. As the population and land patents increased along the coastal plain, the Europeans pushed west, and their migration can be traced out of Philadelphia into this Piedmont region, and eventually over the mountains into the Cumberland Valley. The community of Gettysburg was settled in the 1780s, and it originally was called Marsh Creek Settlement. During the 1790s, Gen. James Gettys laid out a town that he called Gettys-town. In 1800, when Pennsylvania allocated funds for a courthouse for the new Adams County, the village was renamed Gettysburg. It was incorporated in 1806. Gettysburg remained relatively obscure until the summer of 1863. The three-day Battle of Gettysburg, considered one of the most significant engagements in the Civil War, catapulted this obscure village into international fame.

Getting Here

Gettysburg is 30 miles south of Harrisburg, PA, 53 miles west of Lancaster, PA; 118 miles west of Philadelphia; 65 miles east of Breezewood (the junction of I-70 and I-76, the Pennsylvania Turnpike); and 54 miles north of Baltimore, MD. This tour route suggests traveling to Gettysburg on US 15 south out of Harrisburg, PA.

DIRECTIONS

Harrisburg, PA to Gettysburg Information Center

Take US 15 south out of Harrisburg to Gettysburg. Continue south on US 15 for 30 miles to Gettysburg's exit for Lincoln Highway: US 30. Take the exit ramp for US 30, and go west (right) 2 miles to downtown Gettysburg. US 30 becomes York Street. Continue two blocks on York Street to the main, downtown traffic circle — Lincoln Square. Turn right (north) at the circle onto Carlisle Street and go one block to the Gettysburg Information Center on the right. Parking is available adjacent to the building, and along the city streets.

GETTYSBURG INFORMATION CENTER

Gettysburg Travel Council
35 Carlisle St.
Gettysburg, PA 17325   717-334-6274
                    Fax 717-334-1166

The Information Center, operated by the Gettysburg Travel Council, is a good place to start your experience in this historic community. The center is open every day — except major holidays — from 9 AM to 5 PM. This is an opportune time to go over your lodging and dining arrangements, and to get information on other sights and attractions in the vicinity.

DIRECTIONS

Gettysburg Information Center to Gettysburg National Military Park

Return south on Carlisle Street one block to the downtown traffic circle. Go half-way around the circle, continuing south on US 15 BUS, or Baltimore Street, for five blocks, shift right onto Steinwehr Avenue (US 15 BUS). The Gettysburg National Military Park's Visitors Center is two blocks down Steinwehr Avenue on the left.

GETTYSBURG NATIONAL MILITARY PARK

P.O. Box 1080
Steinwehr Ave.
Gettysburg, PA 17325   717-334-1124

This visitors center is open daily from 8 AM to 5 PM, except on Thanksgiving Day, Christmas Day, and New Year's Day. There is ample parking. For those who want to stroll the grounds, the battlefield is open from 6 AM to 10 PM. This center is one of the best equipped in the nation. It has an information desk, a book store — with ample materials for adults and children — and two floors of exhibits on uniforms, rifles, pistols, sabers and swords, cannon and a simulated Civil War tent and field display. There is a large collection of Civil War memorabilia on display in the center, which also features a tribute to the African-American soldiers who fought in the Union Army. A separate room houses an electronic map that vividly demonstrates troop movements during the Battle of Gettysburg (there is a fee for the electronic map demonstration, which runs about every 45 minutes). The center's cyclorama has a free, 10-minute film. A sound-and-light program is available (there is a fee). There are separate, informative brochures on the "High Water Mark" walking tour and the National Cemetery. Make sure you get the

Lemoyne, PA

Lemoyne is located on US 15 in Cumberland County, PA, just across the Susquehanna River from Harrisburg. Lemoyne is named for an anti-slavery advocate, Francis LeMoyne. This town is the site of Fort Washington, the northernmost point that Confederates reached during the Civil War. On June 29, 1863, just two days before the Battle of Gettysburg, Confederate cavalry under CSA Col. Jenkins exchanged shots with Union troops defending the state capital. Today, Fort Washington is located at 8th and Ohio Sts. in Lemoyne.

Harrisburg Side Trip

Ghosts

During the first day's fighting at Gettysburg, Confederate troops under Gen. Alfred Iverson unwittingly exposed their flank and walked into a slaughter from Union troops hiding behind stone walls along today's Doubleday Avenue (see Doubleday Inn in the accommodations listing). The field was strewn with the bodies of more than 450 dead Confederate soldiers, who were hastily buried on the scene after the battle. The bodies were exhumed in 1871. A farmer who owned the field said he was unable to get farmhands to work because of the "perturbed spirits" that were reported to be roaming in the area. It took years before crops grew on the sacred land. The farm owner later planted a vineyard in the depression left at the site, now known as "Iverson's Pit."

Gettysburg Personalities

John Burns

John Burns, over 70 years old, strolled into the area of the 7th Wisconsin mid-day on the first day of Gettysburg and joined in the fighting. Burns was a veteran of the War of 1812, the Seminole wars, and the Mexican War. He was wounded three times during the three-day battle. He barely escaped the hangman's noose after he was captured and charged with being out of uniform. Burns became known as "The Old Hero of Gettysburg." He lived nearly another decade, and died in 1872.

Gettysburg Personality

Photo: Richmond Newspapers

Virginia's Monument at Gettysburg Battlefield.

NPS's general brochure — it contains valuable information on how to get around the historic area, as well as important rules and regulations. The brochure also provides an excellent capsulated history of the three important days in Gettysburg's history — in July 1863.

In early June 1863, a month after The Chancellorsville Battle in Virginia, CSA Gen. R. E. Lee marched his Army of Northern Virginia west, through the gaps of the Blue Ridge Mountains, and north into Maryland and Pennsylvania. On his heels was the Union Army of the Potomac, commanded by USA Gen. Meade. The two armies met in the vicinity of Gettysburg quite by accident. The little village was home to a half dozen tanneries, and a Confederate brigade was searching for new shoes and supplies when it chanced upon Union cavalry commanded by USA Gen. Buford.

On the first day, July 1, Confederates attacked Northern troops on McPherson Ridge, just west of town. The outnumbered Union troops were overpowered and driven to Cemetery Hill, south of town.

During the second day at Gettysburg, the two armies were situated about a mile apart on parallel ridges: the North was on Cemetery Ridge, and the South was on Seminary Ridge. CSA Gen. R. E. Lee ordered an attack against both Union flanks. CSA Gen. Longstreet hit the Federal left, leaving the base of Little Round Top in shambles. Here, Longstreet left Union dead strewn about the Wheatfield, and he overran the Peach Orchard. To the north, CSA Gen. Ewell struck the Union right in the evening at East Cemetery Hill and Culp's Hill.

On Gettysburg's third day, July 3, CSA Gen. Lee's artillery bombarded Federal lines on Cemetery Ridge and Cemetery Hill. This resulted in a thundering, two-hour duel by the cannon on both sides. Later in the day, Lee ordered some 12,000 South-

Cornelia Hancock

Cornelia Hancock was young and attractive — two attributes that otherwise might have dissuaded Dorothea Lynde Dix from using Hancock at the Gettysburg battlefield. But Hancock was a hard working Pennsylvania Quaker, and Dix overlooked her less important qualifications. Hancock remained a nurse throughout the remainder of the war. Dix was the Union's superintendent of women nurses. In her early 60s, Dix played a significant role in reforming prisons and insane asylums.

Gettysburg Personality

Thomas Leiper Kane

Thomas L. Kane, a native Philadelphian, began building his home in northwest Pennsylvania in 1860, but he was interrupted by the outbreak of the Civil War. Dropping construction plans, he organized a regiment of woodsmen, called the Bucktails. Kane fought in 35 battles — he was wounded in five — and was brevetted a major general for his service at Gettysburg. The community of Kane, in northwest Pennsylvania, is named for this Gettysburg veteran.

Gettysburg Personality

Photo: Richmond Newspapers

George Edward Pickett

In 1851, a decade before the Civil War began, George Edward Pickett had reason to celebrate. He was 25 years old when he married his sweetheart, Sally Minge, who — like Pickett himself — was a Richmond, VA, native. But Pickett's marital bliss was short-lived. His wife died after only 11 months of marriage. An 1846 graduate of West Point, the last in his class of 59, Pickett immediately saw action in the Mexican War. At the outbreak of the Civil War, Pickett was promoted to CSA colonel and then brigadier general, and he saw action during the 1862 Peninsular Campaign against USA Gen. George McClellan. Pickett was severely wounded at Gaines' Mill east of Richmond in June 1862. The following year, at Gettysburg, CSA Gen. Pickett's men took part in the famous "Pickett's Charge." Pickett didn't actually command the attack. His troops made up a large part of the assault. Later in the war, Pickett saw action at Drewry's Bluff south of Richmond in May 1864, and he surrendered his division along with CSA Gen. Longstreet at Appomattox. A dapper man, Pickett had shoulder-length hair worn in long, perfumed ringlets. He was a Norfolk insurance agent until he died in July 1875, a decade after Appomattox. The veteran's body was placed in a temporary vault until October that year, when his remains were borne to his native Richmond. He was buried at Hollywood Cemetery with full military honors.

erners to advance across a mile-long, open field toward the center of the Union line. This assault became known as "Pickett's Charge," in which only one in three Confederate soldiers survived.

Some consider Gettysburg the most significant battle of the Civil War. It certainly was costly: the South suffered more than 30,000 killed, wounded or missing during the three days; the North another 23,000. The battle also is called the "High Water of the Confederacy" — it marked the end of the Confederate's second and final invasion of the North. After the three-day struggle, CSA Gen. Lee's army moved south, and USA Gen.

Meade later was criticized for failing to pursue the Southerners.

Meanwhile, Gettysburg was in shambles. The townspeople were left to care for over 50,000 dead, wounded and ill. Many of the casualties were put to rest in hastily dug graves; some were just not buried. The situation so distressed Pennsylvania Gov. Andrew Curtin that he convinced a Gettysburg attorney to buy land for a proper burial ground for Union dead. This became Gettysburg National Cemetery.

The cemetery was dedicated in November, just four months after the famous battle. The main speaker, Edward Everett, delivered a two-hour address. President Lincoln followed

President Lincoln's Gettysburg Address

"Fourscore and seven years ago, our fathers brought forth on this continent a new nation, conceived in liberty and dedicated to the proposition that all men are created equal. Now we are engaged in a great civil war, testing whether that nation or any nation so conceived and so dedicated can long endure. We are met on a great battle field of that war. We have come to dedicate a portion of that field, as a final resting place for those who here gave

Photo: Richmond Newspapers

their lives that this nation might live. It is altogether fitting and proper that we should do this. But, in a larger sense, we can not dedicate — we can not consecrate — we can not hallow — this ground. The brave men, living and dead, who struggled here, have consecrated it, far above our poor power to add or detract. The world will little note, nor long remember, what we say here, but it can never forget what they did here. It is for us the living, rather, to be here dedicated to the unfinished work which they

who fought here have thus far so nobly advanced. It is rather for us to be here dedicated to the great task remaining before us — that from these honored dead we take increased devotion to that cause for which they gave the last full measure of devotion — that we here highly resolve that these dead shall not have died in vain — that this nation, under God, shall have a new birth of freedom — and that government of the people, by the people, for the people, shall not perish from the earth."

Everett at the podium to deliver a few appropriate remarks. "Four score and seven years ago," the President began his now-famous Gettysburg Address. He spoke just two minutes and uttered a mere 272 words. He considered the talk a failure. The world has judged it an eloquent masterpiece.

Today, the Gettysburg battlefield is America's most tangible link to those three hot days in July 1863. Much of the landscape and park property looks just as it did 130 years ago. There is a self-guided auto tour book available at the visitors center, and the drive around the historic area

includes numbered stops with markers that describe battle action. Or you can take an auto tour with a licensed guide (there is a fee). Walking about the battlefield, you can follow specially marked routes that include the High Water Mark Trail, Big Round Top Loop Trail, Billy Yank Trail, Johnny Reb Trail, and paths to Devil's Den and Point of Woods.

In 1993, Turner Network Television (TNT) completed work on a major motion picture, *Gettysburg*. Begun as a television mini-series project, it featured such notable stars as Martin Sheen — who por-

Gettysburg Side Trip

Hanover, PA

This side trip is only for the most hardy Civil War enthusiast, because there is little evidence of a June 30, 1863 battle — the first war action north of the Mason-Dixon line. Hanover is 15 miles east of Gettysburg on US 30 and PA 94. CSA Gen. Stuart's cavalry division faced USA cavalry under Gen. Kilpatrick. Stuart and his men captured a number of prisoners in Hanover's streets before the Northerners mounted a counterattack. Stuart, riding his thoroughbred, Virginia, escaped almost certain capture by jumping a ditch. The engagement kept Stuart from reaching Gettysburg on time. His arrival, a day after Gettysburg fighting began, meant that General Lee was deprived of the "eyes of his army."

Gettysburg Side Trip

Cashtown, PA

This, too, is a side trip for Civil War enthusiasts only. Cashtown, 15 miles west of Gettysburg on US 30, is in the South Mountains. Confederate troops, on the way over the mountains from Chambersburg, assembled in late June 1863 before advancing to Gettysburg. Just west of Cashtown is Caledonia Furnace. During the Gettysburg campaign in 1863, CSA Gen. Early destroyed the charcoal iron furnace — leaving only the stacks. The site now is a state forest park.

The furnace belonged to noted radial Republican Senator Thaddeus Stevens. When told of the complete destruction of his property, Stevens is said to have asked, "Did they burn the debts, too?"

trayed Robert E. Lee. The film is based in part on the 1974 Pulitzer Prize-winning book, *The Killer Angels*, by Michael Shaara. The book is a must-read; the film a must-see. Both, in their own way, helped "humanize" the three days at Gettysburg, especially Pickett's Charge.

Gettysburg Accommodations

Refer to the Foreward for an explanation of the rating system for both the accommodations and restaurants.

THE DOUBLEDAY INN
BED AND BREAKFAST

104 Doubleday Ave.
Gettysburg, PA 17325   717-334-9119
$$$$

In 1986, Sal and Joan Chandon, a young professional couple from Long Island, NY, were looking for some investment property. What they found, instead, was a delightful residence that literally is on the Gettysburg battlefield. Joan's brother, a tour guide at Gettysburg, helped them see the potential in the house, so they — along with Joan's mother, Olga Krossick — turned it into a bed and breakfast. Their Doubleday Inn opened for business in 1987, and Joan and Sal hosted their 10,000th guest in June 1992. Among their more notable guests are actor Bob Hope and his wife, Delores. The inn is named for USA Gen. Abner Doubleday, and each of the dozen rooms has a special Civil War name with accompanying decor. The inn is full of battle memorabilia, documents, weaponry and books. Sal, Joan and Olga serve a full breakfast, and the specialty is — honest — "blue and grey pancakes," made with a specially-colored flour and blueberries. A stay here is like, well, visiting family. From Lincoln Square downtown, take US 30 west (Chambersburg Street and Buford Avenue) for 1 mile beyond the Gettysburg College stadium area to the traffic signal, then right on Reynolds Street for a quarter-mile and over the railroad bridge, and right onto Wadsworth Street for a quarter-mile to the Doubleday Inn on the right (adjacent to marker 3 on the auto tour).

THE BRAFFERTON INN
44 York St.
Gettysburg, PA 17325   717-337-3423
$$$$

"When we turned 50, we decided to do something different," says Jane and Sam Back. The two dropped their administrative positions at Choate Rosemary Hall prep school in Connecticut and purchased the historic, old Brafferton Inn from their long-time friends, Mimi and Jim Agard. This all happened in early 1993, so the Backs have just completed their first year as the Brafferton's new owners. The Backs may be new in the business, but they have a gem of a place from which to learn. Their inn in on the National Registry of Historic Places. During the first day's fighting at Gettysburg, Union troops pushed through the village. Passing an old stone house — site of the present-

day inn — the troops opened fire, and a bullet pierced the glass of an upstairs window and lodged in the fireplace mantel. The bullet scar remains for guests to see today. Many of the inn's collectibles are the Back's family heirlooms, some dating back about 200 years. One breakfast specialty of the Brafferton is "Peaches and Cream French Toast." The inn has 10 rooms, all air conditioned, with individual baths. Children over ten are particularly welcome. From Lincoln Square downtown, walk a half-block east on York Street to the inn at 44 York Street.

GETTYSBURG HOTEL
One Lincoln Square
Gettysburg, PA 17325   717-337-2000
Fax 717-337-6891
$$$

The Gettysburg Hotel is a downtown landmark. It was established in 1797 and has been remodeled several times, most recently in 1991. Now, as a newly-reconstructed historic landmark, the hotel has spacious guest rooms appointed with elegant period furnishings. Some rooms feature a fireplace or a Jacuzzi.

There are many other motels, inns and bed and breakfast facilities in the Gettysburg area. If you have questions, or if you need help making a reservation, talk with the travel counselors at the Gettysburg Information Center (see listing in this tour), or call them at 717-334-6274; 717-334-1166 (Fax).

Gettysburg Restaurants

HISTORIC FARNSWORTH HOUSE
401 Baltimore St.
Gettysburg, PA 17325   717-334-8838
$$

Built in 1810, Historic Farnsworth House is located four blocks south of Lincoln Square, at the corner of Baltimore and South streets. The restaurant here features Gettysburg's only authentic Civil War dining — that is, game pie, peanut soup, spoon bread and pumpkin fritters. It also features 100 visible bullet holes, allegedly from the Civil War action in the vicinity. Owned by Loring and Jean Schultz since 1972, the Shultz's daughter, Pattie O'Day, tells ghost stories in the basement (Tuesday through Friday at 9:30 PM; Saturday at 8:00 and 9:30 PM, $5 for adults, $4 for students, children younger than 6 free). Farnsworth only serves dinner. It has a children's menu. Open 5 to 9 PM, seven days a week, closed only on Thanksgiving Day, Christmas Day and New Years Day.

LINCOLN ROOM
Gettysburg Hotel
One Lincoln Square
Gettysburg, PA 17325   717-337-2000
                        Fax 717-337-6891
$$$

This is an elegant dining room located off the main lobby of the Gettysburg Hotel. The furnishings are quiet and tasteful. This restaurant features outstanding beef, veal, and chicken. It's open 5 to 9 PM, seven days a week. A $6 breakfast buffet is served daily from 7:15 to 10:20 AM.

LINCOLN DINER
32 Carlisle St.
Gettysburg, PA 17325
$

Located across the street from the Gettysburg Information Center (see listing), this little spot isn't found in the travel brochures and visitor guides. Nick Arahovas has operated his diner for 16 years, and locals flock here — 24 hours a day — for the usual diner fare: burgers, chicken and especially the desserts. There's even a no-smoking room.

HOSS'S STEAK AND SEA HOUSE
1140 York Rd.
Gettysburg, VA 17325   717-337-2961
$$

A couple and their young son — obvious tourists — walked into the crowded Hoss's Steak and Sea House. Immediately, the dining room manager, Deborah Patton, reminded the youngster to tie his loose shoe laces. Then, the embarrassed Patton justified herself — "I'm a parent" — to the youngster's parents, who were genuinely pleased with the personal attention. That's Hoss's trademark: personalized service. This restaurant is part of a chain, but it's a local chain, with fresh-cut steaks, seafood and chicken meals that you choose from the big board at the front door. There's a 100-item salad bar, and fresh bread that's baked locally. Hoss's has a children's menu, and it offers discounts to seniors. It's open daily for lunch and dinner and closes only on Thanksgiving Day, Christmas Day and New Year's Eve. The restaurant is located 1.5 miles east of Lincoln Square on US 30 (York Road), just a half-mile from US 15.

Other Gettysburg Attractions

Gettysburg is unique in that almost all its points of interest are related to the town's 1863 Civil War action. No question, Gettysburg is a "tourist mecca," with sights and attractions to interest all ages. Try to stay several days here — Gettysburg grows on you. For questions or reservations, ask for help at the Gettysburg Information Center (see listing).

Annual Events: The Apple Blossom Festival is held the first weekend in May, and the Apple Harvest Festival is held the first two weekends in October. Bluegrass festivals are held in May and September. Outdoor antique shows are held annually in May and September. Gettysburg Civil War Heritage Days are held annually the last weekend in June and the first week in July—coinciding with the actual dates of the 1863 battles. This event features living history encampments, band concerts, a lecture series and battle reenactments. And there's the annual observance of President Lincoln's Gettysburg Address, in November at the Gettysburg National Cemetery.

Antiques: Ask any Gettysburg local: for antiques you can shop 'til you drop in the little Victorian village of New Oxford, 10 miles east of Gettysburg on US 30. The Gettysburg Information Center can help you justify the trip to New Oxford— its on the Historic Conewago Tour, a two-hour driving loop that passes by East Cavalry Battlefield, churches and farms in the Adams County area east of Gettysburg.

Arts: There are a number of galleries and print shops in and around the Gettysburg area. Dale Gatton Historical Art has Civil War art and prints. This shop is located at 777 Baltimore Street, 717-334-8666. The Gettysburg Dinner Theater, complete with Civil War musicals and authentic period music, is located near the entrance to the Gettysburg National Military Park on Steinwehr Avenue.

Historical Sites: Most of Gettysburg's historical sites relate to the community's rich Civil War history. Take advantage of auto and bus tours, steam train rides, a diorama at Battle Theatre, a park-cyclorama with a sound-and-light program, the Confederate States Armory and Museum (Baltimore Street), General Lee's Headquarters (just west of Lincoln Square), and the National Civil War Wax Museum (Steinwehr Avenue). You'll have to hunt for something that's not Civil War oriented. One place is a gem: Eisenhower National Historic Site, the home and property where President Dwight Eisenhower and his wife, Mamie, retired after serving in the White House. After leaving Washington, President Eisenhower was reinstated as General of the Army, and he proudly flew the five-star flag that represented his rank. Today, a five-star emblem is used to mark tour stops of Eisenhower's Gettysburg farm.

Shopping: There are countless shops that offer Civil War memorabilia and souvenirs. Countless. Pick

Photo: Handy from Culver Service

Dead from both armies strew the field of Gettysburg at dawn, July 5, 1863.

THE MUSEUM AND WHITE HOUSE OF THE CONFEDERACY

"**The Museum of the Confederacy is for me an exhilarating and uplifting experience.**" — Ken Burns, creator of the PBS series *The Civil War.*

"**A visit to Richmond —indeed to all the South — is incomplete without a visit to The Museum of the Confederacy and the adjacent White House of the Confederacy.**" — Michael Gleason, author of *The Insiders' Guide to the Civil War, Eastern Theatre*

The critics have spoken! Include the world's largest Confederate collection in your Civil War explorations. The Museum of the Confederacy's exhibits include the original icon of the South "The Last Meeting of Lee and Jackson," an unmatched array of Confederate battle flags, the anchor of the *C.S.S. Virginia,* and the artifacts of many Southern leaders, including Lee's colt revolver, riding boots, saddle, frock coat and sword. Next door, you can see the Civil War through a president's eyes as you experience the elegantly restored White House, home to Jefferson Davis and his family during the Civil War.

Twelfth and Clay Streets
Mon.-Sat. 10:00-5:00
Sun. 12:00-5:00

(804) 649-1861
Part of Richmond's
Historic Court End Tour

---

up a Gettysburg travel guide book at the Gettysburg Information Center (see listing) for all the scoop. Here are a few of our favorites:

The Horse Soldier (Old Gettysburg Village, 777 Baltimore Street) sells weapons, documents, photographs, Civil War relics and other memorabilia. To contact the shop, call 717-334-0347. For souvenirs, the place to visit is the Gettysburg Gift Center, one of the area's largest stores to offer shirts, hats, flags and other Civil War gift items. The center is located in the National Civil War Wax Museum (297 Steinwehr Avenue), or call 717-334-6245. The

Gettysburg area is rich in German history, so take a look at Das Gift Haus, which sells nutcrackers, souvenirs and Amish items. The store also has a Christmas shop (244 Steinwehr Avenue, 717-334-5993). If you're looking for antiques, the place to go is New Oxford — a little Victorian village, 10 miles east of Gettysburg on US 30. Ask any Gettysburg local about antiques and they'll suggest this place, which is located on the Historic Conewago Tour, a two-hour driving loop that passes by East Calvary Battlefield, churches and farms in the Adams County area.

TOUR 6

Gettysburg, PA to Frederick, M

Tour 6:
Northern Piedmont

About This Tour

This tour route covers the Pennsylvania and Maryland Piedmont area. It begins in Gettysburg, PA, and concludes 25 miles to the south, in Frederick, MD. This tour route is one of four that covers the Piedmont region of the Mid-Atlantic. These four include the preceding tour — Gettysburg — and the next two: Tour 7: Middle Piedmont, and Tour 8: Southern Piedmont.

This tour route concludes at Frederick, where we suggest you plan evening dining and lodging.

Travel Tips

US 15, a continuation of Tour 5, is a dual-lane, divided highway in this section of southern Pennsylvania and central Maryland.

History, Geography

The geography and history of this tour route is similar to the preceding chapter, Tour 5: Gettysburg. Native Americans lived and traveled in this region long before Anglo pioneers arrived in the mid-18th century. This area was settled mainly by German and Scotch-Irish pioneers, who landed at Philadelphia and pushed west across the Piedmont to the Cumberland and Shenandoah Valleys in the mountains. Above Gettysburg, the Piedmont region is a watershed for the Susquehanna River. South of Gettysburg, the Piedmont is drained by the Monocacy River — which flows through Frederick, beyond the site of the famous battle named for the river, and to the Potomac River.

Frederick was the scene of frequent Civil War action. CSA Gen. R. E. Lee, after his victory at Manassas in August 1862, marched his Army of Northern Virginia into Maryland to look for vitally needed men and supplies. USA Gen. McClellan followed Lee. Here, in Frederick, McClellan fell upon a copy of a Confederate battle plan, known as "Lee's Special Order Number 191." McClellan pushed 12 miles farther west, to the passes through South Mountain, in pursuit of Lee (see Tour 7: Middle Piedmont). The Battle of Antietam was fought just southwest of Frederick (see Tour 2: Middle Valley). In June 1863, just before the Battle of Gettysburg, USA Gen. Meade assumed command of the Army of the Potomac from USA Gen. Hooker. The event took place at Prospect Hall, just west of Frederick. CSA Gen. Early, on his march toward Washington in July 1864, paused here in the town prior to the noted Battle of the Monocacy — the "Battle that Saved Washington" (see Tour 7: Middle Piedmont). While in Frederick, Gen. Early demanded and received a $200,000 ransom from the townspeople.

Getting Here

This tour route is a natural continuation of the previous tour — Tour 5: Gettysburg. Today, U.S. 15 runs the length of this Piedmont section, and it is the primary link between Gettysburg, PA, and Frederick, MD. Frederick is 50 miles east of Winchester, VA, 150 miles north of Richmond, VA, and 100 miles west of Lancaster, PA.

DIRECTIONS

Gettysburg, PA to Thurmont, MD

Take US 15 BUS south to US 15 and continue south toward Maryland. A mile south of the US 15 BUS/US 15 interchange is the Mason-Dixon Line — the border between Pennsylvania and Maryland and the dividing line between the North and South during the Civil War. This line was surveyed in the 1760s by two Englishmen, Charles

Mason and Jeremiah Dixon (see Tour 1: Cumberland Valley, for a detailed history of the Mason-Dixon Line). Here, you enter Frederick County, Maryland's largest county and one of the most historic. Continue south on US 15. A mile beyond the Mason-Dixon Line is Emmitsburg, MD. Samuel Emmit, an Irishman, got a land patent in the mid-18th century and laid out a town in the 1780s. Originally the community was known as Silver Fancy. Union forces moved through Emmitsburg just days prior to Gettysburg. Eight miles south of Emmitsburg is Thurmont, MD.

DIRECTIONS

Thurmont, MD to Frederick, MD

Continue south on US 15. Four miles south of Thurmont is Catoctin Furnace, established during the American Revolution. Iron from these mountains was used to produce arms during the Revolutionary War and the Civil War. Catoctin is an Algonquin word that means "speckled mountain" — and that accurately describes the rock from this region. In fact, columns in Statuary Hall in the U.S. Capitol are made of Catoctin stone. Continue south on US 15 for 6 miles to

Catoctin Mountain Park

Thurmont, MD, is the gateway to Catoctin Mountain Park, a scenic and historical site that is home to Camp David, the U.S. Presidential retreat. The park, administered by the National Park Service, offers walking trails, scenic drives, camping and water sports. Camp David is not visible from the roadways and it is closed to the public. To reach the park's visitor center, take the MD 77 exit off US 15 at Thurmont, go west on MD 77 2 miles to the visitor center on the right.

Thurmont Side Trip

the northern limits of Frederick. US 15 south cuts through the heart of Frederick. To reach the visitor center, take Exit 6 for Patrick Street east (US 40A east, MD 144 E). Take West Patrick Street east toward downtown — after 0.7 mile the street becomes one-way at South Street. Continue 0.8 mile to the intersection with Market Street, turn left (north) onto one-way Market Street (MD 355 N) and go two blocks to Church Street. Turn right on Church Street; the visitor center is on the immediate left, at 19 E. Church Street.

FREDERICK VISITOR CENTER
Tourism Council of Frederick County
19 E. Church St.
Frederick, MD 21701   301-663-8687
                           800-999-3613

This visitor center is conveniently located amid a host of downtown attractions, all within a 33-block historical district. The center is open from 9 AM to 4:30 PM every day except New Year's Day, Easter, Thanksgiving Day and Christmas Day. The center has abundant information on attractions, as well as dining and lodging facilities in the area. Group tours can be arranged, as well as guided walking tours (from April to December) and carriage rides. We strongly recommend you buy a walking tour brochure of the Frederick historical sites — it costs a mere 50-cents. Most of Frederick's attractions can be observed by simply taking a casual stroll about the old town area. A few other sites require motoring outside the downtown area.

Frederick is the seat of Frederick County. This village was settled by German immigrants who arrived here in mid-1700s. Then, an Irishman, Daniel Dulaney, laid out Frederick in 1745. A half-century later it was called Fredericktowne. Incorporated in 1817, Frederick was named either for Frederick Calvert, the sixth Lord Baltimore, or for Frederick, the Prince of Wales, who was a friend of Lord Baltimore.

Photo: Tourism of Frederick County, Inc.

Re-enactment of the battle of South Mountain in Frederick County, MD. (See page 107)

Frederick is conveniently located in the Maryland Piedmont — several highways intersect here: I-70, I-270, US 40, US 15, and US 460. Frederick was a strategic location in the 1860s, and that's one reason why the community experienced considerable Civil War action.

Today, the Frederick community is excited about the city's recently announced plans to establish a National Museum of Civil War Medicine. The city will convert the old Goodwin Building on E. Patrick Street into a visitor facility that will detail Frederick's role in caring for so many Civil War wounded after the battles at Antietam and the Monocacy. The museum will be opened sometime in late 1994 or early 1995. The city also has plans to establish a separate downtown walking tour of noted historic Civil War sites.

DIRECTIONS

Frederick Visitor Center to Kemp Hall

Begin your downtown walking tour with Kemp Hall, which is located across Church Street from the visitor center, on the southeast corner of E. Church and N. Market streets.

KEMP HALL
E. Church and N. Market Sts.
Frederick, MD 21701

Maryland was a border state during the Civil War, and there were factions in the state that supported both Union and Confederate interests. During the earliest days of the Civil War, new President Lincoln asked the Maryland Civil War Legis-lature to vote on the issue of secession. He purposefully asked the legislature to leave Annapolis and meet here, in Frederick, so that a number of Maryland's southern delegates — proponents of secession — would be unable to attend. Frederick historians say Maryland may well have shifted its allegiance to the South had it not been for this early meeting at Kemp Hall. The building is marked with a bronze plaque.

DIRECTIONS

Kemp Hall to Evangelical Lutheran Church

Walk back across E. Church Street, and go just beyond the visitor center to Evangelical Lutheran Church.

EVANGELICAL LUTHERAN CHURCH
35 E. Church St.
Frederick, MD 21701

This church was organized in 1738 by German-Lutheran pioneers and built of logs. This particular, handsome German Gothic structure was built in 1854, less than a decade prior to the Civil War. The spires, outstanding Lutheran architecture, were among those referred to by John Greenleaf Whittier when he wrote the ballad of "Barbara Fritchie" (see reference to Barbara Fritchie later in this tour).

DIRECTIONS

Evangelical Lutheran Church to St. John the Evangelist Roman Catholic Church

Continue walking two blocks east on Church Street, turn left (north) on Chapel Alley, and go a short block to E. 2nd Street. The church is located at 116 E. 2nd Street.

ST. JOHN THE EVANGELIST ROMAN CATHOLIC CHURCH
116 E. 2nd St.
Frederick, MD 21701

This church, and the Lutheran church preceding it, are good examples of the rich ethnic roots in old Frederick. This church was built by Irish immigrants in 1837, and it is the oldest Catholic Church in the nation. During the 1860s, Civil War soldiers were held as prisoners in this church.

DIRECTIONS
St. John Church to St. John Cemetery
Walk north on Chapel Alley to E. 3rd Street. Turn right (east) on 3rd Street, and walk a block to East Street. The cemetery is on East Street, between E. 3rd and E. 4th streets.

ST. JOHN CEMETERY
East and 3rd Sts.
Frederick, MD 21701

Open dawn to dusk, this cemetery includes the graves of Roger Brooke Taney, former chief justice of the Supreme Court, and a number of Maryland Civil War soldiers, including USA Pvt. George Washington of the 23rd U.S. Colored Troops.

DIRECTIONS
St. John Cemetery to Old City Hall
Backtrack down Chapel Alley to E. 2nd Street, and walk west on 2nd Street toward Market Street. Old City Hall is located at the intersection of Market and 2nd streets.

OLD CITY HALL
124 N. Market St.
Frederick, MD 21701

This is the site of Frederick's Old City Hall, which boasts a dubious Civil War distinction. CSA Gen. Early and his troops entered Frederick in July 1864, on their way to invade Washington, DC. Early demanded $200,000 in cash — or its equivalent in supplies — or he'd torch the town. Local bankers scrambled to honor his request. From here, Early's men moved south of Frederick and encountered Union troops in the noted Battle of the Monocacy (see listing in Tour 7: Middle Piedmont).

DIRECTIONS
Old City Hall to Ramsey House
Continue west on 2nd Street, cross over Market Street to the Frederick Presbyterian Church at 115 W. 2nd Street.

FREDERICK PRESBYTERIAN CHURCH
115 W. 2nd St.
Frederick, MD 21701

This particular church was built in 1845, although the congregation dates to the American Revolution. This was a hospital during the Civil War. An interesting note: during the Civil War, the Presbyterian minister's wife was a close friend of CSA Gen. Stonewall Jackson's wife. And just prior to the Battle of Antietam, Gen. Jackson stopped here to deliver a letter from his wife to the minister's wife.

DIRECTIONS

Frederick Presbyterian Church to Ramsey House
Continue west on 2nd Street, and turn left on Record Street. Ramsey House is a quarter-block up Record Street on the right.

RAMSEY HOUSE
119 Record St.
Frederick, MD 21701

USA Gen. Hartsuff, recuperating from injuries he received at the Battle of Antietam, was a guest here in the fall of 1862. President Lincoln, after an inspection of the noted battlefield on Antietam Creek, returned east through Frederick in October 1862, and stopped at this house to visit the ailing Gen. Hartsuff. The president stepped outside and spoke to a small group assembled on Record Street.

DIRECTIONS

Ramsey House to Dr. John Tyler's Home
Continue south down Record Street to Church Street. Across from the City Hall and Courthouse Square is Dr. John Tyler's Home.

DR. JOHN TYLER'S HOME
108 W. Church St.
Frederick, MD 21701

Dr. Tyler was a noted ophthalmologist who had a pet dog, named Guess. Guess was the model for the black, cast iron dog at the front of Dr. Tyler's house. This cast iron model was stolen in 1862 by Confederate soldiers, who apparently planned to melt it down to make bullets. But the plan went awry. Guess — the model — was found near the Antietam Battlefield and safely returned to his home on Church Street.

DIRECTIONS

Dr. John Tyler's Home to Courthouse Square
Walk across Church Street to Courthouse Square.

COURTHOUSE SQUARE
101 N. Court St.
Frederick, MD 21701

The City Hall was built in 1862, which means the Victorian building was here during various Civil War actions in the Frederick area. In the courthouse square are two busts: Thomas Johnson, Maryland's first governor, and Roger Brooke Taney, chief justice of the Supreme Court.

DIRECTIONS

Courthouse Square to Evangelical Reformed Church
Continue east on Church Street, back toward Market Street, to the Evangelical Reformed Church at 15 W. Church Street.

EVANGELICAL REFORMED CHURCH
15 W. Church St.
Frederick, MD 21701

This Greek Revival church was built in 1848. Barbara Fritchie was a member of this church. CSA Gen. Stonewall Jackson worshiped here on the Sunday prior to the Battle of Antietam in 1862.

DIRECTIONS

Evangelical Reformed Church to Barbara Fritchie Replica House and Museum
Walk south on Market Street a block, and turn right (west) on W. Patrick Street. Go two blocks to the Barbara Fritchie House on the left.

BARBARA FRITCHIE REPLICA HOUSE AND MUSEUM

154 W. Patrick St.
Frederick, MD 21701   301-698-0620

This house is a reconstruction of Barbara Fritchie's house. She was immortalized in John Greenleaf Whittier's poem as the woman who challenged Confederate troops who were in Frederick in September 1862 during the Battle of Antietam. Whittier wrote that she said, "Shoot if you must, this old gray head, but spare your country's flag." Hours: April to September, open Monday, Thursday, Friday and Saturday, from 10 AM to 4 PM; Sunday from 1 to 4 PM; closed Tuesday and Wednesday October and November; open Saturday from 10 AM to 4 PM; Sunday from 1 to 4 PM; closed weekdays except by appointment. Closed December to March.

DIRECTIONS

Barbara Fritchie House to B & O Railroad Station
Backtrack on Patrick Street to Market Street. Turn right and go south on Market Street one block to All Saints Street. The old B & O Station is on the southeast corner of S. Market Street and E. All Saints Street.

Barbara Fritchie (Mary Quantrill)

Barbara Fritchie was 95 years old when John Greenleaf Whittier immortalized her name. But her instant immortality may have been a mistake. Civil War scholars think it was Mary Quantrill — not Fritchie — who was defiant with CSA Gen. Stonewall Jackson's troops. Mrs. Quantrill and her daughter stood at the gate of her house and waived several U.S. flags at Jackson's Confederates. Union troops,

Photo: Tourism Council of Frederick County, Inc.

in town after the Confederates left, got word that Mrs. Fritchie had challenged the Rebels. Someone gave Fritchie a fresh, new American flag, which she waved triumphantly at the Northern soldiers. USA Gen. Jesse Reno tried to buy the flag from Mrs. Fritchie, but he was unsuccessful. Ironically, Gen. Reno was killed days later while fighting in the South Mountains west of Frederick. Meanwhile, through mistaken identity, Fritchie was the name passed on to poet Whittier —and it was Fritchie, not Quantrill, that became a household word.

Frederick Personality

B & O Railroad Station

S. Market and E. All Saints Sts.
Frederick, MD 21701

In October 1862, following his tour of the Antietam Battlefield southwest of Frederick, President Lincoln spoke to a crowd from his train at the old station here. Following his speech, Lincoln returned to Washington. The old station now is the home of the Frederick Community Center.

DIRECTIONS

B & O Railroad Station to Frederick Visitor Center

Backtrack north on Market Street two blocks to Church Street, turn right on E. Church Street and return to the visitor center.

In order to exit downtown Frederick by automobile it is good to remember that E. Market Street in this area is one-way headed north. To exit town to the south, drive east on Church Street for three blocks to Carroll Street. Turn right onto Carroll Street — which runs parallel to Market Street — and go south three blocks to South Street. Turn right on South Street and return to Market Street. At this intersection, Market Street is a two-way street, and you can exit town either north or south. Exiting town on S. Market Street, you will pass Mt. Olivet Cemetery.

Mount Olivet Cemetery

515 S. Market St.
Frederick, MD 21701   301-662-1164

This cemetery, established in 1852, is open from dawn to dusk. Those buried here include Francis Scott Key, author of the "Star Spangled Banner," former Maryland Gov. Thomas Johnson, Barbara Fritchie and more than 800 Union and Confederate soldiers who fell in battle at Antietam and the Monocacy.

Photo: Tourism Council of Frederick County, Inc.

The Barbara Fritchie House is a replica of the famous heroine's home that was destroyed by flood.

Frederick Accommodations

THE TYLER SPITE HOUSE

112 W. Church St.
Frederick, MD 21701   *301-831-4455*
$$$$

Dr. John Tyler (see listing for Dr. John Tyler House in this tour) was a man of prominence and obvious power in old Frederick. He built this Church Street house solely to prevent Record Street from being cut across Church Street to W. Patrick Street. He had the house foundation built overnight. Thus, this house has become known as Tyler's "Spite" house. Today, this grand old house is a bed and breakfast. Bill and Andrea Myer are the hosts. Rooms have 13-foot ceilings, elegant antique furnishings and fine woodwork and moldings. The house has five chandeliers and eight fireplaces — many with imported carved marble mantles. Plan to tackle a multi-course breakfast and a 4 PM tea amid white linens, fresh flowers and silver service.

HAMPTON INN FREDERICK

5311 Buckeystown Pike
Frederick, MD 21701   *301-698-2500*
                             800-HAMPTON
$$

In the midst of so many "brand name" lodging facilities, this Hampton Inn is a welcome, familiar site. This motel has 165 rooms. Doubles cost $55 to $59; kings cost $60 to $64. The Hampton Inn has ten King Deluxe rooms with Jacuzzis for $60 to $64. As with all Hampton Inns, this motel offers a free continental breakfast. There are no-smoking rooms available. The inn includes an outdoor pool and an exercise room. And a special "preferred guest dining certificate" is offered which provides a discount on meals at eight Frederick-area restaurants, including both The Brown Pelican and The Province (listed in this tour). From downtown, take Market Street south beyond I-70, and keep right onto Buckeystown Pike (MD 85). Continue on Buckeystown Pike a mile and just beyond the interchange with I-270.

There are many other motels, inns and bed and breakfast facilities in the Frederick area. If you have questions, or if you need help making a reservation, talk with the travel counselors at the Frederick Visitor Center (see listing in this tour), or call them at 301-663-8687 or 800-999-3613.

Frederick Restaurants

THE BROWN PELICAN

5 E. Church St.
Frederick, MD 21701   *301-695-5833*
$$

David Sexton and Jeff Reinhard are two young, hard-working owners — as well as managers and chefs — at the Brown Pelican. They've turned this down-the-stairs restaurant into a place talked about as far away as Baltimore and Washington. Folks accustomed to "big city" prices will be amazed at what you get here for a few dollars: a grilled salmon entree in lemon pepper butter for $9.95, for example. Or, a walnut bourbon chicken, served with apples, walnuts and cream, for $8.50. And the atmosphere is cozy. Open for lunch Monday to Friday from

11:30 AM to 3 PM. Open for dinner seven days a week from 5 to 9:30 PM.

The place is too small to have a separate no-smoking room — but Sexton and Reinhard know their smoker-regulars, and try to keep them seated away from other diners.

THE PROVINCE
131 N. Market St.
Frederick, MD 21701   301-663-1441
$$

Back in 1767, when Fredericktowne was just two decades old, a local blacksmith built the first building where the Province Restaurant now stands. In those early days, the community was part of the Province of Maryland — thus the restaurant's name. The Province has been owned and managed for 15 years by Nancy Gleason Floria and her husband, Bill Floria. They constructed a smoke-free garden dining room in 1980, decorated with handmade quilts, a flower and herb garden, and snowshoe chairs. Pick from among grilled chicken, roast pork, pasta and — a special treat — Maryland Crab Cake. Lunch is served Monday to Saturday from 11:30 AM to 3 PM and Sunday from 11 AM to 2:30 PM. Brunch is served on Saturday and Sunday. Dinner is served Tuesday to Thursday, from 5:30 to 9 PM; Friday and Saturday from 5:30 to 10 PM; and Sunday from 4 to 8 PM. Closed Monday night.

THE PROVINCE TOO!
12 E. Patrick St.
Frederick, MD 21701   301-663-1441
$

The owners of The Province Restaurant started this little deli/coffee shop in the downtown historic area. This is where the restaurant gets its own homemade desserts, pies, breads, buns and cookies. Managed by Caroline Murphy, the shop is ideal for early morning coffee and pastries, bagels, and biscuit sandwiches. Try their lunchtime soup-and-half-sandwich, with a cookie and drink, all for $3. Open year round, Monday to Friday, from 7 AM to 5 PM; Saturday from 9 AM to 4 PM; Sunday from 8 AM to 3 PM.

LEGENDS
Hampton Inn
5311 Buckeystown Pike
Frederick, MD 21701   301-698-2500
$$

This restaurant is part of the Hampton Inn facility (see listing in this tour). A typical restaurant-bar-lounge, it offers an American menu. Open seven days a week, the restaurant serves both lunch and dinner. The restaurant is open 11 AM to 9 PM. The lounge is open Sunday to Tuesday from 9 PM to midnight; and Wednesday to Saturday from 9 PM to 2 AM.

Other Frederick Attractions

The Frederick area boasts three centuries of Anglo pioneer history. For questions or reservations, ask for help at the Frederick Visitor Center (see listing).

Antiques, Shopping: Besides the downtown historic district, there are four other shopping areas of note. Everedy Square and Shab Row is a revitalized old 19th-century factory located in the vicinity of St. John Cemetery (see listing in this tour). There are 35 specialty shops located at 8 East Street. The Francis Scott Key Mall is located on Buckeystown Pike in the vicinity of the Hampton Inn Frederick (see listing in this tour). The mall has 75 stores and is open seven days a week. The Frederick Towne Mall is located on US 40 W, just to the west of downtown. Over 60 stores and shops are located in the Frederick Towne Mall. North of Frederick, at Thurmont (see listing in this tour), the Historic Cozy Village has 12 specialty shops just off US 15 on MD 806.

Arts: The Delaplaine Visual Arts Center is located at 112 E. Patrick Street. It has visual arts displays and workshops. The Weinberg Center for the Performing Arts, at 20 W. Patrick Street, is an old movie house redesigned to house year round performing and visual arts programs.

Historic Sites: If you're looking for something other than specific Civil War-related sites, visit the Hessian Barracks on the grounds of the Maryland School for the Deaf at 101 Clark Place — four blocks south on downtown on S. Market Street. The stone building was built in 1777 during the American Revolution. German-Hessian mercenaries captured at Saratoga, NY, and Yorktown, VA, were imprisoned here. It was a hospital during the Civil War. This building is open only to groups by appointment. Rose Hill Manor Museum, a mile north of downtown at 1611 N. Market Street, is the site of the home of Thomas Johnson, Maryland's first governor. Johnson lived here for a quarter of a century, beginning in 1794. Open daily from April to October, the home is now a children's museum and has historic period furnishings. The Schifferstandt Architectural Museum, 1110 Rosemont Avenue — just west of downtown, off W. 2nd Street — is located at a former 1756 manor house and is considered a fine example of German colonial architecture. Ask travel counselors at the visitor center to call ahead for tours and hours at the museum.

TOUR 7

Frederick, MD to Manassas, VA

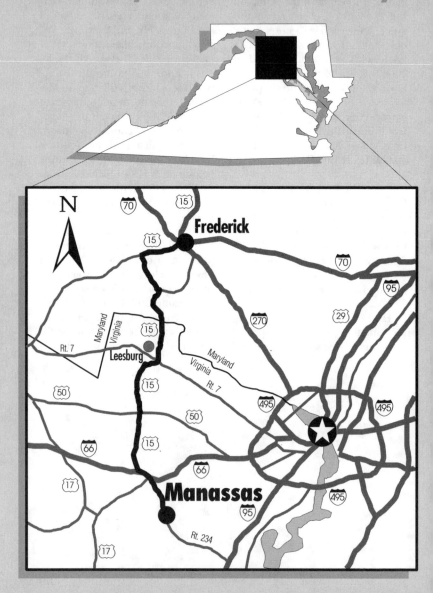

Tour 7:
Middle Piedmont

About This Tour

This tour route is a continuation of Tour 6: Northern Piedmont. It begins in Frederick, MD—where Tour 6 ended—and continues through the Piedmont area of Maryland and Virginia, concluding at Manassas, VA. Thus, this tour route is the third of four in succession that covers the Piedmont of Pennsylvania, Maryland and Virginia, along the eastern slopes of the Appalachian Mountains.

This tour ends at Manassas, where we suggest you plan evening dining and lodging.

Travel Tips

This tour route begins with the busy, downtown streets of Frederick, MD; continues south of Frederick to the site of the Battle of the Monocacy; stretches south through the countryside on US 340/US 15; crosses the Potomac River into Virginia via US 15; includes a stop — for a walking tour — in Leesburg, VA; and winds its way through the Virginia hunt country to Manassas, on the fringe of the Washington, D.C. suburbs.

History, Geography

The Middle Piedmont, a continuation of the two previous tour chapters — Tour 5: Gettysburg and Tour 6: Northern Piedmont — runs north-to-south through a natural valley along the eastern slopes of the Blue Ridge Mountains. This Piedmont valley is drained by the Monocacy River, which flows through Frederick, beyond the site of a famous battle named for the river, to the Potomac River. As with the previous two tour chapters, this region was settled in the mid-18th century by German and Scotch-Irish pioneers, who migrated west out of Philadelphia in search of land, and eventfully established home sites and farms in the Piedmont and valley regions of Pennsylvania, Maryland, and Virginia. Farther south, in Virginia, the Piedmont area also was settled by western-moving settlers from the historic Tidewater region along the Atlantic coastline.

There was Civil War action in this region. There was fighting in the gaps of South Mountain west of Frederick in 1862. The Battle of the Monocacy, just south of Frederick, was fought in 1864. There were several skirmishes in the Leesburg, VA, vicinity during the war. Farther south, at the end of this tour route, Manassas, VA, was the scene of two famous encounters, in July 1861 and August 1862.

Getting Here

This tour route is a natural continuation of the previous tour — Tour 6: Northern Piedmont. Frederick is 50 miles east of Winchester, VA, 150 miles north of Richmond, VA, and 100 miles west of Lancaster, PA.

DIRECTIONS

Frederick, MD to Monocacy National Battlefield

From downtown Frederick, take S. Market Street (MD 355) south for half a mile across I-70. Continue south of MD 355 (Urbanna Pike) for another 2 miles to the stone marker on the right side of the road.

MONOCACY NATIONAL BATTLEFIELD
4801 Urbana Pike
Frederick, MD   *301-662-3515*

Although this locale has been designated a national battlefield, there is no permanent visitor center on site. A temporary center is situated here, along Urbana Pike, but it has irregular hours: open 8 AM to 4:40 PM during tourism season, but closed on Monday and Tuesday.

The battle here on the Monocacy River on July 9, 1864, quite possibly saved the nation's capital, Washington. For that reason — not because of the battle's size — this conflict is considered among the Civil War's more noted battles. CSA Gen. Early was on his way east from the Shenandoah Valley to raid Washington. His troops were met by Union solders under the command of Gen. Wallace. Essentially, the battle cost Early a day's march and a chance to capture Washington. Thwarted, the Confederates turned back to Virginia, thus ending the South's last big chance to carry the war above the Potomac.

Early's raid was part of a scheme to divert the North from CSA Gen. R.E. Lee's army at Richmond and Petersburg, VA. Pushing north through the Shenandoah, Early entered Winchester, VA, in early July, plundered Federal stores at Harpers Ferry, WV, crossed the Potomac River into Maryland at Sharpsburg — the site of a bloody battle two years before — and moved into Frederick. Early's threat to Washington forced USA Gen. Grant to dispatch forces toward Frederick. Until these reserves arrived, however, the only barrier to Early was a force of 2,300 raw, unseasoned men under the command of USA Gen. Wallace.

Frederick Junction — or Monocacy Junction — was located 3 miles southeast of Frederick. Wallace, who trained Union recruits in Baltimore, was unsure whether Early would attack Washington or Baltimore. So, Frederick Junction was his logical choice as a place to defend either city. The Georgetown Pike to Washington, as well as the National Road to Baltimore, crossed the Monocacy River at this place.

While a contingent of troops was rushed by rail out of Baltimore to back up Wallace, the Union officer stretched his small army over 6 miles of the river to cover the bridges of both turnpikes. On Saturday, July 9, the two armies collided along the banks of the Monocacy River, along the Georgetown Pike, and on the National Road. It was only a matter of time before Early's 18,000 Confederates overpowered the 5,800 Union soldiers. By late afternoon, the Federals began a retreat toward Baltimore, leaving behind over 1,600 dead, wounded, and captured. The Confederates reported 1,300 dead and wounded. Later, Wallace gave orders to collect the bodies of the dead in a burial ground on the battlefield where he proposed a monument to read: "These men died to save the National Capital, and they did save it."

The next morning, Early was inside the District of Columbia at Fort Stevens. But, having lost a precious day's time, and his men exhausted, Early could only watch as fresh Union troops arrived to thwart his advance on Washington. Early succeeded in drawing some of Grant's forces away from Lee, but he lost his chance to capture the capital city. That night, Early and his men retreated to Virginia.

Of the two days, Gen. Grant later wrote, "If Early had been but one day earlier, he might have entered the capital before the arrival of the reenforcement I had sent." He added, "General Wallace contributed on this occasion, by the defeat of the troops under him, a greater benefit to the cause than often falls to the lot of a commander of an equal force to render by means of a victory." In time, Wallace went on to literary fame as the author of *Ben Hur.*

DIRECTIONS

Monocacy Battlefield to Balls Bluff, VA
Return north 2 miles on MD 355 to I-70. Get on I-70 west, here at exit 54, and go west two interchanges to exit 52 — the Catoctin Mountain Highway, US 15/US 340. Follow signs to the left, for US 15/340 south. Four miles south of the interstate, US 15/US 240 splits — take the left fork at this split and continue south on US 15.

To the west (right) is South Mountain. In the mountain gaps, in September 1862, CSA Gen. Robert E. Lee tried to block the Federals pushing west out of Frederick.

Battles took place at Turner's, Fox's, and Crampton's Gaps. Lee split his army in order to send CSA Gen. Jackson to capture Harpers Ferry. So, Lee could only hope to delay the Northerners. CSA Gen. McClellan forced his way through these gaps, and by the next afternoon both armies were established along battlelines west and east of Antietam Creek, near Sharpsburg (see Tour 2: Middle Valley).

On US 15, 7 miles south of the US 15/US 340 split, is Point of Rocks, MD, and the Potomac River. Alexander Brown opened a post office at Point of Rocks in 1832. This place is a natural cut in the Catoctin Mountains, created by the Potomac River.

In this general vicinity, Northern and Southern troops often forded the Potomac River on their way into either Virginia or Maryland. Southern troops crossed the Potomac headed into Maryland in September 1862. CSA Gen. Early, on his return from raiding the outskirts of Washington in July 1864, passed this area, too.

DIRECTIONS

Continue south on US 15, which is known in this vicinity as the Point of Rocks Turnpike. Along the highway, just south of the Potomac River, are sites where Confederates often camped. CSA Gen. Stonewall Jackson camped in this vicinity in September 1862 prior to Antietam. Ten miles south of the Potomac River crossing on US 15, the highway splits — US 15 Business continues straight, while Leesburg, VA's US 15 Bypass goes slightly left. Take the bypass and continue south a mile to the Leesburg town limit sign. Just to the south is the turn sign for Balls Bluff Regional Park. Turn left on Battlefield Parkway and go 0.3 miles into a subdivision to Balls Bluff Road, turn left on Balls Bluff Road and go an additional 0.3 miles to road's end. Walk to the Balls Bluff Cemetery, which is located in Balls Bluff Regional Park.

BALLS BLUFF NATIONAL CEMETERY
Leesburg, VA

Here on a ridge above the Potomac River, Northern and Southern troops met on October 21, 1861. It was one of the Union's first disasters of the war. The Federal troops were led by President Lincoln's close friend, ex-Congressman Edward D. Baker, who commaanded his men into an ambush that claimed nearly 50 lives — including Baker's. Some of the Union troops drowned in the Potomac, and a few bodies floated downriver to Washington, D.C. The cemetery is open dawn to dusk.

DIRECTIONS

Balls Bluff to Loudoun Visitors Center, Leesburg, VA
Backtrack down Balls Bluff Road and Battlefield Parkway to US 15, turn left onto US 15 Bypass, and go south 1.2 miles to the interchange with VA 7 BUS west. Take the right exit ramp, and turn right at the traffic signal on VA 7 toward downtown Leesburg. Continue west for 2.7 miles on VA 7 BUS, along the outskirts of Leesburg, to Loudoun Street, which veers to the left. Take Loudoun Street for 0.1 mile to Harrison Street. Turn left onto Harrison Street and into Market Station, the site of the Loudoun Visitors Center.

LOUDOUN VISITORS CENTER
Market Station, Loudoun and Harrison Sts.
Leesburg, VA 22075   703/777-2176

The visitors' center is open from 8 AM to 6 PM daily. Admission is free. The center offers exhibits, displays, information, and rest rooms.

Leesburg is the county seat of Loudoun County. The county gets its name from John Campbell, the fourth earl of Loudoun, who was commander of British forces in North America during the early part of the French and Indian War. Loudoun was governor of Virginia from 1756 to 1759, during which time the county was founded.

In 1758, a year after Loudoun County was cut from western Fairfax County, Francis Lightfoot Lee, one of several prominent and politically active brothers, inherited land in the new county. Soon, "Frank" Lee was a member of the colonial legislature from Loudoun. He was teased by his family and friends in the legislature for living so far from eastern Virginia, and they jokingly called him Francis Loudoun or Col. Frank Loudoun. Still, the House of Burgesses authorized a bill to establish a county seat in Loudoun and name it Leesburg in Frank's honor. He later served with his brother Richard Henry Lee in the Continental Congress, and he was a signer of the Declaration of Independence. CSA General Lee — a distant relative of Francis Lightfoot Lee's — moved through the Leesburg area on his first march into the north in September 1862.

CSA Gen. Early's troops passed this way in July 1864 for the Shenandoah Valley, via the Snickers Gap Turnpike, after an attempted raid on Washington. The road from Leesburg to Alexandria, now VA 7, was a major route during the war. The single most active and partisan Confederate in this region was John Singleton Mosby. So popular were his exploits that the area around Leesburg became known as "Mosby's Confederacy."

DIRECTIONS

Loudoun Visitors Center to Loudoun Museum
From the visitors center at Market Station, walk two blocks west on Loudoun Street to 16 W. Loudoun Street.

LOUDOUN MUSEUM
16 W. Loudoun St.
Leesburg 22075   703/777-0519

This museum is open Monday through Saturday from 9 AM to 5 PM, and Sunday from noon to 5 PM. Admission is free. A room here is devoted to Loudoun County's Civil War history, and there are many artifacts and exhibits related to the war. Particular attention is given to Loudoun's war hero, Confederate "Gray Ghost" John Singleton Mosby. There is mention, too, of the Loudoun Rangers, a group of German farmers recruited by the Union.

Painting: Dale Gallon

John Singleton Mosby

Mosby's aggressiveness — and creativity — were demonstrated early in life. He shot and wounded a fellow student at the University of Virginia in Charlottesville. It was a fight over a young woman. He made friends with his defense counselor and the judge by explaining his interest in studying law, and that enabled him to survive the trial with a six-month jail sentence and a $1,000 fine.

He was a Bristol lawyer when Virginia seceded in 1861, and he enlisted in the Confederate cavalry. He participated in war action at 1st Bull Run, and then rode with CSA Gen. Stuart on the Virginia Peninsula and at Manassas and Antietam. In 1863, he was allowed to organize a group known as "partisan rangers," who went on a guerrilla rampage in an area stretching from Leesburg to Warrenton to Fairfax Courthouse. He also led forays into Maryland and Pennsylvania prior to Gettysburg, and in the Shenandoah Valley in 1864.

Mosby, a 125-pound blond, wore a scarlet-lined gray cape that he draped over his shoulder, and an ostrich plume in his hat. He was clean shaven except during the war, when he wore a full beard. He became known as the "Gray Ghost."

In March 1863, he and his men crept inside Union lines near Fairfax County Courthouse and captured USA Gen. Stoughton and 100 soldiers. Mosby roused Stoughton from his bed, awakening the groggy general by slapping him on his backside. He and his men are credited with prolonging the war — at least a little while. During the Wilderness Campaign near Fredericksburg, the Union wasted considerable time and energy in an attempt to track Mosby down.

In April 1865, Mosby disbanded his troops rather than surrender. He returned to law practice. Later, he supported his old adversary, USA Gen. Grant, for president — a move that gained Mosby little popularity in the South. He served as consul in Hong Kong and later returned to Virginia to write his memoirs. He died in May 1916 in Washington and was buried in Warrenton.

DIRECTIONS

Loudoun Museum to Loudoun Courthouse

From the museum, walk one block north on Wirt Street, and one block east on W. Market Street, to the courthouse at the corner of King and Market streets.

LOUDOUN COURTHOUSE

King and Market Sts.
Leesburg, VA 22075

The courthouse was built in 1759 and replaced in 1811 and again in 1894. A statue honoring Loudoun war veterans graces the front lawn.

DIRECTIONS

Courthouse to Loudoun Visitors Center

From the courthouse, walk east one block on E. Market Street, and south one block on S. Church Street, returning to Market Station.

Resume your automobile tour at this point.

DIRECTIONS

Leesburg to Gilberts Corner

From the visitors center, take Loudoun Street two blocks to King Street, and turn left (south) on King Street. This becomes US 15 south (in this area the roadway is known as Aldie Pike). Continue 10 miles

south out of Leesburg on US 15 to Gilberts Corner, at the intersection of US 15 and US 50. Along the way is Oatlands, an estate originally owned by George Carter, great-grandson of Virginia's famous Robert "King" Carter. Oatlands escaped serious Civil War damage, and today it is a popular attraction that is administered by the National Trust for Historic Preservation. It is open to the public (there is an admission charge) from April to December, on Monday through Saturday from 10 AM to 4 PM, and on Sunday from 1 to 4 PM.

GILBERTS CORNER

CSA Gen. Jackson's mother, Julia Beckwith Neale, was born in the vicinity of this crossroads on leap year day, Feb. 29, 1798. She married Jonathan Jackson in 1818.

DIRECTIONS

Gilberts Corner to Manassas National Battlefield Park

Continue south on US 15 for 7 miles to the intersection at VA 234. Turn left onto VA 234 and go 6 miles to US 29. Cross over US 29 and go a half-mile on VA 234 S to the Manassas Battlefield Visitors Center entrance on the left. Incidentally, US 29 in this vicinity was — and still is — known as the Warrenton Turnpike, which is noted in the his-

— continued on next page

Loudoun Personalities: Loudoun Rangers

A few months after the Civil War began, the Union Army found recruits among the German settlers in Loudoun County. This force was called the Loudoun Rangers. Later in the war, in an attempt to field a regular force in pursuit of Mosby, the Union mobilized the rangers against the "Gray Ghost," but they were no more successful than anyone else in catching him.

Leesburg Personalities

— continued from previous page

tory of both 1st and 2nd Manassas. And the stone house at the intersection of US 29 and VA 234 served as a field hospital during both engagements. The house is part of a driving tour of the 2nd Manassas battlefield (see the next listing).

Aldie, Middleburg

This is a side trip of limited value. It is ideal for avid Civil War buffs and for those interested in seeing the gorgeous countryside that leads into Middleburg, the "capital of Virginia's hunt country." From Gilberts Corner take US 50 W. (John S. Mosby-James Madison Highway), 0.8 mile to Aldie. A turnpike — one of the nation's first — was built along this route (US 50) from Aldie Mill east to Alexandria, VA. It was named the Little River Turnpike, and today it follows US 50, VA 236, and Duke Street through Fairfax County to the Potomac River port.

Aldie is a little community at the base of the Bull Run Mountains. (In Virginia, a "run" is another name for a small creek, and these mountains are the point of origin of Bull Run, a creek that lent its name to the famous Civil War battles at Manassas Junction, just to the east. See the Manassas listing later in this tour route.) Virginia Congressman Charles Mercer laid out Aldie in the early 19th century. The village is best known for Aldie Mill, situated on US 50 at the Little River. Union soldiers lodged inside the mill during their raids in this vicinity. At the present time, only the mill's exterior is available for viewing by visitors. A cavalry battle was fought in the Aldie vicinity in October 1862. The next year, opposing cavalry and artillery fought a spirited battle here in June 1863, just prior to Gettysburg. The fight came as CSA Gen. Longstreet was shifting northwest, from Culpeper to the Shenandoah Valley, prior to moving into Maryland and Pennsylvania.

Five miles farther west of Aldie on US 50 is Middleburg, located halfway between Winchester in the Shenandoah Valley and Alexandria on the Potomac—thus the name. This community and the surrounding countryside is known for its horse breeding, fox hunting, and steeplechase racing. More than 250 Union soldiers from Rhode Island were surrounded by Confederates near here in a series of clashes in mid-June 1863 — related to the action in Aldie. Fewer than 10 percent fought their way out of town. The Red Fox at Washington and Madison Streets is one of the oldest taverns and inns in the county.

A mile west of Middleburg on US 50 is Atoka — a little intersection also known as Rectors Crossroads. This is where a company of CSA Col. Mosby's "partisan rangers" was organized in 1863. A highway marker notes the historic significance. Seven miles farther west on US 50 is Upperville, located in the upland foothills of Fauquier County — therefore, its name. In June 1863, after clashes in Aldie and Middleburg, federal troops put a push on Confederates, including CSA Gen. Stuart's cavalry. Stuart's back was to the Blue Ridge Mountains. Union forces tried driving his men into the Shenandoah Valley. This action was a prelude to Gettysburg a week later in Pennsylvania.

MANASSAS NATIONAL BATTLEFIELD PARK VISITOR CENTER

12521 Lee Hwy.
Manassas, VA 22110   703-754-1861

This National Park Service (NPS) visitor center is open every day, except Christmas Day, from 8:30 AM to 5 PM. During daylight saving's time, the visitor center remains open until 6 PM on weekends. The center offers a museum, slide programs, maps, and a publications display. Definitely get the NPS's free brochure on Manassas — it is an excellent publication. It includes a walking tour of the 1st Manassas Battlefield and a driving tour of the 2nd Manassas Battlefield. Follow the NPS suggested routes for either the walking or driving tours.

Before getting into the Civil War history here, let's cover two topics that raise questions: the origin of the name Manassas, and the names of the two battles that were fought here. Historians aren't sure how Manassas got its name, but they think it comes from the word Manassash in the Bible. The North and South used different names for the battles fought here, just as they did at Antietam (see Tour 2: Middle Valley). The first battle, a skirmish on July 18, 1861, was called the "Affair at Blackburn's Ford" by the North and the "First Battle of Bull Run" by the South. Three days later, the main engagement was called "1st Manassas" by the Confederates, and the "1st Bull Run" by the Federals. The North often used geographical features — in this case, the little creek, Bull Run — to designate battles, while the South relied more on familiar community names. In August 1862 the fighting was called "2nd Manassas" by the South, and either "2nd Bull Run" or simply "Manassas" by the North.

In the early 1860s, Manassas was a major rail stop, where lines from the Shenandoah Valley and central Virginia joined for a last leg into Alexandria and Washington. The rail routes were vital supply lines for whichever army could maintain its control. The Bull Run, a creek that originates in the Bull Run Mountains to the west, flows along the northern portion of the community.

A week prior to the first battle, USA Gen. McDowell was ordered to force CSA Gen. Beauregard's troops out of the vital rail center at Manassas Junction. McDowell reached Centreville, north of Manassas in Fairfax County, and led his troops into action at Blackburn's Ford, down river on the Bull Run east of Manassas.

CSA Gen. Johnston was in the Shenandoah Valley when he received word of McDowell's advance. From early in the morning, Johnston hurried his Confederates through Ashby Gap — in the Blue Ridge Mountains to the west — and then by rail to Manassas. It was an unusually quick response, and it was one of the first times in history that a rail line was used by a military force for mobility.

Fighting took place on a hot summer day, July 21, 1861, in an area bordered roughly by today's Gainesville, Sudley Springs, and Manassas in Prince William County, and Centreville in Fairfax County. Both armies on the field at Manassas were mainly raw recruits or short-term soldiers whose release from the army was counted in days. Given the general lack of experience, the advantage was in the hands of the defenders — in this case, the Southerners. In late afternoon, McDowell's troops retreated from the field, moving north back to Centreville and to the safety of Washington.

The Confederates were successful again a year later, in August 1862 at 2nd Manassas. The action was part of a three-pronged campaign designed by CSA Gen. Lee that included CSA Gen. Jackson's Shenandoah Valley Campaign in the spring, and Lee's own Seven Days' Battles east of Richmond in late June. Again, the Southerners pushed the Federals back to Washington and proved the Confederate leaders' superiority at this early stage of the war.

During the first day's fighting, USA Gen. Pope's troops outnumbered CSA Gen. Jackson's men by three-to-one. Still, Pope couldn't move Jackson. The next day, Pope mistook Jackson's maneuvers as a retreat, and Pope's men were overcome by CSA Gen. Longstreet's troops and forced to retreat over the old stone bridge at Bull Run. The

Manassas Personality

CSA Gen. Barnard Elliott Bee

Barnard E. Bee was a South Carolinian who graduated from the U.S. Military Academy at West Point in 1845. He was wounded during the Mexican War. His father was secretary of state in the new Republic of Texas. When the Civil War began, Bee resigned as a U.S. Army captain and became a Confederate major. He was promoted to brigadier general just a month before 1st Manassas. At the battle, Bee led a brigade of Confederates in march to support Southerners embroiled in a struggle at Matthews Hill. Bee was trying to rally his men when he spotted a newly-arriving Confederate brigade, led by CSA Gen. Thomas Jonathan Jackson. Pointing to Jackson, Bee yelled to his men: "There stands Jackson like a stone wall! Rally behind the Virginians!" In time, the Southerners held back the Union assault. Ironically, Bee was seriously wounded on the battlefield that day. He died the next day, never realizing that his rallying call would immortalize Jackson's nickname.

Manassas Personality

Kady Vivandiere Brownell

Born in Africa while her father was on duty as a British officer, Kady Vivandiere married an American named Brownell. She was just 19 when the Civil War began. And when her husband joined a Rhode Island regiment, she decided to go with him into battle. Observers said she was proficient with both a sword and a rifle. She and her husband fought side-by-side at 1st Manassas. And when the husband's short enlistment was up, he re-upped in another Rhode Island unit — and so did Kady. In 1863, after her husband was discharged with a serious wound, Mrs. Brownell returned to the North and resumed housekeeping. She took along the unit colors she carried at Bull Run, as well as a discharge signed by USA Gen. Burnside.

During the Wilderness campaign, Union troops wasted considerable time and energy chasing Confederate Col. John Singleton Mosby. (See page 110)

next day, the North suffered losses in a fight at Chantilly in Fairfax County, west of Centreville. The victory at 2nd Manassas set the stage for Lee's first push into the north.

DIRECTIONS

Manassas Battlefield Visitor Center to Manassas Museum
From the visitor center at the Manassas Battlefield, take Sudley Road (VA 234) east 4.6 miles to Grant Avenue. Turn right on Grant Avenue and go south nine blocks to Center Street.

Along Grant Avenue, on the right at the intersection with Lee Avenue, is the old Prince William County Courthouse. This red brick building was the site of a July 1911 celebration in honor of the 50th anniversary of 1st Manassas. With a theme of a Re-United States, President Taft was the main speaker. The cannon, anchor, and monument commemorate the event, which was attended by both Union and Confederate veterans.

DIRECTIONS

Continue south to Center Street, turn left and go north three blocks to Main Street.. Turn right on Main Street and go one block to Prince William Street and the entrance to Manassas Museum.

MANASSAS MUSEUM
9101 Prince William St., P.O. Box 560
Manassas, VA 22110   703-368-1873
This little, attractive museum is open Tuesday to Sunday from 10 AM to 5 PM. It is closed on all Mondays except federal holidays.

It also is closed on New Year's Day, Thanksgiving, Christmas Eve, and Christmas. The museum has exhibits, travel information and rest rooms. It charges an admission for its exhibits section. This is a great place to learn more about downtown Manassas.

DIRECTIONS

Manassas Museum to Manassas Cemetery
Return on Main Street two blocks to Church Street (VA 28). Turn left on one-way Church Street and go south five blocks (0.6 mile) to the Manassas Cemetery on the left. The cemetery is near where Center Street becomes a two-way street west of downtown.

MANASSAS CEMETERY
Center St.
Manassas, VA 22110
Two years after Appomattox, Confederate veteran W.S. Fewell donated an acre of land for this cemetery. Within a year, more than 250 Southern soldiers were reinterred. In 1887, the Virginia General Assembly gave the Ladies Memorial Association funds to build a monument to Confederate dead. In 1889, the large red sandstone marker was dedicated in a ceremony. Gen. W. H. E. Lee, Robert E. Lee's son, spoke at the ceremony. The cemetery is open from dawn to dusk.

Manassas Accommodations

Refer to the Foreward for an explanation of the rating system for both the accommodations and restaurants.

THE HOLIDAY INN - MANASSAS BATTLEFIELD

10800 Vandor Lane, at I-66 and VA 234
Manassas, VA 22110   703-335-0000
$$ 800-HOLIDAY

Quaint bed and breakfasts are scarce in the Manassas area. This is a familiar, typical Holiday Inn. Here, you have to throw cute to the wind and go with convenience. This motel is listed because it's a stone's throw to the Manassas Battlefield. In fact, the motel's guest jogging path winds its way into the battlefield property. A room with two double beds costs $53, and a king bed costs $59. There is a "great rate" available — sometimes — for as low as $39 to $49. No smoking rooms are available. Conference rooms are named Grant, Jackson, Lee and Lincoln. This Holiday Inn offers a fitness center and an outdoor swimming pool for the hot summer months. To reach this motel, drive east on VA 234 (Sudley Road) from the battlefield visitor center toward downtown Manassas. The left turn into the Holiday Inn is just before the I-66 highway overpass.

COURTYARD BY MARRIOTT - MANASSAS

10701 Battleview Parkway
Manassas, VA 22110   703-335-1300
Fax   703-335-9442
$$$

This, too, is a place exceptionally close to the Manassas battlefield, and it's a good choice. One nice amenity is the indoor pool. Rooms range from $56 to $72, and a weekly rate brings the daily price down to $45 to $53. Drive east on VA 234 (Sudley Road) from the battlefield visitor center toward downtown Manassas. The left turn at Battleview Parkway is just before the I-66 highway overpass.

HOME-STYLE INN

9913 Cockrell Rd.
Manassas, VA 22110   703-369-1603
$ 800-336-8312

This is a little, downtown motel that bills itself, "Your home away from home." Rooms are relatively inexpensive — a single for $29.95, and children younger than 4 stay free. The Home-Style even offers weekly and monthly room plans. Each room features a microwave, refrigerator, stove and sink. The location is close to downtown: take VA 28 (Center Street) south out of Old Town Manassas, and Cockrell Road intersects with Center Street just south of the Manassas Cemetery.

HAMPTON INN-MANASSAS

7295 Williamson Blvd.
Manassas, VA 22110   703-369-1100

Hampton Inn-Manassas offers 125 rooms, 15 of which contain whirlpools, including five whirlpool suites. In addition, the inn offers a free continental breakfast, an outdoor swimming pool, an exercise room and guest laundry facilities. A double for two persons costs $57.00; a king for two costs $59. This inn is located just off busy VA 234, where there are a number of restaurants. Take I-66 to VA 234 (exit 47), go south on VA

234 for a block to Williamson Boulevard, turn left (east) and go to the first turn into the motel parking lot.

There are other motels, inns and bed and breakfast facilities in the Manassas area. If you have questions, or if you need help making a reservation, talk with hosts at the Manassas Museum (see listing in this tour), or call them at 703-368-1873.

Manassas Restaurants

BRADY'S RESTAURANT AND PUB
8971 Center St.
Manassas, VA 22110   703-369-1469
$$

This is a fun spot in downtown Manassas. Dennis Brady opened the restaurant in 1975; Jim Grafas bought it four years ago. The menu offers some strange but delightful fare: chicken teriyaki club sandwich, a variety of pasta dishes, fish entrees and even a choice of Mexican dinners. Brady's Irish Burger is served with corned beef and topped with cabbage, and it costs $6.50! This is a local hangout, and the bar area is a bit smoky — otherwise, the dining area is pleasant and enjoyable. Open Monday through Saturday from 11 AM to 2 PM, and Sunday from 11 AM to midnight. There's a Sunday brunch from 11 AM to 3 PM. Brady's doesn't accept personal checks, but it takes most credit cards. From the Manassas Museum (see listing in this section) go west a block on Main Street to Center Street. Turn right on Center Street and drive two blocks to the restaurant on the right.

APPLEGATES RESTAURANT
The Holiday Inn - Manassas Battlefield
10800 Vandor Lane, at I-66 and VA 234
Manassas, VA 22110   703-335-0000
$$

This restaurant is convenient to your Civil War tour in the Manassas area. Located in the Holiday Inn, it begins serving hotel guests complimentary coffee at 7 AM. It is open for breakfast until 11 AM. The restaurant offers dinner seven days a week, beginning at 5 PM. The menu is made up of standard American fare. There's live music performed in the lounge section Tuesday through Saturday, after 9 PM.

COURTYARD CAFE
Courtyard by Marriott - Manassas
10701 Battleview Parkway
Manassas, VA 22110   703-335-1300
$$

This motel restaurant is especially known for its morning buffet-style breakfast, seven days a week. The menu is standard American fare. It's open Monday through Friday from 6:30 AM to 11 AM, and again from 5 to 10 PM; Saturday from 7 AM to noon; and Sunday from 7 AM to 2 PM.

Other Manassas Attractions

Annual Events: A barbershop music show, featuring the Bull Troubadours, in February; an antique auto show with rare, old automobiles displayed in Old Town Manassas in June; a Civil War reenactment weekend in August; the Manassas Fall Jubilee, with an old-fashioned streetfest, in Octo-

Civil War Note Cards

produced by the writer of
The Insiders Guide To The Civil War Eastern Theatre
Michael Gleason
Confederate Generals

Pierre G.T. Beauregard	Fitzhugh("Fitz") Lee
Jubal A. Early	Robert E. Lee
Richard S. Ewell	James ("Pete") Longstreet
John B. Gordon	John B. Magruder
Wade Hampton	George E. Pickett
Ambrose Powell ("A.P.") Hill	Stephen D. Ramseur
Thomas J. ("Stonewall") Jackson	Thomas L. Rosser
Joseph E. Johnston	J.E.B. Stuart

Union Generals; Ulysses S. Grant and George B. McClellan

*Available in 8- or 12- card boxes. Order a box of an
individual general — or order an assortment.*

Yes, please send me _____ boxes of the note cards of Civil War generals, at $12.95 for each box of 12 or $9.95 for 8. Virginians include 58 cents (4.5%) for sales tax for each box of 12; or 45 cents for each box of 8 cards. For all orders, include $2.00 per box for shipping and handling.
My check for $_____ is enclosed. Make check payable to "Gleason Publishing Inc.," and send to P.O. Box 25579, Richmond, VA 23260-5579. Or telephone toll-free 800-551-4478.

Name _____

Address _____

City _____ State _____ Zip _____

Cash or Check _____ Mastercard/Visa# _____ Exp. Date _____

---

ber; a Yule house tour and hayrides, both in December.

Antiques, **Arts**: Old Town Manassas has a number of stores, including antique shops, along Center Street downtown. Rohr's Museum and Store is located at the corner of Center and West Streets downtown, and has an extensive collection of antique cars and Americana (fee). The Hayloft Dinner Theatre offers live theater with meals (open Tuesday through Sunday, with cocktails and dinner beginning at 6:30 PM and performances at 8:45 PM; one hour earlier on Sunday).

The dinner theatre is located at 10501 Balls Ford Road, off Sudley Road (VA 234) near I-66.

Shopping: There are several shopping centers and countless stores, fast food restaurants, and shops along Sudley Road (VA 234) between I-66 and downtown Manassas. Another strip of stores can be found north of downtown on Centreville Road (VA 28) beyond Center Street. Pick up a Manassas travel guide book at the Manassas Museum (see listing).

TOUR 8
Manassas to Charlottesville

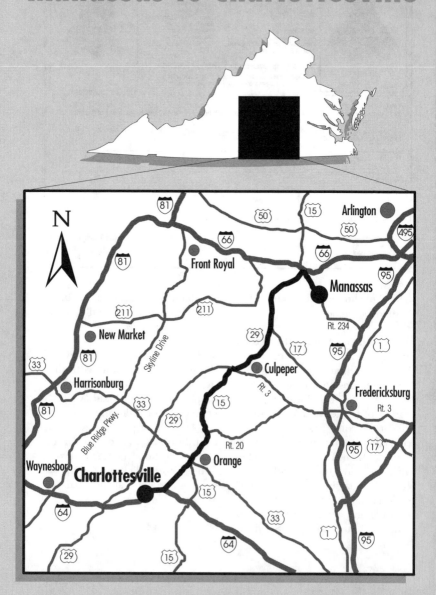

Tour 8
Southern Piedmont

About This Tour

This tour route begins in Manassas, VA, and concludes in Charlottesville, VA. It stretches south through a six-county region of fertile, rolling hills and historic towns along the eastern slope of the Blue Ridge Mountains. The main routes — US 29 and US 15 — take you through a region known for its flourishing farms, orchards and vineyards, and elegant estates. It connects a half dozen small, attractive, historic Piedmont towns.

The tour includes stops in communities that boast multiple attractions, including Warrenton and Charlottesville. It also passes simple, undeveloped sites that contain a mere highway marker. For example, the stop at Brandy Station, the site of a famous Civil War cavalry battle, offers little more than a pastoral setting that has remained virtually unchanged in the past century. Along the way are a handful of side trips: extensions of the main tour route that are designed for the more serious history buff and the less hurried traveler.

This is a one-day tour. In fact, the direct route from start to finish — excluding side trips — is just over 70 miles, so there are plenty of sights and attractions crammed into this relatively short trip. You can expand this tour to two or more days by taking in all the little side trips, and by extending your stay in Charlottesville.

Remember, the recommendations for Manassas appear at the end of Tour 6: Northern Piedmont, which runs from Frederick, MD to Manassas.

Travel Tips

US 29 is a busy dual-lane, divided highway. US 15 is a well-maintained, well-traveled, single-lane road. Congestion is a problem only near Gainesville, VA, where US 29 intersects with I-66 — a major east-west interstate that connects Washington, D.C., with the Shenandoah Valley. Washington commuters pack eastbound I-66 in the early morning, and evening commuters bring westbound I-66 to a virtual standstill. So, plan accordingly.

History, Geography

The Blue Ridge Mountains form the western boundary for this part of Virginia, just as they do for the three previous routes (Tour 5: Gettysburg, Tour 6: Northern Piedmont, and Tour 7: Middle Piedmont). Several prominent rivers cross the Piedmont, flowing westerly from the mountains to the Coastal Plain: the Rappahannock, Rapidan, Anna, Rivanna, and James.

This central Piedmont countryside, which spreads south along the eastern slope of the mountains, was settled mainly by early English pioneers who moved to the "upcountry" from the Tidewater. This region was the home of many prominent Americans, including John Marshall, James Madison, Zachary Taylor, Thomas Jefferson, James Madison, James Monroe, Meriwether Lewis and George Rogers Clark.

The railroad came to Piedmont in the 1840s. One line — the Orange and Alexandria — ran the length of the region, from Lynchburg, VA, on the James River, north through Charlottesville, Gordonsville, Orange, and on to Manassas and Alexandria near Washington.

North of Charlottesville, at Gordonsville, the Orange and Alexandria met the Virginia Central rail line, which ran west from Richmond and Louisa County. Farther north, at Manassas, the Orange and Alexandria met the Manassas Gap line that crossed over the Blue Ridge from the Shenandoah Valley. There was significant Civil War strife along these rail lines.

Because of its central location, between eastern Virginia and the western mountains, Piedmont was the frequent scene of Civil War action. First Manassas was fought in the summer of 1861. The next year, in the spring of 1862, CSA General Ewell crossed the Piedmont on his way west to the Shenandoah Valley to support CSA Gen. Jackson's Valley Campaign. Strategic battles were fought during the summer at Cedar Mountain and, again, at Manassas. In 1863, the cavalry battle at Brandy Station near Culpeper was a prelude to Gettysburg. After Gettysburg, the opposing armies fought battles at Bristoe Station and Rappahannock Station.

In 1864, the last full year of military action, the Wilderness Campaign began as both CSA General Lee and USA General Grant broke winter camp along the east fringe of the Piedmont.

Getting Here

The *Tour 7: Middle Piedmont* route ends here at Manassas.

The *Tour 9: Washington* route ends in Washington, D.C.. The directions from Washington to Manassas: I-66 W to exit 47, VA 234 (Sudley Road).

DIRECTIONS

Manassas to Gainesville, VA
From the visitors center at Manassas National Battlefield Park: west on VA 234 (Sudley Road) for a half-mile to US 29 (Lee Hwy.), left on US 29 and south 4.6 miles to VA 55 in Gainesville.

There was intense fighting in the Gainesville vicinity — and in other communities in the area — before both 1st and 2nd Manassas in 1861 and 1862, and during the Bristoe Campaign after Gettysburg in late 1863. Today, Gainesville is a remote road stop in western Prince William County. The county is named for

DIRECTIONS

From US 29, take VA 55 (Washington Street) west two miles to Fayette Street in Haymarket, left on Fayette Street and one long block to St. Paul's Church.

St. Paul's Church

This red, brick Episcopal Church, used as a Civil War hospital, looks much like it did 130 years ago. The church is used for regular worship services, and is open only on Sundays. Haymarket bears the same name as a famous racecourse in London, England.

DIRECTIONS

Return to US 29, go right and travel south a half-mile to VA 619, go left on VA 619 (Linton Hall Road) and 7 miles — crossing over VA 28 — to Bristow.

Bristow and Catlett

There's little to see in Bristow today. But in 1863 this rail stop — known then as Bristoe, or Bristoe Station — was the scene of action in the Bristoe Campaign. Here, along the Orange and Alexandria rail line, both the Northern and Southern armies shifted south out of Pennsylvania in October and November after fierce summer fighting at Gettysburg, PA. CSA General Lee took an offensive posture against a larger force under USA General Meade, who was forced to retreat.

William Augustus, the Duke of Cumberland, the son of England's King George II. (A fort in western Maryland also was named for this young duke. See Tour 1: Cumberland Valley.) Gainesville now boasts little more than an odd collection of gas stations and fast food marts, which cater to the motorists and commuters that travel along US 29 and I-66. It is a tour stop only because it offers two side trips of moderate significance.

DIRECTIONS

Return a half-mile to VA 28, go left on VA 28 and south 7 miles to VA 806, left on VA 806 and 0.1 mile to the railroad crossing at Catlett.

Like Bristow, there's little to see here in Catlett, which was known as Catlett's Station during the Civil War. In August 1862, Catlett Station was the scene of a dramatic event that became known as Stuart's Catlett's Station Raid. A few days earlier, USA General Pope captured one of Stuart's aides and ran off with the Confederate's hat and cloak. Stuart sought revenge. He found help from an old acquaintance, an unidentified African-American, who helped guide Stuart to Pope's baggage trains. Stuart captured money, papers, clothes — even a handful of Pope's officers. Stuart felt repaid for his earlier loss. Confederate officials put Pope's uniform on display in a store front on Richmond's Main Street. More important, Pope's stolen papers helped

USA General Lee successfully prepare for 2nd Manassas the next week. A year later, on Oct. 14, 1863, a light skirmish was fought on the rail line here at Catlett's Station. Union soldiers beat back an advance by CSA General Stuart's cavalry.

DIRECTIONS

Gainesville to Buckland
US 29 south 3.2 miles to Buckland.

There's an old, restored mill at Buckland on Broad Run, a little creek that crosses the highway here. This old mill site was the scene of a cavalry clash in October 1863. CSA Gen. Stuart's cavalry thoroughly defeated USA Gen. Kilpatrick's cavalry as part of the Bristoe Campaign. Stuart's men, who chased the Federals from the site, jokingly called it the "Buckland Races."

DIRECTIONS

Buckland to Warrenton, VA
From Buckland, continue south on US 29.

Just south of Buckland this tour route crosses into Fauquier — pronounced "Fawk-year" — County, which was formed in 1759 and named for Francis Fauquier, Virginia's royal governor at the time. Prior to the Civil War, the county was best known as the home of Chief Justice John Marshall. Today, it boasts large farms and horse-breeding estates. It's a rural haven for Washington-bound commuters who enjoy the country setting away from the big city.

DIRECTIONS

Continue south on US 29 for 7 miles to Warrenton. Follow signs for US 29/US 15 BUS (the old bypass), continue along US 29/US 15 BUS for a half-mile to Blackwell Road (US 15/US 211 BUS), left on Blackwell Road for 1 mile to downtown Warrenton, left on Main Street for one block to 1st Street, left on 1st Street into the municipal parking lot.

From the parking lot, begin a walking tour of downtown Warrenton. Walk back to Main Street, and go right (west) a half-block to the Fauquier Courthouse.

FAUQUIER COUNTY COURTHOUSE

Warrenton, the Fauquier county seat, gets its name from a Revolutionary War hero, Dr. Joseph Warren, who was killed at the Battle of Bunker Hill. CSA General Stuart began his raid on Catlett Station from Warrenton in August 1862.

The county courthouse survived the Civil War, only to be destroyed by fire in the late 19th century. It was rebuilt almost immediately, and it looks much like the original. A statue of John Marshall — not of a Civil War soldier as you'd expect on a Virginia courthouse lawn — stands here. On the building's west side is a stone marker that honors local Civil War hero John Singleton Mosby. (For more about Mosby, see Leesburg in Tour 6: Northern Piedmont, and Charlottesville later in this tour.)

Today, Warrenton is a busy, prosperous community. Local farmers and the "horsey set" visit downtown to shop or conduct county business. Most travel-oriented businesses, mainly fast-food restaurants and motels, are crowded along the "old bypass," and this leaves the downtown courthouse area as host to a nice collection of many old, well-maintained homes and a couple of fine restaurants. President Clinton visited here in January 1993 as part of his pre-inaugural ceremony.

DIRECTIONS

Courthouse to Warren Green Hotel
From the courthouse, walk one block south on Court Street to Hotel Street and the Warren Green Hotel site.

WARREN GREEN HOTEL
This former hotel, which predates the Civil War, is a fine example of 19th-century architecture. This is where USA General McClellan reportedly relinquished his command of the Army of the Potomac in November 1862 to USA General Burnside. The transfer of leadership, directed by President Lincoln, took place after the Battle of Antietam in Maryland. Legend says McClellan delivered a farewell address to his troops here. Today, this renovated building is used for offices by the Fauquier County School Board.

DIRECTIONS

Warren Green Hotel to Warrenton/Fauquier County Visitors Center
From the hotel, walk three blocks south on Culpeper Street to W. Shirley Avenue (US 29, US 17), turn right (north) on W. Shirley Avenue and go one block to Keith Street. Turn right on Keith Street — a short, half-block street — to 183-A Keith Street.

WARRENTON/FAUQUIER VISITORS CENTER
183-A Keith St.
Warrenton, VA 22186   703-347-4414

This visitors center is operated by the Warrenton/Fauquier County Chamber of Commerce and is tucked away in an old residence. Travel counselors have an ample supply of brochures on attractions, lodging, dining and other points of interest. It is open Monday through Friday from 9 AM to 5 PM.

DIRECTIONS

Visitors Center to Warrenton Cemetery

From the visitors center, return by US 29 to Culpeper Street. Turn left (north) on Culpeper Street and walk three blocks to Lee Street. Turn left (west) on Lee and go five blocks to the cemetery at the intersection of Chestnut and Lee streets.

WARRENTON CEMETERY

Chestnut and Lees Sts.
Warrenton, VA 22186

The Warrenton Cemetery is open sunup to sundown. Admission is free.

Confederate "Gray Ghost" John Singleton Mosby lived in Warrenton after the Civil War and is buried in this cemetery. Mosby's simple tombstone is located near the base of the tall shaft that honors the hundreds of unknown Southern soldiers also here.

DIRECTIONS

Warrenton Cemetery to Parking Lot

From the cemetery, walk east on Lee Street to 1st Street, turn left and walk north across Main Street and back to the municipal parking lot, where you began your walking tour.

DIRECTIONS

Warrenton to Rappahannock River

Leaving the parking lot, return on 1st Street to Main Street, turn left and go east on Main Street. Four blocks down, in the 100 block of Main Street, is the white house where Confederate John Singleton Mosby lived.

RESIDENCE OF MOSBY AND HUNTON

This residence is privately owned; it is not open to the public. The house was also owned by CSA General Hunton, who saw action at 1st Bull Run, Balls Bluff, Antietam, the Wilderness, Cold Harbor, and Petersburg. Hunton was injured while leading a Virginia regiment during "Pickett's Charge" at Gettysburg in 1863, but he survived and later served as a U.S. Senator from Virginia.

DIRECTIONS

From the Mosby Home, continue east four blocks to Meetze Road (VA 643), turn left on Meetze Road and go a half-mile to the US 29 eastern bypass, turn right on the US 29 bypass and go 13 miles south to the bridge over the Rappahannock River.

RAPPAHANNOCK RIVER CROSSING

This river — actually a swift little creek — is pronounced "Rap-ah-Hannock." It springs from the crest of the Blue Ridge Mountains, 40 miles to the west, flows east across the Virginia Piedmont to the "Fall Line" at Fredericksburg, where it broadens on its way to the Chesapeake Bay. Old-line, tradition-oriented Virginians consider this river the unofficial boundary between "real Virginia" to the south and the "foreign," Washington-oriented Northern Virginia.

This was a major river crossing during the Civil War. In early November 1863, there was a struggle here during the Bristoe Campaign. There was a bayonet fight during a rare nighttime attack by Union troops. More than 60 Southerners were captured.

Crossing this river, this tour route enters Culpeper County, which was formed in 1748 and named for Thomas, the second Baron Culpeper, who was Virginia's colonial governor in the 17th century.

This tour site offers a significant side trip.

Rappahannock River Side Trip

DIRECTIONS

Crossing the bridge, take US 29 south for 1.7 miles to VA 674 (Kelly's Ford Road), left on VA 674 and 4 miles east to the parking area on left. VA 674 is unsurfaced for the last portion of the ride. Don't take this road during times of high water.

Kelly's Ford

Kelly's Ford is located down a rutted, dirt path toward the Rappahannock River. In March 1863, Union cavalry under USA General Averell marched toward Confederates positioned to the south near Culpeper. The Northerners crossed over the river at this site. An all-day fight followed, and among the mortally injured was CSA General Pelham. There's a marker near here to honor Pelham, although there's some debate about the exact site of his fatal injury. Kelly's Ford was also the scene of action in June 1863, during fighting to the north at Brandy Station and west at Stevensburg. And in November 1863, two regiments of Union troops — more than 2,000 men — were captured by Southerners in an incident that thoroughly stunned Federal army leaders.

Kelly's Ford Personality

John Pelham

John Pelham was an Alabama officer. He resigned from West Point in May 1861, just as the Civil War began, and worked his way back through Federal lines to the Confederacy. He was described as blond, blue-eyed, and handsome—an obvious sensation with Southern ladies. CSA General Lee once described Pelham as "gallant." Serving in CSA General Stuart's cavalry, Pelham was struck by a shell fragment and killed here at Kelly's Ford. Countless women went into mourning, and the "Gallant Pelham" was posthumously promoted to lieutenant colonel.

MAJOR JOHN PELHAM, C.S.A. COMMANDING THE STUART HORSE ARTILLERY, WAS MORTALLY WOUNDED AT THIS SITE IN THE BATTLE OF KELLY'S FORD MARCH 17, 1863. ERECTED 1951 BY ADMIRERS OF THE GALLANT PELHAM

Photo: Richmond Newspapers

DIRECTIONS

Rappahannock River to Brandy Station

Returning on VA 674 to US 29, go south (left) on US 29.

About a quarter-mile on the right, at VA 685, is a marker that honors CSA General Pelham.

Continue south on US 29 for 1 mile to VA 663, turn left on VA 663 and zigzag east for a quarter-mile to Bailey's Store at Brandy Station.

BAILEY'S STORE

Brandy Station, VA   703-825-9169

There's no visitors center in the Brandy Station battlefield vicinity, so this little country store serves as an unofficial information post. It is open Monday through Saturday from 6:30 AM to 8 PM, and Sunday from 6:30 AM to 7 PM. It offers groceries, drinks, hardware, souvenirs and — of course — information.

Brandy Station got its name in the early 19th century, in a time when a local inn and tavern served — obviously — brandy. Legend says soldiers frequented the tavern, and when the bar ran out of the popular spirit, the men got angry and wrote "BRANDY" on the outside wall. Just before the Civil War, when the rail line from Orange to Manassas was laid through the area, this place became known as Brandy Station.

A major Civil War battle — considered the war's major cavalry action — was fought here in June 1863. Today, only a few highway road signs mark the scene of this famous event. The battle was fought on the vast expanse of farmland that surrounds Bailey's Store. It's all in private hands — there's no National Park Service facility here. In late 1993, a Bethesda, MD, developer announced plans to develop a $10 million, three-mile For-

Painting: Dale Gallon

Dale Gallon's "Ride to Glory"

mula One car-racing track, complete with a restaurant, retail facilities and a grandstand for thousands of spectators. Area preservationists and Civil War enthusiasts are concerned about the fate of this battle site.

In May 1863, on the heels of victory at Chancellorsville to the east, CSA General Lee decided to move his great army northwest, from the "Fall Line" near Fredericksburg to the Shenandoah Valley, into the rich farmland of southern Pennsylvania. USA General Hooker, whose Army of the Potomac lost at Chancellorsville, learned that some of the western-moving Confederates were camped here, just north of Culpeper, on the Orange and Alexandria Railroad line.

On June 5, 1863, Hooker ordered a reconnaissance of the area around Deep Run, a creek that feeds the Rappahannock River in southeastern Fauquier County. Opposing forces fought a skirmish, and the Union soldiers took three dozen prisoners. USA General Sedgwick, located just to the east, made observations in this vicinity, leading the Union army to plan its attack at Brandy Station.

On the morning of June 8, 1863, 11,000 Union cavalry troops left Falmouth near Fredericksburg to attack the Confederates here. At 4 AM the next day, under the cover of an early morning haze, the Union cavalry forded the Rappahannock River and struck the Southerners with a surprise, two-column attack. USA General Buford assembled his troops northeast of the rail town at Beverly Ford, crossed the river and struck CSA General W. E. Jones' cavalry, pushing the Confederates back from Fleetwood Hill toward Brandy Station. Fleetwood Hill changed hands several times.

Nine miles downstream, at Kelly's Ford, a Union cavalry division under USA General Gregg circled south of Brandy Station and struck CSA General Stuart's soldiers from the rear. Stuart drove Gregg back, while Fleetwood Hill was saved by a counterattack by CSA General Hampton.

Union cavalrymen, previously inferior to Southern horsemen, developed confidence early on this spring day in the Virginia Piedmont. The Gettysburg Campaign was under way, and the 11-hour battle later

DIRECTIONS

From Bailey's Store, take VA 663 south for 5 miles.

Stevensburg

Stevensburg was the scene of a separate cavalry action during the Battle of Brandy Station in which USA General Duffie's division captured half a Virginia regiment. The battle took up precious time for the Northerners, and they were delayed in participating in the main part of the Brandy Station fight. Union cavalry reassembled here after Brandy Station. USA General Grant camped his 2nd Corps here during the winter of 1863. In May 1864, Union forces moved from here to Germanna Ford, to the southeast, to begin the Wilderness Campaign near Fredericksburg.

Brandy Station
Side Trip

became known as the largest cavalry engagements ever fought in North America.

DIRECTIONS

Brandy Station to Fleetwood Hill

From Bailey's Store, take VA 663 north, cross over US 29 on VA 663 to the Frontage Road, turn right and drive one mile up the hill to a memorial marker.

The marker here on the south side of the road honors the cavalry action at Fleetwood Hill, a part of the Brandy Station battle.

DIRECTIONS

Brandy Station to Culpeper

Return on the Frontage Road and VA 663 to US 29, turn right on US 29 and continue south 2.5 miles to the first Culpeper exit (US 29/US 15 BUS).

Along this leg of the tour, just south of Brandy Station on US 29, is the site where CSA General Lee reviewed his cavalry on June 8, 1863 — the day before Brandy Station. This is the same place where CSA General Ewell camped, and then began his march after Brandy Station to Pennsylvania.

DIRECTIONS

From US 29, go right on US 29/US 15 BUS and 4 miles into downtown Culpeper. This route becomes Main Street downtown.

Culpeper is the county seat of Culpeper County. It is the birthplace of CSA Gen. A.P. Hill (see Tour 14: Southside). Like other communities along this tour route, Culpeper was frequently in the path of both Northern and Southern armies that shifted east or west during the Civil War. It, too, was a rail head of the Orange and Alexandria Railroad. Culpeper is sometimes called the "Cavalry Capital of the Civil War," mainly because of the action at nearby Brandy Station. A number of commercial buildings were used as hospitals for wounded soldiers, and soldiers — both Union and Confederate — are buried in downtown cemeteries. Today, Culpeper remains a quaint, charming community. President Clinton stopped here in January 1993 to attend a church service as part of his pre-inaugural ceremony.

DIRECTIONS

At the intersection of Davis and Main Streets, go left on Davis Street for a half block to the museum on the left

MUSEUM OF CULPEPER HISTORY
140 E. Davis St.
Culpeper, VA 22701

This community museum is a modest facility — the exhibits are few, but they are interesting. Civil War artifacts and memorabilia are part of its local history interpretation. It is open Tuesday to Saturday from 11 AM to 4 PM, and Sunday from 1 to 4 PM. It is closed on Monday from April to October. Admission is free, but donations are welcome.

DIRECTIONS

Culpeper to Cedar Mountain
From the Culpeper Museum, take Davis Street back to Main Street, turn left on Main Street and go east for a half mile to the traffic light, go left at the traffic light onto US 15 and zigzag south of Culpeper toward Cedar Mountain. Continue south on US 15 (James Madison Highway) through a rural area for 6 miles to a pull-off on the right side of the highway.

There's no need to stop here very long. Cedar Mountain can be seen across the farmland to the north, and there are three highway markers here that commemorate a significant battle on Aug. 9, 1862.

CSA General Jackson's troops fought with Union soldiers under USA General Pope, and Jackson was able to hold his positions until troops arrived to swing the tide to the Southern side. Jackson drove the Union forces back to the northwest. This action, sometimes called "Slaughter Mountain," rather than Cedar Mountain, took place as both armies shifted into position for 2nd Manassas, later in August 1862.

DIRECTIONS

Cedar Mountain to Orange
Continue south on US 15 (James Madison Highway).

Along the way, 4 miles south, is a highway pull-off and marker at Locust Dale. On August 9, 1862, hours before the Battle of Cedar Mountain, CSA General Jackson crossed the Rapidan River here on his way north.

Culpeper's Memorial to its Confederate soldiers.

DIRECTIONS

Continue on US 15, and 3 miles south, at the intersection of VA 622, are signs for Woodberry Forest School.

This famous boarding school was founded in 1889 by Robert Stringfellow Walker, who served as an officer in CSA Colonel Mosby's Rangers. The original estate was once owned by President James Madison's brother, William.

A mile farther south is the Rapidan — pronounced "Rap-a-Dan" — River. A marker here honors Confederate veteran James Lawson Kemper, who is buried nearby. Kemper was seriously wounded while leading his brigade of Southern troops in Pickett's Charge at Gettysburg in July 1863. Later in the Civil War, he was promoted to major general, and he was governor of Virginia from 1874 to 1878.

Crossing the Rapidan River, this tour route enters Orange County, which was established in 1734. That year, Princess Anne, the eldest daughter of England's King George II, married William IV, the Prince of Orange-Nassau — so the county was named in his honor. Orange County, during the first decade of its existence, stretched west to the Appalachian Mountains. The county was the home of two former U.S. presidents: James Madison and Zachary Taylor.

Two miles south of the Rapidan, US 15 becomes Madison Street in downtown Orange. This little community is the county seat of Orange, and the courthouse is located at the intersection of Madison and Main Sts.

ORANGE COUNTY COURTHOUSE

The Orange County Courthouse looks much as is did during the Civil War. Southerners used the basement of this old building as an arsenal during the war. Not surprisingly, a Confederate statue is located on the front lawn.

DIRECTIONS

Orange Courthouse to St. Thomas' Church

From the courthouse, go north on Main Street two blocks to Caroline Street (VA 20), turn left on Caroline Street and go a half-block to St. Thomas' Church on the left.

ST. THOMAS' CHURCH

Caroline St.
Orange, VA

CSA President Davis and General Lee occasionally attended services in this attractive, old Episcopal church. It remains open on Sundays.

DIRECTIONS

St. Thomas' Church to Orange Town Limits

From St. Thomas Church, continue south on Caroline Street (VA 20) for a quarter-mile to the southern town limits and the intersection of US 15 and VA 20. At this intersection, where VA 20 shifts north, continue south on US 15.

Lee's Camp and Jackson's Camp

Only an avid historian will want to take this side trip. It's out of the way, and there's only the landscape to see. Turn here on VA 20 and go north. A mile north of this intersection, CSA General Lee camped for the winter from December 1863 until May 1864 and the beginning of the Wilderness Campaign.

Four miles farther north, CSA Generals Jackson, Ewell, and A.P. Hill camped a week, beginning Aug. 15, 1862, between the Battles of Cedar Mountain and 2nd Manassas.

Orange Side Trip

DIRECTIONS

Orange to Gordonsville

Continue south on US 15. Just south of Orange, CSA General Jackson camped in August 1862 just after the Battle of Cedar Mountain.

US 15 continues south for 8 miles to Gordonsville. There's a traffic circle at the intersection of US 15 and US 33. Go three-quarters around the circle and follow the signs for US 33 east into downtown.

Gordonsville traces its name to an inn built by Nathaniel Gordon in the late 18th century. By the 1840s, this little community was a regular stop on the Orange and Alexandria rail line that ran from Charlottesville north to Manassas. Another rail line, the Virginia Central, ran west out of Richmond and Louisa County and intersected here.

DIRECTIONS

On US 33, about a quarter-mile east of the traffic circle, is the Gordonsville Presbyterian Church.

GORDONSVILLE PRESBYTERIAN CHURCH

US 33
Gordonsville, VA

CSA Gen. Jackson, who visited Gordonsville no fewer than 18 times during the Civil War, often worshiped here. The church is still open on Sundays.

DIRECTIONS

Presbyterian Church to Exchange Hotel Museum

Continue four blocks east on US 33 to the Exchange Hotel Museum, on the left, beside the railroad tracks.

EXCHANGE HOTEL MUSEUM

US 33
Gordonsville, VA   *703-832-2944*

Originally a hotel for rail passengers, this two-story museum houses an exceptional Civil War exhibit. It is open Tuesday through Saturday from 10 AM to 4 PM, and Sunday (in the summer) from 12:30 to 4:30 PM. It is closed January 1 through March 15, and on Independence Day, Labor Day, Thanksgiving and Christmas. There is an admission fee. This old Exchange Hotel is a fine example of Greek Revival architecture. It became a hospital during the war.

Wounded soldiers from Cedar Mountain, Chancellorsville, Mine Run, Brandy Station and the Wilderness were transported by train and treated at the hospital here. In 1864, after the Wilderness, no fewer than 6,000 men were brought here to the hospital in just a single month. Soldiers who died at this old hospital were buried behind the building, and later reinterred in nearby Maplewood Cemetery. Plan enough time to thoroughly visit the Civil War artifacts displayed here.

DIRECTIONS

Gordonsville to Charlottesville

From downtown Gordonsville, return on US 33 to the major traffic circle, take VA 231 south.

Just south of Gordonsville, this tour route crosses into Albemarle County. Pronounced "Al-ba-Marle," this historic county was established in 1745 and named for Virginia's governor, the Earl of Albemarle. Thomas Jefferson was born in Albemarle, and this region is affectionately known as "Jefferson's Country." He made his home at Monticello. James Monroe lived in Albemarle, too, at Ash Lawn-Highland. Jefferson designed and built the University of Virginia, and he was joined by Monroe and James Madison in laying the school's cornerstone and serving on the first board of visitors. Today, Albemarle County boasts countless horse farms and elegant estates. The real estate here is quite expensive.

DIRECTIONS

Continue on VA 231 south for 10 miles to VA 22.

Just before VA 22 is the site of Castle Hill, the home of Thomas Walker. The guardian of Thomas Jefferson, Walker was the explorer who "discovered" the Cumberland Gap in 1750 and became known as the "Father of Kentucky." Castle Hill is privately owned and not open to the public.

DIRECTIONS

Continue south on VA 22 five miles to US 250 W, and then west on US 250 for two miles to I-64.

DIRECTIONS

Return west on US 33, back through downtown Gordonsville, beyond the traffic circle at US 15, and continue a half-mile west of the circle on US 33 to Maplewood Cemetery on the right.

Maplewood Cemetery

This little cemetery is open from sunup to sundown. A number of Civil War dead, especially those treated and buried at the Exchange Hotel hospital, were reinterred here. Over 700 Southern soldiers, mainly from Georgia and North Carolina, are buried in the back of the cemetery. A simple marker notes where the mass grave is located.

Gordonsville Side Trip

CSA Gen. Stonewall Jackson often attended the Gordonsville Presbyterian Church.

A highway marker along this section of US 250 notes the location of Shadwell, the place where Thomas Jefferson was born. Just west of Shadwell is Monticello Mountain, the site of Jefferson's home.

DIRECTIONS

At I-64, take the left turn (westbound, sign for Staunton) and go 2 miles west on the interstate to exit 121 (VA 20). Follow blue signs for Visitors Center/Museum. At the end of the exit ramp, turn left on VA 20 (Scottsville Road) and go south a half-mile to the traffic light and the visitors center entrance on the right.

CHARLOTTESVILLE/ALBEMARLE CONVENTION AND VISITORS BUREAU
VA 20 South
Charlottesville, VA 22901   804-977-1783

This visitors center was built in the 1970s as part of western Virginia's observance of the American Bicentennial. It is open every day from 9 AM to 5:30 PM. It closes at 5 PM during the period from November to April. It is closed on New Year's Day, Thanksgiving and Christmas. Admission is free. The center offers information on area attractions, including lodging and dining. The staff here helps travelers make reservations for dining and accommodations. The center also has a museum and gift shop operated by Monticello, the home of Thomas Jefferson. Rest rooms are available. Access is by a series of steps; an elevator is available for the disabled.

Charlottesville, the county seat of Albemarle, was established in 1763 and named in honor of England's new, 17-year-old queen, Charlotte of Mecklenberg-Stretilz in Germany. This is central Virginia's largest city south of Washington. It is a cosmopolitan city, thanks mainly to the University of Virginia, one of the state's — and nation's — top institutes of higher learning. The university draws an impressive faculty and student body.

DIRECTIONS

Visitors Center to Historic Downtown

From the visitors center, turn left (north) and follow VA 20 toward downtown. VA 20 becomes Monticello Avenue and Avon Street. Continue 2 miles to Belmont Bridge over the railroad tracks. Across the bridge, at the traffic light, turn right on Market Street and follow the signs for Water Street — the route makes three quick right turns around a parking garage and back under the bridge, past the old railroad station. Continue west on Water Street, under the bridge, where there are several blocks of municipal parking facilities on the left side of the street. Park in one of the lots.

As early as August 1861, Charlottesville was "a vast hospital for the sick and wounded," according to one newspaper. A number of public buildings and private homes in the downtown area were put to use to tend to Civil War casualties. During the four years of the war, nearly 23,000 were treated in this town.

CSA Gen. Jackson's troops were in the Charlottesville vicinity in 1862 during his Shenandoah Valley Campaign. Two years later, on leap year day, Feb. 29, 1864, there was a skirmish a few miles north of town at Rio Hill — or Rio Mill. USA Gen. Custer led a small force south from Culpeper with a plan to destroy a bridge over the Rivanna River (site of today's Charlottesville Reservoir, off US 29 N). A Confederate artillery unit, in winter camp on the south bank of the river, received an early warning. The battle was brief but Custer's men succeeded in burning down the bridge.

DOWNTOWN MALL

A block north of the Market Street parking area is the Charlottesville Mall — formerly old Main Street. Stroll along the pedestrian walkway and experience the combination of old town architecture and modern-day shopping amenities. This seven-block mall was dedicated in 1976, and it forever altered the city's old downtown Main Street. The brick pedestrian walkway is lined with trees, flower planters, art and benches.

John West

One of Charlottesville's most prominent, early 20th-century African-Americans was a successful businessman named John West. A barber, West was the adopted son of Jane West, the community's richest free black in 1860. Young West inherited a house and $3,200 from his mother when she died in 1869. He, in turn, left a sizable estate when he died 60 years later, in 1929: 20 houses, 20 lots, several commercial buildings, thousands of acres of farmland throughout Albemarle County, over $23,000 in cash, and another $26,000 in bonds.

One afternoon in 1865, young West was standing outside a store on Main Street — today's Mall — when two strangers rode up, handed him the reins to their horses, and went inside a tailor's shop. Moments later, West was startled by a man running down the street, yelling for Confederate "Gray Ghost," John Singleton Mosby. Northern troops were invading Charlottesville from the north. Realizing he held the reins to Mosby's horse, West ran inside to alert the riders.

The elusive Confederate rushed from the store, flipped West a silver dollar as thanks, and headed west up 5th Street on a dead run. West ran behind to make sure Mosby escaped, and noticed that the Confederate was able to "clear High Street at one jump with mud flying to heaven." In a flash, Mosby was gone; the Yankees, meanwhile, were too busy looting downtown to notice.

Forty years after the incident, in the early 20th century, Mosby was in Charlottesville and re-met West. The barber showed the old Confederate the same silver dollar, and asked him if he remembered the incident. Mosby replied that, while he had been busy looking at the endless number of Union blue coats, he had some recollection of the day.

DIRECTIONS

Mall to Court Square
Two blocks north of the Mall, up either 4th Street or 5th Street, is the old Albemarle County Courthouse and historic Court Square.

The courthouse is located on Jefferson Street, between 4th and Park streets. Thomas Jefferson sometimes visited this old building, which was used in earlier days for Sunday church services. A Civil War statue and a pair of cannons graces the front of the building.

DIRECTIONS

Court Square to Jackson Park
Adjacent to the Courthouse, at 4th and Jefferson streets, is Jackson Park.

This small, urban plot features a fine equestrian statue of CSA General Stonewall Jackson by noted sculptor Charles Keck.

DIRECTIONS

Jackson Park to Lee Park
Walk two blocks west on Jefferson Street to 2nd Street to Lee Park, which features an equestrian statue of CSA General Lee.

DIRECTIONS

Lee Park to Water Street Parking Lots
Walk three blocks south, back across the Mall, to the municipal parking lots on Water Street, where you began your walking tour.

DIRECTIONS

Water Street to University of Virginia
Driving west from the parking lot, go west on Water Street until it merges with Main Street.

Here, a statue atop Vinegar Hill honors Virginia explorers Meriwether Lewis and William Clark, and their Native American guide, Sacajawea.

DIRECTIONS

Continue west 2 miles on Main Street (US 250 W BUS), which becomes University Avenue as it enters the University of Virginia environs.

Take a few moments to visit the university here. The buildings, including the Rotunda and the pavilions along the Lawn, were designed by the university's founder, Thomas Jefferson, and they are considered the best collection of architecture in the nation. Incidentally, the University of Virginia may be the only educational facility that avoids using the word "campus." Say "grounds," instead. CSA Colonel John Singleton Mosby made local history during his college days here when he shot and injured a fellow student during a quarrel over a young lady friend. A sympathetic judge saved Mosby from a severe sentence.

John Singleton Mosby

John Singleton Mosby grew up just south of Charlottesville, and he attended the University of Virginia. (See more on Mosby in Tour 6: Northern Piedmont.) A popular story is that, once in 1896, Mosby was visiting Charlottesville and was severely injured when he was kicked in the face by a horse. Unconscious, he was rushed to the University of Virginia infirmary. As Mosby returned slowly to consciousness, an intern leaned over to check him: "What's your name?" "None of your damned business," the old Confederate replied. A surgeon, in the room to operate, spoke up, "He's conscious all right."

University Personality

DIRECTIONS

University to University Cemetery

Continue west on University Avenue through the grounds of the University of Virginia, across Emmet Street (US 29 BUS). This route becomes Ivy Road (US 250). Four blocks west of US 29 is Alderman Road — the University Hall athletic complex on the right. Turn left at the traffic light onto Alderman Road, and go a half-mile to the University Cemetery on the left, at the intersection with McCormick Road.

UNIVERSITY CEMETERY
Alderman and McCormick Rds.
University of Virginia
Charlottesville, VA 22903

This cemetery, located in the midst of student dormitories, features a large statue honoring over 1,000 Confederate graves. The statue reads, "Fate denied them victory but clothed them with glorious immortality."

DIRECTIONS

From University Cemetery, return north on Alderman Road a half-mile to Ivy Road (US 250 BUS). To return to downtown Charlottesville, turn right and retrace the route along Ivy Road, University Avenue and Main Street. To go to the Farmington Country Club entrance, turn left on Ivy Road and go west 1.6 miles to the club entrance, at the railroad tracks on the right.

Farmington Country Club Entrance

In March 1865, USA Gen. Custer was in Charlottesville with the war's end only six weeks away. USA Gen. Sheridan had just handed a final defeat to CSA Gen. Early at Waynesboro, over the Blue Ridge. Custer, one of Sheridan's commanders, pushed through Rockfish Gap in the Blue Ridge Mountains and entered the town from the west. The Charlottesville mayor met Custer here at the present-day entrance to Farmington and turned over the keys to the town.

Charlottesville Side Trip

Sarah Ann Strickler

Nineteen-year-old Sarah Ann Strickler went to Charlottesville from Madison County to attend the Albemarle Female Institute. Strickler was an avid Confederate. She wrote in her diary, "Oh, if I were only a boy, to fight [Sheridan's men] — it chafes me sorely to have to submit to their insolence."

No one was thinking of school, she wrote, and 2,000 Northern soldiers rode through her front yard. She stood in her window and spoke to one of the enemy soldiers. He told her he was in town to "tear up the railroad." Then, he added, "If you live in Richmond you can go with us, we'll be there in a few days."

Then, the young student wrote, "I told him never, that if they fought ten million of years they could not conquer us. He rode away, and some of them actually waived their hats at us." She and a fellow student clinched their fists and shook them at the soldiers.

In 1867, after having been severely chastised by townspeople for shaking her fist at the enemy, she married a Southern veteran named Robert Herndon Fife. The Fife's moved into Oak Lawn south of town and raised nine children.

Charlottesville Accommodations

Our thanks to the authors of the *Insiders' Guide to Virginia's Blue Ridge* for their listings for Charlottesville.

BOAR'S HEAD INN

US 250 West
Charlottesville, VA 22905   804-296-2181
$$$$ 800-476-1988

The Boar's Head Inn is a resort complex, with 175 rooms located beside a duck pond on several manicured acres just west of the city. The inn and sports club were the dream of the late John Rogan, a prominent businessman who loved the history of the surrounding countryside of Albemarle County. Rogan designed the buildings, and coordinated its construction. He utilized traditional architecture. Once, he went out in the countryside, found an old mill, took it down piece by piece, and used it to create the impressive, main floor dining room called the Old Mill Room. It's modern, too, and caters to every fancy — particularly the expensive ones. Want a massage? Want to play golf or racquet sports? This is one of the top lodging facilities in Virginia, and it offers several separate dining rooms and lounges. The Boar's Head sounds expensive — and it is. But ask them about special rates and packages. And pamper your family. From the University area, take US 250 W BUS (Ivy Rd.)

OMNI CHARLOTTESVILLE

235 W. Main St.
Charlottesville, VA 22901   804-971-5500
$$$$ 800-843-6664

Back in the mid-1970s, during the American Bicentennial celebration, city officials went to work sprucing up the downtown, Main Street corridor. The downtown mall is the result.

USA General Custer entered Charlottesville after Sheridan's victory in Waynesboro, receiving the keys of the city from the town's mayor.

Then, the city decided to get a prominent, successful hotel facility to help anchor the west end of the mall. And the Omni Charlottesville is the fruit of that labor. The Omni is relatively expensive — but it's convenient to so many downtown attractions and amenities. It has an attractive, multi-story atrium inside. The Omni has more than 200 rooms, restaurants, a lounge, a sauna and health club and — a first for downtown — an indoor/outdoor pool.

BEST WESTERN CAVALIER
105 Emmet St.
Charlottesville, VA 22901   804-296-8111
$$ 800-528-1234

If you want to be near the University of Virginia, and you want to stay at a moderately priced motel, then the Best Western Cavalier is a good choice. (The University of Virginia mascot is the "Cavalier" — thus the name of this locally owned Best Western.) This motel is located at one of the University's busiest intersections: Emmet Street (US 29 BUS) and Ivy Road (US 250 BUS). You can walk to the university's oldest, most historic attractions. It has more than 100 rooms, two suites, and three meeting rooms. It's basic, the parking is cramped, and it can get a little noisy, especially after UVa wins a basketball or football game. But you can't beat the location — or the prices.

CLIFTON COUNTRY INN
VA 729
Charlottesville, VA 22901   804-971-1800
$$$$

This fine old country bed and breakfast dates to 1800. The white-columned estate and its 48-acre spread are especially inviting. It is located east of Charlottesville, near Thomas Jefferson's birthplace at Shadwell. *Country Inns* magazine named this inn one of the 12 best in the nation. Each room has a private bath and fireplace. Guests can use the kitchen, swim in a lap pool or practice tennis. Many bed and breakfasts discourage children, but youngsters are welcome here — mainly because the extensive rolling hills offer plenty of space to romp and play. Take US 250 west 10 miles toward Richmond. Just past Shadwell, turn right (south) on VA 729. The inn is located a half-mile down VA 729, across from Stone Robinson Elementary School.

There are many other motels, inns and bed and breakfast facilities in the Charlottesville area. If you have questions, or if you need help making a reservation, talk with the travel counselors at the Charlottesville/Albemarle Convention and Visitors Bureau (see listing in this tour), or call them at 804-977-1783.

Charlottesville Restaurants

C & O RESTAURANT
515 E. Water St.
Charlottesville, VA 22901   804-971-7044
$$$$

About 20 years ago, a local entrepreneur took an old, downtown greasy spoon and turned it into one of the best restaurants in the Mid-Atlantic. It gets its name from the old Chesapeake and Ohio train station just across the street. Satisfied customers? The exterior is unimpressive, even deceptive. Inside, the upstairs dining room offers French cuisine that — well, try it yourself. The menu varies, but anything — everything — is first rate. The C & O has been honored by almost all the food critics, including the reviewers from *Bon Appetit, Food & Wine Magazine,* the *New York Times* and *The Washington Post.* Make your dinner reservations far, far in advance. This is a choice selection for a couple interested in a quiet, candlelight dinner on a white tablecloth. Located one block south of the downtown Mall, across from the old C&O depot and near City Hall. Call now.

BLUE RIDGE BREWING CO.
709 W. Main St.
Charlottesville, VA 22901   804-977-0017
$$

Blue Ridge Brewing Co. is located in an old building on the stretch of Main Street between downtown Charlottesville and the University of Virginia. It bills itself as Virginia's first "brew pub." It smells like a brewery — which it is. Beer is made on the premises and labels include Hawksbill Lager, Piney River Lager, and Afton Ale. (Piney River is a mountain creek in Nelson County; Afton is a Blue Ridge mountain and gap just west of the City.) Oh, yes, there's food, too. The varied menu caters to UVa students and townspeople, as well as travelers. The restaurant is open on Monday from 5 to 10 PM. It is open Tuesday through Sunday from 11:30 AM to 2 PM, and from 5 to 10 PM. The bar is open each night until 2 AM. This is a choice selection for anyone interested in eating and drinking late.

THE COFFEE EXCHANGE
120 E. Main St.
Charlottesville, VA 22901   804-295-0975
$

Located on the downtown mall, near 1st and Main streets, the Coffee Exchange is a European-style cafe. This is especially nice for lunch. It offers fresh-baked breads, homemade soups and fresh salads. This bakery and cafe is a popular spot for lunch. The atmosphere is fresh and bright; the smell of roasted coffee fills the air. It's open seven days a week and offers a weekend brunch.

COURT SQUARE TAVERN
Court Square
Charlottesville, VA 22901   804-296-6111
$

The Court Square Tavern is a longtime, downtown fixture, located in the basement of the old Monticello Hotel. The hotel has gone the way of law offices and condominiums, but the tavern lingers on. Located across the street from the courthouse, at the corner of 5th and Jefferson streets, this is a perfect Insiders' haunt. It is small and cramped, as you'd expect an English pub to be. It's a popular hangout for local attorneys, real estate agents, and other court square patrons and offers simple, appealing sandwiches, crab cakes — even Shepherd's Pie, a tavern favorite.

THE HARDWARE STORE RESTAURANT
316 E. Main St.
Charlottesville, VA 22901   804-977-1518
$$

When the city converted its old downtown Main Street into a mall, the Hardware Store Restaurant became a popular addition. A local businessman took an ages-old hardware store and turned it into a fun place to eat. Visitors — especially kids — will get a kick out of the decor that includes old hardware store drawers and ladders. The menu is exceptionally varied, with everything from "low cal" salads to bugers and fries. Located on the downtown Mall, near E. 3rd and Main streets.

MICHIE TAVERN

VA 33
Charlottesville, VA 22901   804-977-1234
$$

Located on VA 53 near Monticello, Thomas Jefferson's home, this building is a fine example of an early Virginia tavern and inn. The interior looks like an tavern, complete with hosts and hostesses in colonial garb. Visitors, especially youngsters, will enjoy the fried chicken buffet that is served daily. Don't miss one Southern specialty: black-eyed peas with sweet stewed tomatoes. From I-64, follow directions for the Charlottesville/Albemarle Visitors Center, and then head up Monticello Mountain a mile on VA 53.

Other Charlottesville Attractions

So, here you are in "Mr. Jefferson's Country" with a day or two to see all the sights and do a little shopping. You could really take a week or two, but here is a thumbnail report on some of the area's other, "must see" attractions. For questions or reservations, ask for help at the Charlottesville/Albemarle Convention and Visitors Bureau. And, we

also recommend that you pick up a copy of the *Insiders' Guide to Virginia's Blue Ridge* at your area bookstore. It contains all the information you'll need to thoroughly enjoy the area.

Annual Events: The Dogwood Festival and Garden Week are both observed in the spring. The Ash-Lawn Highland Summer Opera Festival is conducted in June. The Virginia Festival of American Film is held in October. The Foxfield Races, which offers steeplechase and flat races, holds events in the spring and fall. Of course, the University of Virginia provides exciting college basketball, football and lacrosse.

Antiques: There are no fewer than two dozen antique shops in and around Charlottesville — far too many to select one or two. Local tour guide books list many of these shops, along with their telephone numbers and addresses. Remember, though, that these shops vary in quality and service. Generally, antiques — really good antiques — found in this community are expensive.

Arts: The McGuffey Art Center, located in a former elementary school in the downtown historic area, has 20 working studios for artists. The center is open to the public. The Bayly Art Museum is located near the grounds of the University of Virginia and offers ongoing art exhibits. The university's Heritage Repertory Theatre offers rotating plays during the summer at Culbreth and Helms theaters. And the Virginia Discovery Museum hosts a hands-on program that features history, art and science through interactive exhibits. This is especially fun for young people and their parents. It is located on the downtown mall, across from City Hall.

Dr. Don Nidiffer is a dealer of American historical documents, and is particularly interested in Civil War-era papers. He can be contacted by writing P.O. Box 8184, Charlottesville, VA 22906, or by calling 804-296-2067.

Historical Sites: Monticello, the home of Thomas Jefferson, is one of the nation's premiere presidential homes. Be prepared for a long wait, especially in the summer. The Charlottesville/Albemarle Convention and Visitors Bureau building has a Monticello exhibit and gift shop. Check in there about tour times and availability at the estate on top of Monticello Mountain. Ash Lawn-Highland is the restored summer home of President James Monroe. It is located 2 miles west of Monticello. Montpelier, the home of President James Madison, is located near Orange.

Shopping: You will find concentrated shopping areas downtown, uptown near the University of Virginia, and northwest of the city along the US 29 (Emmet Street) corridor. The Charlottesville area has countless shops, boutiques and stores, offering such specialty items as needlecrafts, jewelry, sports equipment, designer clothes, art and quilts. The area has three major shopping centers.

Vineyards: Albemarle and Orange counties boast several vineyards, including Oakencroft, Simeon Vineyards, and Montdomaine. Most offer tours, tastings and sales, but it is best to check ahead for specifics.

TOUR 9
Washington, DC

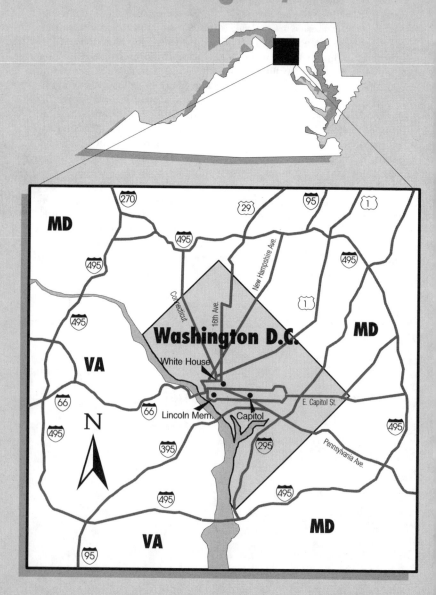

Tour 9
Washington, DC

About This Tour, Travel Tips

This tour route covers Washington, DC Motoring into Washington is a tedious task, at best. If possible, avoid rush-hour traffic that clogs roadways into the city in the morning and out in the evening. Radio traffic reports are especially helpful. Remember, too, that traffic is particularly busy — and often snarled — during unusual weather conditions, particularly winter snows and heavy summer rains. There is one consolation for visitors: many Washingtonians leave town for vacation during the summer tourism season.

If you must drive in Washington, there are a few easy guidelines. The city's four quadrants — northwest, northeast, southwest, and southeast — are centered on the U.S. Capitol. Thus, the Capitol building is the point where the north/south and east/west axes meet. The dividing lines for these four quadrants are North, South, and East Capitol Streets and the Mall. Most places cited in this tour guide are in the vicinity of the Capitol and in the northwest quadrant. East/west streets run in alphabetical order, beginning with single letters (like A Street), then two syllable words (like

Adams Street), then three syllable words (like Albemarle Street). Watch out near the Capitol — there is an A Street in each of the four quadrants. North/south streets are numbered, beginning with 1st. Diagonal streets are named for states of the Union.

Actually, while in the DC area, it's simply best to avoid motoring. The best alternative is the Metro subway system, a clean, efficient, and safe way to see Washington without the confusing traffic patterns and other driving hassles, finding and paying for parking, or getting lost. Thus, each attraction listing also includes the appropriate Metro rail stop. The Metro has several rail lines — which are color-coded and easy to decipher. The Red Line serves the northern section of the district and Montgomery County, MD. The Green Line serves the district's eastern section, including Prince Georges County, MD. The Orange Line serves the eastern and western sections of the district, from Fairfax County, VA, to Prince Georges County, MD. The Blue Line runs from National Airport in Alexandria, VA, through the heart of the district, to Capitol Heights, MD. The Yellow Line runs from center city to Huntington, south of Alexandria, VA. The Metro has a $5 one-day, all-you-can-ride fare that is ideal for visitors. The special fare is good all day (until midnight) on weekdays, weekends and holidays, however you must board after 9 AM on weekdays. For information on the Metro, telephone 202-637-7000. Metro ridership information is available by telephoning 202-637-7000 — a line that is available 6 AM to 11:30 PM every day. You can purchase the special ticket at Metro Center at 13th and F streets NW in the district, and at the Concourse at the Pentagon in Arlington, VA. It also is available at some grocery stores in the Washington metropolitan area. Up to two children under the age of 5 can ride free on Metro with an accompanying adult. All riders 5 years of age and older must have their own Metro ticket.

There's another way to see Washington's historic attractions: Tourmobile. This is a convenient way to see 18 major sites along Washington's Mall and into Northern Virginia. Tourmobile charges a fee, but it offers free reboarding throughout its tour route. Tourmobile even offers special vehicles for the mobility impaired. For information, telephone 202-554-7950.

Washington is a tourist attraction and visitors are welcome. Still, it makes good sense to be cautious, particularly in areas outside the immediate downtown area. When motoring or walking, go during daylight hours and take along companions.

History, Geography

Washington, DC, the nation's capital, straddles the Potomac and Anacostia Rivers, along the "fall line."

It is rich in American history and offers countless attractions. Once the home of Native Americans, the land around the Potomac and Anacostia rivers — both names are of Native American origin — was surveyed by Anglo settlers almost immediately after the founding of Jamestown, VA, in 1607. Near the end of the 18th century, with the formation of the new federal government, the site for the new federal city was established here on the "fall line" of the Potomac. Maryland and Virginia contributed portions of their land for the creation of the District of Columbia, a ten-square mile diamond-shaped territory. The capital city, named in honor of Virginian George Washington, transformed farmland, fields and river bottomland into a bustling community with a single commodity: politics.

By the time President Lincoln was inaugurated in 1861, the Washington population topped 60,000. Months later, Civil War-related activities swelled the city to twice its usual population. Naturally, Washington was a busy place during the Civil War. Federal troops built forts and guarded major buildings and roadways entering and leaving the city. From the war's beginning, there were threats and rumors of Confederate invasions, although Southern troops made only one major thrust, when CSA Gen. Early's raid closed in on Fort Stephens in 1864.

Today, Washington's population is ten times greater than it was in 1860. The Metropolitan Statistical Area is the third largest in the nation, stretching from the Pennsylvania border north of Baltimore, to

Spotsylvania County, VA, near Fredericksburg.

Getting Here

Use interstate highways whenever possible to enter Washington: I-270 from the northwest, I-95 from the northeast or south, and I-66 from the southwest. These routes converge at the Capital Beltway, which circles the district. This tour route is a natural continuation of either Tour 6: Northern Piedmont, or Tour 7: Middle Piedmont. Tour 6 concludes at Frederick, MD — from there, Washington is a brief jaunt down I-270. Tour 7 concludes in Manassas, VA — from there, Washington is an equally quick trip east on I-66.

DIRECTIONS

Tour 9: Washington
This tour route begins in the vicinity of the U.S. Capitol [Metro's Blue-Orange line, Capitol South stop; or Red line, Union Station stop].

U.S. CAPITOL
1st and A Sts., Constitution and Independence Aves.
Washington, DC 20510   202-225-6827

This is the most recognizable building in the nation — perhaps the world. The cornerstone was laid by President Washington in 1793. In 1800 Congress moved into the first completed section, now the old Senate wing. Two years later, the House of Representatives met in a makeshift building put up on the foundation of its wing. By 1811, both the House and Senate wings were completed, and rebuilt, before they were damaged by the British during the War of 1812. The reconstruction led to several alterations, plus the construction of a wooden dome.

In the 1840s, Congress moved to enlarge the Capitol, and by 1859 — on the eve of the Civil War — both the House and Senate relocated into new wings. In addition, plans were made to replace the old dome with a larger structure, and work continued on that project through the Civil War.

Here, in the years preceding the Civil War, this remarkable building was forever linked with the nation's most significant legislation — and its most significant lawmakers (see Prelude to the War section in the Overview chapter). Presidents are inaugurated here. Familiar legislators included South Carolina Sen. John C. Calhoun; Kentucky Sen. Henry Clay, the "Great Compromiser"; Illinois Sen. Stephen Douglas, the "Little Giant"; and Massachusetts Sen. Daniel Webster. Here, Congress debated major issues and legislation, including the Missouri Compromise of 1820, the Compromise of 1850, nullification, secession, and the Kansas-Nebraska Bill. The Thirteenth Amendment, which prohibited slavery in the nation, was adopted in 1865. The U.S. Supreme Court, which met in the Capitol until its own building was constructed across 1st Street in 1935, issued its famous 1857 Dred Scott Decision here. Beginning in the 1850s, arguments over slavery intensified. Members of Congress began carrying pistols and canes; fights broke out.

As Southern states seceded, their representatives escaped the Washington madness. The Capitol became a Union Army barracks, and troops camped in the Rotunda. Supplies were stored in the legislative chambers, and an oven was set up in the basement to bake the Union soldiers' daily 10-ounce bread ration. Soldiers drilled on the east lawn. Later, during the war, the Capitol was used as a hospital. Meanwhile, work continued on the 250-foot dome, and the famous crowning statue of "Freedom" was installed in December 1863. The statue was refurbished in 1993. There are a number of statues of Americans associated with the war, especially in Statuary Hall and the Rotunda.

Free tours are conducted from 9 AM to 3:45 PM, seven days a week except New Year's Day, Thanksgiving Day and Christmas Day. The line forms on the East Front. The Capitol also offers a variety of places to dine and shop, and hours vary according to the Congressional schedule and season of the year.

DIRECTIONS

US Capitol to Library of Congress

From the East Front, cross 1st Street SE to the corner of 1st Street and Independence Avenue SE [Blue-Or-ange line, Capitol South stop].

LIBRARY OF CONGRESS

101 Independence Ave. SE
Washington, DC 20540   202-707-5000

This is the nation's foremost library and collection of important manuscripts and papers, including materials related to the Civil War. The main building of this complex was constructed in 1896. Before that, the library housed its vast collection in the U.S. Capitol. Today, the library is housed in three separate buildings: Jefferson, Madison, and Adams. The Jefferson Building is undergoing extensive renovation in 1994, and the Adams Building is used solely for research purposes, so visitors' services are centered on the Madison Building. Its entrance is on Independence Avenue SE.

A variety of exhibits are offered at any given time and usually are free. A free tour is conducted Monday through Friday at 10 AM and at 1 and 3 PM, except federal holidays. (Groups over nine people should check in advance.) A free orientation film is shown every half hour from 9 AM to 9 PM, Monday through Friday. It is also shown on Saturday from 8:30 AM to 5 PM, and Sunday from 1 to 4:30 PM. Tours are free but restricted to groups of 50 per tour. A gift shop is located off the Madison Building lobby, and is open Monday through Saturday from 9 AM to 5 PM. The library cafeteria is open to visitors for lunch Monday through Friday from 12:30 to 3 PM.

DIRECTIONS

Library of Congress to Old Capitol Prison Site

West on 1st Street to present U.S. Supreme Court site [Blue-Orange line, Capitol South stop; or Red line, Union Station stop].

OLD CAPITOL PRISON SITE
1st and A Sts. NE

Located on the site where the U.S. Supreme Court now sits, this also was the site of the Old Brick Capitol that Congress used after the British trashed the Capitol during the War of 1812. With the Capitol under reconstruction, President James Monroe was inaugurated in 1817 on a platform outside the Brick Capitol. The structure also was used as a hotel, and it was converted to a prison during the Civil War. Among its more famous prisoners was Belle Boyd, a Confederate spy (see Tour 2: Middle Valley).

DIRECTIONS

Old Capitol Prison Site to Douglass Home Site
The Douglass Home Site is a block directly behind the present Supreme Court building. From 1st Street, go to East Capitol Street, go left one block to 2nd Street, go left one block to A Street, and turn right onto A Street [Red line, Union Station stop].

DOUGLASS HOME SITE
A Street NE, 300 block

This is the site of Frederick Douglass' first Washington residence. A former slave, this famous abolitionist was a minister to Haiti

Lincoln Park and Stanton Park

Here are two more places that have Civil War-related names — one includes a significant statue that might justify a separate visit. Lincoln Park, E. Capitol Street and 11th Street NE, features Emancipation Statue, which honors Lincoln's freeing of the slaves. The statue was dedicated in April 1876 with President Ulysses Grant and noted African-American leader Frederick Douglass in attendance. Speaking at the dedication, Douglas said of Lincoln, ". . . under his rule and the fullness of time, we saw [him] . . . penning the immortal paper, making slavery forever impossible in the United States."

Stanton Park, Maryland and Pennsylvania avenues NE, honors President Lincoln's secretary of war, Edwin McMasters Stanton. An Ohioan, he was U.S. attorney general under President Buchanan. Serving throughout Lincoln's two administrations, he also was secretary of war briefly under President Andrew Johnson. When he opposed Johnson's reconstruction plans, he was asked to resign; when he refused, Johnson suspended him. After Johnson replaced him with former Gen. Ulysses Grant, the U.S. Senate named him back to his old post. Again the president tried to remove him; again the Senate overruled Johnson. He resigned after the president was impeached. In 1869, newly-elected President Grant appointed him to the U.S. Supreme Court, but the jurist died four days afterwards.

Stanton, a northwest Pennsylvania town, is named in his honor. Simon Cameron, who served briefly before Stanton as President Lincoln's secretary of war, was a Pennsylvania native. Cameron, a town on the Susquehanna River in Pennsylvania — and Cameron County — are named in his honor.

Capitol Side Trip

Seward Square, Garfield Park

There are two places in this vicinity that have Civil War-related names —but nothing more, so skip the visit. Seward Square, at Pennsylvania and North Carolina avenues SE, honors William Henry Seward, a New Yorker, who was President Lincoln's Secretary of State. He was injured by an accomplice of John Wilkes Booth during the Lincoln assassination. A Whig, he was a former governor of New York, and twice was passed over by Republicans as a possible candidate for president. Garfield Park, at New Jersey Avenue and F Street SE, also honors President James A. Garfield, a veteran of the Civil War.

DIRECTIONS

Douglass Home Site to the Garfield Monument
The Garfield Monument is located on the Reflecting Pool at 1st Street and Maryland Avenue [Blue-Orange line, Federal Center stop].

GARFIELD MONUMENT
Maryland Ave. and 1st Street SW,
Reflecting Pool

This monument honors President Garfield, who was a Civil War veteran.

DIRECTIONS

Garfield Monument to Grant Memorial
The Grant Memorial is on the opposite side of the reflecting pool from the Garfield Monument [Blue-Orange line, Federal Center stop].

GRANT MEMORIAL
1st Street SW, Reflecting Pool

This equestrian statue is one of the largest in the world. It was dedicated in April 1922, on the centennial of USA Gen. Grant's birth. The memorial's sculptor took more than 22 years to complete this tribute to Grant, which includes a dozen horses, nearly as many soldiers, and four lions.

DIRECTIONS

Reflecting Pool to Smithsonian Institution
Before leaving the area of the reflecting pool, in front of the U.S. Capitol, it should be noted that the Smithsonian Institution has a number of buildings along the Mall.

SMITHSONIAN INSTITUTION
1000 Jefferson Dr. SW, on the Mall
Washington, DC 20560   202-357-2700

This is America's "attic," and the Smithsonian offers an array of exhibits, places to dine and shop, and other visitor amenities. There is a wealth of American history depicted in the Smithsonian. In particular, the Museum of American History, at the corner of Constitution Avenue and 14th Street NW, has an exhibit on the Civil War. The Smithsonian's facilities are open free seven days a week (except Christmas) from 10 AM to 5:30 PM. There are extended hours in the summer tourism season [The Blue-Orange line, Smithsonian stop].

Photo: Richmond Newspapers

Frederick Douglass was born into slavery and taught himself to read.

Meade Statue Side Trip

Judiciary Square

There are three sites of note in the area of Judiciary Square. The Lincoln Statue is located at Judiciary Square and D Street NW. The National Building Museum, formerly the Pension Building, is at F and 4th Sts. NW, and has a frieze that depicts Civil War troops. The National Portrait Gallery, at 7th and G streets NW, formerly the U.S. Patent Office, is a fine example of Classical Revival architecture. It was used as a Civil War hospital. The gallery is open free from 10 AM to 5:30 PM every day except Christmas [Red line, Judiciary Square stop].

DIRECTIONS

Grant Memorial to Meade Statue

Meanwhile, from the West Front of the Capitol, walk northwest down Constitution Avenue to Pennsylvania Avenue [Green-Yellow line, Archives-Navy Memorial stop].

MEADE STATUE

Pennsylvania and Constitution Aves.

Located in front of the U.S. Court House, this statue honors Union Gen. George Gordon Meade. Born in Spain to American parents, Meade was appointed to West Point from Pennsylvania. He participated in the Peninsular Campaign, 2nd Manassas, Antietam, Fredericksburg and Chancellorsville, and he commanded the Army of the Potomac from just before Gettysburg until the end of the war. He died of pneumonia in 1872, at the age of 57, having never fully recovered from a wound he received at White Oak Swamp just east of Richmond during the Seven Days' Battles of the Peninsular Campaign.

Here, along Pennsylvania Avenue in May 1865, more than 150,000 Union soldiers marched in review before President Andrew Johnson and Northern generals. The parade included the Armies of the Potomac, Tennessee, and Georgia. Soldiers marched 12 abreast for over eight hours straight.

DIRECTIONS

Meade Statue to Hancock Statue

Walk west on Pennsylvania Avenue to 7th Street NW [Green-Yellow line, Archives-Navy Memorial stop].

HANCOCK STATUE

7th and Pennsylvania Ave. NW

This statue honors Union Gen. Winfield Scott Hancock, a Pennsylvania native. He participated in McClellan's Peninsular Campaign in 1862, and saw action at Chickahominy, Golding's Farm, Savage's Station and White Oak Swamp. He also saw action at Antietam, Fredericksburg, Chancellorsville, and Gettysburg, where he was seriously injured. After the war, Hancock was an unsuccessful candidate for president in 1880, losing to President Garfield. He died in 1886.

DIRECTIONS

**Hancock Statue to
National Archives**

National Archives is on Pennsylvania Avenue at 7th Street NW [Green-Yellow line, Archives-Navy Memorial stop].

NATIONAL ARCHIVES

8th and Pennsylvania Ave. NW
Washington, DC 20108   202-501-5400

In addition to housing some of the nation's most precious documents, the National Archives has an extensive collection of military service records.

DIRECTIONS

**National Archives to J. Edgar
Hoover FBI Building**

The J. Edgar Hoover FBI Building is located between 9th and 10th streets on Pennsylvania Avenue [Blue-Orange line, Federal Triangle stop].

J. EDGAR HOOVER FBI BUILDING

9th and Pennsylvania Ave. NW

Completed in 1975, this building cost $126 million dollars. The Pennsylvania Avenue facade of the building features a block-long, ten-foot tall exhibit to eight American presidents and their relationship with the "Main Street of America." President Lincoln is among the eight presidents featured.

DIRECTIONS

**J. Edgar Hoover FBI Building
to Ford's Theater National
Historical Site**

From the J. Edgar Hoover FBI Building, walk a block north on 10th Street to E Street NW [Blue-Orange line and Red line, Metro Center stop].

FORD'S THEATER
NATIONAL HISTORICAL SITE

511 10th St. NW, at E St.
Washington, DC 20004   202-426-6927

President Lincoln was shot at Ford's Theater on Good Friday, April 14, 1865, five days after the Confederate surrender at Appomattox. He was attending a performance of "Our American Cousin," and was shot just before 10 PM by John Wilkes Booth. The president died the following morning. Booth masterminded the plot the previous year with several accomplices.

The theater has been recreated to look as it did the night Lincoln was fatally wounded. It is open free from 9 AM to 5 PM every day except Christmas. Performances are still held in the theater section, and it sometimes closes briefly for pre-performance set up. There is a museum of assassination-related memorabilia located on the floor beneath the theater. Adjacent to the museum is a book store, open from 9:30 AM to 4:15 PM.

DIRECTIONS

**Ford's Theater to
Petersen House**

The Petersen House is across the street from Ford's Theater [Blue-Orange line and Red line, Metro Center stop].

PETERSEN HOUSE

516 10th St. NW
Washington, DC 20004   202-426-6830

This house is where President Lincoln was taken after being shot. He died the next morning in a back bedroom. The house has been preserved and restored to its original

John Wilkes Booth

John Wilkes Booth was born and raised near Bel Air, MD, north of Baltimore. His father, Junius Brutus Booth, was thought to be insane, which may explain his son's strange and unbalanced behavior. John regularly exterminated cats on his family's farm, and he often ran away from home to play among Chesapeake Bay oystermen.

Photo: Wide World Photo

He was attracted to the stage at an early age, starring in a Baltimore performance at the age of 17. In four short years, he was playing leading Shakespearian roles in Richmond, and his career was on the rise. A dark and handsome actor, he was romantically linked with a number of women. Despite his astonishing stage career, and its accompanying success, Booth became interested in politics and the issues of the day. Unlike his other Maryland family members, his loyalties were with the South and the institution of slavery. He saw the Civil War as simply a fight between tyranny and freedom, a position that prompted his brother, actor Edwin Booth, to describe as unquestioned insanity.

In 1859, as a member of a Virginia militia unit, he took part in the arrest and execution of John Brown, the abolitionist who raided Harpers Ferry (see Tour 2: Middle Valley). A year before the Civil War ended, he apparently developed his daring plan to kidnap President Lincoln. This, he figured, might bring about the war's end or — at least — the exchange of prisoners. He sought out two former schoolmates, ex-Confederates Samuel Arnold and Michael O'Laughlin. During the last two months of 1864, Booth surveyed the roads of southern Maryland and those leading out of Washington.

Booth also made friends with John Surratt, a Confederate dispatch rider who operated between Richmond and Washington. Surratt was the son of Mary Surratt, a widow, who later sold her tavern in Prince Georges County, MD, just east of the district, and began operating a Washington boarding house. John Surratt brought in two more accomplices: an unbalanced 19-year-old named David Herold, and a coach-maker and Confederate sympathizer named George Atzerodt. In March 1865, Arnold and O'Laughlin moved to Washington, and Booth lined up another conspirator, Lewis Powell Payne, a poor, crazy, teenage Confederate veteran who was injured at Gettysburg and later escaped the military.

On March 20, 1865, the wild band tried to capture Lincoln as he rode by carriage near the Old Soldier's Home north of the city. But the president didn't make the trip that day, and Booth's party was foiled. Thinking their plot was suspected, the group split up, with Arnold and O'Laughlin heading back to Baltimore, and Surratt scattering to Richmond and then Canada. Early the next month, the North captured Richmond and the Confederates surrendered at Appomattox. Five days later, on April 14, the conspirator made his final plans after he heard the president planned to attend a performance at Ford's Theater, five blocks east of the White House.

Booth, himself, planned to assassinate the president. Atzerodt would kill Vice President Johnson in his Kirkwood Hotel room, and Payne and Herold would assassinate Secretary Seward at home. Having rigged the president's box at the theater, Booth slipped in during the performance and shot Lincoln in the head. He stabbed Major Henry Rathbone, who was in the box with the president and their two wives. Then, Booth leaped onto the stage, shouting "Sic semper tyrannis" — the Virginia motto. He added, "the South is avenged." His spur caught in the folds of the flag draping the box. He fell and broke his left leg.

Atzerodt, assigned to Vice President Johnson, got scared and never took part in the plot. Herold deserted Payne, who succeeded in wounding Seward. Herold, meanwhile, met up with Booth as he escaped the city on horseback. Meeting at the Anacostia River bridge near the Navy Yard, the pair headed southeast out of the city; they were hunted down in Caroline County, VA.

appearance. It is open, free of charge, from 9 AM to 5 PM every day except Christmas.

DIRECTIONS

Petersen House to Willard Hotel
From 10th Street, return to E Street NW and turn right (west). Go five blocks west on E. Street to 14th Street NW and the Willard Hotel [Blue-Orange line, Federal Triangle stop].

WILLARD HOTEL
14th and Pennsylvania Ave. NW

This is where President-elect Lincoln lived before his inaugural ceremony in March 1861. Lincoln and his wife, Mary, accompanied by President James Buchanan, left the Willard Hotel on the morning of the inauguration, and rode by open carriage up Pennsylvania Avenue to the Capitol for the ceremony. During the war, a Union vigilante group was stationed here. A popular myth is that Julia Ward Howe composed the "Battle Hymn of the Republic" at the hotel, but she probably wrote her classic

Willard Hotel Side Trip

Treasury Department Building

The Treasury Building, at 1500 Pennsylvania Avenue, is located adjacent to the White House. This is the third oldest building in Washington. Construction began in 1836 on the site chosen by President Andrew Jackson. The building ruined the long vista between the Capitol and the White House. In 1861, after word spread of possible Confederate attacks, the building was put under heavy Union guard [Blue-Orange line, McPherson Square stop].

while visiting a Union campsite somewhere in the Washington vicinity (see Richmond Personality: William Steffe in Tour 12: Richmond).

DIRECTIONS

Willard Hotel to Sherman Statue

From the Willard Hotel, walk a block west to 15th Street NW and the Ellipse behind the White House [Blue-Orange line, McPherson Square stop].

SHERMAN STATUE

President's Park, Ellipse

This statue honors Union Gen. William Tecumseh Sherman. A native of Ohio, he saw action in the Western Theater. He is known for his march on Atlanta and his "March to the Sea" and Carolina campaigns. In 1869, Sherman succeeded Union Gen. Grant as commander in chief of the army, a position he held for 14 years. He died in 1891.

DIRECTIONS

Sherman Statue to American National Red Cross Building

Walk to the west side of the Ellipse, to 17th Street NW. The American National Red Cross Building is located at 17th and D streets NW [Blue-Orange line, Farragut West stop].

AMERICAN NATIONAL RED CROSS BUILDING

17th and D Sts. NW
Washington, DC 20006   202-737-8300

This building was completed in 1929. It has an inscription over the portico, "In Memory of the Heroic Women of the Civil War." The Red Cross has exhibits on the first and second floors. The building is open free of charge from Monday through Friday, 9 AM to 4 PM, and closed on federal holidays.

DIRECTIONS

American National Red Cross Building to the White House

Walk north on 17th Street NW four blocks to Pennsylvania Avenue. Turn right (east) on Pennsylvania Avenue and go half a block to the White House [Blue-Orange line, Farragut West stop].

WHITE HOUSE

1600 Pennsylvania Ave. NW
Washington, DC 20500   202-456-7041

This is the official residence of the president and first family. Construction began in 1792 and President John Adams' family was the first resident. Originally the President's House, it was painted to hide evidence of the fire set by the British

Women Nurses

Susan Brownell Anthony, a feminist reformer in her 40s, was a teacher, lecturer and suffragette. She was an organizer of the Women's Loyal League that supported Lincoln.

Mrs. Stephen Barker was a nurse who went to Washington from Massachusetts in 1861 with her husband, a Union chaplain. She worked her way up to become superintendent of several Washington infirmaries. A lecturer who traveled throughout New York to raise funds for the Sanitary Commission, she stayed in Washington after the war's end to aid returning Union veterans.

Clara Barton, also in her 40s, was a Massachusetts woman working at the U.S. Patent Office in Washington when the war began. She helped get medicine and care to Union soldiers. An active philanthropist, she became the first president of the American Red Cross in 1882.

Clara Barton

Dorothea Lynde Dix was the Union superintendent of women nurses during the war. Born in 1802, Dix was active in movements to reform prisons and insane asylums.

Isabella Fogg, a native of Maine, became a nurse after her son enlisted in the Union Army. Going to work in Washington, she later saw action during the Peninsular Campaign, Fredericksburg, Chancellorsville, Gettysburg, and the Wilderness. She collapsed from overwork after nursing her son — a war casualty — to health. In January 1865, four months before Appomattox, she fell and was permanently crippled.

Harriett Hawley was a Union army nurse from Connecticut. Working mainly in the South, she moved to Washington in 1864 when her husband was assigned to USA Gen. Butler's command on the James River in Virginia.

Dorothea Lynde Dix

Mary Morris Husband, a Pennsylvania native, worked on hospital boats operated by the Sanitary Commission. She helped care for Union soldiers injured on Virginia's Peninsula. She then worked in Washington until May 1865.

during the War of 1812. Then, it was renamed the White House. President Lincoln moved in here in 1861. Within months, the official residence was turned into an army barracks as war fever hit Washington. Union soldiers drilled and slept in the East Room. From here, Lincoln issued his famous Emancipation Proclamation in September 1862 after the Battle of Antietam. The president prepared the proclamation's final draft at his summer cottage on the grounds of the U.S. Soldiers' Home. The official document applied only to areas still in rebellion — where the Union government had no authority. It said that, beginning January 1, 1863, "all persons held as slaves within any State, or designated part of a State, the people Whereof shall then be in rebellion against the United States, shall be then, henceforward, and forever free." Tours are available free at the White House on Tuesday through Saturday from 10 AM to noon. Admission tickets are required, however, and may be obtained at the ticket booth on the Ellipse beginning at 8 AM on the morning of the tour.

White House Personalities

Vice Presidents Hamlin and Johnson

Hannibal Hamlin was President Lincoln's first vice president. He was an antislavery Democrat who left his party over the issue. Bored during his vice presidency, he joined the Maine coast guard and served as a mere private during its 1864 Summer drill. Lincoln replaced him in 1864 with Andrew Johnson. Hamlin returned to Washington in 1869 as a senator and radical reconstructionist. He died in 1891. Two Pennsylvania communities bear Hamlin's name.

Photo: Bettman Archive

Andrew Johnson

Andrew Johnson was born in Raleigh, NC, in 1808. He settled in Tennessee and learned to read from his wife, Eliza McCardle Johnson, whom he married in 1827. A Democrat, he held a number of public positions in Tennessee: mayor, legislator, governor, congressman and U.S. senator. He supported Kentuckian John C. Breckenridge against Lincoln in the 1860 presidential election. Despite having once held slaves, he opposed secession. In 1862, President Lincoln appointed him the military governor of Tennessee. Two years later, the president picked him to replace Hamlin as vice president. After Lincoln's assassination, he served the remainder of the president's term. He fought off a resolution of impeachment, which failed in Congress by a single vote. Returning to Tennessee, he was reelected to the U.S. Senate in January 1875, and he died six months later. His wife died the next year.

Elizabeth Keckley

Born a slave, Elizabeth Keckley purchased her freedom and served as a seamstress for both Mrs. Jefferson Davis and Mrs. Lincoln. In 1868, she published *Behind the Scenes*, about her experiences in Lincoln's White House. She wrote about a "sad, anxious day" in 1863, when the Confederates — obviously before Gettysburg — were "flushed with victory." She wrote:

One day he came into the room where I was fitting a dress on Mrs. Lincoln. His step was slow and heavy, and his face sad. Like a tired child he threw himself upon a sofa, and shaded his eyes with his hands. He was a complete picture of dejection. Mrs. Lincoln, observing his troubled look, asked, "Where have you been father?" "To the War Department," was the brief, almost sullen answer. "Any news?" "Yes, plenty of news, but no good news. It is dark, dark everywhere." He reached forth one of his long arms, and took a small Bible from the stand near the head of the sofa, opened the pages of the holy book. . . . I discovered that Mr. Lincoln was reading the divine comforter, Job.

DIRECTIONS

White House to Blair House

Walk across Pennsylvania Avenue to the Blair House at 1651 Pennsylvania Avenue [Blue-Orange line, Farragut West stop].

BLAIR HOUSE

1651 Pennsylvania Ave. NW

Adjacent to Lafayette Park, this is the guest quarters for the White House. The home of Francis Preston Blair, President Lincoln's postmaster general, this is the place where the president offered Rober E. Lee the command of the Union army This building is closed to the public.

Francis Preston Blair

Francis Preston Blair descended from a long line of prominent Virginians. His great-grandfather, family progenitor John Preston, was one of the earliest Irish settlers of Virginia's Shenandoah Valley. Preston's daughter, Anne, married Francis Smith of Orange County, VA. The Smith's daughter, Elizabeth, married a western Virginia attorney, James Blair. Their son, Francis Preston Blair, was born in Abingdon, VA, in April 1791.

A Kentucky lawyer-turned-journalist, Blair strongly opposed nullification. In 1830, he was invited to Washington by President Andrew Jackson to start a pro-administration newspaper. In 1836, he purchased a President's Square residence. Blair also had a summer home, located in the country outside Washington, which he named "Silver Spring" — the origin of the name of the present-day Maryland suburb.

Active in Republican politics, Blair presided over the 1856 meeting that organized the new party. In January 1865, he met with Confederate President Jefferson Davis, and he initiated plans for a "peace conference" held in the Hampton Roads, VA, region and attended by President Lincoln and Confederate Vice President Alexander Stephens. He died at Silver Spring in 1876.

The Blair House in Washington is where Robert E. Lee was offered the command of the Union Army.

White House Side Trip

Lafayette Square

Across Pennsylvania Avenue from the White House, Lafayette Square was home to a number of Washington personalities, including William Henry Seward, Lincoln's secretary of state, and South Carolina Senator John C. Calhoun. The Hay-Adams Hotel, at 1 Lafayette Square (800 16th Street NW), was the residence of John Milton Hay, who was President Lincoln's assistant private secretary while he was in his 20s. Hay later wrote a 10-volume biography of the president, and he served as ambassador to Great Britain and secretary of state under Presidents McKinley and Theodore Roosevelt. Hay died in 1905.

St. John's Church, at 16th and H streets NW, is known as the "Church of the Presidents." Built in 1816, it was designed by Benjamin Latrobe, who served as the first organist. The church is open without charge to small groups of visitors, Monday through Saturday from 8 AM to 4 PM. It closes after noon service on Sundays, and for most holidays.

White House Side Trip

DIRECTIONS

From Lafayette Square, walk north on 17th Street NW two blocks to Farragut Square (K and 17th streets NW).

Farragut Square, McPherson Square, Thomas Circle, Scott Circle, DuPont Circle, McClellan Monument, Sheridan Circle

This statue, square and park honor Tennessean David Glasgow Farragut, a Union admiral. Born in 1809, he entered the navy at the tender age of nine. Three years later, while still a preteen, he was prize master of a ship captured

— continued on next page

— continued from previous page

in the Pacific during the War of 1812. A Union sympathizer, he was married twice — both wives were Norfolk, VA, natives — and left his home in Tidewater Virginia when the South began secession talks. He was a hero of Southern naval battles during the war.

In 1864, returning to a hero's welcome in New York City, he received $50,000 from city officials to buy a home, plus a promotion to the newly created rank of vice admiral. In 1865, he was one of the first Union men to enter Richmond when it fell, and the next year he became the first person in U.S. Navy history to be promoted admiral. He died in 1870.

President-Veterans

Besides Ulysses Grant and Andrew Johnson, four other U.S. presidents — residents of the White House — were veterans of the war:

Rutherford Hayes, a Union officer from Ohio, saw action at Winchester, Cedar Creek, and South Mountain, where he was wounded in the arm. He served in Congress from Ohio and supported President Johnson's impeachment. He was elected twice as governor of Ohio. In 1876, he became the 19th president, succeeding President Grant, after a disputed vote count and a special electoral commission awarded him a razor-thin victory. Hayes ended Reconstruction in the South by withdrawing the last of Union troops. He served one term in the White House and later died in Ohio in 1893.

James Garfield, another Union officer from Ohio, saw action in the war's Western Theater. A member of Congress, he was on the special electoral commission that voted for Hayes in 1876. Elected president in 1880, to succeed Hayes, he was inaugurated in March 1881 and shot three months later while entering a Washington train station. He died in September 1881 in New Jersey and was buried in Cleveland.

Benjamin Harrison, like Garfield, was a Union officer from Ohio and saw action in the Western Theater. He was the great-grandson of a Virginia signer of the Declaration of Independence, and the grandson of President William Henry Harrison. An attorney and U.S. senator, he defeated incumbent President Grover Cleveland, who received more popular votes than Harrison but fewer Electoral College votes. Harrison lost to Cleveland in the presidential race four years later. He died in Indianapolis in 1901.

William McKinley, another Ohioan, enlisted in Rutherford Hayes' 30th Ohio regiment at the age of 18. He served in West Virginia, Antietam, and Shenandoah Valley campaigns. After the war, he served in Congress and as governor of Ohio. He was elected president in 1896, and reelected in 1900. He was shot by an anarchist at the Pan-American Exposition in Buffalo, NY, in September 1901, and he died a week later.

DIRECTIONS

From Farragut Square, walk east on K Street NW for two blocks to McPherson Square (K and 15th streets NW).

McPherson Square

This statue and square honor James Birdseye McPherson, a Union general from Ohio. He saw action in the Western Theater, and was killed in the Battle of Atlanta in July 1864. He was only 35.

DIRECTIONS

From McPherson Square, walk north on Vermont Avenue for two blocks to Thomas Circle (Vermont and Massachusetts avenues NW).

Thomas Circle

This statue and circle honor "The Rock of Chickamauga," Union Gen. George Henry Thomas. A Virginian, he graduated from West Point and remained loyal to the North. He saw action in the Western Theater, and was one of only 15 Union officers to receive Thanks of Congress for his war action and heroism. He died on active duty in 1870. The junction for four major city streets, the circle now has a traffic tunnel underneath.

DIRECTIONS

From Thomas Circle, walk west two blocks to Scott Circle (Massachusetts Avenue and 16th Street NW).

Scott Circle

This circle and statue honor Virginia-born Winfield Scott, a hero of the Mexican War, and general-in-chief of the U.S. Army at the beginning of the Civil War. He was born in Dinwiddie County, VA, in 1786, a year before the U.S. Constitution was adopted. He died at West Point at the age of 90, the only Southern non-West Pointer who remained loyal to the North. The statue of Scott, erected in 1874, was cast from cannon captured in the Mexican War. Also in Scott Circle is the Daniel Webster Statue, which honors the noted senator from Massachusetts. The statue was cast in bronze and erected in 1900.

DIRECTIONS

From Scott Circle, walk west three blocks to DuPont Circle (Connecticut Avenue NW at P Street).

DuPont Circle

This circle has a fountain that honors Union Rear Adm. Samuel Francis duPont, a veteran of war action in the South. He was president of the board that met in Washington in June 1861 to plan the Union's naval operations. He died in June 1865, two months after the war's end, while still on active duty. Originally Pacific Circle, DuPont Circle was graced with a statue of duPont in 1884. Later, his family moved the statue to Delaware and commissioned Daniel Chester French to design the fountain.

DIRECTIONS

From DuPont Circle, walk north on Connecticut Avenue for seven blocks to the McClellan Monument (Connecticut Avenue and California Street NW).

Painting: Dale Gallon

"Tomorrow...We Must Attack Him"

McClellan Monument

This equestrian statue honors Union Gen. George Brinton McClellan. A Pennsylvania native, McClellan succeeded the venerable Winfield Scott as commander and chief of the army. He was called the "Young Napoleon" during the early stages of the war. But after Antietam, Lincoln appointed Union Gen. Burnside to replace McClellan as commander of the Union Army of the Potomac. McClellan ran unsuccessfully against Lincoln for president in 1864.

DIRECTIONS

From the McClellan Monument, return south on Connecticut Avenue for five blocks to R Street NW. Turn right (west) on R Street and walk four blocks to Sheridan Circle (Massachusetts Avenue and 23rd Street NW).

Sheridan Circle

This circle honors Union Gen. Philip Henry Sheridan, who was known during the war as "Little Phil." A New Yorker of Irish descent, he saw action at the Wilderness and

Maynard, Brady and Ericsson

Dr. Edward Maynard, a Washington dental surgeon, obtained a patent in 1845 for a "primer tape," similar to the caps used in today's toy cap guns. Rifles used in the war were made — or modified — to accommodate this tape, which became known as "Maynard Tape."

Mathew Brady, the noted war photographer, was an astute entrepreneur who created a mobile darkroom for his assistants who worked various battlefields. Brady was quite nearsighted, and seldom did much negative work himself. In fact, he rarely stepped foot out of his two studios, in New York and in Washington.

John Ericsson, a Swede, invented the screw propeller and designed the *Monitor* ironside in 1861. A memorial in West Memorial Park, near the Lincoln Memorial, is dedicated to Ericsson.

Washington Personalities

Baltimore, MD

Baltimore, a Gaelic word, gets its name from Cecilius Calvert, Lord Baltimore, who founded Maryland in the 17th century. The town was founded in 1726 and laid out on Thomas Carroll's land. It was merged with Jones-town in 1745 and incorporated in 1797. Originally called Baltimore City, its name was changed so it wouldn't be confused with Baltimore County.

Four Massachusetts volunteers and a dozen citizens were killed in Baltimore in April 1861, after a group of secessionist sympathizers attacked a train of soldiers from Pennsylvania and New York. The troops were headed for Washington when the riot broke out.

Spotsylvania. He conducted a raid on Richmond in May 1864, during which time CSA Gen. J.E.B. Stuart was killed. Sheridan's Shenandoah Valley Campaign raged from August 1864 until nearly the end of the war. He was with USA Gen. Grant at Appomattox in 1865.

Washington Accommodations

The rate charges for a double room, not including taxes, are a bit higher in the DC area than in most of our other tour areas, so we changed the rating scale to better reflect what you will pay:

$	Under $80
$$	$81 to $120
$$$	$121 and up

Our thanks to the authors of *The Insiders' Guide to Metro Washington, DC* for their suggestions of accommodations and restaurants.

THE MAYFLOWER
1127 Connecticut Ave., NW
Washington, DC 20036   202-347-3000
$$$

This is a much-revered Connecticut Avenue landmark, a place to see and be seen. The Mayflower lobby takes up an

entire block; it has two restaurants and a lounge. This facility, a former Stouffer hotel, has more than 800 units—some with kitchenettes. Dignitaries often stay here. Indeed, the White House is just four blocks away.

THE WILLARD INTER-CONTINENTAL
1401 Pennsylvania Ave., NW
Washington, DC 20005   202-965-2300
$$$

The Willard (see listing in chapter listing) is a Washington landmark that almost fell victim to the wrecking ball before it was renovated and reopened in 1986. A short walk from the White House, the Treasury Department, National Theater and the Mall, the Willard has two lounges, a cafe and a formal restaurant, the Willard Room.

BED 'N' BREAKFAST LTD. OF WASHINGTON, DC
P.O. Box 12011
Washington, DC 20005   202-328-3510
$-$$

From budget to luxury offerings, Bed 'N' Breakfast Ltd. of Washington can connect you with an array of private-home lodgings, guests houses and inns. They even know about some apartments available for family groups and extended-stay guests.

Washington Restaurants

There are so many wonderful restaurants in the Washington, D.C. area that we are hard-pressed to pull out a few for you here. But, that is our task, so you'll find some of our favorites here, from glamorous to just plain good.

The ratings scale for restaurants also reflects prices that are a bit higher than in most our other tours, so we are providing a different scale. These rates are for a dinner meal for two, not including taxes, tips, or alcoholic beverages.

$	Under $30
$$	$31 to $60
$$$	$61 to $100
$$$$	$101 and up

BLACKIE'S HOUSE OF BEEF
1217 22nd St., NW
Washington, DC 20037   202-682-1840
$$$

This Washington landmark dates to 1946. It is located just off M Street between Georgetown and downtown. Blackie's features antiques, paintings and cozy rooms with fireplaces. As its name suggests, this restaurant features beef and more beef — from thick steaks to succulent roast beef.

CLYDE'S OF GEORGETOWN
3236 M St., NW
Washington, DC 20007   202-333-9180
$$

Another Washington institution, Clyde's is a street-front saloon on busy M Street in popular Georgetown. A fun, dependable place with broad appeal — patrons likely include grad students, yuppie couples and old-line establishment types. Beyond the bars, for drinks and raw seafood, a back dining area offers fresh pasta and seafood, Clyde's own brand of award-winning chili, steaks, sandwiches and homemade desserts.

THE MONOCLE
107 D St., NE
Washington, DC 20002   202-546-4488
$$

This trendy restaurant is located a half-block from the U.S. Senate office buildings on Capitol Hill. It is the place to see a number of Hill notables — particularly when Congress is in session. Catch your favorite Senator or a lofty lobbyist having a quick respite at the bar or dinner with friends and colleagues. Owner/manager John Valanos and his friendly associate, Nick Selimos, greet each guest at the door as if they're a future President (which some guests undoubtedly are).

Other Washington Attractions

There is much to see and do in Washington, DC Again, we recommend our sister guide, which covers annual events, arts, historical sites, places to shop, dine and stay the night, embassies, and a thorough appraisal of the attractions scene.

Annual Events: The Cherry Blossom Festival in April is beautiful. Independence Day on the Mall in

Photo: Matthew Brady

Ulysses S. Grant at the close of the Civil War wearing the four stars of a full general.

July is spectacular, and it's accompanied by the Smithsonian Institution's Folk Life Festival. Other major holidays — including Memorial Day and Veterans Day — mean a grand parade, usually along Constitution Avenue. In December, as the nation's capital celebrates the holiday season, the Pageant of Peace features a giant evergreen tree on the Ellipse at the White House.

Arts: Washington is the nation's center for museums and galleries, including the Corcoran Gallery of Art, National Air and Space Museum, National Gallery of Art, National Museum of American History, National Museum of American Art — and much, much more. The newest arrivals: the U.S. Holocaust Memorial Museum, at Independence Avenue and 14th Street NW, and the National Postal Museum, at 2 Massachusetts Avenue NE. Also new are the Sailor's Memorial on Pennsylvania Avenue and a statue honoring women veterans at the Vietnam Veterans Memorial near the Lincoln Memorial. Washington is also home of the Kennedy Center, Arena Stage, National Theater, Warner Theater, Ford's Theater (see listing in this chapter), and Folger's Shakespeare Library. For the latest in political parody and satire, take in the Capitol Steps, a group of current and former Capitol Hill employees that performs weekends at Chelsea's Restaurant in Georgetown.

Shopping: The nation's capital can be a shopper's paradise. From elegant boutiques to souvenir shops, Washington has it all. For starters, there's Georgetown Park in Georgetown, the Shops at National Place (adjacent to the downtown Marriott on Pennsylvania Avenue), and the old Post Office Pavilion (also on Pennsylvania Avenue). Each section of Washington offers a unique shopping experience, like Filene's Basement, a bargain-hunter's delight, across the street from the Mayflower. Near Capitol Hill, the renovated Union Station rail center has a number of fancy shops and restaurants. The building itself is worth a visit.

TOUR 10

Arlington to Fairfax

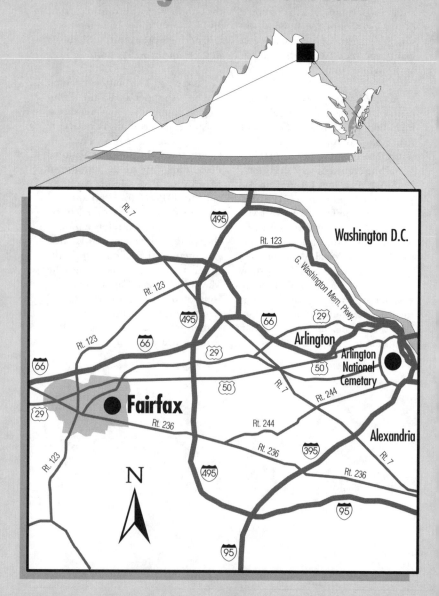

Tour 10
Northern Virginia

About This Tour

This tour route covers Arlington and Fairfax counties, and the cities of Fairfax and Alexandria — all Northern Virginia suburbs of Washington, D.C.

Travel Tips

This section of the Washington Metropolitan area is heavily congested, especially during morning and evening rush hour periods. Be especially careful on the highways and roads of Northern Virginia, particularly the Washington Beltway, I-395 and I-95 south.

There's another way to experience some of Northern Virginia's historic attractions: Tourmobile. This is a convenient way to see 18 major sites along Washington's Mall and into Northern Virginia. Tourmobile charges a fee, but it offers free reboarding throughout its tour route. Tourmobile even offers special vehicles for the mobility impaired. For information, telephone 202-554-7950.

History, Geography

Before the Civil War, Northern Virginia was oriented to the south — toward Richmond. During the Civil War, all the region in this tour route, including Fairfax County and the City of Alexandria, was occupied by Union forces. Only after the war's conclusion, and the influx of an increased population — including Union sympathizers from the North and African-Americans from the "liberated" South — did Northern Virginia become reoriented more to the whims and politics of Washington, D.C.

This region traces its origins to Anglo pioneers from Virginia's Tidewater. In 1649, King Charles II of England granted land patents between the Potomac and Rappahannock rivers to a handful of Englishmen, mainly ancestors of Thomas, sixth Lord Fairfax, for whom Fairfax County is named. In time, the Virginia area along the Potomac River was settled by a number of illustrious families — including Washington, Mason, Carter, Fitzhugh and Lee. Mount Vernon, on the Potomac, was the home of Lawrence Washington and, later, of his half-brother, George Washington. Nearby was Belvoir, the home of George William Fairfax, a cousin of Lord Fairfax. Gunston Hall was the home of George Mason, one of many Virginians involved in the American struggle for independence. Arlington was the estate of George Washington Parke Custis, the step-grandson of George Washington.

Tobacco was the principal crop of colonial Northern Virginia, and warehouses were located all along the Potomac. Roads leading from the hinterland farms, including the now famous Little River Turnpike, led west-to-east to the river. These port sites became the locations of such prominent communities as Alexandria in Fairfax County, and Dumfries, Occoquan and Woodbridge in Prince William County. The main route between Northern Virginia and Richmond generally followed the "fall line" — the geographic division between the coastal plain and the rolling piedmont. The fall line marks the end of tidal movement and the head of navigation for the rivers of the coastal plain.

In the late 18th century, a portion of Northern Virginia land was donated to the new federal government for the establishment of the District of Columbia, the seat of government. The new federal city, which bore the name of Northern Virginian George Washington, was a ten-mile square, overlapping Maryland, Virginia and the Potomac River. The Virginia portion of the district took in the community of Alexandria, the county seat of Fairfax at the time. With this decision, the Fairfax county seat was moved west, to a place called Providence — now known as the City of Fairfax. In 1846, Virginia retroceded its portion of the land within the District of Columbia, and the returned land was named Alexandria County — the county was renamed Arlington in the 20th century.

In the 1850s, two major rail lines were constructed in Northern Virginia. One ran from Alexandria to Leesburg. The other ran from Alexandria to Gordonsville, through a small Prince William County community known as Manassas Junction. The railroad greatly reduced Alexandria's prestige as a major river trading center. By this time, Richmond and Baltimore already were drawing business away from Alexandria, and tobacco and wheat were dropping in popularity. Alexandria developed the dubious distinction as being a major trade center for African American slaves.

When Virginia seceded from the Union, in the spring of 1861, Union soldiers poured into Northern Virginia to occupy jurisdictions along the Potomac River. Skirmishes were less prevalent here, thanks in part to a series of forts, including Fort Ward in Alexandria, that encircled the nation's capital. In 1863, when the new state of West Virginia was established, Alexandria became the location of the "restored" government of Virginia under federal control. Because of this "occupation," Northern Virginia recovered more quickly than other Southern locales after the surrender at Appomattox.

Getting Here

DIRECTIONS

Lincoln Memorial (Washington) to Arlington National Cemetery

This tour route is a natural continuation of Tour 9: Washington. The first stop on this route is Arlington National Cemetery, just across Memorial Bridge from Washington's Lincoln Memorial. This tour route also can be accessed from Manassas, VA — the end of Tour 7: Middle Piedmont. From Manassas, take I-66 east toward Washington to exit 72, Spout Run Parkway. At the end of the exit ramp, turn right (north) onto US 29 (Lee Highway) and go one block to VA 124. Turn left onto VA 124 (Spout Run Parkway) and go one mile to the merge with southbound George Washington Memorial Parkway. Take the George Washington Memorial Parkway south for 1.8 miles to the right exit for Memorial Bridge and Arlington Cemetery. The exit ramp makes a 180-degree loop and up to Memorial Drive. Turn left on Memorial Drive and go one block to Arlington Cemetery entrance.

LINCOLN MEMORIAL

Located on the Mall at the end of Memorial Bridge, the Lincoln Memorial is one of Washington's most recognizable attractions. An appropriate memorial to President Abraham Lincoln was debated almost immediately after his assassination. There was talk of a memorial roadway between Washington and Gettysburg, and of monuments near the Capitol and Union Station. Finally, a site was chosen in the swampy overgrowth along the Potomac River, and the monument was dedicated in 1922.

Outside, the 36 columns signify the number of states in the Union during Lincoln's presidency. The columns tilt inward to avoid the allusion of bulging at the top. Inside, on the south wall, Lincoln's Gettysburg Address is carved into the marble. Interestingly, this memorial faces across the Potomac toward Arlington House, Robert E. Lee's former residence. The memorial is open free daily from 8 AM to midnight. A gift shop and book store operate on an abbreviated schedule, depending on the season.

Cross the Potomac River from Washington into Virginia on the Memorial Bridge and Memorial Avenue, which symbolically links the North and the South. At the Washington side of the neoclassical bridge is the Lincoln Memorial. At the Virginia side is Arlington House. The bridge is the northern terminus of the Mount Vernon Memorial Highway, which extends south along the Virginia and District of Columbia shore of the Potomac to the home of George Washington.

ARLINGTON NATIONAL CEMETERY
Arlington, VA 22211

More than 225,000 veterans and their family members are buried at Arlington, the best known of the country's 100-plus national cemeteries. The cemetery traces its origins to the Civil War and to the efforts of Army Quartermaster Gen. Montgomery Meigs, who schemed to use

200 acres of CSA Gen. Robert E. Lee's family property to bury Washington's overwhelming Civil War casualties. By 1865, more than 16,000 graves were scattered about Arlington House, the Lee mansion overlooking the Potomac River.

In 1882, Lee's son, George Washington Custis Lee, ceded title of the Arlington House property to the federal government for the cemetery, despite a U.S. Supreme Court ruling that the government improperly took the land.

The cemetery includes the Tomb of the Unknown Civil War Dead, and the remains of more than 2,000 Union soldiers, as well as a Confederate Monument and a section for the burial of Confederate soldiers. Oliver Wendall Holmes Jr., a U.S. Supreme Court Justice and a Civil War veteran (see Hagerstown, MD, in Tour 1: Cumberland Valley), also is buried here. Also buried at Arlington are Presidents John F. Kennedy and William Howard Taft. The cemetery has memorials to the crew of the space shuttle *Challenger*, servicemen killed in the hostage rescue attempt in Iran, and nurses from the Spanish-American War to the present.

Arlington National Cemetery is open every day from 8 AM to 5 PM from October to March, and from 8 AM to 7 PM from April to September. There is a parking facility at the cemetery (a fee is charged), which also can be reached by the Washington Metro blue line. A visitors center is open seven days a week. Handicapped visitors and persons who want to visit a private grave site may get a temporary pass to drive into cemetery. Otherwise, vehicle traffic is prohibited. The Tourmobile, a concession-operated service (fee) provides access to Arlington House. It operates from 8 AM to 7 PM April through September and from 8 AM to 5 PM October through March.

Arlington Cemetery Side Trip

Freedman's Village

Efforts are under way to improve an area within Arlington National Cemetery that once was the site of Freedman's Village, a flourishing town for 10,000 freed African-American slaves. The village, complete with houses, farms, businesses, school and hospital, was built in 1863 on land that was part of Robert E. Lee's estate, Arlington House.

Originally, Freedman's Village was developed to house the thousands of former slaves who crowded into Washington after President Lincoln abolished slavery in the city—a year before the Emancipation Proclamation freed slaves in the South. The village grew to epic proportions. Two African American churches in Arlington County can trace their roots to Freedman's Village. But there's very little other evidence of the town.

Arlington Cemetery includes the graves of 3,800 freed slaves and 1,200 African-Americans who fought in the Union Army. The village location will be included in the guided tour of the cemetery. Names and histories of those buried at the site will be recorded.

ARLINGTON HOUSE,
THE ROBERT E. LEE MEMORIAL
Arlington, VA 22111

In 1824, the Marquis de Lafayette visited Arlington House and described the view across the Potomac to Washington as the finest in the world. George Washington Parke Custis, President George Washington's step-grandson, built Arlington House in the early 1800s. It was named for the Custis family homestead on Virginia's Eastern Shore. Robert E. Lee married Custis' daughter, Mary Anna Randolph Custis, at Arlington House in 1831, and the estate became their home for the next 30 years.

Lee lived here when he received word of Virginia's secession in April 1861. And it was here at Arlington that Lee decided to resign his U.S. Army commission to join the Confederate army. Soon, federal troops occupied the house. In 1864, the 1,100-acre Arlington House estate was designated a national cemetery. Ironically, Arlington Cemetery would be the final resting place for so many federal solders who opposed Lee.

Ironically, too, Arlington House estate was never located in its namesake: Arlington County. The mansion was a part of Virginia land ceded to the District of Columbia. Then, the estate was located in Alexandria

Robert E. Lee

Robert E. Lee, born Jan. 19, 1807 at Stratford in Westmoreland County, VA, spent his youth and adult life in Northern Virginia. He was only 3 years old when his family moved up the Potomac River to Alexandria, a busy river port and thriving commercial center of 7,500. A few miles up the Potomac from Alexandria was Arlington House estate, home of George Washington Parke Custis. Custis was like a father to Robert E. Lee, who married Custis' daughter in 1831 at the estate.

Throughout Lee's career in the Army, and until the beginning of the Civil War, Arlington House remained his home. It was a haven where he could lay down his disappointments, his frustrations, and his anxieties.

In 1861, Lee was forced to decide between his nation and state. On April 18, he rode from Arlington into Washington to visit Virginian Winfield Scott (see Petersburg Personality in Tour 13: Petersburg), general in chief of the U.S. Army, and Francis Blair (see Blair House Personality in Tour 9: Washington), President Lincoln's advisor. Blair told Lee that Lincoln was willing to give him command of a 100,000-man federal army. The next day, a Baltimore mob killed three Union soldiers, and by 2 PM their bodies were lying in state at the U. S. Capitol. That afternoon Lee received news from Richmond that a Virginia convention had voted to secede from the Union. War was imminent. Sitting alone at Arlington, Robert resigned his U. S. Army commission. The next day, he attended church in Alexandria, where a Richmond contingent arrived to say that Virginia wanted him to be major general of the state's army.

On April 22, Lee left for Richmond, never to return to Arlington. Later, he commented on his resignation from the U.S. Army: "I did only what my duty demanded."

Arlington House Personality

County — the Virginia part of the District retroceded to the Commonwealth in 1846. It was a part of federal property in 1920 when Alexandria County was renamed Arlington by the Virginia General Assembly to honor Robert E. Lee and his estate. In 1925, the U.S. Congress designated Arlington House and its grounds as the Robert E. Lee Memorial, with Memorial Bridge to link memorials to President Lincoln and Lee.

Arlington House is operated by the National Park Service. A tour includes most of the estate's 26 rooms, including bedrooms, the Morning Room, the family dining room, the guest chamber and the Lee's Chamber, where General Lee wrote his U.S. Army resignation. Arlington House is open from 9:30 AM to 6 PM from April to September, and from 9:30 AM to 4:30 PM October through March. Access to Arlington House is by parking at the Arlington Cemetery and walking to the house. The Tourmobile (see above) also provides access.

DIRECTIONS

Arlington Cemetery to Lee's Boyhood Home

Return north on Memorial Drive to the traffic circle at Memorial Bridge. Go three-quarters of the way around the circle — as if you're heading west — and then take the left exit ramp (signs for I-395, Alexandria and Mount Vernon) that loops back onto the George Washington Memorial Parkway south toward Alexandria and National Airport. Continue south on the parkway for 1.5 miles to the I-395 interchange, another 1 mile to the National Airport

entrance, and then another 3 miles to the northern city limits of Alexandria. Here, at the first traffic signal, the parkway becomes Washington Street through downtown Alexandria. Proceed through six more traffic signals (0.8 miles) to Oronoco Street. Turn left — across northbound parkway traffic — onto Oronoco Street. The Boyhood Home of Robert E. Lee is in the first block of Oronoco Street.

BOYHOOD HOME OF ROBERT E. LEE
607 Oronoco St.
Alexandria, VA 22314   703-548-8454

Robert E. Lee lived with his mother, brothers and sisters in several Alexandria houses, beginning about 1810, including this stately, brick Federal-style house, owned by a relative, William Henry Fitzhugh.

DIRECTIONS

Lee Homes to Christ Church

From Oronoco Street, return to Washington Street and turn left (south) on Washington Street. Go three blocks (0.2 miles) to Cameron Street. Christ Church is on the right side of Washington Street at Cameron Street. Turn right on Cameron Street and go one block to Columbus Street. A public parking lot and on-street parking is available on Columbus Street. Enter the church grounds from Columbus Street.

CHRIST CHURCH
118 N. Washington St., at Cameron St.
Alexandria, VA 22314

This attractive, 18th-century Episcopal Church is one of Alexandria's

The stairway at Robert E. Lee's boyhood home shows furnishings at the Federal-style Alexandria townhouse.

— and Virginia's — most famous landmarks. Many of Alexandria's famous families, including the Washingtons and Lees, worshipped here. The church cemetery was the town burying ground until 1815. Robert E. Lee was confirmed at Christ Church, and this is where he attended church as a youth and young adult. It's said that on the third Sunday in April 1861, the day after he resigned his commission in the U.S. Army, Lee left church services here and was met by a contingent from Richmond. The men reported that Virginia wanted Lee to be major general of the state forces. Within days, Lee was on his way to Richmond — and the Civil War.

DIRECTIONS

Christ Church to Infantry Monument

From Christ Church, go south one block on Columbus Street to King Street. Turn left on King Street and go one block to Washington Street. Turn right on Washington Street and go one block to Prince Street. The Infantry Monument sits in the middle of this intersection. The Lyceum, located on the southwest corner of this intersection, has a visitor's parking lot.

INFANTRY MONUMENT

Washington and Prince Sts.
Alexandria, VA 22314

The Confederate monument in the middle of Washington Street honors the men of Alexandria's 17th Va. Infantry Regiment. This is the place where a number of these Confederate infantrymen assembled, then marched down Duke Street

and boarded an Orange and Alexandria Railroad train headed for Manassas Junction. At Manassas, they joined Confederate forces for the Battle of 1st Manassas.

The statue was dedicated in a ceremony in 1889. Virginia Governor Fitzhugh Lee, a former officer in the Army of Northern Virginia and General Robert E. Lee's nephew, delivered the address. The area around the monument once measured 40 by 60 feet, and it included a fence with ornamental gas lamps.

The statue's island was reduced in size as automobile traffic increased along Washington Street, especially in 1932 after construction of the George Washington Memorial Parkway. Since then, on occasion, the statue has been struck by an errant automobile.

LYCEUM

Washington and Prince Sts.
Alexandria, VA 22314

The Lyceum, a good example of Greek revival architecture, was established in 1839 as a cultural and scientific center. Its origins are traced to the efforts of Quaker educator Benjamin Hallowell, who ran an Alexandria school a decade earlier and helped Robert E. Lee prepare for West Point. During the Civil War, the Lyceum was used as a hospital. Then, after being used as a private residence and offices, it became a state center for the American Bicentennial celebration in the 1970s.

Today, the old Lyceum is home of Alexandria's History Museum. And it now looks more like it did in 1839, thanks to a fresh coat of paint — an

Henry "Light-Horse Harry" Lee, Ann Carter Lee

January 1807 was not the best of times for Ann Hill Carter Lee. She had just lost her father, Charles Carter of Shirley Plantation (see Tour 15: Peninsula), and her husband Harry — Henry "Light-Horse Harry" — Lee was known to disappear frequently. Ann, who was pregnant, caught a bad cold riding a coach through wet and cold weather from Shirley to her Westmoreland County home. Alone at Stratford, she gave birth to a son on Jan. 19. She named the new baby after her brothers Robert and Edward: Robert Edward Lee.

The boy was the fourth child for Ann and her husband, Henry "Light-Horse Harry," a veteran of the

Henry "Light-Horse Harry" Lee

Revolution, a member of the Continental Congress, and Virginia Governor. He commanded U. S. soldiers in the Whiskey Insurrection in 1794, and delivered President Washington's eulogy before both houses of Congress. Light-Horse Harry also suffered financial reversals, and he reportedly spent time in jail twice for debt. In 1813, during the War of 1812, Light-Horse Harry sailed to the Caribbean, either to relieve his family of the burdens of his illness, or to avoid public embarrassment for his poor finances. Five years later, on his way home, he died at Georgia's Cumberland Island.

The Lee children — Charles Carter, Anne, Sydney Smith, Robert, and Mildred — were raised by their mother, who was forced to use her family trust income to sustain the household. During the economic depression following the War of 1812, Ann ran the family on about $600 a year. She lived long enough to see her children grown, and when she died in 1829, Carter was an attorney, and young Anne was married to William Marshall, a clergyman-turned-lawyer. Smith was in the Navy, and Robert had only recently graduated second in his class from West Point. Mildred later married and settled in Europe.

Ann Hill Carter Lee hosted the Marquis de Lafayette at this house during the Frenchman's visit to America in the 1820s. George Washington Parke Custis, the man who built Arlington House, married Mary Lee Fitzhugh in the drawing room here. Later, the Custis' daughter married Robert E. Lee at Arlington House.

The house is listed in the National Register of Historic Places and as a Virginia Historic Landmark. It is furnished with authentic period pieces. This home is open on Sunday from 1 to 4 PM, and all other days from 10 AM to 4 PM. It is closed Easter, Thanksgiving Day, and on some other special occasions. It is open only by appointment during the period December 15 to January 31. A fee is charged.

Alexandria Side Trip

Old Town Alexandria

This pharmacy, at 107 S. Fairfax Street, was founded in 1792 — the year the cornerstone was laid at the President's House (later the White House) in Washington, D.C. The shop's original furnishings and glassware remain intact today.

In the fall of 1859, J.E.B. Stuart — then a U.S. Army lieutenant — went to the apothecary shop to find another U.S. Army officer, Col. Robert E. Lee, and deliver a message from the secretary of war. Lee was told to rush to Harper's Ferry to put down a disturbance started by abolitionist John Brown (See Harper's Ferry in Tour 2: Middle Valley).

DIRECTIONS

Walk north one block to Washington and King streets. Turn right (east) on King Street and walk four blocks to Fairfax Street. Turn right (south) on Fairfax Street and go a quarter-block to the Stabler-Leadbeater Apothecary Shop.

On the northeast corner of King and Fairfax streets is the William Ramsey House, built in 1724 by Alexandria' first mayor and now the city's visitor's center. Just north of the William Ramsey House, at the corner of Fairfax and Cameron streets, is Carlyle House, built in 1753. Carlyle House served as the headquarters for British Gen. Braddock during the French and Indian War.

Across the street from the Carlyle House and the William Ramsey House, facing King Street, is Alexandria City Hall. A block west of City Hall, at the corner of King and Pitt streets, was the site of the Marshall House Incident in 1861.

historical shade of yellow-orange. The color was chosen after extensive research that included analysis of original paint scrapings.

DIRECTIONS

Return to the Lyceum to continue this tour route by automobile.

Infantry Monument to Alexandria National Cemetery
Go south on Washington Street one block to Duke Street. Turn right (west) on Duke Street and go four blocks to S. Henry Street (US 1 one-way south). Turn left (south) on US 1 one-way south, and go one block to Wilkes Street. Turn right (west) on Wilkes Street and go six blocks west into the gates of Arlington National Cemetery.

ALEXANDRIA NATIONAL CEMETERY
Wilkes St.
Alexandria, VA 22314

Nearly 4,000 Civil War dead—mostly Union soldiers — are buried in this, one of the nation's first national cemeteries. It is open from dawn to dusk.

DIRECTIONS

Alexandria National Cemetery to Fort Ward Museum and Historic Site
Backtrack east on Wilkes Street six blocks to Patrick St (US 1 one-way north). Turn left (north) on Patrick Street and go three blocks to King Street. Turn left (west) on King Street (VA 7) and go west for 0.5 miles to Union Station, Alexandria's main railroad station. Beyond the railroad station, beyond the underpass, turn left (south) onto Callahan Road.

USA Col. Ellsworth and Secessionist Jackson

Ephraim Elmer Ellsworth organized the Chicago Zouave Cadets, a group of soldiers who modeled themselves after French Algerian infantrymen — known as Zouaves. A New York native, Ellsworth moved to Chicago in the 1850s — a time when newspapers reported on the exploits of the French Zouaves in the Crimean War. Ellsworth was fascinated with the North African uniforms and the Zouave reputation for drill and weapons precision.

Ellsworth and his Chicago group put on a number of exhibitions, including visits to West Point and the White House in Washington. President Lincoln has been quoted as saying that Ellsworth was "the greatest little man I ever met."

In the first year of the Civil War, Ellsworth and his men were organized as a U.S. regiment and stationed at the U.S. Capitol. Soon, Ellsworth's regiment was part of a 13,000-man Union contingent ordered across the Potomac to occupy Alexandria. What caught Ellsworth's eye was an exceptionally large flag that flew from the Marshall House, a hotel then located at King and Pitt streets.

The Marshall House manager, Virginian James William Jackson, was an ardent secessionist. His large flag, designed after the Confederate "Stars and Bars," could be seen as far away as the White House across the Potomac.

Ellsworth decided to capture the flag. He and a group of followers entered the Marshall House, went to the roof, hauled down the flag, and began their escape. But Jackson, armed with a double-barreled shotgun, met the group in the stairway. USA Corporal Francis E. Brownell used his rifle to deflect Jackson's shotgun, but the Southern's weapon discharged. Ellsworth was struck and killed instantly. In turn, Brownell fired his rifle at Jackson, who was struck in the head and fatally injured.

The incident was witnessed by a New York newspaper correspondent, and soon the two deaths were sensationalized by Northern and Southern sympathizers alike. Souvenir-seekers stole pieces of the Marshall House stairway where the two died. Ellsworth's funeral, held in the East Room of the White House, was attended by a bereaved President Lincoln.

The Marshall House incident inspired patriotic poems and songs, and Ellsworth was hailed in the North as "the first to fall." The 44th New York Regiment, known as "Ellsworth's Avengers," was raised in his honor. The regiment adopted a commemorative ballad, of which a stanza said:

> "First to fall, thou youthful martyr,
> Hapless was thy fate;
> Hastened we, as thy avengers,
> From thy native State,
> Speed we on, from town and city,
> Not for wealth or fame,
> But because we love the Union,
> And our Ellsworth's name."

The Marshall House site is the present-day location of the Holiday Inn on King Street in Old Town Alexandria.

Union Station, Potomac Yard

The 88-year-old Union Station is the only surviving rail station of four that once served Alexandria. The City of Alexandria has received a $14 million federal grant to renovate this old station.

Just north of Union Station is Potomac Yard, nearly a century old, which traces its origins to Alexandria's emergence as a regional railroad center. Beginning in the 1840s, and continuing through the Civil War, Alexandria's reputation as a major river port declined as it became known as a national rail center.

Alexandria became directly involved in construction projects for five major railroad lines — some that vanished in time, others that formed the foundation for such prominent rail companies as the Southern, C&O, Pennsylvania, and the Richmond, Fredericksburg, and Potomac (RF&P). It was 1872 before a north-south rail link was completed from Washington to Richmond. The Pennsylvania Railroad took over the old Alexandria and Fredericksburg Railroad and built a line to Quantico, connecting with the RF&P to Richmond. By the turn of the century, both Alexandria and Washington were important railroad centers.

Alexandria was filled with remnants of classic old rail lines — the Alexandria and Harpers Ferry, which grew to become the Washington and Old Dominion; the Orange and Alexandria, which later merged with the Manassas Gap to become the Orange, Alexandria, and Manassas; the Alexandria and Fredericksburg, which merged with the Alexandria and Washington to become the northern most part of the RF&P. In Washington, from the northern end of the "Long Bridge" over the Potomac to the Capitol, there were freight yards, a freight station, a passenger depot, and grade crossings for the Pennsylvania, Southern, and Baltimore and Ohio railroads.

In 1907, Washington opened its new Union Station. To eliminate the number of freight yards previously located throughout Washington, a major new rail yard facility was built south of the Potomac. Situated between the Long Bridge and Alexandria's northern city limits, it was called Potomac Yard. It opened in August 1906, and by World War II it was the busiest rail classification center in the nation.

Observe the Washington Masonic Temple across Callahan Road from the railroad station. The temple is a Masonic shrine to President Washington, and is located in Shooter's Hill, a Civil War fortification.

DIRECTIONS

Continue south on Callahan Road one block to Duke Street. Turn right (west) on Duke Street (VA 236 W) and go west 1.3 miles to Quaker Lane. Turn right (north) on Quaker Lane and go 1.2 miles to Braddock Road. Observe the Fort William historical marker on the west side of Quaker Lane, just 0.2 miles from Duke Street. Fort William was one of the earthworks built as a circle of defense around Washington during the Civil War. At Braddock Road, turn left and go 0.7 miles to Fort Ward Museum and Historic Site on the right.

FORT WARD MUSEUM
AND HISTORIC SITE
4301 W. Braddock Rd.
Alexandria, VA 22304   *703-838-4848*

Fort Ward was the fifth largest — and, now, the best restored — of the more than 150 earthwork forts and batteries that formed the Defenses of Washington. This fort, like numerous others, was constructed soon after Virginia voted in early 1861 to secede from the Union. It guarded Alexandria's western approaches — like the Alexandria-Leesburg Turnpike and the Little River Turnpike.

The fort was named for Commander James Harmon Ward, the first Union naval officer killed in the Civil War. The museum is pattered after a Union headquarters building. It houses a collection of Civil War artifacts. A self-guided tour leads along the fort's preserved earthwork walls, of which 95 percent are visible.

The museum is open Sunday from noon to 5 PM and Tuesday to Saturday from 9 AM to 5 PM. The 45-acre historic site is open daily from 9 AM to sunset. They are closed on Mondays and on New Year's Day, Thanksgiving Day and Christmas Day. The facility is owned and operated by the City of Alexandria, which charges no admission but gladly accepts well-deserved donations from visitors.

DIRECTIONS

Fort Ward to Fairfax Courthouse

Leaving Fort Ward, turn right (west) on Braddock Road and go a half block to Howard Street. Turn left (south) on Howard Street and go four blocks to Seminary Road. Turn right (west) on Seminary Road and go four blocks to I-395 (Shirley Highway). Turn left and follow signs for I-395 south (toward Richmond). Go south on I-395 for 4 miles to I-495 (Washington Beltway). Take I-495 north (exit 1-C for Rockville), and go 7.7 miles to I-66. Follow signs for I-66 west, left lane exit, and continue west on I-66 for 4.5 miles to VA 123 (exit 60, Chain Bridge Road). Take VA 123 south— 1 mile to US 29, and another 1 mile to Main Street (VA 236) in downtown Fairfax. Cross over Main Street on VA 123, go one block, and turn right into the Fairfax Courthouse parking lot.

This monument, at the Fairfax County Courthouse, commemorates one of the first battles in the Civil War.

FAIRFAX COURTHOUSE

4000 Chain Bridge Rd.
Fairfax, VA 22030

The historic community around Fairfax Courthouse was the scene of numerous skirmishes throughout the Civil War. In fact, some historians say a battle here on June 1, 1861, technically was the "first battle of the war" (see Big Bethel in Tour 15: Peninsula). That's when former Virginia Gov. "Extra Billy" Smith took charge of the Warrenton (Fauquier County, VA) Rifles after the commander, Capt. John Q. Marr, was killed during USA Lt. Thompkins' cavalry raid. Marr is honored by a plaque on the courthouse grounds. There was another significant battle in the vicinity in late June 1863 — days before the Battle of Gettysburg in Pennsylvania.

This building is on the National Register of Historic Places. George and Martha Washington's wills were recorded here. Two blocks west of the courthouse is the site where Confederate "Gray Ghost" John Singleton Mosby captured USA Gen. E. H. Stoughton.

DIRECTIONS

Across Main Street from the courthouse was the home of Antonia Ford, an alleged Confederate spy.

Fairfax Personality

USA Gen. E. H. Stoughton

Brig. Gen. Edwin Henry Stoughton was a youthful 25 years old when he was captured near the Fairfax Courthouse by CSA Col. Mosby. A Vermont native, born in 1838, Stoughton saw action in USA Gen. McClellan's Peninsular Campaign and was promoted to brigadier general in 1862 — at the age of 24.

In March 1863, he and a number of his men were captured by Mosby, who crept inside Union lines near the courthouse. The sleeping Stoughton was awakened when Mosby slapped him on his backside (see Leesburg Personality in Tour 7: Middle Piedmont). Mosby allegedly said, "Get up, general, and come with me." Stoughton replied, "What is this? Do you know who I am, sir?" Mosby answered: "I reckon I do, general. Did you ever hear of Mosby?" "Yes," said Stoughton, "have you caught him?" Mosby answered, "No, but he has caught you!" Mosby also stole away with 58 Union horses.

When President Lincoln learned of Gen. Stoughton's capture, he reportedly commented in disgust that he could create another general with the stroke of a pen, but he hated to lose the horses. Mosby escorted Stoughton to Culpeper, well behind Union lines. The Union officer was shipped to Richmond, where his brigadier general commission expired while he was being held in Libby Prison.

Exchanged and with no military status, he practiced law in New York City until his death in 1868.

Antonia Ford Willard

Two days after CSA Col. Mosby captured USA Gen. Stoughton, a 19-year-old Fairfax woman, Antonia Ford, was arrested and put in prison on charges of being a Confederate spy. Miss Ford lived on Chain Bridge Road (the two-story brick house is located at 2977 Chain Bridge Road), just north of Main Street and the courthouse. Union soldiers searched her house and found an honorary aide-de-camp commission she received from CSA Gen. J.E.B. Stuart. Antonia was sent to the Old Capital Prison (see Tour 9: Washington).

The story has a happy ending: Union Maj. Joseph C. Willard, a former provost marshall at the Fairfax Courthouse, fell in love with Antonia and negotiated her release from prison. He married her after the war. Major Willard was co-owner of the famous Willard Hotel in Washington, D.C. He and Antonia had just one child, a son, Joseph E. Willard, who served as lieutenant governor of Virginia and U.S. minister to Spain. Joseph was considered the most influential political figure in Fairfax County in the early 1900s.

Fairfax Personality

DIRECTIONS

Two miles west of the courthouse, beyond I-66 and W. Ox Road, and adjacent to Fair Oaks Mall, is Chantilly, the place where USA Gens. Kearny and Stevens were killed.

DIRECTIONS

Fairfax Courthouse to Fairfax Station

From the courthouse return to VA 123 (Chain Bridge Road) and turn right (south). Take VA 123 south for 3.3 miles to Fairfax Station Road (VA 660).

USA Gen. Kearny

Gen. Philip Kearny, a New Yorker, joined the U.S. Army in 1837 at the age of 23 after studying law at Columbia University. He lost his arm while fighting with USA Gen. Winfield Scott in the Mexican War. He resigned from the army in 1851 to travel in Europe; a decade later, with the onset of the Civil War, he was commissioned a brigadier general.

In September 1862, General Kearny rode into a line of CSA Gen. Jackson's soldiers at Chantilly, VA, just west of W. Ox Road. Ordered to surrender, Kearny tried to fight his way out of the trap and was fatally injured. Later that year, the officers who served under Kearny devised a gold medal — the "Kearny Medal" — to award to those who honorably served in Kearny's command. The next year, another medal — the "Kearny Cross" — was developed for Union enlisted men who distinguished themselves in battle. More than 300 Kearny Medals were awarded; two women were among the recipients of the Kearny Cross. Kearny, NJ, bears the general's name.

Fairfax Personality

FAIRFAX STATION

Fifty yards south of Fairfax Station Road on VA 123 is the original rail bed of the Orange and Alexandria Railroad, which served as a link between Alexandria and Manassas Junction. A quarter-mile west on Fairfax Station Road (VA 660) is St. Mary's Church, the oldest Roman Catholic church in Fairfax County. This church was built in 1758 for the Irish immigrants who came to this area to build the railroad line. In August 1862, after 2nd Manassas, wounded Union soldiers were brought here by rail, on their way to Alexandria. Here, nurse Clara Barton — founder of the American Red Cross — tended to the war wounded (See Women Nurses in Tour 9: Washington). Two miles north of Fairfax Station is Burke's Station, the next stop on the Orange and Alexandria Railroad. CSA Gen. Stuart captured a telegraph station operation at Burke's Station in December 1862.

DIRECTIONS

Return to Alexandria

For lodging and dining in Alexandria, backtrack on VA 123 (Chain Bridge Road) for 2.5 miles to Braddock Road. Turn right on Braddock Road and go 5.5 miles to I-495 (Washington Beltway). Take right ramp onto the Washington Beltway (follow signs for Washington, Alexandria), and go 9.5 miles to exit 1B (US 1 north into Alexandria historic district).

Northern Virginia Accommodations

As was the case in our last tour in Washington, D.C., we think your best bet for negotiating the options for dining, resting, and playing in Northern Virginia is to have a copy of our sister publication, the *Insiders' Guide to Metro Washington, D.C.* in hand. It will provide detailed information on this Northern Virginia area (as well as to D.C. and Suburban Maryland). But, to get you started, here are a few of our favorite accommodations.

The rate charges for a double room, not including taxes, are comparable in this area to those in D.C.:

$	Under $80
$$	$81 to $120
$$$	$121 and up

OLD TOWN HOLIDAY INN

480 King St.
Alexandria, VA 22314   703-549-6080
$$

The Old Town Holiday Inn offers the best location, and one of the top values, in Alexandria's famed historic district. Rooms are colonial-themed, and they have hair dryers and speaker phones with computer modem capability. Its a short walk to a number of Old Town Alexandria's attractions, including galleries, shops, restaurants and the Potomac waterfront. This inn provides free transportation to National Airport (2 miles away) and Metro's King Street Station.

MORRISON HOUSE

116 S. Alfred St.
Alexandria, VA 22314   703-838-8000
$$$

A celebrated inn, the Morrison House is an elegant mansion in the heart of Alexandria's Old Town. There are 45 rooms, and each is decorated with Federal-period antiques. Several rooms have fireplaces and four-poster canopy beds. The inn's restaurant and lounge enhance the romantic atmosphere, making it the perfect urban getaway for honeymoons or romantic weekends.

OLD COLONY INN

N. Washington and 1st Sts.
Alexandria, VA 22314   703-548-6300
$$

Less glamorous than our other Alexandria choices, the Old Colony Inn still is practical, accommodating, and convenient. Located north of historic Old Town, on the George Washington Memorial Parkway, this inn is a short trip south — to Old Town and the heart of Alexandria, and north — to National Airport, the Pentagon, and the District of Columbia. The Old Colony has motor court-style rooms, as well as high rise rooms and a conference center. It also features an outdoor swimming pool.

BAILIWICK INN

4028 Chain Bridge Rd.
Fairfax, VA   703-691-2266
$$

Bailiwick Inn is a 19th-century brick house, located in the center of Fairfax's historic district. Actually, the inn is located across Chain Bridge Road from the historic Fairfax County Courthouse (see listing). The inn has 14 rooms — some with feather beds and others with whirlpools and fireplaces. The Bailiwick provides an opportunity to stroll along Fairfax's Main Street. George Mason University is nearby.

Northern Virginia Restaurants

The ratings scale for restaurants also reflects prices that are a bit higher than in most our other tours. These rates are for a dinner meal for two, not including taxes, tips, or alcoholic beverages.

$	Under $30
$$	$31 to $60
$$$	$61 to $100
$$$$	$101 and up

KING STREET BLUES

112 N. St. Asaph St.
Alexandria, VA 22314   703-836-8800
$

King Street Blues is, interesting, not on King Street — but on St. Asaph Street, a half-block off the main drag of Old Town. Professionals, yuppies and other hungry Alexandrians like King Street Blues for its barbecue, burgers, salads and soups.

HARD TIMES CAFE

1404 King St.
Alexandria, VA 22314   703-683-5340
$

Anyone with a hankering for mouth-watering chili should put Hard Times on their list of "must-sees." The exterior appearance is unassuming, and the dining area is full of clanging beer bottles, cigarette smoke, and NOISE. Still, the chili — Texas-style, Cincinnati-style, and vegetarian — spaghetti, and beer-batter onion rings make the visit worth the stop. The decor is uniquely western.

FISH MARKET
105 King St.
Alexandria, VA 22314   703-836-5676
$$

The First Market is located along lower King Street in Old Town — the historic district that stretches along the Potomac River. The restaurant is busy and exciting. Tops on the menu are the oysters, spicy shrimp, and a rich clam chowder — which is especially nice on a snowy, winter evening. During the summer, try a "schooner" of beer. It helps eliminate the drudgery of the metropolitan area's exceptionally humid afternoons.

RED, HOT AND BLUE
1600 Wilson Blvd.
Arlington, VA 22209   703-276-7427
$$

The late Lee Atwater, the Republican political strategist who swept into Washington during the Reagan-Bush years, is credited with getting this barbecue place going in the metropolitan area. No question, Atwater knew his barbecue! Red, Hot and Blue is located on ground floor of an Arlington high rise office building, and the interior is glitz, lights and music. But don't let the aesthetics fool you: this is THE place for Memphis-style barbecue ribs, platters and sandwiches. It's simply

the best barbecue this side of . . . Memphis.

PEKING GOURMET INN
6029-6033 Leesburg Pike
Falls Church (Baileys
Crossroads), VA 22041   703-671-8088
$$

Located in a small, obscure strip mall in busy Baileys Crossroads, this Chinese restaurant is the choice of top politicians and locals alike. Former President Bush's motorcade zipped into the parking lot on several occasions (President and Mrs. Bush's photographs adorn the walls inside, along with those of other current and past notables.)   The service is elegant and the food is divine. Ask for the Peking Duck.

Other Northern Virginia Attractions

Annual Events: George Washington is Alexandria's most famous local hero. The City hosts a grand parade each year in February to honor Washington's birthday. Alexandria also is rich in Scottish and Irish history. Thus, the City features a great St. Patrick's Day parade in March, and an equally exciting Scottish Christmas program in December.

Antiques: There are a number of antique shops in Northern Virginia, and especially on the back streets of Old Town Alexandria. Prices are steep. Beware.

Arts: The top arts attraction in northern Virginia is Wolf Trap Farm Park, a nationally ranked center for performing arts administered by the

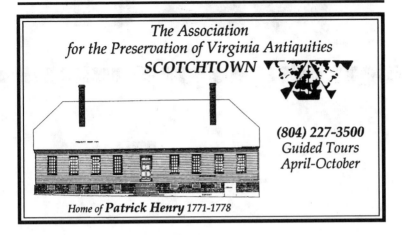

The Association
for the Preservation of Virginia Antiquities
SCOTCHTOWN

(804) 227-3500
Guided Tours
April-October

Home of **Patrick Henry** 1771-1778

National Park Service. Wolf Trap offers top name entertainers throughout the year, but the specialties are featured during the summer. Locals take blankets and picnic dinners to lounge on the grassy lawn and enjoy musical programs. The Patriot Center at George Mason University in Fairfax features a number of top name attractions throughout the year.

Historical Sites: Besides Civil War attractions, northern Virginia has a number of prominent historical sites. Remember, Alexandria is George Washington's home town. His famous estate, Mount Vernon, is located just south of the city along the Potomac River. Nearby are Woodlawn Plantation, carved from the Mount Vernon property, and Gunston Hall, the home of George Mason. Sully Plantation, the home of Richard Bland Lee, is located at Chantilly near Dulles Airport. It is a fine example of an 18th-century county farmhouse.

Shopping: The urban sprawl of northern Virginia offers one unique advantage: a proliferation of top-quality shopping malls. In Arlington — Ballston Common, Glebe Road at Wilson Boulevard, and Fashion Centre at Pentagon City, just off I-395 near the Pentagon. In Fairfax County — Seven Corners Shopping Area, VA 50 and VA 7; Fairfax Square, VA 7 at Tysons Corner; Tysons Corner Center, VA 7 and VA 123; Galleria at Tysons II, VA 7 and VA 123; Reston Town Center, Reston; Fair Oaks Mall, VA 50 and I-66; and Springfield Mall, Franconia Drive at I-95. On I-95, 20 miles south of Alexandria, is Potomac Mills Mall (Exit 52), one of the top outlet mall attractions in the nation.

TOUR 11

Alexandria to Fredericksburg

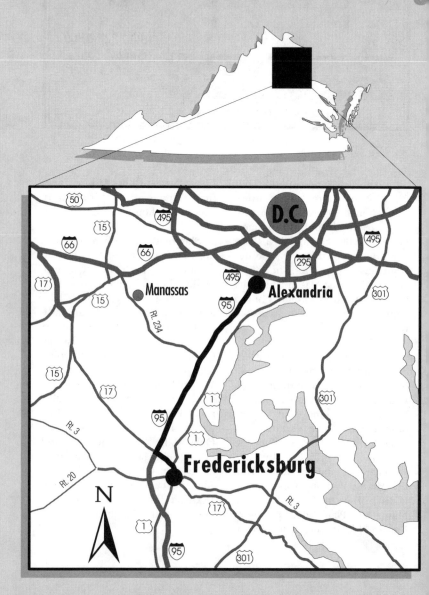

Tour 11:
Fredericksburg

About This Tour

This tour route is a continuation of Tour 10: Northern Virginia. This route begins in Northern Virginia and runs the length of I-95 from the Washington Beltway in Northern Virginia south to Fredericksburg, VA. This tour route concludes in the Fredericksburg area, where we suggest you plan evening dining and lodging.

Travel Tips

I-95 is part of the busy north-south corridor of Virginia that stretches along the "fall line." Be on the lookout for heavy, fast-moving traffic along this major interstate route. Be especially alert to traffic along the beltway and I-95. Avoid rush-hour traffic that clogs the southbound interstate in the evening. Radio traffic reports are especially helpful. Remember, too, that traffic is particularly busy — and often snarled — during unusual weather conditions, particularly winter snows and heavy summer rains. During heavy congestion, consider using US 1 South as an alternate route. US 1 runs parallel to I-95 and, despite its many traffic signals, it can be a wise alternative to hours sitting in bumper-to-bumper traffic on the interstate.

History, Geography

The stretch between Washington and Fredericksburg was originally settled by Native Americans, and their place names still are in evidence today: the town of Occoquan, for example, Aquia Creek, and the Potomac and Rappahannock rivers. Jamestown's Capt. John Smith explored the upper reaches of the Rappahannock and Potomac as early as 1608. English settlers in Virginia's Tidewater began pushing west late in the 17th century, and they settled a number of community's along the "fall line" of Virginia's principal rivers. Spotsylvania County was established in this area in 1720 and named for Alexander Spotswood, who was Virginia's lieutenant governor from 1710 to 1722. At about the same time, the community of Fredericksburg was established on the Rappahannock fall line and named — like Frederick County, VA, mentioned in Tours 2 and 3 — for Frederick Louis, England's Prince of Wales and the oldest son of King George II.

George Washington lived as a youth at Ferry Farm, located just across the Rappahannock River from Fredericksburg in Stafford County. Washington's only sister, Betty Washington Lewis, lived with her husband, Fielding Lewis, at Kenmore in Fredericksburg. Washington's mother, Mary Ball Washington, lived in Fredericksburg until her death in 1789. During the American Revolution, the community bustled with activity. After the war, James Monroe was an attorney in Fredericksburg prior to moving to Washington, D.C., to begin a lengthy service in the federal government.

In 1861, Fredericksburg was a quiet community of just 5,000. But its strategic location, half way between Washington and Richmond, made it a critical focal point during the Civil War. Today, the Fredericksburg and Spotsylvania National Military Park commemorates four major Civil War actions: the Battle of Fredericksburg in 1862; the Chancellorsville Campaign (including Chancellorsville, Second Fredericksburg, and Salem Church) in April and May 1863, the Battle of the Wilderness in early May 1864, and the Battle of Spotsylvania Court House in mid-May 1864. By war's end, more than 100,000 soldiers were killed or wounded in these four campaigns.

Getting Here

I-95 runs north-south along Virginia's fall line. This tour route, a continuation of Tour 10: Northern Virginia, suggests traveling to Fredericksburg from I-95 south out of Northern Virginia.

DIRECTIONS

Alexandria to Spotsylvania County, VA

Begin from Alexandria, VA, and take US 1 south to the Washington Beltway (I-495 west, I-95 south). Take the beltway south (follow signs for Richmond), and go 6.0 miles to the intersection of I-495, I-95 and I-395. This is one of the busiest intersections along the entire north-south stretch if I-95. Here, at milepost 167, take I-95 south, and continue south through Fairfax County, VA, into Prince William County.

Prince William County Side Trip

Occoquan, VA

Occoquan (I-95, milepost 160) is a quaint village on the banks of the Occoquan River in Prince William County. It looks much as its did more than a century ago, in December 1862, when CSA Gen. Hampton led raids against Union wagon trains, capturing prisoners and wagons near here and at Dumfries to the south. Then, CSA Gen. Stuart, joined by Hampton's men, led raids on Dumfries and Occoquan, beginning the day after Christmas 1862. This engagement became known as Stuart's Dumfries Raid. After a successful operation, Stuart moved west to Burke's Station on the Orange and Alexandria Railroad. He captured the telegraph station operator before an alarm could be tapped out on the telegraph to Washington. According to one of several conflicting stories, Stuart had one of his men — an accomplished telegraph operation — tap out a message to USA Gen. Meigs, the quartermaster-general in Washington, complaining about the quality of mules furnished for his men. Stuart, it is said, told Meigs that the mules were so inferior that they embarrassed him in moving his captured wagons!

DIRECTIONS

Continue south on I-95, through Prince William and Stafford counties, across the Rappahannock River bridge, and into Spotsylvania County. Don't be confused by visitors center directional signs along I-95 — our tour route continues south on I-95 to exit 126-B, the location of the Spotsylvania Visitors Center. At exit 126-B (US 1), take the right exit and stop at US 1. Turn right on US 1 and go 0.2 miles to the traffic signal at Southpoint Parkway. Turn left onto Southpoint Parkway and go 0.2 miles to the Spotsylvania Visitors Center on the left.

SPOTSYLVANIA VISITORS CENTER

4704 Southpoint Parkway
Fredericksburg, VA 22407   703-891-TOUR
800-654-4118

This visitors center, operated by the County of Spotsylvania, has a small display of Civil War memorabilia, maps, and a complete list of brochures and travel materials. Plan your Spotsylvania County accommodations and dining details from here. In addition, you can obtain information about Civil War-related attractions and points of interest east of Fredericksburg — particularly the "Northern Neck" region of Virginia — that are not in this tour route. For example, VA 3 east out of Fredericksburg winds its way through King George and Westmoreland counties, through the Northern Neck, and includes such stops as Robert E. Lee's birthplace at Stratford. And US 17 south out of Fredericksburg goes through Caroline County, spans the length of Virginia's Tidewater, and passes

near the place where John Wilkes Booth was captured after assassinating President Lincoln in 1865. Travel counselors at the Spotsylvania Visitors Center can help you with information on these, and other, points of interest.

DIRECTIONS

Spotsylvania Visitors Center to Fredericksburg Battlefield Visitor Center

From the Spotsylvania Visitors Center, return 0.2 miles on Southpoint Parkway to US 1. Turn right on US 1 and go north (toward downtown Fredericksburg) for 1.6 miles — four traffic signals — to Lafayette Boulevard (US 1 business). Turn right on Lafayette Boulevard and go east 3.3 miles to the Fredericksburg Battlefield Visitor Center on the left. Turn left and park behind the visitor center building.

FREDERICKSBURG BATTLEFIELD VISITOR CENTER

Lafayette Boulevard, US 1 Business
Fredericksburg, VA 22405   703-373-6122

The National Park Service (NPS) operates a complex, 7,700-acre battlefield system in the Spotsylvania/Fredericksburg area. This national military park system includes battle sites in and around the community of Fredericksburg, with four significant locations: Fredericksburg, Chancellorsville, the Wilderness and Spotsylvania Court House. In addition, the NPS incorporates information on Chatham (an estate just east of town), Old Salem Church (west of Fredericksburg), and Guinea Station (a shrine to Stonewall Jackson located south of town). The NPS has an extensive brochure that offers a complete tour of the battlefields, with 16 individual tour stops (the name and number of each stop are shown in red on the map). This self-guided tour of the four battlefields and three buildings begins at this visitor center. A special recorded cassette tape of the tour also is available. Our tour route generally follows the NPS brochure, but we do suggest a few variations along the way. This visitor center is open from 9:00 AM to 5:00 PM daily except New Year's Day and Christmas, and park rangers are on duty to provide information. There is ample parking. Rest room facilities are provided. In addition, there are information publications for sale, picnic tables, and facilities to assist handicapped visitors.

This NPS facility is convenient to a number of important sites associated with the Fredericksburg Battlefield. In fact, the first four stops of the self-guided tour are in this vicinity. These sites, besides the visitor center itself, are Lee Hill Exhibit Shelter, Federal Breakthrough and Prospect Hill. These locations help interpret the important Civil War battle that was fought at Fredericksburg, December 11 through 13, 1862.

Fredericksburg is like a natural amphitheater, with the land rising up on either side of the Rappahannock River. USA Gen. Burnside set up a position east of town, on Stafford Heights, in mid-November 1862. But it was a month later, on December 11, before Union troops crossed the Rappahannock River on pontoon bridges to attack a

Confederate contingent that was firmly set on the high ground west of the town. The Federals advanced west, across the river, through the town, and beyond the north-south tracks of the RF&P (Richmond, Fredericksburg and Potomac) Railroad. Pushing uphill on the west, Burnside made two attacks. USA Gen. Meade made an assault on the left, attacking CSA Gen. Jackson at Prospect Hill. Jackson eventually pushed Meade back. The other Union assault struck at Lee's main defense at Marye's Heights. Northerners were slaughtered by Confederate artillery fire and by thousands of infantrymen behind a stone wall in the vicinity of the "sunken road." It was a devastating loss for both armies: more than 17,000 casualties. The ultimate Confederate success was CSA Gen. Lee's most one-sided victory of the Civil War. Civil War action took place in Fredericksburg again in 1863 as part of the Chancellorsville Campaign.

DIRECTIONS

Fredericksburg Battlefield Visitor Center to Fredericksburg Visitor Center

From the battlefield visitor center, continue north on Lafayette Boulevard (US 1 Business) for 1.7 miles — through four traffic signals — to Caroline Street in downtown Fredericksburg. Turn left (west) on Caroline Street and go two blocks to the Fredericksburg Visitor Center on the left. Follow signs for free visitor parking.

WhetherYour Outlook Is Blue Or Gray,You'll Find Colorful History Here.

Grant, Lee, Lincoln, Davis, Clara Barton, Walt Whitman. These are just a few of the thousands who played a part in Fredericksburg's illustrious history during the Civil War.

The stories and places are still here today for you and your family. Just take the Route 3 exit off I-95. That's 50 miles south of Washington, or 55 miles north of Richmond—depending on which side you're coming from.

Fredericksburg,Virginia

Call 1-800-678-4748. Or write Visitor Center, Box PT3, 706 Caroline St., Fredericksburg, VA 22401.

FREDERICKSBURG VISITOR CENTER

706 Caroline St.
Fredericksburg, VA 22401   *703-373-1776*
          800-678-4748

This visitor center is operated by the Fredericksburg Department of Tourism. There are a number of historic attractions in the downtown Fredericksburg area (see listing at end of this chapter for other attractions not related to the Civil War), and travel counselors can help you with information and materials. Of particular interest is the Presbyterian Church of Fredericksburg, at the corner of Princess Anne and George streets. Built in 1833, the church was a hospital during the Civil War for soldiers from both the Union and Confederacy. Clara Barton (see Tour

9: Washington) went to the church in 1862 to nurse soldiers after the Battle of Fredericksburg.

DIRECTIONS

Fredericksburg to Chatham

From the Fredericksburg Visitor Center, continue west on Caroline Street for three blocks to William Street (US 3 east). Turn right on William Street (US 3 east), cross over the Rappahannock River bridge, and then turn left on White Oak Road (VA 218). Go a block to the entrance to Chatham on the left. Take the Chatham entry road a half-mile to the estate.

CHATHAM

120 Chatham Lane
Falmouth, VA   703-373-4461

Chatham, a fine old Georgian mansion, once was the home of wealthy Virginian William Fitzhugh. Interestingly, Fitzhugh, one of Robert E. Lee's ancestors, was the father of Mary Fitzhugh Custis, the first mistress of Arlington House (see Tour 10: Northern Virginia). Lee courted his wife, the former Mary Custis, at Chatham. By the 1860s, J. Horace Lacy owned Chatham, so it became known as the Lacy House when Union officers used it as a headquarters in 1862. It also was used as a Union hospital. Once encompassing more than 1,000 acres, the estate declined after the Civil War to barely 30 acres. It was donated to the National Park Service (NPS) in the 1970s. There is a great view of Fredericksburg from the front lawn. Park rangers are on duty to provide information and interpretation of the overall battlefield park story. The NPS has information materials for sale, and picnic tables are available. The estate is open from 9:00 AM to 5:00 PM every day except New Year's Day and Christmas Day.

DIRECTIONS

Chatham to Old Salem Church
Exit Chatham and return to US 3. Cross back (west) over the Rappahannock River bridge. Follow signs for US 3 west. At the end of the bridge, turn right and go a short block, then turn left (west) on Amelia Street. Follow Amelia Street through downtown to Washington Avenue. From Washington Avenue, continue on to Old Salem Church. Go a half-block south to William Street (US 3) and turn right on William Street (US 3 west). Go 2 miles, beyond the I-95 interchange and Spotsylvania Mall (on left), to the intersection of US 3 and VA 639 (Salem Church Road) Heavy development and business growth along this stretch of US 3 result in heavy congestion and frequent road improvement projects. Avoid this section of US 3 during late afternoon, when commuters make they way home. Watch for road realignments and widening projects. Old Salem Church is located on the south side of US 3 at this intersection.

OLD SALEM CHURCH

This old church was built just two decades before the Civil War. During the Battle of Fredericksburg in December 1862, a number of women and children escaped battle-torn Fredericksburg and sought refuge in the church, located west of the town. During the Chancellorsville Campaign, in May 1863, fighting raged in the vicinity of the church, and Confederate surgeons treated soldiers at this site after the fight subsided.

Washington Avenue Side Trip

Confederate Cemetery

In 1865, the year the Civil War ended at Appomattox, the Fredericksburg Ladies Memorial Association established the Confederate Cemetery. More than 2,000 Southern soldiers, most unidentified, are buried in the cemetery. It is open free from dawn to dusk.

Source: Richmond Newspapers

The Battle of Chancellorsville took the life of Stonewall Jackson in May 1863.

DIRECTIONS

Old Salem Church to Chancellorsville Visitor Center

From Old Salem Church, take US 3 west for 6.6 miles to the Chancellorsville Visitor Center on the right.

CHANCELLORSVILLE VISITOR CENTER

Park rangers at this National Park Service (NPS) facility offer information on Civil War sites related to the Chancellorsville Campaign. The NPS self-guided tour, including the tape cassette tour, continues at this battlefield site. Tour stops 5 through 9, including the visitor center site itself, are in this vicinity. This center has a museum, auditorium, restrooms and a picnic area. There are special facilities for handicapped visitors. Publications can be purchased. It is open every day of the year from 9:00 AM to 5:00 PM except New Year's Day and Christmas Day.

After suffering serious losses at the Battle of Fredericksburg, in December 1862, the Union Army welcomed a new commander when President Lincoln dismissed USA Gen. Burnside and replaced him with USA Gen. Hooker. In the spring of 1863, Hooker moved his army upriver on the Rappahannock to near the crossroads at Chancellorsville — not a town, but a brick estate, complete with a veranda, in the area known as the Wilderness. CSA Gen. Lee moved his Confederate troops into positions to thwart the Union attack. Hooker's men were struck on May 2 in a surprise flank attack led by CSA Gen. Jackson. The day ended in tragedy, however, when Jackson was shot and seriously wounded by a group of his own soldiers. Jackson's arm was amputated and buried near this site. (CSA Gen. Lee sent word to Jackson, "You have lost your left arm; I have lost my right." Jackson died several days later from his wounds. Lee, meanwhile, struck repeatedly at the

Federals, and drove the enemy back across the Rappahannock after three long days of fighting.

WILDERNESS EXHIBIT SHELTER

This is stop number 10 on the National Park Service (NPS) self-guided tour of the regional battlefields. The wooded area in this section of western Orange County was so thick that it became known as the Wilderness. The trees in this wilderness were literally set on fire by the weapons discharges in early May 1864 when CSA Gen. Lee met USA Gen. Grant in the Battle of the Wilderness. This was the first of many renowned encounters between these two generals. The opposing armies fought along the Orange Turnpike (present-day VA 20) for the better part of two days. Fighting to a draw, Grant moved his army southeast toward the Spotsylvania County Courthouse. Grant suffered more than 17,000 casualties. Lee suffered about half that amount.

USA Gen. Ulysses S. Grant

Ulysses Simpson Grant was born in April 1822 at Point Pleasant, Ohio, a community east of Cincinnati and just across the Ohio River from Kentucky. His father, tanner Jesse Root Grant, and his mother, the former Hannah Simpson, baptized him Hiram Ulysses Grant. Later, when he registered as a young cadet at West Point, he inverted his name — Ulysses Hiram Grant — because he thought the initials, "H.U.G." would be ridiculed. Days later, he learned his congressman had listed his name as Ulysses Simpson Grant, which erroneously incorporated his mother's maiden name, so Grant lived with the name change.

He was the best horseman at West Point, but nothing else distinguished him at the service academy. He asked for a commission in the cavalry, but there were no vacancies, so he ended up in the infantry. During the Mexican War, Grant served with two distinguished generals, Zachary Taylor and Winfield Scott, both of whom — ironically — were Virginia natives.

Later, stationed in California, he survived dreary military conditions, alone without his wife, and took up drinking. Chastised by his commanding officer for excessive drinking, Grant resigned his commission. His resignation was accepted by the Secretary of War, Jefferson Davis, the future president of the Confederacy.

Following a decade of insignificant business dealings, Grant rejoined the Army at the outbreak of the Civil War and was sent to duty in Missouri and Illinois. Slowly, Grant worked his way up the U.S. Army hierarchy, and he saw extensive action in the Western Theater.

In the spring of 1864, President Lincoln promoted Grant general-in-chief of the Union Army. It was left to Grant to establish a concerted effort of all Union forces. He set about a three pronged attack against the Confederates: USA Gen. Meade's Army of the Potomac against CSA Gen. Lee, USA Gen. Butler's Army of the James against Confederate communications and Richmond, and USA Gen. Sherman's Army of Tennessee against CSA Gen. Johnston's army and Atlanta.

Grant himself took up headquarters with the Army of the Potomac, and encountered his first head-on collision with CSA Gen. Lee at the Wilderness. A year later, in April 1865, Grant accepted Lee's surrender at Appomattox.

Three years after Appomattox, Grant gave up a comfortable Army position — including its $25,000 annual salary — to enter the world of politics. He was the Republican party's nominee for the presidency, and he took the electoral votes of all but eight states. Grant's White House was filled with a number of his military cronies. His father-in-law, Col. Frederick Dent, an unreconstructed Southerner, visited often.

Grant served two terms as president, took his family on a two-year whirlwind tour of Europe, and settled in New York City. Overcome by throat cancer, he earned an income writing his personal memoirs, which he finished just before he died. He was buried in a granite mausoleum on New York's Riverside Drive. President Lincoln once summed up Grant's service, saying, "He fights."

SPOTSYLVANIA EXHIBIT SHELTER

This is stop number 13 on the National Park Service (NPS) self-guided tour. There are three other NPS stops in this vicinity. "I will fight it out on this line if it takes all summer," wrote USA Gen. Grant to USA Gen. Halleck, who had been appointed Grant's chief of staff only weeks before. The phrase was part of a communication written on May 11, 1864, from Spotsylvania. Grant was determined to move on to Richmond, despite the heavy losses his army received at this old county courthouse. Both armies were dug in here after the Wilderness.

The day after Grant sent his letter to Halleck, two Union corps charged Confederates in a dense fog. The Southerners had wet gunpowder, which enabled the Union soldiers to make a successful, initial assault. But Confederate reinforcements counter-attacked and the opposing troops fought a fierce, 20-hour battle, often resorting to hand-to-hand combat. This fighting, much of which took place at the now famous "Bloody Angle," prompted Grant to write his communication to Halleck. Grant eventually abandoned the field on May 21.

Spotsylvania Personalities

Mountain Rifles

The Mountain Rifles was a unique Confederate unit. Mustered in 1861 at Green Bank in Pocohantas County, West Virginia, its 100-plus recruits were all over six feet tall. Most of these mountaineer giants were killed at the Bloody Angle at Spotsylvania.

Massaponax Church

Massaponax (Mass-ah-pon-ex) Baptist Church was built just before the Civil War. Being on the main route between Richmond and Washington — present-day US 1 — the church was on the path of major troop movements by both armies. A famous Civil War photograph shows USA Gen. Grant and several of his officers sitting on church pews in the yard at Massaponax Church.

DIRECTIONS

Massaponax Church to Stonewall Jackson Shrine, Guinea Station

From this intersection of VA 608 and US 1, turn south (away from Fredericksburg) on US 1 and go 4.3 miles to the village of Thornburg. From Thornburg, turn left (east) on VA 606 and go 5.7 miles to Guinea Station. (On US 1, less than a mile south of Massaponax Church, VA 607 runs east toward Guinea Station. This route is marked on the National Park Service (NPS) self-guided tour map. This continues the route used by CSA

Gen. Jackson's ambulance wagon when it transported him to Guinea Station after Chancellorsville. VA 607 is a small, narrow state route; we recommend you go farther south, through Thornburg, to reach Guinea Station.

Stonewall Jackson Shrine, Guinea Station

The Jackson Shrine is open daily during the summer. There are reduced hours the rest of the year. Walking tours, living history talks, and other interpretive programs are presented during the summer months. A variety of informational publications concerning Civil War history are available for purchase, and picnic tables are available.

CSA Gen. Jackson, following his accidental wounding at Chancellorsville on the night of May 2, 1863, was removed to a field hospital near Wilderness Tavern where his arm was amputated. Two days later, he was taken overland by an ambulance wagon to the house, here, at Guinea Station — then known as Guiney's Station — on the

---

Guinea Station Personality

Stonewall Jackson

Thomas Jackson was born Jan. 21, 1824 near Clarksburg, Virginia (in present-day West Virginia). He was the third child — second son — of Julia Beckwith Neale Jackson and lawyer Jonathan Jackson. Tom's parents died in poverty while he was still young, and he was raised by an uncle, Cummins Jackson. As a young adult, Thomas honored his late father by taking the name Jonathan as his middle name. A noted Southern officer in the Civil War, Jackson was nicknamed "Stonewall."

Photo: Richmond Newspapers

On April 20, 1863, in the midst of an afternoon downpour at Guiney's Station south of Fredericksburg, Jackson rushed aboard the train from Richmond to greet his family. His wife, Anna, traveled from her parent's home in North Carolina for the Confederate officer to see his 5-month-old daughter, Julia, for the first time. Jackson was excited to see his "little angel," Julia. He, himself, was orphaned at the age of 7, and he spent his youth crisscrossing Virginia, living with relatives, and dreaming of a family of his own. Young Julia was named for his late mother. After being shot by "friendly fire" at the Battle of Chancellorsville, Jackson was taken to the railhead, where he developed pneumonia. On May 9, 1863, Jackson called for his little Julia. He caressed her with his wounded right hand and prayed while the little girl cooed. He died the next day.

Julia Jackson grew up, married a Richmond newspapers man, William Edmund Christian, and had a son and a daughter. She died at the age of 27, leaving her mother to raise the two children.

RF&P railroad. Jackson was placed in a field office. But his wounds were complicated by pneumonia, and he died on May 10.

Fredericksburg/ Spotsylvania Accommodations

Refer to the Foreword for an explanation of the rating system for both the accommodations and restaurants.

LaVista Plantation Bed and Breakfast

4420 Guinea Station Rd.
Fredericksburg, VA   703-898-8444
$$

This little bed and breakfast, in an 1838 Classical Revival home on historic Guinea Station Road, offers two suites, complete with private baths, fireplaces and televisions. A fresh egg breakfast is served each morning.

ROXBURY MILL BED AND BREAKFAST
6908 Roxbury Mill Rd.
Spotsylvania, VA   703-582-6611
$$

This house, built as the working mill for Roxbury Plantation which dates to the 1720s, offers two guest rooms, one suite and a children's room. All the rooms are decorated with antiques, and each has a deck and view of the mill race and nearby dam.

COMFORT INN SOUTHPOINT
5422 Jefferson Davis Highway
Fredericksburg, VA 24407   703-898-5440
$$

This familiar facility offers 175 rooms, a restaurant on the premises, and an outdoor swimming pool. Some non-smoking rooms and two handicapped rooms are available.

Fredericksburg/
Spotsylvania
Restaurants

GOOLRICH'S MODERN PHARMACY
901 Caroline St.
Fredericksburg, VA   703-373-3411
$

Located in the historic old downtown section, on Caroline Street, this is one of the last great drug stores with a lunch counter. Perfect for a quick lunch: a sandwich and the best milk shake in Virginia! Open only for lunch.

VIRGINIA DELI
101 William St.
Fredericksburg, VA   703-371-2233
$

This is a sandwich shop conveniently located in the historic old downtown section — near the Rappahannock River Bridge. This deli offers a wide selection of specialty sandwiches along with soft drinks, waters and juices. The deli also sells a selection of Virginia-made products. Open Monday through Thursday from 8:00 AM to 5:00 PM, Saturday from 8:00 AM to 6:00 PM, and Sunday from 10:00 AM to 5:00 PM.

MORRISON'S CAFETERIA
3104 Plank Rd. (US 3)
Fredericksburg, VA   703-786-6535
$$

An excellent choice for a family outing, particularly when children are included. Morrison's is a chain that serves home-style cooking cafeteria-style. (Don't let the long cafeteria line deter you — it moves very quickly.) Daily specials offer a complete meal for under $7 — children for under $2.50. Meals are ideal for the hungry traveler. Open Sunday through Thursday from 11:00 AM to 8:30 PM, and Friday and Saturday from 11 AM to 9:00 PM.

CRACKER BARREL
OLD COUNTRY STORE
5200 Southpoint Parkway
Fredericksburg, VA 24407   703-891-7622
$$

Located across from the Spotsylvania Visitor Center (see listing), and adjacent to the Massaponax Outlet Center, this restaurant offers country cooking. Breakfast is served all day. Chicken and beef are dinner staples. The Cracker Barrel is open Sunday through Thursday from 6:00 AM to 10:00 PM, and Friday and Saturday from 6:00 AM to 11:00 PM.

Other Fredericksburg/ Spotsylvania Attractions

For questions or reservations, ask for help at either the Spotsylvania Visitor Center (see listing) or the Fredericksburg Visitor Center (see listing).

Annual Events: President's Day and George Washington's Birthday are special events in the Fredericksburg area in February, Market Street Fair is a springtime celebration in May, the Fredericksburg Art Festival is held in June, and Kenmore's gingerbread house contest and exhibit is conducted in December.

Antiques: Caroline Street in downtown Fredericksburg is an antique-lover's heaven. No fewer than 20 shops offer antiques and memorabilia — mainly Civil War-related. Browse along the stores and window shop for brief, unexpected history lessons.

Historical Sites: Four prominent structures in downtown Fredericksburg are on the list of state or national landmarks: The Mary Washington House, 1200 Charles Street in Fredericksburg, the place where George Washington's mother lived for 17 years until her death in 1789; Kenmore, 1201 Washington Street, completed in the 1750s by Fielding Lewis for his wife, Betty, George Washington's only sister; the Rising Sun Tavern, 1306 Caroline Street, built in the 1760s by George Washington's younger brother, Charles; and the James Monroe Law Office, 908 Charles Street, which has a number of Monroe's personal possessions. Check at the Fredericksburg Visitor Center for a "Hospitality Pass," which is a combined admission to these four sites and three others, including the Fredericksburg Area Museum and Cultural Center. Also ask at the Fredericksburg Visitor Center about carriage tours of the historic district. Ferry Farm, George Washington's home when he was a youngster, is located across the Rappahannock River in Stafford County.

Source: Richmond Newspapers

Robert E. Lee and Stonewall Jackson together led the
Confederacy to several early victories.

Stratford Hall Plantation

Birthplace of Robert E. Lee

- Located just 40 miles east of Fredericksburg on Route 3
- One of America's finest 18th century historic houses
- Facilities include: 1600 acre working plantation with grist mill, reception center video, colonial gift shop and plantation dining room
- Annual Civil War reenactment first weekend in June

Robert E. Lee Memorial Association, Inc.
Stratford Hall Plantation • Stratford, Va. 22558
For brochure or information Phone (804) 493-8038

Shopping: Caroline Street in downtown Fredericksburg is a bustling, active place with dozens of shops and stores. Along this busy street you will find Becks Antiques and Books (708 Caroline Street, 703-371-1766), which sells new, used and rare Civil War books. Next door, Staley's Sundries (710 Caroline Street, 703-899-6464) specializes in Civil War gifts and music. Also, Valor Art and Frame Ltd. (718 Caroline Street, 703-372-3376) has Civil War limited edition prints, original art, artifacts, books and custom framing.

At 401 William Street is The Pickett Post (703-371-7703), an antique shop that specializes in Civil War-era items, including collectibles, edged weapons, firearms, buttons, reference books and metal detectors. Near the Fredericksburg Battlefield Center is The Galvanized Yankee, which specializes in military artifacts. It is located at 1016 Lafayette Boulevard (703-373-1886).

North of Fredericksburg, across the Rappahannock River, is Falmouth Trading Post (256 Cambridge Street, 703-771-3309), which specializes in Civil War military collectibles. West of Fredericksburg, on the route toward Chancellorsville, is Stars and Bars Military Antiques (9832 Plank Road, Spotsylvania, VA, 703-972-1863), a shop definitely worth a visit.

Suburban shoppers converge at Spotsylvania Mall, just off I-95 on US 3 west (Plank Road). Value shoppers go to the Massaponax Outlet Center at Southpoint (just off I-95 at exit 126-B), which offers a wide variety of discount outlet stores. The ultimate in outlet shopping, Potomac Mills, is located north of Fredericksburg on I-95 (exit 156). This is the number one attraction in Virginia, and the largest outlet center in the world. It offers more than 200 stores.

TOUR 12
Fredericksburg to Richmond

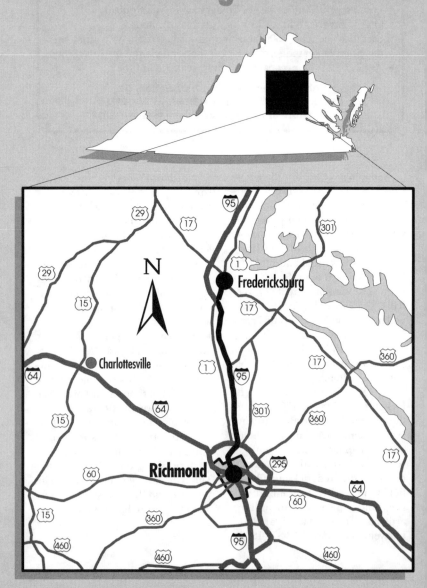

Tour 12
Richmond

About This Tour

This tour route is a natural continuation of Tour 11: Fredericksburg. It begins in Fredericksburg, VA, and leads to downtown Richmond, VA, where it concludes. We suggest you plan evening dining and lodging in Richmond.

We also recommend you get a copy of *The Insiders' Guide to Richmond*, which will provide detailed information about all the Richmond area has to offer the visitor. This book is available at your local bookstore.

Travel Tips

I-95 is part of the busy north-south corridor of Virginia that stretches along the "fall line." Be on the lookout for heavy, fast moving traffic along this major interstate route. If I-95 is particularly congested, try US 1 as an alternative. US 1 runs parallel to I-95.

History, Geography

Richmond, which sits on the James River "fall line" was named by William Byrd II after the borough of Richmond, England. Byrd himself laid out the village in 1737. More than 40 years later, in 1779, Richmond was designated the Virginia state capital.

Richmond experienced action during the American Revolution.

In 1785, the James River Company was established for the purpose of building a 200-mile canal from Richmond to the Appalachian highlands. George Washington was honorary president of the effort that later became known as the James River and Kanawha Canal project. Chief Justice John Marshall was a longtime resident of Richmond, which was the site of Aaron Burr's famous treason trial in 1807.

Richmond was the primary objective of the Union army for four years — the cry was "On to Richmond!" After all, Richmond was the Confederate capital, and it served as the South's main manufacturing and medical center. The supply depots here served the entire Eastern Theater. Twice, Union forces advanced dangerously close to the capitol. There was USA Gen. McClellan's Peninsular Campaign (See Tour 15: Peninsula) and USA Gen. Grant's assault in 1864.

The infamous Libby and Bell Isle prisons were two of several prisons located in Richmond for a time. Here, too, were the Tredegar Iron Works and the Richmond Armory and Arsenal, which together accounted for half of the ordnance issued by the Confederacy. Tredegar was owned by Joseph Reid Anderson, a graduate of West Point. Anderson built the Valley Turnpike between Staunton and Winchester. Commissioned a brigadier general, and wounded during the Peninsular Campaign, Anderson returned to work at Tredegar in 1862 and stayed. Barely a business or residence in Richmond escaped the horrors of war. Today, the state capital is rich in Civil War heritage.

Getting Here

I-95 (north-south) and I-64 (east-west) converge in Richmond, the Virginia capital city. This tour route suggests traveling to Richmond from I-95 south out of Fredericksburg, VA.

DIRECTIONS

Fredericksburg to Ashland

From Fredericksburg, take I-95 south toward Richmond. Along this route are a number of historical sites related to the Civil War. At Ladysmith (on US 1, just off exit at milepost 110), Confederate troops often camped en route north or south. At Carmel Church (also on US 1, just off the exit at milepost 104), USA Gen. Grant moved through in May 1864, taking Confederate earthworks and establishing his headquarters in a church. Near Doswell (also on US 1, just off exit 98), on the North Anna River, is where CSA Gen. Lee almost trapped USA Gen. Grant in 1864.

At Ashland (in Hanover Co., just off milepost 92), both CSA Gens. Jackson and Stuart camped in the vicinity in June 1862, and CSA Gen. Lee made his headquarters nearby in May 1864.

Hanover County Personality

USA Lt. Thomas Farrell

An historic Southern church, destroyed by Confederate cannon fire in 1864, may be rebuilt from the sketches of a Union spy and artist, Thomas Farrell. Hanover County's Polegreen (or Pole Green) Church, built in the 1740s, was the home pulpit of Samuel Davies, a Presbyterian who protested the Virginia colony's church policies.

In 1862, Farrell was a young Union Navy lieutenant and busy at work in Hanover, drawing sketches in preparation of USA Gen. McClellan's pending Peninsular Campaign. Farrell, 17, was President Lincoln's bodyguard at the beginning of the Civil War. Farrell sketched the Hanover landscape and took time to draw a few exterior and interior scenes of Polegreen Church. But his efforts were useless, because the Union never struck Hanover during the campaign.

In 1864, the historic church was struck by Confederate cannon fire during the Battle of Cold Harbor. It burned to the ground. William S. White, a member of the 3rd Richmond Howitzers during the June 1864 battle, wrote in his diary that it was his cannon that struck the famous, simple, box-shaped church.

More recently, a printer found Farrell's faded church sketches in a grocery bag stored in the basement of his grandfather's Philadelphia row house. Now, the artwork may fulfill a purpose. The Polegreen Foundation plans to use the drawings as part of an effort to reconstruct the historic building.

Henry Clay

Five miles east of Ashland is the birthplace of Kentucky statesman Henry Clay. He was born on April 12, 1777, during the American Revolution. Clay traced his family's roots to English settlers who arrived in the Virginia colony shortly after Jamestown. This area of Hanover

Source: Richmond Newspapers

County was known as "the Slashes" — a term that describes the wet, swampy terrain that often is overgrown with scrub pines and bushes.

With the aid of his stepfather, Henry Watkins, Clay took a job in 1792 in Richmond, where he soon caught the attention of jurist George Wythe. By 1797, Clay was practicing law and feeling the lure of the new state of Kentucky. Settling in Lexington, KY, he became a prominent criminal lawyer and quickly climbed the ladder of political success.

In 1803, at the age of 26, he was elected to the Kentucky legislature. Three years later, he was elected to the U.S. Senate to fill the unexpired term of John Adair, taking office in November despite being under the minimum Constitutional age limit of 30. In and out of both the U.S. Senate and House, including a tenure as speaker of the House of Representatives, he also was secretary of state under President John Quincy Adams and an unsuccessful candidate for president in 1824, 1832, and 1844.

Clay was the chief architect of the Compromise of 1850 (see section, "Prelude to the War"), and for this he became known as the "Great Compromiser." He also was known at various times as the "Mill Boy of the Slashes," "Prince Hal" (for having a personality similar to Shakespeare's King Henry V), "Harry of the West," and the "Great Pacificator" (for his efforts to wrangle peaceful relations among his fellow legislators). Clay died in Washington, D.C., on June 29, 1852, and funeral services were held in the old U.S. Senate chambers.

DIRECTIONS

Ashland to Metro Richmond Visitor Center

Continue south on I-95 to the interchange with I-295 (mile-post 89)Continue south on I-95 and take exit 78 (Boulevard, milepost 78). Take the exit ramp to the stop sign, turn right (west) on Boulevard, and go to the first traffic signal at Ellen Street. Turn left (south) on Ellen Street, adjacent to the stadium complex, and go 0.1 mile to the Metro Richmond Visitor Center on the left.

Yellow Tavern, Stuart Monument

Yellow Tavern was a stop on the main highway (present-day US 1) between Richmond and Fredericksburg. On May 12, 1864, Confederate cavalry leader J.E.B. Stuart was shot by 48-year-old Union marksman John Huff (who, ironically, was shot and killed less than two weeks later at Haw's Shop, VA). Stuart died the next day of the wound he received. A monument was dedicated in June 1888 by Gov. Fitzhugh Lee — himself a Civil War veteran — just 30 feet from the spot where Stuart was shot. Stuart was born in Virginia on Feb. 6, 1833. Known by his West Point classmates as "Beauty," the attractive Stuart had a long beard that concealed his youthful image. He was just 31 when he died. To see the monument, exit I-95 at milepost 89, and take I-295 west. Exit immediately at US 1 (follow sign for Ashland), go north on US 1 for 0.1 mile, and turn right (east) on the Virginia Center Parkway. Take the parkway east for 0.5 mile to Telegraph Road on the right. Turn right on Telegraph Road and go 0.2 miles to the monument on the right. Backtrack on Virginia Center Parkway, US 1, and I-295 to return to I-95 south.

METRO RICHMOND VISITOR CENTER
1710 Robin Hood Rd.
Richmond, VA 23219   804-358-5511

This facility is operated by the Metro Richmond Convention and Visitor Bureau, and it offers brochures and maps on attractions, lodging, dining and shopping in the greater Richmond area. Travel counselors help visitors with lodging reservations and directions, and special discounted lodging rates are sometimes available. The visitor center also offers specialty gifts and souvenirs. Open daily 9:00 AM to 5:00 PM. Hours are extended in the summer until 7:00 PM.

DIRECTIONS

Metro Richmond Visitor Center to Museum of the Confederacy

Return to I-95 south and go 4.0 miles to exit 74-C. Follow signs for Broad Street west and the Museum of the Confederacy. Turn right onto Broad Street and go west to 11th Street. Turn right on 11th Street and go two blocks to Clay Street. Turn right on Clay Street and go two blocks to the Museum of the Confederacy. Park in the lot at the end of Clay Street. The lot is designated for the Medical College of Virginia; the Museum of the Confederacy validates parking.

MUSEUM OF THE CONFEDERACY
1201 E. Clay St.
Richmond, VA 23219   *804-649-1861*

A visit to Richmond — indeed, all the South — is incomplete without a visit to the Museum of the Confederacy and the adjacent White House of the Confederacy. These two points of interest are located in Richmond's historic Court End district, a few blocks from the Virginia State Capitol. Clay Street is a gorgeous site amid the tall, overpowering structures of the Medical College of Virginia. The Museum of the Confederacy offers self-guided tours of exhibits on the South's role in the Civil War. Here's what you see: CSA Gen. Robert E. Lee's surrender sword from Appomattox, CSA Gen. Stuart's plumed hat, and the coat worn by CSA President Davis when he was captured in 1865. The museum's vast collection of Civil War art includes the original oil titled "The Last Meeting of Lee and Jackson." The museum is open Sunday from noon to 5 PM, and Monday through Saturday from 10 AM to 5 PM. It is open every day except New Year's Day, Thanksgiving Day and Christmas Day. There is an admission charge: Adults pay $4.00 for either the Museum of the Confederacy or the White House of the Confederacy (see listing below), or $7.00 for both. Children's admission is $2.25 for either attraction, or $3.50 for both. Seniors pay $3.50 for either, or $5.00 for both. College students pay $2.50 for either, and $4.50 for both. A small gift shop is on site.

The museum's well-trained staff of historians and researchers frequently sets up special exhibits. Recently, the museum offered an exhibit on Confederate flags, including the battle flag of the Army of Northern Virginia — commonly called the Confederate Flag. The exhibit, "Embattled Emblem," examined the flag's origins, how it was designed and where it flew during the Civil War. It covered the flag's design, which includes the blue St. Andrew's Cross on a red field. The Confederacy's first national flag featured three horizontal stripes — two red, one white — and a blue field with stars arranged in a circle. The national flag of the South resembled the U.S. flag, and that created confusion at 1st Manassas in 1861. As a result, the ANV's battle flag was adopted for military use. The exhibit also examined 20th century adoption of the "Confederate Flag" by divergent political, social and heritage groups. A third exhibit section presented recent local, regional and

Jefferson Davis

Jefferson Davis was born June 3, 1808, in Christian County (now Todd County), KY. He was the tenth child of Jane Cook Davis and her husband, Samuel, son of a Welsh emigrant and a Revolutionary War veteran. Later, Jefferson Davis moved with family to Mississippi. Nominated for an appointment to West Point, Davis graduated from the academy in 1828. He had the distinction of attending West Point with Robert E. Lee, a fellow cadet, and later of taking part in the Black Hawk War with Abraham Lincoln, a fellow officer.

Photo: Library of Congress

In 1833, Davis was stationed at a Wisconsin fort commanded by Col. Zachary Taylor of Orange County, VA. Davis fell in love with Taylor's daughter, Sarah Knox Taylor, and despite her father's disapproval, the pair was married in Mississippi. Three months later, however, Sarah died of malarial fever.

Davis later remarried, was elected to the U.S. House, and served in the Mexican War under his former father-in-law — and later president — Gen. Zachary Taylor. Gen. Taylor appointed his former son-in-law as one of the commissioners to negotiate the surrender of Monterey. In time, Davis returned to Washington as a U.S. Senator, with a break in service as secretary of war in President Franklin Pierce's cabinet. After Mississippi's secession, which Davis announced on the Senate floor, he retired to the South and was elected president of the Confederate States of America.

On Feb. 11, 1861, Jefferson Davis said good-bye to his family at Brierfield Plantation and began his trip to Montgomery, AL, for his inauguration as president of the Confederate States of America. Davis, traveling alone, took a boat to Vicksburg, MS, and traveled through Jackson, MS, Chattanooga, TN, and Atlanta on his way to Alabama. His indirect route was caused by the lack of direct railroad lines in the South. Davis eventually moved to Richmond.

Ironically, also on Feb. 11, a crowd of a thousand supporters rallied in a morning drizzle at the train station in Springfield, IL, as President-elect Abraham Lincoln — on the eve of his birthday — departed for his inaugural in Washington, DC. Lincoln told the crowd, "I now leave, not knowing when, or whether ever, I may return, with a task before me greater than that which rested upon Washington. Without the assistance of that Divine Being, who ever attended him, I cannot succeed. With that assistance I cannot fail."

Confederate White House Personality

Joe Davis

On April 30, 1864, Jefferson Davis' young, 5-year-old son, Joe Davis, died after falling off the veranda of the Confederate White House. Thus, the presidents of both the South and the North — Abraham Lincoln and Davis — lost sons while in the service of their countries.

national controversies that surround public display of the flag. Also, the museum recently featured an exhibit of flags carried by CSA Gen. Picket's Virginia Division at Gettysburg. Eleven of the 12 flags carried into battle, as well as two not captured, are in the museum collection.

WHITE HOUSE OF THE CONFEDERACY

1201 E. Clay St.
Richmond, VA 23219   804-649-1861

The White House of the Confederacy was the executive mansion for CSA President Davis and his family. A National Historic Landmark, the house has been restored to its mid-19th century appearance. Guides lead tours through the house during museum hours, with some exceptions. The admission fee is:

Adults pay $4.00 for either the White House of the Confederacy or the Museum of the Confederacy, or $7.00 for both. Children's admission is $2.25 for either attraction, or $3.50 for both. Seniors pay $3.50 for either attraction, or $5.00 for both. College students pay $2.50 for either, or $4.50 for both.

DIRECTIONS

White House of the Confederacy to Virginia State Library and Archives

Backtrack west on Clay Street to 12th Street. Turn left on 12th Street and go two blocks to E. Broad Street. Park along E. Broad Street or in a public parking lot in the vicinity. The Virginia State Library and Archives is located on E. Broad Street at Capitol Square (at 12th Street).

VIRGINIA STATE
LIBRARY AND ARCHIVES

11th St. at Capitol Square
Richmond, VA 23219-3491 804-786-8929

This library has a vast collection of books and artifacts. In addition, it frequently offers exhibits on various Virginia history topics. The library has an extensive collection of state government records, including those related to the Civil War.

DIRECTIONS

**Virginia State Library to
Virginia State Capitol**
The Virginia State Capitol is located adjacent to the Virginia State Library and Archives.

VIRGINIA STATE CAPITOL

Capitol Square
Richmond, VA 23219   804-786-4344

This, the Virginia State Capitol, was the Capitol of the Confederacy. This is the meeting place of the Virginia General Assembly, the oldest lawmaking body in the western hemisphere. The building was designed by Thomas Jefferson, while he was minister to France. For his model, Jefferson chose "La Maison Carree," a Roman temple built in Nimes, France, in the first century of the Christian era. He called the structure "the best morsel of ancient architecture now remaining." The capitol cornerstone was laid in August 1785, and the assembly held its first session in 1788. The portico was added in 1790, and the walls were stuccoed in 1800. The marble

City of Monuments

Living, breathing monuments. From Patrick Henry's "Give me liberty, or give me death" speech at St. John's Church to dramatic re-enactments at world famous battlefields.

METROPOLITAN
RICHMOND
800-365-7272

statue of George Washington in the capitol's rotunda was sculpted by Jean Antoine Houdoun. It is considered one of the most precious statues in the nation.

The Virginia secession convention was held in the building in 1861, and Gen. Robert E. Lee appeared before the session to accept command of the armed forces of Virginia.

The Hall of the House of Delegates was restored in 1929. It contains numerous pieces of statuary, including those of CSA Gens. Stonewall Jackson, J.E.B. Stuart, Joseph E. Johnston and Fitzhugh Lee. There is a statue, too, of Matthew Fontaine Maury. There are busts of CSA President Jefferson Davis and Vice President Alexander H. Stephens.

Next door, the Executive Mansion has been the official residence of Virginia governors since 1813. The old bell tower was completed in 1824. It is the oldest continuously occupied governor's residence in the nation.

The statuary on the capitol grounds include those of Dr. Hunter Holmes McGuire, the surgeon who served as Jackson's medical director (see Tour 3: Shenandoah Valley); William "Extra Billy" Smith, a brigadier general in the Confederacy and governor of Virginia during the Civil War; and CSA Gen. Stonewall Jackson. In fact, this Jackson statue was the first Confederate hero's monument erected in Richmond.

CSA President Davis delivered his inaugural address from the Washington statue on the capitol grounds. And the body of CSA Gen. Stonewall Jackson was brought to the Executive Mansion to lie in state.

Capitol tours are given on Sunday from 1 to 5 PM and Monday through Saturday from 9 AM to 5 PM. Groups are asked to make reservations.

The Executive Mansion also offers tours, but hours vary, and reservations are required. For more information, telephone 804-371-2642.

DIRECTIONS

Virginia State Capitol to St. Paul's Church

St. Paul's Church is located across the street from Capitol Square, at the corner of 9th and Grace streets.

Robert E. Lee

When Robert E. Lee appeared before the Virginia secession convention in 1861, he delivered a brief speech in accepting command of Virginia's Confederate forces. He said:

"Mr. President and Gentlemen of the Convention. Profoundly impressed with the solemnity of the occasion, for which I must say I was not prepared, I accept the position assigned me by our partiality. I would have much preferred had your choice fallen on an abler man. Trusting in Almighty God, an approving conscience, and the aid of my fellow-citizens, I devote myself to the service of my native State, in whose behalf alone will I ever again draw my sword."

Lee's remarks are inscribed on the base of his statue in the old Hall of the House in the capitol.

Virginia State Capitol
Personality

Governor William "Extra Billy" Smith

Smith got the name "Extra Billy" from the days when he ran a mail-coach service from Washington, D.C. to Georgia. As business grew, Smith demanded and got extra payment from the government.

A lawyer-turned-politician, he served in the Virginia legislature and then as Congressman, before his election as governor in 1845. He served three years until he moved to California in 1849. Out west, Smith refused to run for state office because he refused to give up his Virginia residency. Back in Virginia, he was elected to Congress again — a position he held nine years until Virginia's secession in 1861.

He served at 1st Manassas (see Fairfax Courthouse in Tour 10: Northern Virginia), and then got himself elected to the Confederate Congress, attending political meetings when his military schedule permitted. Appointed a brigadier general, Smith was elected governor of Virginia in May 1863, but he decided to fight at Gettysburg the next month, so he didn't take office until January 1864. After the war, Smith lived near Warrenton. He served in the Virginia Assembly into his 80s, and he died in 1887 at the age of 91.

St. Paul's Church

815 E. Grace St.
Richmond, VA 23219   804-643-3589

CSA President Davis and Gen. Robert E. Lee attended this Greek Revival church, so it became known as the "Cathedral of the Confederacy." Pews used by both Davis and Lee are marked. During worship services the first Sunday in April 1865, Davis received a note that Gen. Lee's lines were broken at Petersburg — the Confederate president was advised to evacuate Richmond immediately. Today, the church has a large, active congregation. It is open daily from 10 AM to 4 PM. A brief church tour is offered each Sunday following the 11 AM worship service.

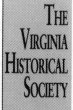

LEONIDAS N CREEKMORE
CO H
8 FLA REGT
CSA
AUG 9 1825
MAY 24 1865

Photo: Richmond Newspapers

There are 18,000 Civil War veterans buried in Hollywood Cemetery.

DIRECTIONS

St. Paul's Church to Holly-wood Cemetery

Walk back to the parking area on Broad Street. Drive west on Broad Street for 15 blocks to Belevedere Street. Turn left (south) on Belevedere Street and go eight blocks — over I-195 — to Spring Street. Turn right on Spring Street and go three blocks to Cherry Street. Turn right on Cherry Street and go a block to Hollywood Cemetery on the left.

HOLLYWOOD CEMETERY

412 S. Cherry St.
Richmond, VA 23220   804-648-8501

This elegant cemetery was established in 1847 and named for its prolific holly trees. More than 100 acres in size, the cemetery includes the burial site of CSA President Jefferson Davis and his family, and CSA Gens. J.E.B. Stuart and George Pickett. Two Virginia-born U.S. Presidents — James Monroe and John Tyler — are buried here, too. More than 18,000 Confederate soldiers are buried in Hollywood, including many who were removed from Gettysburg. There is no charge to enter the grounds. The cemetery is open Sunday from 8 AM to 6 PM and Monday through Saturday from 7 AM to 6 PM.

DIRECTIONS

Hollywood Cemetery to Monument Avenue

Leaving Hollywood Cemetery, go north on Cherry Street to Idlewood Avenue. Turn right on Idlewood Avenue and go two blocks back to Belvidere Street. Turn left on Belvidere Street and go six blocks to Grace Street. Turn left (west) on Grace Street and go six blocks to Lombardy Street. Turn left on Lombardy Street and go a block to Monument — turn right and continue west on Monument.

MONUMENT AVENUE

Laid out in 1889, Monument Avenue is a leading symbol of Richmond. The broad avenue offers an architecturally diverse mix of "classic revival" buildings, built in harmony with rows of maples and oaks. Since 1907, the roadway has been paved in asphalt block. The avenue has been a ceremonial entry to downtown Richmond, with such notables as William Howard Taft, Winston Churchill and Charles Lindbergh entering the city by this boulevard. Here's a list of the significant monuments:

LOMBARDY STREET: a monument to CSA Gen. J.E.B. Stuart, who was considered "the best cavalry officer in America." He was just 31 when he was wounded at the battle of Yellow Tavern (see listing above) north of Richmond in Hanover County. He died the next day at his brother-in-law's home, located on nearby Grace Street. This statue was dedicated in 1907.

ALLEN AVENUE: a monument to CSA Gen. Robert E. Lee. A 60-foot monument, it has a simple inscription: "Lee." It was unveiled in 1890, when the area was an open field. During the Civil War, Lee's family rented a house at 707 E. Franklin Street.

DAVIS AVENUE: near the old outer defenses of Richmond, a monument to CSA President Jefferson Davis. This statue was designed by one of

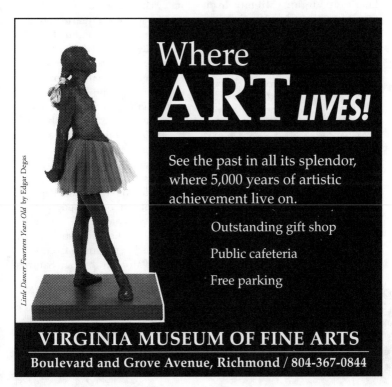

Richmond's own: Edward Virginius Valentine. It was unveiled in 1907. Valentine's studio was located on E. Clay Street — today the site of the Valentine Museum, a block west of the Museum of the Confederacy. He also designed the statue of Thomas Jefferson that can be seen in the lobby of the Hotel Jefferson in downtown Richmond.

BOULEVARD: a monument to CSA Gen. Stonewall Jackson. This statue was unveiled in 1919.

BELMONT AVENUE: a monument to oceanographer Matthew Fontaine Maury, known as the "Pathfinder of the Sea." The statue was dedicated in 1929. Maury, who taught at Virginia Military Institute after the Civil War, also is buried in Hollywood Cemetery.

DIRECTIONS

Monument Avenue to Virginia Historical Society

Turn around on Monument Avenue and head east to Boulevard. At Boulevard, turn right (west) and go two blocks to the Virginia Historical Society on the right. Parking is available in front of the society building.

VIRGINIA HISTORICAL SOCIETY
428 N. Boulevard
Richmond, VA 23221-0311 804-358-4901

The Virginia Historical Society is the oldest continuously operating cultural institution in Virginia, and it has the largest collection of Virginia history materials anywhere. It boasts more than 7 million processed manuscripts, more than 125,000 books, 5,000 maps, and nearly 800 portraits.

Founded in 1831, the society conducts programs, conferences and lectures around the state for schools, museums, libraries and local historical societies. In addition, it has sponsored more than 100 teacher recertification workshops, seminars and conferences in the past three years. In 1993, the society distributed specially designed teaching kits to more than 1,000 state school teachers.

The state headquarters, built in 1912 and refurbished in 1992, was originally a memorial to the Confederate soldier. "Battle Abby" is well known for its monumental murals, called the "Seasons of the Confederacy" and developed by Frenchman Charles Hoffbauer in the 1920s. Admission to the historical society museum is $3.00 for adults, and $2.00 for children and students up to the university level. The society offers "Senior Tuesday": senior citizens on Tuesdays pay only $1.00. Admission is free for members of the historical society. The society is open Sunday from 1 to 5 PM, and Monday through Saturday from 10 AM to 5 PM.

Richmond Personality

William Steffe

Julia Ward Howe is credited with writing new lyrics to the "Battle Hymn of the Republic" for a piece of music made popular by a singing quartet of the 12th Mass. Volunteers (see Julia Ward Howe in Tour 9: Washington). In fact, the new lyrics were published in the *Atlantic Monthly* in early 1862. However, the original camp meeting song was written by William Steffe of Richmond.

Association for the Preservation of Virginia Antiquities

The Association for the Preservation of Virginia Antiquities (APVA), headquartered in Richmond, has broadened its scope by forming a new branch to identify and preserve endangered Civil War sites. The branch is named for noted historian Douglas Southall Freeman. It announced plans in 1993 to focus first on battlefield sites in central Virginia, and it will work with other APVA branches, historical organizations, individuals and local governments and agencies. The APVA is 104 years old, has 5,000 members, and owns or administers 35 historic properties in Virginia.

Richmond Personalities

Elizabeth Van Lew

Elizabeth Van Lew — alias "Crazy Bet" and "Miss Lizzie" — was a Union spy. Van Lew was a member of a well-known Richmond family. She was called "Crazy Bet" because she acted rather nutty — probably to disguise her spy work. She helped Northern soldiers escape through a tunnel at her home on Grace Street. After the war, she was appointed Postmistress of Richmond by Ulysses Grant. She is buried in Richmond.

Richmond Personality

Sallie Putnam

Sallie Putnam lived in Richmond throughout the war. On April 3, 1865, as Union forces moved in on Richmond, she wrote:

As the sun rose on Richmond, such a spectacle was presented as can never be forgotten by those who witnessed it. . . . All the horrors of the final conflagration, when the earth shall be wrapped in flames and melt with fervent heat, were, it seems to us, prefigured in our capital. . . . The roaring, crackling and hissing of the flames, the bursting of shells at the Confederate Arsenal, the sounds of the instruments of martial music, the neighing of the horses, the shouting of the multitudes . . . gave an idea of all the horrors of Pandemonium. Above all this scene of terror, hung a black shroud of smoke through which the sun shone with lurid angry glare like an immense ball of blood that emitted sullen rays of light, as if loath to shine over a scene so appalling. . . . [Then] a cry was raised: 'The Yankees! The Yankees are coming.'

Richmond Personality

There are numerous Civil War attractions located south and east of downtown Richmond. To the south, Drewry's Bluff and Hopewell, as examples, are covered in the next chapter — Tour 13: Petersburg. Much of the Civil War action east of Richmond relate to USA Gen. McClellan's Peninsular Campaign of 1862 or USA Gen. Grant's march on Richmond in 1864. The area east of Richmond is covered in this book's last chapter — Tour 15: Peninsula. The visitor center at the Richmond National Battlefield Park, located on E. Broad Street in Richmond, is included as the first stop in Tour 15.

Richmond Accommodations

JEFFERSON HOTEL
Franklin and Adams Sts.
Richmond, VA   804-788-8000
$$$$

For years, the Jefferson Hotel has been a Richmond landmark. A large stairway connects the upper and lower lobby areas, which feature a statue of the hotel's namesake, Thomas Jefferson. The Jefferson was built in 1895 and renovated just over a decade ago. It has 274 rooms, meeting space and a top-rated restaurant, Lemaire.

MARRIOTT RICHMOND
500 E. Broad St.
Richmond, VA   804-643-3400
$$$$

The Marriott, located in the heart of downtown Richmond, offers more than 400 rooms, a number of hospitality suites, and three separate restaurants in this 30,000-square-foot complex adjacent to Richmond Centre. There's an indoor pool, weight room, saunas, and aerobics instruc-

tion. Parking is available free in a 1,000-space lot next door.

LINDEN ROW INN
100 E. Franklin St.
Richmond, VA   804-783-7000
$$$$

Seven antebellum townhouses, three buildings and a carriage house have been restored into this 70-room inn located in historic downtown. Rooms include Empire furnishings. Guests enjoy a continental breakfast, while the dining room serves lunch and dinner. Meeting rooms are available.

BENSON HOUSE

Benson House is a bed and breakfast reservation service. It assists travelers with b&b accommodations in the Fan District and on Monument Avenue in Richmond, as well as in Fredericksburg, Williamsburg and Petersburg, VA. For more information, contact the service at 2036 Monument Avenue, Richmond, VA, 23220, or call 804-355-4885 or 804-353-6900.

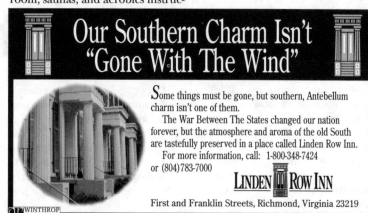

Richmond Restaurants

TRAVELLER'S RESTAURANT

707 E. Franklin St.
Richmond, VA   804-644-1040
$$$

Traveller's is a fine place for lunch or dinner in downtown Richmond. The restaurant is significant, not only for its beef, pork and seafood, but because it's located in the house where Robert E. Lee's family lived during the Civil War. Lee himself returned here after the war's end. The restaurant is open Monday through Friday from 11:30 AM to 2:30 PM and from 5:30 to 10:30 PM. It is open Saturday from 5:30 to 10:30 PM and closed on Sunday.

EXTRA BILLY'S STEAK AND BAR-B-QUE

5205 W. Broad St.
Richmond, VA   804-282-3949
$

This restaurant has a history connection, too. William "Extra Billy" Smith was Virginia's governor during the Civil War (see listing under Virginia State Capitol above). Located near the shopping center at Willow Lawn, Extra Billy's serves a variety of bar-be-que dishes. This is a large, busy restaurant that's ideal for families with children. Open Monday through Thursday from 11:30 AM to 10:00 PM, it stays open an extra half-hour on Friday. Saturday hours are 5:00 to 10:30 PM. It is closed on Sunday.

THE TOBACCO COMPANY

1201 E. Clay St.
Richmond, VA   804-782-9431
$$

Located in an old tobacco warehouse in Richmond's historic Shockoe Slip, the Tobacco Company offers cocktails, dinner and dancing. It features a three-story atrium and antique furnishings. Better known for its entertainment than its food, the Tobacco Company is a magnet for young adults interested in tasting Richmond's night life. Open until 2:00 AM each night, there's a varying cover charge (for men only) on certain nights.

In 1919 this statue stood over a tobacco field.

Other Richmond Attractions

For questions or reservations, ask for help at the Metro Richmond Convention and Visitor Bureau (see listing). The convention and visitors bureau also operates a booth at the Sixth Street Marketplace, 550 E. Marshall Street, in downtown Richmond (Box C-250, Richmond 23219, telephone 800-365-7272 or 804-782-2777).

Annual Events: A partial listing of recurring events in the Richmond area includes the Virginia Spring Show (March), the Virginia State Horse Show and Historic Garden Week (April), June Jubilee, Virginia Food Festival (August), Autumn Harvest Grand Illumination Parade and Richmond Children's Festival (October), Richmond Craft Show (November) and house tours and open houses (December).

Arts: Cultural and performing arts abound in the Richmond area. There's the Richmond Ballet, the Richmond Symphony, the Virginia Opera, Theatre IV, TheatreVirginia, and Hanover County's Barksdale Theatre. The Virginia Museum of Fine Arts is located at Boulevard and Grove avenues, and is open every day but Monday. The Valentine Museum, near the Museum of the Confederacy, features the life and history of Richmond and is open daily. The convention and visitors bureau has telephone numbers and schedules for these and other arts activities.

Entertainment: Looking for something else fun to do? Try a riverboat cruise on the Annabel Lee (call 222-5700 for details), the Science Museum of Virginia, Kings Dominion, hot air ballooning, NASCAR racing, whitewater rafting or ice hockey. The Lora Robins Gallery of Design from Nature has a top-notch collection of fine minerals, gems, fossils and rare seashells.

Historical Sites: Pick from a list of dozens of important sites in Richmond. There's the Maggie Walker National Historic Site, Maymont, the John Marshall House, Black History Museum and Cultural Center of Virginia, Agecroft Hall, Wilton House, the Edgar Allan Poe Museum and Old Stone House, to name only a few. Various tours are available. Ask for details at the convention and visitors bureau.

Shopping: Owens Books, 2728 Tinsley Drive (804-272-8888) has Civil War publications, maps, and new, used, rare and out-of-print books. The Richmond Arsenal, 7605 Midlothian Turnpike (804-272-4570), buys, sells and trades Civil War artifacts.

The propietor is almost as well known as the equipment at Bob Moates Sports Shop (10418 Hull Street, Midlothian, 804-276-2293). Moates often portrays CSA Gen. Robert E. Lee in Civil War functions.

Downtown 6th Street Marketplace covers three blocks between the Coliseum and Grace Street. The Shops of Libbie and Grove avenues in the West End sell jewelry, antiques and gift items. Also in the West End is Carytown, a stretch of Cary Street near I-195 with blocks of unique stores and shops. Regency Square, in the West End, and Willow Lawn, on Broad Street nearer downtown, are two malls with hundreds of places to shop and dine.

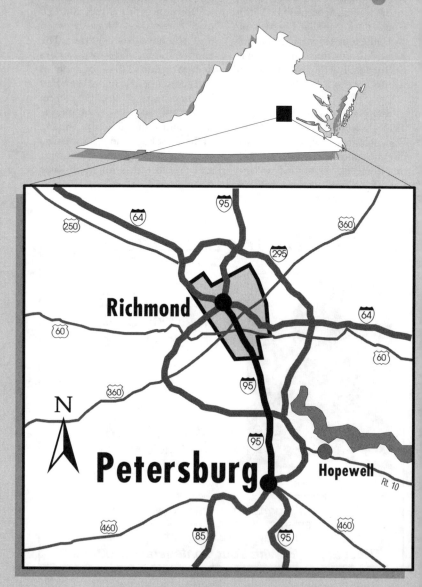

TOUR 13
Richmond to Petersburg

Tour 13
Petersburg

About This Tour

This tour route covers the city of Petersburg, VA, and its environs. This tour continues after Tour 12: Richmond. In fact, this route begins just south of Richmond. There is a side trip to City Point in Hopewell, and the remainder of the tour has stops in downtown and surrounding Petersburg. This tour route concludes in Petersburg, where we suggest you plan evening dining and lodging.

Travel Tips

This tour route begins on busy I-95. It is best to avoid this heavily used interstate during morning and evening rush-hour periods. As with other tours along interstate highways, this route uses convenient mile markers as guide posts for making exits and measuring distances. Petersburg is a busy place, and traffic often is congested, particularly in the downtown area.

History, Geography

Petersburg, like Washington, Fredericksburg and Richmond, sits on the "fall line" — the natural dividing line that separates the coastal plain to the east and the rolling piedmont to the west. Hopewell and Colonial Heights, two separate cities located between Richmond and Petersburg, sit along the banks of the Appomattox River, which joins the James River at Hopewell. Petersburg, also a port city on the Appomattox, traces its origins to the mid-1600s, when Abraham Wood established Fort Henry as a trading post in the far "western" reaches of colonial, tidewater Virginia. Capt. Peter Jones married Wood's daughter, and he developed the settlement at Fort Henry. In time, it became known as Peter's Point — and, later, Petersburg. In 1781, British Gen. Benedict Arnold raided the community during the American Revolution. Gen. Lafayette, a Frenchman serving the colonial forces, camped across the Appomattox River at Colonial Heights. Eventually, Petersburg became a major commercial center, serving as a central hub for Southside Virginia farmers who shipped their crops — mainly tobacco — to eastern markets. With the advent of the railroad, Petersburg rivaled Richmond as a major transportation center that linked points throughout Virginia.

In the summer of 1864, Union and Confederate troops clashed at Petersburg. It was the beginning of a long Union siege that lasted until the spring of 1865. CSA Gen. Robert E. Lee began his final retreat from the Petersburg area in March 1865, and surrendered to USA Gen. Grant at Appomattox in April that year.

Getting Here

Petersburg is just south of Richmond. This tour route suggests traveling south from Richmond to Petersburg on I-95.

DIRECTIONS

Richmond to Drewry's Bluff
Exit Richmond on I-95 south, crossing the James River at mile marker (MM) 74. Continue south 7 miles to Chippenham Parkway at MM 67. Take the Chippenham Parkway west a mile to the US 1/301 intersection, and continue south on US 1/301 for 2.4 miles to VA 656. Take the left turn (east) onto VA 656 (Bellwood Road), and go half a mile, just beyond the I-95 overpass, to Fort Darling Road. Turn left (north) on Fort Darling Road and continue parallel to I-95 for half a mile to the entrance to Drewry's Bluff, which is part of the Richmond National Battlefield Park.

DREWRY'S BLUFF

This site, with a 90-foot bluff and a commanding view of the James River, was named for a local landowner, Capt. Augustus H. Drewry. The James River was navigable from Hampton Roads at Norfolk to Richmond, and this made the threat of a Union attack on Richmond a continuous threat during the Civil War. A Confederate fortification was constructed at Drewry's Bluff during the first month of the war, and it remained in existence throughout the war's four years. Confederate naval vessels fought off Union boats at the base of Drewry's Bluff in May 1862, saving Richmond from a Union assault.

Until the spring of 1864, Drewry's Bluff was used for naval training and as a Richmond fortification. Union Gen. Butler advanced within 3 miles of this area in May 1864, but his troops were stopped by a counterattack by CSA Gen. P.G.T. Beauregard. In early April 1865, soldiers and sailors defending Drewry's Bluff were part of the mass Confederate retreat that ended at Appomattox. That month, President Lincoln passed by Drewry's Bluff on his way up the James River.

This fortification also was known as Fort Darling by the Federals. Today, Drewry's Bluff is part of the Richmond National Battlefield Park system (see Tour 12: Richmond).

DIRECTIONS

Drewry's Bluff to Petersburg
Continue south on US 1/301 to the intersection with VA 10. Turn left (west) on VA 10 a half-mile to I-95.

CITY POINT UNIT, PETERSBURG NATIONAL BATTLEFIELD

Cedar Lane
Hopewell, VA   *804-458-9504*
For nearly ten months, beginning in June 1864, USA Gen. Grant made his headquarters here. Grant moved his Army of the Potomac to Hopewell after major fighting at the Wilderness, Spotsylvania Court House and Cold Harbor. Grant

City Point, Hopewell

From VA 10 and I-95 (exit 61-A), take VA 10 east 7.5 miles across the Appomattox River and into downtown Hopewell on Randolph Road. Just inside the downtown area, take Main Street north (left) a block to Appomattox Street, and north on Appomattox Street for one mile to Cedar Lane. Go left on Cedar Lane two blocks (0.3 miles) to City Point Unit, which is part of the Petersburg National Battlefield system.

Petersburg
Side Trip

chose City Point for a reason: this small river port community was connected to Petersburg by rail, and the town gave him a strategic link with both Hampton Roads to the east and Washington, D.C. to the north.

Grant set up his headquarters at Appomattox Manor, the home of Dr. Richard Eppes. The homesite was a century old by the time Grant erected his tent on the front lawn. Here, Grant coordinated an operation that included constructing buildings and new wharves, as well as a major telegraph system to relay information from Washington to the battlefield and back. Almost overnight, this sleepy community of about 100 residents was turned into a supply center for 100,000 Union soldiers.

Members of a Confederate Peace Commission visited Grant at his headquarters in January 1865. The meeting was an attempt by Southern leaders to negotiate an end to the four-year-old Civil War. From here, Grant had the Confederates escorted to Hampton Roads for a meeting with President Lincoln.

The president visited City Point twice. He joined Grant in June 1864 for a visit to the Petersburg front. The president was back in March 1865, and spent two weeks in meetings with Grant, USA Gen. Sherman, and USA Adm. Porter on the

Photo: Richmond Newspapers

Guns like this one at Drewry's Bluff stopped Union gunboats from moving up the James River toward Richmond.

president's ship, the *River Queen*, docked just off shore. A day after the meeting, Grant moved closer to the Petersburg front and began his final spring offensive against Petersburg. Richmond and Petersburg fell to Grant's troops less than a week later.

City Point is open from 8 AM to 4:30 PM every day except Christmas and New Year's Day.

DIRECTIONS

Leaving City Point

Return on Cedar Lane and Appomattox street to Randolph Street and VA 10 to I-95.

From I-95 and VA 10 (exit 61-A), continue south on I-95 to Petersburg and take exit 52. Off the exit ramp, go west (right) onto Washington Street and continue three blocks to Sycamore Street. Turn right (north) on Sycamore Street and go five blocks to Old Street. Make a right on Old Street and go a block to the Petersburg Visitor's Center parking lot. There are ample directional signs throughout downtown to the parking area.

SEE HOW
THE CIVIL WAR
WAS WON
VISIT
CITY POINT,
VIRGINIA

1-800-863-TOUR

A NATIONAL
HISTORIC DISTRICT IN
HOPEWELL, VIRGINIA

PETERSBURG VISITOR'S CENTER

425 Cockade Alley
Petersburg, VA 23804   *804-733-2400*
800-368-3595

This visitor's facility is located in the attractive McIlwaine House, which was built in the early 1800s by Petersburg Mayor George Jones. The center is open seven days a week — except Thanksgiving Day and Christmas Day — from 9 AM to 5 PM. There is ample parking in the lot across from the center, and the center offers three hours of parking free. Tour guides are available.

A fire in 1815 wiped out much of Petersburg's Old Towne. Once a collection of wooden warehouses and homes, the community rebuilt after the fire, and a number of handsome Federal style brick buildings from this time survive. Petersburg was a major river port trading center during the Civil War.

At the beginning of the Civil War, Virginia had an African American population of nearly a half million, including 490,000 slaves and more than 50,000 free blacks. Half of Petersburg's 18,000 population was African American; about 15 percent were free black. Thus, Petersburg had more free blacks than any Southern city at the time the war began.

"The key to taking Richmond is Petersburg," said USA Gen. Grant, referring to the four rail lines and major roads that converged at Petersburg and provided supplies and equipment to Richmond and the Confederacy. Grant and his counterpart, CSA Gen. Robert E. Lee dug in at Petersburg. The result: a 10-month struggle in which Grant slowly forced Lee to retreat. The Petersburg experience has been called the longest siege in American warfare.

Petersburg was stuck by a major tornado in the summer of 1993. The natural disaster leveled a number of prominent downtown businesses and homes. Nevertheless, the Petersburg community has united to rebuild — again. Following the disaster, billboards throughout town featured a brief message from City Manager Valerie Lemmie: "We will rise and we will prosper."

DIRECTIONS

Petersburg Visitor's Center to Siege Museum

Walking west from the visitor's center, stroll along Old Street back to Sycamore Street, and go south (left) on Sycamore Street and up the hill a block to Bank Street. Turn right (west) on Bank Street and go half a block to the Siege Museum.

SIEGE MUSEUM

15 W. Bank St.
Petersburg, VA 23803   804-733-2404

This museum is located in the old Exchange Building, which was built in 1839 as a commodities market. It was restored in 1976-1977. The museum tells how the people of Petersburg lived before, during and immediately after the Civil War. There are a number of excellent exhibits, including such subjects as manufacturing, tobacco, cotton, foundry products, transportation, the care of the wounded during the war, and the role of women during the war. A film is shown regularly. This museum is open from 10 AM to 5 PM every day except New Year's Day, Thanksgiving Day, and Christmas Day. Admission is charged: $2.00 for adults and $1.50 for seniors and children ages 6 to 12. Childen younger than 6 are admitted for free.

DIRECTIONS

Siege Museum to Centre Hill Mansion

From the Siege Museum, return to Sycamore Street, turn right (south) on Sycamore Street and walk two blocks up the hill to E. Tabb Street — which is adjacent to the Petersburg Courthouse. Turn left (east) on E. Tabb Street and walk a block to Adams Street. There are 19 steps leading up the hill to Centre Hill Mansion.

CENTRE HILL MANSION

1 Centre Hill Circle
Petersburg, VA 23803   804-733-2401
                              800-368-3595

Richard Bolling, a member of a prominent Petersburg family, built Centre Hill Mansion in 1823. It was

A Pennsylvania Chaplain

There is one exhibit at the Siege Museum that features a letter written in April 1865 by an unidentified Pennsylvania chaplain. It reads:

"On April 3, 1865, the guns fell silent. The great feature of the road between here and Petersburg is the debris of two armies. Broken guns, castaway garments, dead horses and mules, broken down wagons, etc., are strewn all over the ground. Many of the houses are burned.... The few inhabitants remaining are old men and women, children, and Negroes.... It will take a generation to repair the loss."

Siege Museum Personality

constructed of oversize brick in Flemish bond. Later, the 25-room house was remodeled in the Greek Revival design of the 1840s. Downstairs is a view of a tunnel that once connected the mansion with the Appomattox River. The mansion was visited by President Lincoln and USA Gen. Grant. Recently, an adjacent five-story apartment building was demolished, giving the mansion a panoramic view of downtown Petersburg. Open 10 AM to 5 PM every day except Christmas. The mansion has a guided tour, a museum, and a gift shop. Admission is $2.00 for adults and $1.50 for seniors and children 6 to 12. Children younger than 6 are admitted for free.

DIRECTIONS

Centre Hill Mansion to Petersburg Visitors Center
Return to the visitor's center by taking E. Tabb, Sycamore and Old streets.

DIRECTIONS

Petersburg Visitor's Center to Blandford Church
From the visitor's center resume your Petersburg tour by automobile. Take Old Street back to Sycamore Street, and turn left (south) on Sycamore Street. Continue on Sycamore for five blocks, one block beyond Washington Street (one-way west) to Wythe Street (one-way east). Turn left (east) on W. Wythe Street and continue a block beyond the I-95 overpass to Crater Road (US 360 south). At Crater Road, turn right (south) and go 0.2 miles to Blandford Church on the left.

BLANDFORD CHURCH, RECEPTION CENTER

111 Rochelle Lane
Petersburg, VA 23805   *804-733-2396*

Built in 1735, this fine old church was abandoned when the town of Blandford was absorbed by Petersburg. In 1901, the Ladies Memorial Association of Petersburg developed Blandford Church into a Confederate shrine for the 30,000 Southern soldiers buried — by the state — in the church cemetery. That's when Louis Comfort Tiffany was called on to design a series of breathtaking stained glass windows. Each window was donated by a Confederate state in honor of native sons who died in the Civil War. Over the main door is the only Tiffany window in the world that features the Confederate battle flag.

Behind the church, along with the Confederate buried, are a number of weathered old tombstones that date to the early 18th century. Confederate Memorial Day, June 9, is observed here each year. The church has a visitor center and small gift shop. The church can be seen daily from 10 AM to 5 PM. Admission is $2.00 for adults and $1.50 for seniors and children ages 6 to 12. Children younger than 6 are admitted for free.

DIRECTIONS

Blandford Church to Petersburg National Battlefield
Return north 0.2 miles on Crater Road to Wythe Street. Turn right (east) on Wythe Street (VA 36) and continue east 2 miles (Wythe Street leads to E. Washington Street, or VA 36 east) to the Petersburg National Battlefield entrance.

Photo: City of Petersburg Department of Tourism

The Blandford Church, built in 1735, was restored as a Confederate shrine in 1901, honoring the 30,000 soldiers buried in the surrounding churchyard.

Blandford Church
Personality

Mary Logan

U.S. Congressman John Alexander Logan, a former Union general, and his wife, Mary Logan, visited Petersburg in 1867. They were taken by the sight of children placing flowers on the graves of Civil War casualties at Blandford Church. Returning to Washington, Mrs. Logan urged her husband to establish a national observance in honor of Civil War dead, and it led to a proclamation issued in early 1868 by the Grand Army of the Republic. Later that year, on May 30, 1868, Decoration Day — later known as Memorial Day — was celebrated nationally for the first time. Two years earlier, in May 1866, the first known Southern memorial day was observed on the second anniversary of the Battle of New Market in Virginia's Shenandoah Valley (see Tour 3: Shenandoah Valley).

PETERSBURG NATIONAL BATTLEFIELD
Va. 36
Petersburg, VA 23804   804-732-3531

This major facility, operated by the National Park Service (NPS), contains nearly 2,500 acres just east of downtown Petersburg. The visitor center is open daily from 8 AM to 5 PM. It is closed only on New Year's Day and Christmas Day. An admission fee is charged. The NPS offers exhibits, a film, and a small publications center. There is a 16-mile driving tour that covers all the major historical sites at Petersburg Battlefield. The NPS offers a superb brochure that includes detailed information on more than 15 separate sites, including Fort Sedgwick, Poplar Grove Cemetery, Fort Fisher, Fort Gregg, and Five Forks.

Department of Tourism
800-368-3595

PETERS BURG VIRGINIA

UNEXPECTED PLEASURES...
Petersburg National Battlefield

DIRECTIONS

Petersburg Battlefield to Fort Lee Quartermaster Museum

From Petersburg Battlefield on VA 36, go east a half mile to the main entrance to Fort Lee, a U.S. Army installation. Enter Fort Lee on Lee Avenue and turn left at the first intersection — A Avenue. Take A Avenue one block to the Quartermaster Museum on the left. Parking is to the museum's side and rear.

U.S. ARMY QUARTERMASTER MUSEUM

A Ave., Fort Lee
Petersburg, VA 23801   804-734-4203

The U.S. Army Quartermaster Corps was founded in 1775, just two days after the U.S. Army itself was established. Today, Fort Lee is the U.S. Army Quartermaster Center. The museum has a number of exhibits on military uniforms, flags, transportation equipment, food services, and memorial activities. Among the items featured at the museum are Gen. Dwight D. Eisenhower's uniforms and Gen. George Patton's World War II jeep. There is a gift shop.

The Quartermaster Museum is open Tuesday to Friday, 10 AM to 5 PM, and Saturday and Sunday from 11:30 AM to 4:30 PM. It is closed on Mondays, New Year's Day, Thanksgiving, and Christmas. There is free admission.

DIRECTIONS

To return to downtown Petersburg, drive west on VA 36, which becomes Washington Street, into town.

Coal Miners and African American Troops

One Union regiment, the 48th Pa., included a number of coal miners from the mountains of Pennsylvania. The regiment was commanded by Lt. Col. Henry Pleasants, a mining engineer before the Civil War. Pleasants devised a unique plan, approved by his superior officers, that his miner/troops dig a mine under a Confederate fort and trenches, fill it with powder, and set off an explosion.

The 500-foot tunnel was completed after a month's work in the summer of 1864. Then, USA Gen. Burnside was given the task of attacking the enemy through a gap made by the mine's explosion. African American troops were specially trained for the mission, but later were withdrawn after Union officers feared political repercussions. Looking for white soldiers to replace the black troops, Burnside ordered three division commanders to draw straws to determine who would lead the mine assault.

After a faulty fuse failed to set off the 320 kegs — 8,000 pounds — of explosives, two miner/soldiers succeeded in lighting the powder at sunrise on July 30. The destruction left a crater more than 150 long, 60 feet wide and 30 feet deep. More than 250 Confederates were killed or wounded. Fighting ensued, and a Union assault combined with a Southern counterattack left thousands of casualties on both sides. A number of Union officers later were found to be responsible for the "stupendous failure," as Grant deemed the events at the crater.

Petersburg Battlefield Personalities

Winfield Scott

Virginia-born military hero Winfield Scott died in May 1866 at West Point, 15 days shy of his 80th birthday. Some of the most illustrious public figures of the day attended his funeral He was the only Southern, non-West Point general who remained loyal to the Union during the Civil War.

Scott was born in Dinwiddie County, near Petersburg, in June 1786 — a year before the U.S. Constitution was adopted. In 1807, at the age of 21, he rode to Richmond to observe the famous trial of Aaron Burr.

He was a hero of several American military conflicts, particularly the Mexican War. During the Mexican War, Scott had the distinction of commanding two young officers named Ulysses S. Grant and Robert E. Lee. In 1861, nearly 75 years old, he was general-in-chief of the U.S. Army at the beginning of the Civil War.

He was an associate of every president from Thomas Jefferson to Abraham Lincoln. Known as "Ol' Fuss and Feathers," he played a role in ending two wars, saved the country from several others, and made a number of scholarly contributions to military tactics and procedures. Frequently mentioned as a presidential candidate, his one significant campaign ended in defeat to President Franklin Pierce.

Eight years after his death, in 1874, a statue of Scott was erected at Scott Circle in Washington, D.C. It was cast from cannon captured in the Mexican War (see Tour 9: Washington).

On April 1, 1865 the Battle of Five Forks was fought 5 miles north of Dinwiddie County Court House. The battle — known as the "Waterloo of the Confederacy" — broke the siege of Petersburg and led to the ultimate fall of Richmond. The next day, Confederates evacuated Richmond and Petersburg; Union troops occupied Richmond the day after that.

Petersburg Accommodations

Refer to the Foreward for an explanation of the rating system for both the accommodations and restaurants.

MAYFIELD INN BED AND BREAKFAST
3348 W. Washington St., P.O. Box 2265
Petersburg, VA 23804   804-733-0866
$$$ 804-861-6775

If you've dreamed of staying in an elegant, historic Southern home, this bed and breakfast offers you the perfect chance. Built in the 1750s, Mayfield is the oldest existing brick house in Dinwiddie County. It's a state and national historic landmark, and is considered one of the finest mid-18th century residences in the state. Two defense lines were established on Mayfield property during the siege of Petersburg in the Civil War. Jamie and Dot Caudle have restored and furnished Mayfield with antiques and period reproductions. The owners offer two double bedrooms and two suites, along with four acres of attractive grounds, a

40-foot outdoor heated pool, and a full country-style breakfast. Take Washington Street (US 1/460 west) 3 miles west of downtown to Petersburg's western city limits. The inn is on the left.

COMFORT INN
11974 S. Crater Road
Petersburg, VA 23805   804-732-2900
$$

Built just five years ago, this 96-room Comfort Inn is pleasant and inviting. Located in a quieter section of Petersburg, away from interstate traffic, this facility offers a continental breakfast and an outdoor pool. From downtown, take South Crater Road (US 301 South) 6 miles south.

HOLIDAY INN
I-95 and Washington St.
Petersburg, VA 23803   804-733-0730
$$ 800-HOLIDAY

Located along the heavily traveled I-95 corridor, this Holiday Inn is just a half mile north of the interchange of I-95 and I-85. Rooms at this Holiday Inn were only recently remodeled. A full-service Mini-Mart offers snacks, magazines, and essentials. From downtown, take Wythe Street (one-way east) to Washington Street, and then back track on Washington Street to the Holiday Inn. Better yet, look for the familiar Holiday Inn logo sign.

Petersburg Restaurants

NANNY'S FAMILY RESTAURANT
11900 S. Crater Road
Petersburg, VA 23805   804-733-6619
$

This is the place for excellent food, family atmosphere, friendly service and inexpensive dinners — it's a real gem. Linda Stewart, her husband, Ronnie, and their two college-age sons, Tim and Jeff, serve some of the finest barbeque and chicken around. Remember, this is Brunswick Stew area, and Nanny's has a great recipe. *The New York Times* mentioned Nanny's Brunswick Stew in a 1993 article. With seating for more than 100, including a no-smoking section, this is a very popular local hangout. Nanny's also has banquet facilities and a catering service. You don't need reservations because there's plenty of room. Your Petersburg visit is incomplete until you've dined at Nanny's. Take S. Crater Road (US 301 South) out of downtown. Nanny's is near the Comfort Inn (see listing above).

ALEXANDER'S
101 W. Bank St.
Petersburg, VA 23804   804-733-7134
$$

This is another local hangout, and the food is exceptional. The dining room is cramped, so there's no separate area for nonsmokers. Still, patrons flock to Alexander's for breakfast, lunch and dinner. Family-style dinners include leg of lamb, lasagna, chicken parmesean, and a variety of salads and desserts. Alexander's offers take-out orders and catering. Open Monday and Tuesday from 9 AM to 3:30 PM, and Wednesday through Saturday from 9 AM to 8:30 PM. Alexander's was slightly damaged during the August 1993 tornado, but it reopened 12 days later and operated in the midst of building repair work all along Bank and Old streets. The restaurant is located two doors down from the Siege Museum (see listing).

ANNABELLE'S RESTAURANT AND PUB
2733 Park Ave.
Petersburg, VA 23805   804-732-0997
$$

This restaurant was built within the walls of an old, stone dairy barn. There are a number of old collectibles —including a used gas street lamp— to make the visit intriguing and interesting. The American-style menu offers a variety of choices, from beef and chicken to seafood and pasta. Annabelle's is part of a Southern chain. It's open Monday through Thursday from 11:30 AM to 11 PM; Friday and Saturday from 11:30 AM to midnight; and Sunday from noon to 10 PM. A children's menu and a no-smoking section are available. Take Sycamore Street south from downtown to S. Crater Road. Turn right (south) on S. Crater Road and go past the N&W road overpass and take the third right onto Park Avenue. Annabelle's sits behind Burger King and Kentucky Fried Chicken; it has ample parking.

Other Petersburg Attractions

Petersburg offers a number of unique attractions and points of interest. For questions or reservations, ask for help at the Petersburg Visitor's Center (see listing). Also check in with the Hopewell Visitors Center, 201-D Randolph Square, just off VA 10 in downtown Hopewell (telephone 804-541-2206).

Annual Events: The Appomattox Batteau Day and the Battersea Ball (see Battersea under Historical Sites below) are both held each year in September. In addition, Petersburg offers garden and house tours, sports events, and a candlelight Christmas tour during the year.

Antiques: Old Towne Petersburg, all along Old Street and River Street, has a number of antique shops. In addition, South Side Station on River Street has a flea market that offers crafts, collectibles, maps, memorabilia, Civil War items, gifts and "Made in Virginia" goods.

Arts: The Petersburg Symphony Orchestra offers a season of classical, modern and popular music. Founded in 1978, the Petersburg Symphony is a full symphonic orchestra with 65 musicians. The Petersburg Public Forum offers headline speakers throughout the year. Original art can be purchased in the spring at the Poplar Lawn Art Festival. The Petersburg Art League opens new art exhibits monthly at its warehouse on Rock Street.

Historical Sites: Battersea is a Palladian-style country house that was built in the 1770s by John Bannister, Petersburg's first mayor. The First Baptist Church on Harrison Street is home of the nation's oldest African American congregation. The Trapezium House on Market Street, built in 1817 by Charles O'Hara, doesn't have a parallel wall. O'Hara learned from his West Indian servant that such an odd-shaped structure would prevent evil spirits from settling in.

In Hopewell, a boat tour of historical sites is available aboard the *Pocahontas II*, which seats 90 and operates from April through October. The City of Hopewell operates a visitor center at 201-D Randolph Square. For information on Hopewell's historical sites and other attractions, as well as lodging and dining listings, contact travel counselors at the visitor center (804-541-2206).

Violet Bank Museum (303 Virginia Avenue, Colonial Heights, VA) is owned by the City of Colonial Heights and boasts original woodwork and some of the most beautiful Adams-style ceiling moulding in the nation. The museum is located at the site where CSA Gen. Lee set up his headquarters tent in 1864 and learned of the explosion of the Crater during the Siege of Petersburg. The museum is open Tuesday through Saturday from 10:00 AM to 5:00 PM, and Sunday from 1:00 to 6:00 PM. It is closed on Mondays. For more information, call 804-520-9395.

For more information on the entire area, write Box 35140, Richmond 23235, or call 804-541-2616.

Shopping: The Old Towne and Courthouse historic districts have a wide variety of shops and stores. In addition, there is an extensive collection of businesses along Crater Road South (US 301 South). Take Sycamore Street south from downtown for 4 miles to Crater Road.

Art by H. Kidd

VIOLET BANK MUSEUM
General R.E. Lee's Headquarters • 1864
303 Virginia Ave.   Colonial Heights, VA
1 mi north of Petersburg, off Rt 301 & I-95
Open: Tues-Sat 10-5; Sun 1-6

TOUR 14

Petersburg to Lynchburg

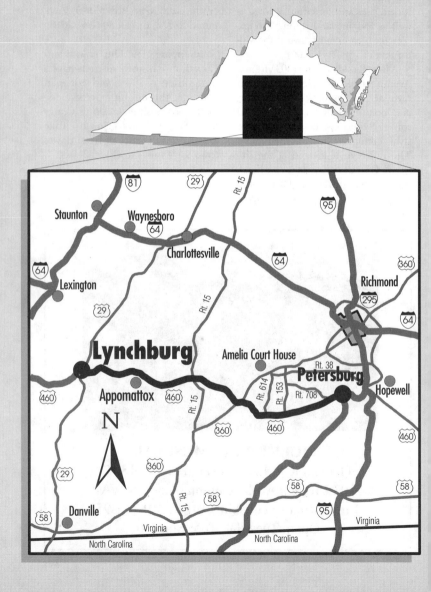

Tour 14
Southside

About This Tour

This tour route is a natural continuation of Tour 13: Petersburg. It begins at Petersburg, VA, and runs west across Virginia's "Southside" to Appomattox, VA. This tour route roughly follows CSA Gen. Robert E. Lee's nine-day retreat that began west of Petersburg and concluded at Appomattox.

This tour concludes at Appomattox, but lodging and dining recommendations are in Lynchburg, VA, a few miles to the west. Our sister publication, *The Insiders' Guide to Virginia's Blue Ridge*, will also be helpful.

Travel Tips

US 460 is a dual-lane, divided highway in this section of southern Virginia. This is tobacco country, with rolling hills along the route from the "fall line" at Petersburg to the base of the Blue Ridge Mountains at Lynchburg.

History, Geography

Virginia's Southside is a wide geographic band that runs west-to-east between the eastern flowing Appomattox River and the Virginia border with North Carolina. Native Americans, mainly the Nottoway and Appomattox tribes, lived in this region prior to the 17th century, after which Anglo Americans pushed west out of the Virginia Tidewater to begin settling the region. The main river in this area is the Appomattox, named for the Native American tribe, which originates in Appomattox County and flows east to Hopewell. County names reflect the region's Native American heritage and the influence of western-moving Anglo settlers.

Nottoway and Appomattox counties, of course, are named for the Native Americans who lived here. Amelia is named for the daughter of England's King George II; Lunenburg is named for one of the German possessions of England's Hanoverian kings; Cumberland is named for Amelia's brother, William Augustus, the Duke of Cumberland and the third son of King George II (see Tour 1: Cumberland Valley); Prince Edward is named for King George III's nephew, Prince Edward Augustus; and Charlotte honors the teenage queen and wife of King George III (see Charlottesville in Tour 8: Southern Piedmont).

In late March 1865, following the fall of Richmond and Petersburg, CSA Gen. Robert E. Lee and his troops began a western retreat. Just over a week later, on April 9, the retreat ended at the small village of Appomattox, on the rail line from Lynchburg to Petersburg. The series of battles that took place during this period are sometimes known as the Appomattox Campaign, and also "Lee's Retreat."

Lynchburg, located west of Appomattox, is known as the City of Seven Hills. This bustling city is located on the James River near the eastern slopes of the Blue Ridge Mountains. In the years preceding the Civil War, Lynchburg's position as a major business hub was enhanced by the railroad line that followed the river bed east to Richmond.

Getting Here

This tour route is a continuation of Tour 13: Petersburg. It begins just west of Petersburg and continues west to Appomattox and, finally, Lynchburg.

DIRECTIONS

Petersburg to Namozine Church, VA
Leave Petersburg on W. Washington Street, or US 1/460. Outside town, and beyond the US 1/460 interchange with I-85, this route is known as the Boydton Plank Road, which leads south to Dinwiddie Courthouse and to Five Forks, scene of a major battle on April 1, 1865. Just beyond I-85, along US 1/460 and just to the north of the highway, is the place where noted CSA Gen. Hill was killed.

Petersburg Personality

Source: Richmond Newspapers

A. P. Hill

Affectionately known as "A.P.," Hill was christened "Ambose Powell." A native of Culpeper, VA, Hill graduated from West Point in 1847 at the age of 22. He served in the Mexican War, and then signed on with the Confederate Army in 1861 as an infantry colonel. He rose to the rank of major general a year later. Hill achieved distinction at Antietam, and in 1863, after Fredericksburg and Chancellorsville, he was promoted to lieutenant general and command of a corps for CSA Gen. Robert E. Lee. A veteran of Gettysburg and the Wilderness, he led a retreat from Petersburg in 1865. Hill was killed near Petersburg on April 2, just days before the Confederate surrender at Appomattox.

DIRECTIONS

Continue on US 1/460 south. Two miles farther south, US 460 splits from US 1. Turn right (west) on US 460 and continue west 6 miles to Sutherland. Take VA 708 (Claiborne Road) to the right (north) for 10.7 miles to Namozine Church. This stretch of VA 708, also known as Namozine Road, is a single lane, rural roadway; the Virginia countryside looks much as it did in Civil War days. The Namozine Church sits on the left at the intersection of VA 708 and VA 622.

NAMOZINE CHURCH

This small, unassuming box-like structure was built in 1847. Events here reflect the quickly changing luck of the retreating Confederates: the church was a Confederate headquarters on the morning of April 3, 1865, and by nightfall, following a cavalry battle, it was a Union stronghold.

DIRECTIONS

Namozine Church to Amelia Courthouse, VA

From the church, continue north on VA 708 (Namozine Road), a small country road. Stay on VA 708 for 6 miles to Mannboro, and 4 more miles to VA 153. Turn right (north) on VA 153 and continue 3 miles to Scotts Fort. At Scotts Fort, turn left (west) on VA 38 and go 6 miles into downtown Amelia Courthouse.

AMELIA COURTHOUSE, VA

This community is the county seat of Amelia County. Confederate forces retreating from both Richmond and Petersburg converged here. CSA Gen. Robert E. Lee spent April 4 and 5 in Amelia, hoping to find cars of badly needed supplies from the Richmond and Danville Railroad. This delay was doubly costly: the supplies never came, and the Confederates lost a full day in their escape from the pursuing Federals. This almost became the site of the Confederate surrender. The statue on the courthouse lawn honors Virginia's Confederate soldiers.

DIRECTIONS

Amelia to Jetersville, VA

From Amelia Courthouse, continue a half-mile on VA 38 to US 360. Turn left (west) on US 360 and continue 7 miles to Jetersville.

JETERSVILLE, VA

USA Gen. Sheridan anticipated that CSA Gen. Robert E. Lee, retreating from Amelia, might shift his forces south toward Danville. So, Sheridan lay in wait at Jetersville (also known as Amelia Springs) for the retreating Lee. Lee countered by shifting north, thus avoiding a major confrontation with Sheridan here at this small railroad stop.

DIRECTIONS

Jetersville to Sailor's Creek Battlefield Historical State Park

Continue west on US 360 for 2.5 miles to VA 307. Turn right (north) on VA 307 (follow signs for Sailor's Creek) and go 6 miles to VA 617. Along the way, this route crosses over Sailor's Creek, the small stream for which the battle is named. Turn right (north) on VA 617 and go 6 miles to the Sailor's Creek Battlefield Historical State Park and the Hillsman House on the right.

SAILOR'S CREEK BATTLEFIELD HISTORICAL STATE PARK

Twin Lakes State Park
Green Bay, VA 23942   804-392-3435

CSA Gen. Robert E. Lee pushed west, avoiding a major confrontation with Union troops at Jetersville. Spring rains turned area streams into mud holes, and Lee's men and their supply wagons got mired at Sailor's Creek. The battle at Sailor's Creek was fought on April 6. It has the dubious distinction of being the last major battle of the Civil War. Meanwhile, Union soldiers fired on Confederates at Hillsman House. In time, CSA Gens. Anderson and Ewell surrendered. Lee lost half his army — the largest unstipulated surrender on the continent. By now, Appomattox was just 72 hours away. The Hillsman House, used as a Civil War hospital, is open for living history programs in the summer months.

DIRECTIONS

Sailor's Creek to Rice, VA

Return south on VA 617 to VA 307. Turn right (west) on VA 307 and go 7 miles to US 460. Go west on US 460 to Rice.

RICE, VA

Rice, known then as Rice's Station, was the scene of minor skirmishing on April 7. Rice was named for William Rice, who built a church here in the mid-18th century.

DIRECTIONS

Rice to Farmville, VA

From Rice, take US 460 west and US 460 BUS, 6 miles to Farmville. Follow signs for Farmville's historic district along US 460 BUS (Third Street).

FARMVILLE, VA

USA Gen. Grant's men burned High Bridge on the Appomattox River near Farmville.

DIRECTIONS

Farmville to Appomattox Visitor Information Center

From downtown Farmville, take US 460 BUS west for 4 miles and get back on US 460 west, a dual lane, divided highway. Continue for 27 miles and follow signs to downtown Appomattox. A mile farther on US 460 (Confederate Blvd.), turn left (south) at the traffic signal onto Court Street, and follow signs for Appomattox Visitor Information Center. Take Court Street for 0.6 mile, and turn right onto Main Street and 0.2 mile to the visitor's center parking lot on the right.

Cumberland Church

Two miles north of Farmville, on VA 45 (the extension of Main Street north), is Cumberland Church in Cumberland County. CSA Gen. Robert E. Lee was at this white-columned church on April 7 when he received USA Gen. Grant's first note that sought a surrender. Return on VA 45 to downtown Farmville.

APPOMATTOX VISITOR INFORMATION CENTER

Main St., P.O. Box 704
Appomattox, VA 24522   804-352-2621

This visitor's center is located in the town's old train depot. It is open seven days a week from 9 AM to 5 PM and is closed on major holidays. This center offers information on various historical sites in the Appomattox area.

Appomattox was a rural county during the days of the civil War. Of the nearly 9,000 county residents, more than 54 percent were African American. Major fighting took place in this vicinity on April 8 and 9. Following the action on April 9, and swift action by USA Gens. Sheridan and Ord to block further escape, CSA Gen. Robert E. Lee realized that surrender was inevitable.

DIRECTIONS

Appomattox Information Center to Appomattox Court House National Historical Park

Return on Court Street to US 460. Turn left (west) on US 460 and go 0.1 mile to VA 24. Turn right (north) on VA 24 and go 2 miles to the National Park Service (NPS) facility entrance on the left.

APPOMATTOX COURT HOUSE NATIONAL HISTORICAL PARK

P.O. Box 218
Appomattox, VA 24522   804-352-8987

CSA Gen. Robert E. Lee surrendered to USA Gen. Grant here on April 9, 1865, ending the four-year Civil War. Three days later, on April 12, soldiers of Lee's Army of Northern Virginia laid down their arms

Photo: Richmond Newspapers

"The Surrender of General Lee to General Grant," was painted by L.M.D. Guillaume.

before Grant's Union army. Lee was on his way to Richmond; Grant already was in Washington.

The visit here begins in the visitor center in the reconstructed courthouse on the NPS grounds. The center offers an information desk downstairs and a museum upstairs. The park facility offers a village of restored and reconstructed buildings, including the McLean House, Meeks Store, the Woodson Law Office, Clover Hill Tavern, the old courthouse, jail, Kelly House, Mariah Wright House, surrender Triangle, Isbell House and Peers House. The NPS is open seven days a week. During summer months the hours are from 8:30 AM to 5 PM; after October the hours are 9 AM to 5 PM. The park charges a $2.00 fee for persons 17 to 61 years of age.

Photo: Ken Cady

The McLean House in Appomattox was the site of Lee and Grant's meeting on April 9, 1865.

Wilmer McLean

Consider the sad story of Wilmer McLean. Prior to the Civil War, McLean owned a house on the Bull Run in Northern Virginia. In 1861, during action at Manassas, an artillery shell fell down McLean's chimney and into a stew being prepared for CSA Gen. Beauregard. Seeking a more tranquil place to live, McLean bought a farm house at — of all places — Appomattox. McLean's house was chosen for the surrender meeting between USA Gen. Grant and CSA Gen. Robert E. Lee. The two military leaders met in McLean's parlor, after which Union officers stripped the room for souvenirs. The house was dismantled in 1893 for a war museum in Washington, D.C. The plan never materialized. The current house at the Appomattox Courthouse National Historical Park is a reconstruction. As for Wilmer McLean, the Civil War began in the kitchen of his first home . . . and ended in the parlor of his second home.

DIRECTIONS

Appomattox to Lynchburg Visitors Center

Return on VA 24 to US 460 in Appomattox. Turn right (west) onto US 460 BUS. After 0.2 miles, take a left and get back on US 460. Go 15.6 miles on US 460 to the Lynchburg city limits. Take the exit for 501 and 460 BUS at Campbell Avenue. Take Campbell for 1.6 miles and stay right on Kemper Street at the fork where Cambell Avenue veers left. Drop down the hill and follow signs for US 29. Take US 29 north (follow signs for Charlottesville), and go north two exits to the Main Street exit to right. Take the second right exit onto Main Street, go three blocks on Main Street to 12th Street, turn left onto 12th Street and go a block to the Visitors Information Center at the corner of 12th and Church streets.

LYNCHBURG VISITORS INFORMATION CENTER

216 12th St. at Church St.
Lynchburg, VA 24504   *804-847-1811*
                          800-849-0722

Lynchburg was chartered in 1786 by John Lynch and the community quickly became a center for the trade of tobacco, iron and agricultural products. Located on the James River, Lynchburg was connected to Richmond by the James River Kanawha Canal. Positioned near the base of the Blue Ridge Mountains, Lynchburg was a major rail and supply base and hospital center for the Confederate army. In June 1864, Union Gen. Hunter's troops were pushed back by soldiers serving with CSA Gen.

Breckinridge. CSA Gen. Early's troops arrived from Charlottesville by train in time to assist Breckinridge in the defense of Lynchburg.

DIRECTIONS

Lynchburg Visitors Information Center to Lynchburg Museum

From the Visitor's Center, go east on one-way Church Street for half a block to 13th Street, turn right on 13th Street and go a block to Court Street. Turn right on Court Street and go to 9th Street.

LYNCHBURG MUSEUM AT THE OLD COURTHOUSE

901 Court St.
Lynchburg, VA 24505   *804-847-1459*

This old courthouse is listed as a Virginia Historic Landmark, and it is on the National Register of Historic Places. Built in 1855 and designed as one of Virginia's outstanding Greek Revival civic buildings, the structure was restored in 1976 as part of Lynchburg's celebration of the American Bicentennial. Lynchburg's rich history is depicted in various exhibits, including one that incorporates Civil War artifacts. The museum is open daily from 1 to 4 PM. It is closed New Year's Day, Thanksgiving Day and Christmas Eve and Day. A fee of $1 for adults and 50 cents for children is charged. Across the street is Monument Terrace, with sculptures and commemorative markers of the Civil War, the Spanish American War and World War I. Lynchburg natives who fought in these wars are honored by a 139-step staircase memorial.

DIRECTIONS

Lynchburg Museum to City Cemetery

From the museum at 9th and Court streets, continue west on Court Street to 5th Street. At 5th Street, turn left (south) and go eight blocks to Taylor Street. At Taylor Street turn right (west) and drive to 4th Street and into City Cemetery.

CITY CEMETERY

Taylor and 4th Sts.
Lynchburg, VA 24505

Open from sunrise to sunset, this old cemetery is a Virginia Landmark and it is listed on the National Register of Historic Places. The first land for this cemetery was given by John Lynch, Lynchburg's founder. Established in 1806, the City Cemetery includes a section where 2,700 Confederate soldiers are buried.

PEST HOUSE MEDICAL MUSEUM

City Cemetery, Taylor and 4th Sts.
Lynchburg, VA 24505

The white farm building here within the grounds of City Cemetery was built in the 1840s. It was the medical office of Dr. John Jay Terrell. "Pest" is short for "pestilence." A number of Dr. Terrell's medical tools and equipment are on display here. The museum is open from sunrise to sunset. It offers self-guided tours, or special tours by appointment.

DIRECTIONS

City Cemetery to Spring Hill Cemetery

Leave the Medical Museum and City Cemetery on the winding, one-way roadway that exits onto Wise Street

at 5th Street. At 5th Street (US 29 BUS), turn right (south) and continue 1.3 miles past E.C. Glass High School and Park Avenue to Oakley Avenue (US 221). Turn left (east) on Oakley Avenue and go to Fort Avenue. The cemetery is located at the corner of Oakley and Fort avenues. To enter the cemetery, turn left from Oakley onto Fort. Avenue and go 100 yards to the cemetery entrance on the right

SPRING HILL CEMETERY

Fort and Oakley Aves.
Lynchburg, VA 24505

CSA Gen. Jubal A. Early, the man who helped save Lynchburg from USA Gen. Hunter's attack in 1864, is buried at Spring Hill Cemetery. Early commanded the 2nd Corps of the Confederate Army of Northern Virginia. After the Civil War, he made his home in Lynchburg, where he died in 1904. A number of other Confederate heroes and soldiers are buried at Spring Hill. The cemetery is open from sunrise to sunset.

DIRECTIONS

Spring Hill Cemetery to Fort Early

Exit the cemetery at Fort Avenue, turn left (south) on (this is also US 29 BUS, US 460 BUS), and continue 0.6 to the intersection of Fort and Memorial avenues and the entrance to Fort Early.

FORT EARLY

Memorial and Fort Aves.
Lynchburg, VA 24505

This is the site of the earthwork fortifications and the command post used by CSA Gen. Early during 1864 action in Lynchburg. The grounds can be toured from 7 AM to 7 PM, but the building, a 20th-century construction, is closed to the public. Across the street from the entrance is an obelisk that honors Early.

Lynchburg Accommodations

THE MADISON HOUSE BED AND BREAKFAST

413 Madison St.
Lynchburg, VA 24504   804-528-1503
$$$

This fine old Victorian home is located just off 5th Street — on the route between Lynchburg Museum and City Cemetery (see listing) — in the Garland Hill Historic District. The bed and breakfast offers antique-filled parlors and a library with numerous Civil War books. The Madison House features the Gold Room, the Blue Room, the Madison Suite, the Rose Room and the Veranda Room. Built by a tobacco baron, the home has original china bathroom fixtures, crystal chandeliers, a stained glass window and an 1850s English banquet table. The Madison House has a no smoking policy. Because of the antiques and

fixtures, the home does not allow children or pets.

LYNCHBURG MANSION INN BED AND BREAKFAST

405 Madison St.
Lynchburg, VA 24504   804-528-5400
$$$$ 800-352-1199

Located next door to the Madison House, this 9,000-square-foot Spanish Georgian Mansion is situated on a half-acre in the same Garland Hill Historic District. Built in 1914, the house features a fifty-foot Grand Hall and cherry and oak woodwork. Then, for wonderful touches, there are the lace bags of potpourri tied to bedposts and satin clothes hangers. Pets are prohibited, but "well behaved" children are welcome. Smoking is allowed only on the veranda. Bob and Mauranna Sherman certainly have a "mansion" here.

HOLIDAY INN CROWNE PLAZA LYNCHBURG

601 Main St.
Lynchburg, Va 24504   804-528-2500
$$

This lengthily named hotel was the Radisson until early in 1994. Located in the downtown business district, six blocks from the Visitors

Danville, VA

It's a long haul — 67 miles south on US 29 — from Lynchburg to Danville. And there's little Civil War history along the way to justify the hour-plus drive. But avid Civil War enthusiasts may want to make this particular side trip, especially to see the site of the last Capitol of the Confederacy. Danville's Sutherlin House, at 975 Main Street, was the place where William Sutherlin hosted Jefferson Davis, Confederate administrative officers and members of President Davis's cabinet as they fled Richmond at the end of the Civil War. One cabinet meeting was held in Danville before CSA Gen. Robert E. Lee surrendered at Appomattox.

Lynchburg Side Trip

Center, this Holiday Inn has more than 240 rooms. Children under 17 stay free with parents. The inn also features a weight room and an outdoor pool for summertime swimming. Non-smoking rooms are available. From the US 29 Bypass, take the Main Street exit and go six blocks west to Main and 6th Street.

Lynchburg Restaurants

SHAKERS

3401 Candlers Mountain Rd.
Lynchburg, VA 24502   804-847-7425
$$

This restaurant, located at the entrance to the River Ridge Mall, is a popular spot for locals. An all-American menu is offered: steaks, chicken, fish, salads, sandwiches and pasta. You'll find plenty of ficus trees and plants. Shakers has a lunch buffet and offers take-out service. There is a children's menu and a no smoking section. Shakers accepts credit cards but no personal checks. It is open Sunday through Thursday from 11 AM to midnight, and Friday and Saturday from 11 AM to 1 AM. Candlers Mountain Road is located off US 460, south of town.

MORRISON'S FAMILY DINING

3405 Candlers Mountain Rd.
Lynchburg, VA 24502   804-237-6549
$$

There's nothing more convenient than fine food served cafeteria style. Morrison's is in the River Ridge Mall and it is part of a chain that offers a wide selection of economy-priced meals. Credit cards are accepted, but only local checks. Open Monday through Friday from 11 AM to 2:30 PM, and 4:30 to 8:30

PM; Saturday from 11 AM to 8:30 PM; and Sunday from 11 AM to 8 PM. Candlers Mountain Road is located off US 460, south of town.

JEFFERSON'S RESTAURANT

Holiday Inn Crowne Plaza Lynchburg
601 Main St.
Lynchburg, Va 24504   804-528-2500
$$

This restaurant is located inside the Holiday Inn — the former Radisson Hotel. American cuisine includes Chicken Blue Ridge, rainbow trout, beef tenderloin and a marinated rib-eye steak. This is a convenient location. There's a no smoking section. Open seven days a week from 6:30 AM to 2 PM and 6 to 10 PM

Other Lynchburg Attractions

Annual Events: Spring Garden Show in April; Festival by the James and Bateau Festival, both in June; Kaleidoscope, a three-weekend arts and crafts festival in September; Harvest Festival in October; Christmas at Point of Honor and Christmas at the Market, both in December.

Arts: The Lynchburg Fine Arts Center, the Lynchburg Symphony Orchestra, the Virginia School of the Arts — a private secondary school that prepares youths for dance, theater and visual arts careers — and the arts programs at four local colleges provide this community with a number of exceptional arts programs.

Historical Sites: Point of Honor (112 Cabell Street) is a 1815 Federal-style house built by Dr. George

Cabell, the personal physician to Virginia patriot Patrick Henry. Riverside Park (along the James River) is hard to find, but a Civil War buff can see the *Marshall*, a passenger packet that plied the James River and Kanawha Canal in the mid-19th century. This packet carried Stonewall Jackson's body to Lexington for burial in 1863. Pulitzer Prize-winning historian Douglas Southall Freeman was born in Lynchburg, and his home is located on Main Street. Poplar Forest, Thomas Jefferson's "home away from home," is located west of Lynchburg in Bedford County.

Patrick Henry's last home and burial site is at Brookneal, a small town 5 miles southeast of Lynchburg. Booker T. Washington, the noted African American author and first president of Tuskegee Institute, was born on a small tobacco farm in Franklin County — about an hour's drive southwest of Lynchburg.

Shopping: Lynchburg offers six shopping centers and malls and an endless number of outlets and specialty shops. Ask for information at the Lynchburg Visitors Center (see listing).

TOUR 15

Richmond to Hampton

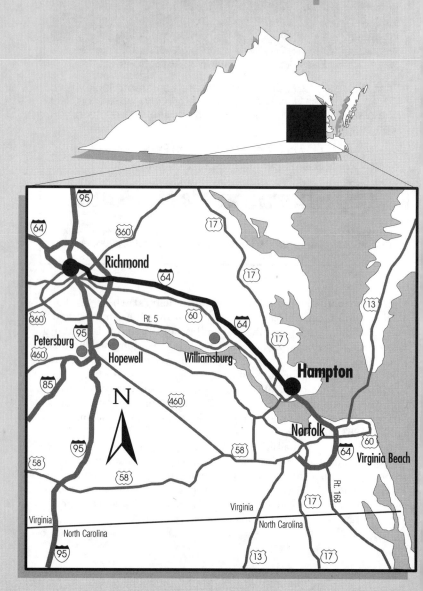

N

Richmond

Petersburg

Hopewell

Williamsburg

Hampton

Norfolk

Virginia Beach

Rt. 5

Rt. 168

Virginia

Virginia

North Carolina

North Carolina

Tour 15
Peninsula

About This Tour

This tour route begins in Richmond, VA, and runs the length of Virginia's "Peninsula," to Williamsburg, Newport News, and Hampton. We suggest you plan evening dining and lodging in Williamsburg.

Three of our sister Insiders' Guides, to Williamsburg, Richmond, and the Virginia Beach/Norfolk area, will also be helpful.

Travel Tips

VA 5, a number of small, state roads, and then I-64 are the principal routes of this tour. Be on the lookout for heavy, fast moving traffic along the major interstates. The state roads are narrow and less-traveled, so use caution.

History, Geography

The long stretch of land known as the Virginia Peninsula stretches from Richmond, east to Hampton Roads and the Atlantic Ocean. It is bordered on the north by the York River and on the south by the James River. This region ranks among the most historic in the nation. The first permanent English settlement in the New World was established at Jamestown, on the James River, in

1607. Williamsburg, once the colonial capital of Virginia, is situated a few miles north of the old Jamestown settlement. Yorktown, which completes the "historic triangle" with Jamestown and Williamsburg, was the site of the British surrender that ended the American Revolution. At the tip of the peninsula are Newport News and Hampton, rich in Virginia maritime history. Fort Monroe, the guardian of the Chesapeake Bay, is located on a spit of land overlooking Hampton Roads.

In 1862, USA Gen. McClellan began his Peninsular Campaign by ferrying a 100,000-man force down the Potomac River from Washington, D.C., into the Chesapeake Bay, and to Hampton, where he began a move upland toward Richmond. CSA Gen. Johnston, who commanded the Southern troops, was injured near Fair Oaks, and CSA Gen. Lee was placed in command of the army. Lee led Confederates against the invading Northerners in what has become known as the Seven Days Battles. In the end, following 35,000 casualties suffered by the opposing armies, USA Gen. McClellan retreated east after getting within 10 miles of the capital city.

Two years later, in 1864, USA Gen. Grant assumed command of the Union forces and began a relentless push to take Richmond. He inched his way south and east from Fredericksburg to the outskirts of Richmond, fighting USA Gen. Lee at every opportunity. In early June, in a fierce battle at Cold Harbor, the Federals lost 7,000 men in less than a half-hour. Afterwards, USA Gen. Grant pushed south across the James River toward Petersburg, and dug in for the last winter of the war.

Richmond was protected by a ring of fortifications that nearly encircled the town. An outer ring, about 16 miles from downtown, stretched more than 65 miles. Another ring of defenses was located inside that circle, about 4 miles from downtown. Forts, trenches and earthworks helped protect the capital of the Confederacy.

Getting Here

This tour route begins at the Richmond National Battlefield Park on E. Broad Street in Richmond. The route shifts east out of Richmond on US 360.

DIRECTIONS

From I-95, take exit 74-C and follow signs for the Richmond National Battlefield Park Visitor Center.

RICHMOND NATIONAL BATTLEFIELD PARK VISITOR CENTER

3215 E. Broad St.
Richmond, VA 23223   *804-226-1981*

The Richmond National Battlefield Park is located at the site of the Confederate's Chimborazo General Hospital. This National Park Service (NPS) facility offers tour informa-

tion, exhibits, a slide presentation, a movie and a bookstore. Uniformed park rangers can answer questions. The NPS also offers living history programs. The visitor center is open free daily from 9:00 AM to 5:00 PM. It is closed on New Year's Day and Christmas Day.

The NPS has an excellent brochure that covers a number of Civil War sites. The brochure includes a self-guided, 80-mile tour running throughout the eastern outskirts of the city. It has color-coded sites to associate them with either the campaigns of USA Gen. McClellan in 1862 or USA Gen. Grant in 1864. There are tape tours of some sites available for rent or sale. Our tour route follows much of the NPS route, with some minor alterations. The NPS tour route and park system features distinctive brown signs.

Chimborazo Hospital, built in 1862 and the largest in the world at the time, served more than 75,000 sick and wounded Confederate soldiers during the Civil War. A model of the hospital is on display in the visitor center.

DIRECTIONS

Richmond National Battlefield Park to Chickahominy Bluff

From the Richmond National Battlefield Park, return west on Broad Street to I-95. Take I-95 north and go 0.5 miles to I-64 east. Take I-64 east 1.0 miles to US 360 east — follow signs for Mechanicsville. Take US 360 east and go 2.0 miles to the Chickahominy Bluff entrance on the right.

CHICKAHOMINY BLUFF

CSA Gen. Lee watched the beginning of the Seven Days' Battles from this place, which offers a nice view of the Chickahominy River to the north and Mechanicsville beyond. The NPS offers interpretive facilities, an audio station, exhibits and a short self-guided trail.

DIRECTIONS

Chickahominy Bluff to Beaver Dam Creek
Continue east on US 360 for 1.8 miles to VA 156. Take the right exit, turn right (south) onto VA 156, and go south 0.6 miles to Beaver Dam Creek facility on the right.

BEAVER DAM CREEK

Beaver Dam (Beaverdam) Creek is a tributary of the Chickahominy River. This stop on the NPS tour was part of the Union line that the Southerners unsuccessfully tried to attack during the Seven Days' Battles. This battle was also known as Mechanicsville.

DIRECTIONS

Beaver Dam Creek to Gaines' Mill
Continue south on VA 156 for 1.4 miles to the traffic signal at Cold Harbor Road. Turn right on Cold Harbor Road (VA 156) and go 2.9 miles to the entrance road on the right. Take a right into the Gaines' Mill entrance and go 0.7 miles to parking lot.

GAINES' MILL

The Confederates attacked the Union line here, as part of the Seven Days' Battles. There were more than 15,000 casualties. The NPS has a short self-guided trail at this tour stop.

DIRECTIONS

Gaines' Mill to Cold Harbor
Return the 0.7 miles to VA 156, turn right on VA 156 and go 0.3 miles to the Cold Harbor entrance on the left. Follow signs for a 1.5 mile loop through the facility.

COLD HARBOR

Along the side of the self-guided tour route are trenches used by Confederates who dug in here in early June 1864 and repulsed a major attack by USA Gen. Grant. Entrenchments like the ones at Cold Harbor, military strategists later learned, are nearly impregnable against frontal assaults. Grant lost 7,000 solders in 30 minutes. There's a small NPS visitor center here, along with picnic facilities. A quarter-mile down the road is the old Gathright House (closed to the public), which served as a hospital. "Cold Harbor" is an old term for a place to stay overnight that doesn't serve hot meals.

DIRECTIONS

Cold Harbor to Fort Gilmer
Take VA 156 south for 4.5 miles to the intersection with I-295. Here, our tour route differs from the NPS self-guided tour. In the vicinity of this interstate intersection, as you'll note on the NPS tour, are Seven Pines, Fair Oaks, Oak Grove and Savage Swamp — all notable locations during the Seven Days' Battles in 1862.

FORT GILMER

Fort Gilmer, along with Fort Harrison, Fort Gregg, and Fort Hoke, were elements of an elaborate system of Confederate breastworks. After Cold Harbor in June 1864, USA Gen. Grant moved his men to this vicinity, crossing the James River to direct his main effort against Petersburg.

DIRECTIONS

**Fort Gilmer to
Fort Harrison**

From Fort Gilmer, continue south on Battlefield Park Drive for 1.4 miles to Fort Harrison. You will pass Fort Johnson on the right.

FORT HARRISON

USA Gen. Grant's men captured Fort Harrison in late September 1864. Fourteen African American soldiers in the Union Army were awarded Medals of Honor. They were among several regiments of African American troops recognized for their bravery. With the capture, Fort Harrison became a part of the Union lines around Richmond. The NPS has interpretive facilities here, including an exhibit and audio station. There is a short self-guided trail as well as picnic facilities.

DIRECTIONS

Fort Harrison to Fort Brady

From Fort Harrison, continue south on Battlefield Park Drive for 1.1 miles to Fort Hoke, then turn left on Hoke-Brady Drive and go 2.8 miles to Fort Brady.

FORT BRADY

Fort Brady was built after the Union Army took Fort Harrison. It was designed to neutralize Fort Darling across the James River on Drewry's Bluff and anchor the Federal line from Fort Harrison. There is a great view of the James River from an overlook at Fort Brady. The NPS offers a short self-guided trail.

DIRECTIONS

Fort Brady to Malvern Hill

Return north on Hoke-Brady Drive for 0.9 miles to Kingsland Road. Turn right (east) on Kingsland Road and go 4.0 miles to VA 5. Turn right (east) on VA 5 and go 3.0 miles to VA 156 north. Turn left (north) on VA 156 and follow signs for 1.4 miles to Malvern Hill on right.

MALVERN HILL

Malvern Hill was the last of the Seven Days' Battles. It was fought on July 1, 1862. USA Gen. McClellan's artillery was lined hub-to-hub to fire on the attacking Confederates. After this battle, USA Gen. McClellan withdrew to his base at Harrison's Landing, down the James River. The NPS has interpretive facilities featuring exhibits and an audio station.

DIRECTIONS

**Malvern Hill to
Frayser's Farm**

Continue north on VA 156 for 1.8 miles to Glendale National Cemetery and Frayser's Farm on the right.

USA Gen. George B. McClellan

George Brinton McClellan was born in Philadelphia in December 1826. His ancestors sailed to New England from Scotland in the early 18th century, and his great-grandfather, Samuel McClellan, served in the American Revolution as a Connecticut officer. In 1842, George McClellan entered West Point and graduated second in his class. For the next two decades, he served in various positions in the U.S. Army, including action in the Mexican War and then in the development of military strategies, training and education.

Photo: Associated Press

In 1857, he resigned his commission to become an executive with the Illinois Central Railroad, where he met the company's attorney, Abraham Lincoln. By 1860, McClellan became president of the Ohio and Mississippi Railroad.

McClellan was a superb military organizer and creator of the Army of the Potomac. Known early in the Civil War as a "young Napoleon," he replaced the aging Winfield Scott as general-in-chief of the Union Army. After 1st Bull Run, McClellan urged President Lincoln to approve a plan by which the Union general would transport troops down the Potomac River and Chesapeake Bay to Fort Monroe, then push up the Virginia peninsula to Richmond. The president reluctantly agreed to the strategy, so long as Washington, D.C., was sufficiently protected.

McClellan eventually instituted his Peninsular Campaign, which ran into delays, first at Yorktown and then in heavy spring rains east of Richmond. The general complained about being outnumbered and not getting adequate troop reinforcements. Finally, after the series of battles within 10 miles of the Confederate capital, he was ordered to withdraw, and his troops were attached to USA Gen. Pope's command.

McClellan got another chance to command the Union Army, but he failed to pursue CSA Gen. Lee following the Battle of Antietam in Maryland. Lincoln then replaced McClellan with USA Gen. Burnside, and the "young Napoleon" never again saw action in the field.

In 1864, he was unsuccessful as a presidential candidate against Lincoln. McClellan spent the next three years abroad before taking a position as chief engineer of the New York City Department of Docks. He was governor of New Jersey from 1878 to early 1881. He died in Orange, NJ, in October 1885, leaving behind a wife, Ellen, a daughter and a son.

Peninsula Personality

Frayser's Farm

In this battle, the day prior to Malvern Hill, Confederate troops unsuccessfully tried to assault the Union position, and the circumstances left CSA Gen. Lee thoroughly disappointed. Just to the north is White Oak Swamp, whose name often is given to this battle.

DIRECTIONS

Frayser's Farm to Shirley Plantation

Backtrack south on VA 156 for 3.2 miles to VA 5. Turn right (east) on VA 5 and go 5.3 miles to VA 608. Turn right on VA 608 and go 1.7 miles to Shirley Plantation.

Shirley Plantation

501 Shirley Plantation Rd.
Charles City, VA 23030   804-829-5121
800-232-1613

Located on the banks of the James River, between Richmond and Williamsburg, the Shirley estate was established only six years after the English settlement at Jamestown. It was the home of two prominent Virginia families, the Hills and the Carters.

Construction of the present house began in 1723 by Edward Hill, a Virginia burgess, for his daughter, Elizabeth, who married John Carter, son of King Carter. Ann Hill Carter, Robert E. Lee's mother, was born at Shirley, and she married Henry "Light-Horse Harry" Lee at the estate. Confederate General Lee received a portion of his schooling at Shirley Plantation. Shirley is open from 9:00 AM to 5:00 PM every day except Christmas Day. The last tour begins at 4:30 PM. Admission is $6.00 for adults, $5.00 for seniors, $4.00 for children over the age of 12, and $3.00 for children ages 6 to 12.

DIRECTIONS

Shirley Plantation to Berkeley Plantation

Backtrack on VA 608 to VA 5. Turn right (east) on VA 5 and go 3.1 miles to Berkeley Plantation entrance on the right.

Berkeley Plantation

VA 5
Charles City, VA 23030   804-829-6018

Berkeley, another fine James River plantation, is an attractive three-story brick house that dates to 1726. The building date and the name of the owners, Benjamin Harrison IV and his wife, Anne, appear in a date stone over a side door. Bricks for the mansion were fired on site. The nation's first ten presidents head a list of distinguished guests who visited the Harrison estate. Benjamin Harrison, the son of the builder of Berkeley, was a signer of the Declaration of Independence and a three-time governor of Virginia. His third son, William Henry Harrison, was born at Berkeley and later became the nation's ninth president. William Henry Harrison's grandson, Benjamin Harrison, was a Union officer and later the 23rd president.

During the Civil War, CSA Gen. McClellan established his headquarters for a time at "Harrison's Landing," as Berkeley was called. President Lincoln visited the Union general and his 140,000 troops here. "Taps" was composed at Berkeley while McClellan's troops were camped at the estate.

USA Gen. Daniel Butterfield

USA Gen. Daniel Butterfield was a 30-year-old, college-educated businessman in New York City when the Civil War began. He moved quickly up the ranks of the Union Army. He was commissioned a lieutenant colonel in May 1861 during the Peninsular Campaign. At the battle of Gaines' Mill, despite an injury, he seized the colors of the 3rd Pa. and rallied the regiment at a critical time in the battle. Years later, he was awarded the Medal of Honor for that act of heroism.

Quartered at Harrison's Landing, or Berkeley Plantation, Butterfield composed "Taps," the familiar military bugle call that is sounded at night as an order to put out lights. The slow, soft bugle call is also sounded at military funerals and memorial services.

Following the Peninsular Campaign, Butterfield served at 2nd Bull Run, Antietam, and at Marye's Heights in the Battle of Fredericksburg. He became a major general and served as the chief of staff of the Union's Army of the Potomac. He was wounded at Gettysburg and then reassigned to the Western Theater.

By war's end, he was breveted to major general of the volunteers. He stayed in the army after the Civil War, serving as superintendent of the army's recruiting service in New York City. In 1870, after resigning from the military, he went to work with the American Express Co. He was in charge of a number of special public ceremonies, including USA Gen. Sherman's funeral in 1889. Married in 1886, at the age of 55, he died in 1901. His tomb is the most ornate in the cemetery at West Point.

The grounds are open 8:00 AM to 5:00 PM daily, and the house is open from 9:00 AM to 5:00 PM, with the last tour beginning at 4:30 PM. Admission to the house and grounds is $10.00. There is a discount for seniors, and a $5.00 charge for children ages 6 to 12. Admission for the grounds only is $5.00 for adults and $2.50 for children 6 to 12. There is a restaurant on the site, which is open daily from 11:00 AM to 4:00 PM.

DIRECTIONS

Berkeley Plantation to Charles City Courthouse
Continue east on VA 5. The Charles City Courthouse is located 6.7 miles east of Berkeley Plantation on VA 5.

North Bend Plantation

Also along VA 5, North Bend Plantation is a Greek Revival-style home built in the early 1800s. USA Gen. Sheridan occupied the estate in 1864. The desk used by Sheridan at North Bend is now a treasured family heirloom. North Bend's present owner, who is related to secessionist Edmund Ruffin, has restored the home and established a bed and breakfast. For more information, contact George or Ridgely Copeland, North Bend Plantation, 12200 Weyanoke Road, Charles City, VA 23030, or telephone 804-829-5176. (See listing in accommodations section at the end of this chapter.)

Charles City Courthouse Side Trip

Evelynton

Along VA 5 is Evelynton Plantation, built in the 18th century of Georgian Revival architecture, was once a part of Westover Plantation. It was named for Evelyn, the daughter of William Byrd II of Westover. The house is furnished with family heirlooms, and it has a boxwood garden and grounds that overlook the James River.

Since 1847, Evelynton has been home for the Ruffin family. The family's patriarch, Edmund Ruffin, was born in Prince George County, VA, in 1794, attended the College of William and Mary, and became known as a writer, agriculturalist, and staunch secessionist. He served briefly in the Virginia Senate, and published a Petersburg, VA, newspaper devoted to agriculture. He was a member of the Palmetto (South Carolina) Guard, and some credit him with firing one of the first shots of the Civil War at Fort Sumter, SC. In June 1865, Ruffin shot himself to death in Amelia County, VA, because of his apparent unwillingness to live under the U.S. — rather than Confederate — government.

Evelynton, the scene of frequent Civil War skirmishes, is open to the public. For more information, write Evelynton Plantation, VA 5, Charles City, VA 23030, or telephone 804-829-5075.

CHARLES CITY COURTHOUSE
Charles City, VA 23030

Charles City County was one of the four old boroughs first established in Virginia in the early 17th century. In 1634, the four boroughs were increased to eight "shires," or counties. This original shire was named Charles City to honor England's Prince Charles, later King Charles I. The county seat was moved to this place in the 1730s and the courthouse was built about the same time. During the Civil War, Union soldiers rifled the building and many of the records were destroyed. The courthouse is still in use today.

DIRECTIONS

Charles City Courthouse to Sherwood Forest

Continue east on VA 5. Three miles beyond Charles City Courthouse, turn right at the entrance sign for Sherwood Forest's parking lot.

SHERWOOD FOREST
Charles City, VA 23030   804-829-5377

Sherwood Forest Plantation was the elegantly furnished home of John Tyler, the tenth president. It is considered the longest frame house in the nation. The home, maintained today by Tyler descendants, has a 68-foot-long ballroom and features an extensive collection of Tyler heirlooms. A national landmark, it is open daily from 9:00 AM to 5:00 PM. The 19th-century Overseer's House Tavern is available for dining, catered meals, box lunches, receptions and meetings.

DIRECTIONS

Sherwood Forest to Colonial Williamsburg Visitor Center

Continue east on VA 5 for 12 miles to the outskirts of Williamsburg. Follow green signs for the Colonial Williamsburg Visitor Center, located off the Colonial Parkway and VA 132.

President John Tyler

John Tyler was born a few miles away, at Greenway, on March 29, 1790. He attended the College of William and Mary, graduated at 17, studied law under his father, and was a practicing attorney by 1809. Two years later, Tyler was elected to the Virginia House of Delegates, where he served on and off for three decades. A Virginia congressman, he served a two-year term as governor beginning in 1825. Afterwards, he served nine years in the U.S. Senate.

In 1840, Tyler was elected vice president on a ticket headed by fellow Virginian William Henry Harrison. This was the one and only time that both members of a presidential ticket were natives of the same state. Harrison, inaugurated in 1841, died after only a month in office, and Tyler became the first vice president to ascend to the presidency.

Tyler's one-term administration was filled with political intrigue and controversy. He did attempt a third party movement in 1844, in an effort to win reelection, but he withdrew after realizing its inevitable failure. The following year, he left Washington, D.C., without attending President James Polk's inaugural, and retired to Sherwood Forest.

Tyler was 23 when he married Letitia Christian in 1813 in New Kent County, VA. The couple were married 23 years and had eight children before Letitia died in the White House in 1842. Two years later, in the waning years of his presidency, Tyler was observing trials on the warship *Princeton* and escaped death when a gun exploded. One of the victims was New York Sen. David Gardiner. Two months later, the widowed Tyler married the late senator's daughter, Julia Gardiner. She retired to Sherwood Forest with her husband in 1845, and together the couple had seven children.

When the first southern states seceded in 1861, Tyler led a compromise movement, and was the leading delegate of a peace convention held in Washington, D.C. When that effort failed, he helped created the Confederacy. Elected to the Confederate House of Representatives, he died in Richmond on Jan. 18, 1862, before he was able to actively serve the Southern cause. Because of his secession activities, his death was not officially recognized in Washington, D.C., and because of his elected position to the Confederate House, it can be said he was the only U.S. president to bear arms against the federal government.

Tyler was buried in Hollywood Cemetery in Richmond (see Tour 12: Richmond). One of Tyler's sons, David Gardiner Tyler, dropped out of Washington and Lee University after his father died and joined the Confederate Army's Rockbridge (County, VA) Artillery. Interestingly, John Tyler's family history spans a century and a half. Tyler was born during the administration of George Washington, the nation's first president, and the last of his children — David's sister, Pearl — died during the administration of Harry Truman, the nation's 33rd president.

Artwork: Virginia Historical Society

The Confederates fought a sharp rear-guard battle at Williamsburg on May 6, 1862, slowing McClellan's advancing forces.

COLONIAL WILLIAMSBURG
VISITOR CENTER

Williamsburg, VA 23185   804-229-1000

There is so much to see and do in the Williamsburg area, so this is the best place to begin your visit — particularly if you need help preparing an itinerary. Colonial Williamsburg is one of the nation's most historic and most beautiful attractions. You can center an entire vacation in this fine community that was known as "Little London" in colonial times.

Williamsburg was colonial Virginia's second capital. Established as Middle Plantation in 1633, the seat of government was moved here from Jamestown in 1698. A year later, the community was renamed Williamsburg, to honor England's King William III. It served as the Virginia capital until 1780, when the seat of government was moved upland to Richmond.

"The saddest year in Williamsburg's history was 1862," writes historian Parke Rouse Jr., a resident of this historic community.

That was when USA Gen. McClellan moved up the Virginia peninsula, defeated Confederates at nearby Fort Magruder, and put Williamsburg under military guard. The 2,000 residents of the town remained under guard for the duration of the Civil War. Benjamin Ewell, a West Point graduate and president of the College of William and Mary, became a Confederate engineering officer and helped establish peninsula defenses against Union attack. Skirmishes were frequent in this quaint, former capital city, which took years to recover after war's end in 1865.

Today, Colonial Williamsburg offers a vast array of attractions. You could spend days visiting the Colonial Capitol, the Governor's Palace, Carter's Grove, and the more than 30 homes, craft shops and public buildings in the historic area. Colonial Williamsburg offers a variety of admission packages, including the Patriot's Pass, the Royal Governor's Pass and the basic admission ticket, which is $23 for adults and $13.75 for children. Ask the travel counselors for assistance. Remember, *Travel and Leisure Magazine* is quoted as saying that it takes three to four days to fully appreciate all that Colonial Williamsburg has to offer.

EAST OF WILLIAMSBURG

There are several other Civil War-related attractions farther east on the Virginia peninsula that justify a second day's tour. These stops are:

COLONIAL NATIONAL HISTORICAL PARK

P.O. Box 210
Yorktown, VA 23690   804-898-3400

This 9,000-acre national park, with sites in both Jamestown and Yorktown, connects the "historical triangle" with a 23-mile scenic roadway. This parkway is a convenient way to reach Yorktown, on the north side of the peninsula at the York River. Rich in Revolutionary War history, Yorktown also was the scene of Civil War action. CSA Gen. Magruder's defenses kept USA Gen. McClellan back for months and delayed his move up the Virginia peninsula toward Richmond. When McClellan finally assaulted Yorktown, the Confederates retreated and left behind land mines, a new technique in warfare.

NEWPORT NEWS PARK

13560 Jefferson Ave.
Newport News, VA 23603   804-886-7912
804-888-3333

Located off exit 250-B on I-64, east of Williamsburg, visitors can see 10 miles of original fortifications along a wooded nature trail. USA Gen. McClellan assaulted the Confederate's defense line at the Battle of Dam No. 1, on April 16, 1862. The first medal of honor was earned at this battle by Vermonter Julian Scott, a drummer boy. Today, the park is equipped with numerous camp sites. The City of Newport News operates a visitor center adjacent to this park.

THE MARINERS' MUSEUM

100 Museum Drive
Newport News, VA 23606   804-595-0368

Take exit 258-A off I-64, and follow signs on US 17 south (Clyde Morris Blvd., Museum Drive) for 2.3 miles to The Mariners' Museum entrance. This museum is one of Virginia's finest attractions and it boasts one of the world's largest maritime collections. See paintings, maps, ship models, watercraft and other maritime memorabilia, including an exhibit on the clash of the Civil War ironsides, the USS *Monitor* and the CSS *Virginia*, formerly the USS *Merrimac*. You could spend all day at this exceptional attraction. The museum is open Monday through Saturday from 9:00 AM to 5:00 PM, and Sunday from noon to 5:00 PM. It is closed only on Christmas Day. A fee of $5 for adults and $1 for children is charged. The museum has a research library and archives, open Monday through Saturday from 9:00 AM to 5:00 PM, and closed on most major holidays. The museum also has a gift gallery.

Source: Richmond Newspapers

The CSS Merrimac's *duel with the USS* Monitor *was a turning point in U.S. naval history.*

USS *Monitor* and CSS *Virginia*

The battle of the *Monitor* and *Merrimac* — the *Merrimac* became the CSS *Virginia* — was fought on March 9, 1862, in Hampton Roads. The battle was indecisive, but it marked a change in naval warfare from wood and sail to iron and steam. The *Monitor* sank off the North Carolina coast on New Year's Eve in 1862, and The Mariners' Museum now is the principal museum for the Monitor National Marine Sanctuary. In addition, a group called the Monitor-Merrimac Memorial Foundation Inc. has proposed a $50 million, ten-year project to build a memorial to honor the two Civil War ironclads. It would be built at one end of the Monitor-Merrimac bridge tunnel span of I-664, which crosses the James River at the site of the ironclad battle.

WAR MEMORIAL MUSEUM OF VIRGINIA

Huntington Park
9285 Warwick Blvd.
Newport News, VA 23607   804-247-8523

From I-64, take exit 263-B (Mercury Boulevard) and follow US 258 south for 3.3 miles to Warwick Boulevard. Turn right (west) on US 60 (Warwick Boulevard) and look for Huntington Park on the south side of the roadway. Be careful — this museum is difficult to find. It is best to go west on Warwick Boulevard for a quarter-mile and U-turn at South Avenue. Return east on Warwick Boulevard to the entrance to Huntington Park on the right. (An alternate way: from The Mariners' Museum, see listing above, return north on Museum Drive a mile and turn right (east) on US 60. Take US 60 south 3.5 miles to Huntington Park on the right. A large railroad locomotive sits beside Warwick Boulevard, and that's a good landmark for Huntington Park.)

Founded in 1923, and operated by the City of Newport News, this museum houses more than 50,000 artifacts related to the nation's war history from the American Revolution to the present. Particularly interesting is the Civil War section of

Site of Big Bethel

From I-64, take exit 261 (Hampton Roads Center Parkway) west. At the end of the exit ramp, and beyond Hampton Woods Plaza, turn right (north) on VA 600. Go 3.0 miles to Big Bethel markers along the roadway. Unfortunately, Big Bethel Reservoir is a manmade lake that has submerged the site of an 1861 skirmish considered the first land battle of the Civil War. A group of untrained Union soldiers from Fort Monroe attacked an equally untrained group of Confederates. The Northerners retreated to Fort Monroe after a confusing, two-hour skirmish.

the museum, with uniforms, weapons and printed materials. The museum also has a gift shop.

FORT MONROE CASEMATE MUSEUM

P.O. Box 341
Fort Monroe, VA 23651   804-727-3391
804-727-3973

From I-64 take exit 268 (VA 169 east). At the end of the exit ramp, turn left (east) on VA 169 (Mallory Street) and go 0.2 miles to VA 143 east (Mullen Street). Turn right on VA 143 and go east through the community of Phoebus for 0.5 miles to the main gate at Fort Monroe. The Casemate Museum is located inside the old fortress at Fort Monroe, so follow signs for one of several bridges over the moat into the enclosed compound.

Named for President James Monroe, this is the nation's largest stone fort ever built. It is located at Old Point Comfort, which traces its history to 1607 when Capt. Christopher Newport's sailing party landed at Cape Henry. The first fort on this site was built in 1609. A new brick fort, named for England's King George II, was built in 1727 after Spain declared war on England. In 1774, during the American Revolution, Virginia built a temporary light on this site to guide ships into Hamp-

ton Roads. In 1800, the federal government completed a permanent light at this site.

During the next two decades this site was witness to considerable history. In 1819, work began on Fortress Monroe — the name later was changed from "fortress" to "fort." Four years later, the fort received its first U.S. Army garrison. A year after that, the Marquis de LaFayette visited during his American tour. In 1828, the garrison included an artilleryman, Sgt. Maj. E.A. Perry, also known as writer Edgar Allan Poe. And in 1831, a young Army engineer named Robert E. Lee arrived on the scene to supervise the construction of the fort's moat.

During the early days of the Civil War, USA Gen. Butler took command of the fort, which was one of few military facilities in the South that the Confederates failed to capture. In 1861, three escaped Virginia slaves made their way to the fort. Rather than returning the trio under the Fugitive Slave Law, Butler declared the slaves "contraband of war" — the first use of the term.

The next year, 1862, was a busy one, too. Fort Calhoun, offshore in Hampton Roads, was renamed for USA Gen. Wool, who was the com-

Harriett Tubman, Nurses

Harriett Tubman was an African American who served as a spy and scout for the Union Army. She was a nurse who cared for a number of individuals who escaped into Union lines at Fort Monroe. Three months after the war's end, in July 1865, she was honored by an appointment as ". . . nurse or matron at the Colored Hospital, Fort Monroe, Virginia." Tubman was but one of many nurses that served on the peninsula during the Civil War. The war lured nurses from around the country, including Helen Gilson of Massachusetts and Amy Bradley of Maine, both of whom served during the Peninsular Campaign of 1862.

The walking tour also provides a glimpse of the quarters used by Army Lt. Robert E. Lee while he was stationed at the fort. The building is a private residence and off limits to visitors. Quarters One, also off limits, is the oldest residence on the post. Its list of distinguished guests includes President Lincoln and the Marquis de Lafayette. The engineer wharf along the waterfront is the place where USA Gen. McClellan began his Peninsular Campaign and where Jefferson Davis came ashore for his imprisonment. The Old Point Comfort lighthouse, in continuous operation since 1802, can be seen but not visited. The Lincoln Gun, the first 15-inch Rodman made, was cast in 1860, named for the president in 1862, and used to bomb Confederate batteries near Norfolk. The entire fort is listed as both a national and state landmark.

Hampton University

In 1868, three years after the Civil War ended, a young Union Army officer, Samuel Chapman Armstrong, established a new school in Hampton, VA, to educate freed slaves. Armstrong created a "normal and agricultural institute" with two teachers and 15 students. Later known as Hampton Institute, the school is now Hampton University. Armstrong was school principal until he died in 1893. Booker T. Washington, a Virginia native, was an 1875 Hampton graduate, and he founded Tuskegee Institute with principles he learned from Hampton. Another Hampton graduate, Robert Tussa Moton, a native of Amelia County, VA, served as the institute's administrator from 1890 to 1915, when he succeeded Booker Washington as president of Tuskegee. Moton, an advisor to five U.S. presidents and founder of the Urban League, retired to Gloucester County, VA, and died in May 1940.

Today, Hampton University has an enrollment of nearly 5,000 students and a faculty of almost 400. The Hampton Institute Museum has a renowned collection of art and artifacts. Also on campus is Emancipation Oak, where Union soldiers announced to Hampton Roads citizens in 1863 the Emancipation Proclamation that freed slaves.

Located at Queen and Tyler streets in Hampton, the school is accessed via I-64, exit 267. For more information, write Hampton University, Hampton, VA 23668, or telephone 804-727-5000.

mander of the Hampton Roads fortifications. President Lincoln visited Fort Monroe to observe the Union attack on Norfolk. Meanwhile, hundreds lined the fort's ramparts and beaches to see naval history when the ironclad vessels fought in Hampton Roads. USA Gen. McClellan used the fort as the springboard for his Peninsular Campaign.

CSA President Jefferson Davis, captured after the Civil War, was returned to Virginia and imprisoned at the fort. He was first kept in a casemate — a wall chamber — before being moved to officers' quarters. He was released two years later.

The Casemate Museum is the starting point of a walking tour around old Fort Monroe. The museum has interesting, graphic exhibits, including the barren casemate where Davis was imprisoned. The museum is free and open daily except on major holidays.

Williamsburg Accommodations

Refer to the Foreward for an explanation of the rating system for both the accommodations and restaurants.

WILLIAMSBURG HOTEL/MOTEL ASSOCIATION
Williamsburg, VA 23185   804-220-3330;
800-446-9244

Choosing just the right lodging in Williamsburg is an almost impossible task. But don't despair — help is available. The Williamsburg Hotel/Motel Association was established in 1976 to help anxious and eager travelers with accommodations planning and reservations as-

sistance. Today, the association represents more than 70 hotels and motels — that's more than 8,000 rooms — in the Williamsburg area, and it handles thousands of information requests each year. Plus, it's easy to contact the travel counselors. Simply telephone the toll free number from anywhere in the country. The help line is also a handy way to check on transportation, dining and entertainment information.

COLONIAL WILLIAMSBURG
Williamsburg, VA 23185   804-229-1000;
800-HISTORY

Colonial Williamsburg offers a wide variety of accommodations. In addition to the popular Williamsburg Inn ($$$$) and Williamsburg Lodge ($$$), a number of individual properties are available in the historic area. For information and assistance, telephone Colonial Williamsburg on its toll-free 800 number.

HAMPTON INN, WILLIAMSBURG
201 Bypass Rd.
Williamsburg, VA 23185   804-220-0880
$$$ 800-289-0880

This motel is one of two Hampton Inns in the Williamsburg area. The sign is a familiar one for traveling families on strict budgets. This inn has more than 120 rooms, and it offers a free continental breakfast and an indoor, heated swimming pool. There are some non-smoking rooms available.

THE CEDARS BED AND BREAKFAST
616 Jamestown Rd.
Williamsburg, VA 23185   804-229-3591
$$$ 800-296-3591

This charming bed and breakfast is located in a residential section near the College of William and Mary. The Cedars is on busy Jamestown Road (VA 5), but it has off-street parking in back. Antiques and reproductions decorate the nine rooms and varied suites. The Cedars offers fresh baked muffins for breakfast, afternoon tea, and evening refreshments by the fireplace. The historic area is a brief walk away; but you might decide not to leave.

NORTH BEND PLANTATION
12200 Weyanoke Rd.
Charles City, VA 23030   804-829-5176
$$$$

There's plenty of history at North Bend (see listing above). Try staying a day — or longer — in the "Magnolia Room," the "Sheridan Room," the "Rose Room" or the "Maids Quarters." Children 6 and older are welcome at North Bend; smoking is restricted to designated areas. George and Ridgely Copeland, the proprietors, think of everything: try a dip in the swimming pool or a game of billiards, croquet or horseshoes. A continental breakfast is served, and the Copelands will help with reservations at nearby historic restaurants and taverns. Above all else, ask to see the desk that USA Gen. Sheridan used during his occupation of North Bend.

LIBERTY ROSE BED & BREAKFAST
1022 Jamestown Road   804-253-1260
$$$$

This bed and breakfast inn offers a romantic, comfortable atmosphere. Sandra and Brad Hirz have completely renovated this 1920s house made from Jamestown brick on a hillside covered with beautiful old

trees one mile from the Historic Area. Inside you'll find English, Victorian, French Country and colonial antiques — a mix of abundant conversation pieces and interesting knickknacks of all kinds. The rich lace and wallpapers contribute to the romantic mood. A grand piano and fireplace in the salon, and gratis soft drinks at any time on the glassed-in breakfast porch are particularly inviting.

Each guest room has its own name — "Rose Victoria," "Magnolias Peach," "Savannah Lace," "Suite Williamsburg," and "Blossom" — all accurate indicators of their charm. All rooms offer television, VCR, movies, lush bathrobes, bubble bath, a silk rose for the lady, a bowl of chocolates, alarm clocks, and gold miniature flashlights. Mention the famous chocolate chips and you will find them outside your door for an evening's snack.

Liberty Rose cannot accept pets, and it is a non-smoking house.

EDGEWOOD PLANTATION
4800 John Tyler Memorial Hwy. (Route 5)
Charles City, VA 23030   804-829-2962
800-296-EDGE

In a countryside filled with the formalities of Georgian and Colonial Revival architecture, Edgewood's Carpenter Gothic style is a truly refreshing offering for you to consider. The plantation has been featured in recent editions of two magazines: the front cover of *Country Victoria* and *Country Inn.*

On one bedroom window upstairs, Elizabeth "Lizzie" Rowland wrote her name with a diamond. Legend has it that she died of a broken heart waiting in vain for her lover to return from the Civil War.

She reportedly still sits, watching from "Lizzie's Room." Don't let the Edgewood ghost intimidate you, however; you'll find comfort, relaxation, and a good night's sleep in any one of the seven bedrooms here.

Special features here include old canopy beds, formal gardens, a swimming pool and hot tub, a candlelight full breakfast, afternoon Victorian teas and tours, and a peaceful, convenient location, about 25 miles from Williamsburg, Richmond and Petersburg.

Williamsburg Restaurants

SHIELDS TAVERN
Duke of Gloucester St.
Williamsburg, VA 23185   804-229-2141
$$

If time is a test of a restaurant's value, then Shields Tavern would win any contest. This restaurant dates to the 1740s, when James Shields had a —yes—tavern. Today, the interior is decorated as it was during Mr. Shield's

day. The menu features the top meal choices of yesterday: spit-roasted beef, seafood soups and a number of hearty dinners. The Shields Sampler is a good choice; it includes chicken fricassee. Reservations are absolutely necessary, especially in the summer season. Contact the restaurant or the Colonial Williamsburg Visitor Center (see listing) for hours and reservation assistance.

TRELLIS RESTAURANT AND GRILL
Duke of Gloucester St.
Williamsburg, VA 23185   804-229-7610
$$$-$$$$

The Trellis has a national reputation, so telephone well in advance for a reservation. Fresh entrees include seafood, beef, poultry and sausage, with excellent soup, salad, dessert and wine choices. This is the ultimate dining experience. *The New York Times* is quoted as saying the Trellis is the "best restaurant in this part of Virginia. . . ." The review is worth editing to say "anywhere in Virginia." Open daily, lunch is served from 11:00 AM to 2:30 PM, and dinner is available from 5:00 to 9:30 PM. An outdoor cafe also serves lunch, weather permitting.

BASSETT'S RESTAURANT
207 Bypass Rd.
Williamsburg, VA 23185   804-229-3614
$-$$

Families with children will particularly enjoy Bassett's with its informal atmosphere and multiple television screens. Bassett's offers a variety of entrees, sandwiches and burgers, and it includes a children's menu. A no-smoking area is available. Young adults migrate to the bar, which is open after the regular restaurant closes. Bassett's is open every day except Thanksgiving Day and Christmas Day. Hours are 11:30 AM to 1:00 AM; the bar remains open until 2:00 AM. During the winter, the bar opens at 3:30 PM, but it still remains open late.

Other Williamsburg and Peninsula Attractions

For questions or reservations, ask for help at the Colonial Williamsburg Visitor Center (see listing).

Arts: Colonial Williamsburg offers the DeWitt Wallace Decorative Arts Gallery, which has one of the largest collections of 18th century English and American textiles, prints, furniture and other art objects. In addition there is the Abby Aldrich Rockefeller Folk Art Center. The College of William and Mary, the nation's second oldest institute of higher learning, offers students, townsfolk and visitors a year-long array of performances, concerts and arts programs.

Entertainment: Yes, there's more to do! Kids like Go-Karts Plus, which offers two separate race tracks. Go-Karts Plus is located at 6910 Richmond Road (US 60) near the Williamsburg Pottery, 804-564-7600. Also on Richmond Road is the Old Dominion Opry, which offers country music and comedy for the entire family. For reservations, telephone 804-564-0200. Water County USA offers water rides and live entertainment. Call them at 804-229-9300.

Photo: Virginia Historical Society

The Battle of Cold Harbor was one of the most devastating conflicts of the Civil War.

The ultimate entertainment experience on the peninsula is available at Busch Gardens, which offers Old World Europe, shows, concerts, dining and much more. Telephone Busch Gardens at 804-253-3350. Golfers can enjoy no fewer than five major golf course facilities in the Williamsburg area. Check in at the Colonial Williamsburg Visitor Center (see listing) for details.

Historical Sites: In addition to the various sites associated with Colonial Williamsburg, the first-time visitor must see Jamestown, the site of the first English settlement in America. Nearby, Yorktown is the site of the British surrender that ended the Revolutionary War.

Numerous historical attractions await you in Newport News, Hampton, and — across Hampton Roads — Norfolk, Portsmouth, Chesapeake and Virginia Beach. Pilot Mitchell Bowman, a Civil War en-

thusiast, operates Historic Air Tours out of Williamsburg. He offers three flights over peninsula battle scenes: the Battlefield Tour, the Capital City Tour, and the Petersburg Siege tour. Each 50-minute flight costs $60 a person — $54 a person in a group. It's a unique, interesting way to learn and appreciate the region's history. Contact Bowman at 804-253-8185.

Or try a historic plantation cruise aboard the *Annabel Lee* out of Richmond. The cruise includes historical narration, demonstrations and reenactments. Lunch, dinner and children's cruises are also offered. For more information, telephone 804-222-5700.

Tidewater Touring Inc. in Williamsburg offers a number of historic and shopping tours in Virginia. For more information, telephone 804-872-0897. Maximum Guided Tours Inc. offers a candlelight tour of "The Ghosts of Williamsburg." This tour includes history stories and interesting trivia about Williamsburg

homes and past residents. For information, telephone 804-565-4821.

The City of Hampton operates the Hampton Convention and Visitor Bureau at 710 Settlers Landing Road (804-727-1102 or 800-800-2202). The visitor bureau has information on the various points of interest in Hampton, and travel counselors can assist you with information on lodging and dining. Ask counselors about the Hampton Boat Tour — a two hours-plus ride that covers much of the Hampton Roads area.

Shopping: The Williamsburg Pottery, located on Richmond Road (US 60) west of town, has served visitors and locals for a half century. This was Virginia's first great "outlet mall" — a collection of several buildings that sells literally everything. Over the years, Richmond Road has developed into a vast collection of outlet malls and stores. This stretch of highway is challenged only by Potomac Mills (see Tour 11: Fredericksburg) as the ultimate shopping experience in Virginia. Otherwise, try shopping in the variety of stores and shops in Williamsburg's historic area. Colonial Williamsburg furniture, crafts and art are available in several stores. Throughout the Williamsburg area are dozens of stores and shops that offer jewelry, antiques and gift items. Several local publishing companies print shopping guides to the Williamsburg area, and these helpful booklets are available at the Colonial Williamsburg Visitor Center (see listing) and at almost every motel, restaurant and attraction.

RESOURCES

ACCESSORIES

**THE REGIMENTAL
QUARTERMASTER**
CIVIL WAR reproduction Muskets,
Revolvers, Carbines, Swords, Uniforms,
Insignia, Leather Goods, Bayonets, Books,
Buckles, Buttons, Tents, Tinware, Tapes,
Equipment, Accouterments, Accessories
and more. Listing $2, Regimental
Quartermaster, Box 553, Hatboro, Pa.
19040-0553. (215) 672-6891.

ACCOMMODATIONS

THE DOUBLEDAY INN
104 Doubleday Avenue,
(717) 334-9119
**The only B&B located directly on the
Gettysburg Battlefield.** Beautifully restored
Colonial with central A/C, period antiques,
authentic Civil War memorabilia and artifacts. Enjoy candlelight country breakfasts,
afternoon tea and hors d'oeuvres, free Civil
War lectures and Gettysburg Library.

ART

**FRAMING FOX ART GALLERY
CIVIL WAR ART**
Kunstler, Trioani, Gallon, plus others. We
buy and sell. Ship anywhere. Layaway
plan. Large inventory of art. Best prices.
Also Greenwich and Millpond dealer. Call
**800-237-6077. FRAMING FOX ART
GALLERY**, P.O. Box 679, Lebanon, N. J.
08833.

ARTIFACTS

**ORIGINAL CIVIL WAR
ANTIQUES FOR SALE!!!**
Muskets, swords, photos, equipment,
drums, flags, relics, etc. **EVERYTHING
FULLY GUARANTEED!** Remit $8.00
for next two illustrated catalogs to: Dave
Taylor's **CIVIL WAR ANTIQUES**, P.O.
Box 87, Sylvania, Ohio 43560. Or call
(419) 878-8355 days, 882-5547 evenings.

ARSENAL ARTIFACTS
Large, active inventory of authentic period
artifacts and ACCENTS & PRINTS limited edition prints featuring conservation mat-
ting & framing. Just off Business I-95.
Professional electrolysis and restoration.
Buying single items or collections. 231
Winslow St., Fayetteville, NC 28301. (910)
483-1111.

ATTRACTIONS

SHENANDOAH VALLEY HERITAGE MUSEUM
Come follow Stonewall Jackson's campaign as explained through the narrative
program of a 12-ft. electronic map where
300 lights follow the movements of the
contending armies.
Summer hours: Mon.-Sat. 9-4, Sun. 1-4
Winter hours: Thur.-Sat. 10-4
382 High Street, Dayton, VA 22821
(703) 879-2681

RESOURCES

BOOKS

RESOURCES

BOOKS

CAPSULE HISTORIES of every Civil War unit, Union and Confederate. Each contains organizational data, engagement lists, maps, etc. Only $10.00 per unit. **John F. Walter, 79-13 67 Drive, Middle Village, NY 11379.**

"FIELD ARTILLERY PROJECTILES OF THE AMERICAN CIVIL WAR," revised 1993 edition. Extensive information, 552 pages, 450 photos, US & CS Army & Navy shells, fuses, grenades, rockets. $39.95 + $4.95 UPS shipping (5 lb. book.) Author's signature.
Peter C. George
P.O. Box 74, Mechanicsville, VA 23111
(804) 321-7272

FLAGS

FLAGS! First, second and third National Confederate, Regulation, Battle, Bonnie Blue and period U.S. flags. Poles and hardware. Miniature gift sets.
THE FLAG CENTER
9 S. Harvie St., Richmond, VA 23220,
355-7801
5813 Grove Ave., Richmond, VA 23226,
285-0427

MUSIC

SINGIN' THE BLUES AND GREYS
Folk group EarthRise sings fourteen Civil War songs. In four-part harmony, as God and the composers intended. Accompaniment: guitar, mandolin, banjo, fiddle, autoharp, recorder, drums. Cassette $10. CreaTech Music, 122 Mallard, Goleta, CA 93117.

REPLICAS AND REPRODUCTIONS

REPRODUCTION UNIFORMS
George C. Dunn
P.O. Box 9203, Richmond, VA 23227
(804) 262-7995

SOUTH BEND REPLICAS, INC.
ANTIQUE ARTILLERY REPRODUCTIONS, miniature to full scale, Civil War and earlier. 128 page reference catalog with text and over 1200 pictures, $7.00; flyer only, stamped and self-addressed envelope. South Bend Replicas, Inc., 61650 Oak Road, South Bend, IN 46614.

Index to Advertisers

Index

C

D

T

U

Who you are and what you think is important to us.

Fill out the coupon and we'll give you an Insiders' Guide® for half price ($6.48 off)

Which book(s) did you buy? _____

Where do you live? _____

In what city did you buy your book? _____

Where did you buy your book? ❑ catalog ❑ bookstore ❑ newspaper ad
❑ retail shop ❑ other _____

How often do you travel? ❑ yearly ❑ bi-annually ❑ quarterly
❑ more than quarterly

Did you buy your book because you were ❑ moving ❑ vacationing
❑ wanted to know more about your home town ❑ other _____

_____

Will the book be used by ❑ family ❑ couple ❑ individual ❑ group

What is you annual household income? ❑ under $25,000 ❑ $25,000 to $35,000
❑ $35,000 to $50,000 ❑ $50,000 to $75,000 ❑ over $75,000

How old are you? ❑ under 25 ❑ 25-35 ❑ 36-50 ❑ 51-65 ❑ over 65

Did you use the book before you left for your destination? ❑ yes ❑ no

Did you use the book while at your destination? ❑ yes ❑ no

On average per month, how many times do you refer to your book? ❑ 1-3 ❑ 4-7
❑ 8-11 ❑ 12-15 ❑ 16 and up

On average, how many other people use your book? ❑ no others ❑ 1 ❑ 2
❑ 3 ❑ 4 or more

Is there anything you would like to tell us about Insiders' Guides? _____

_____

_____

Name _____ Address _____

City _____ State _____ Zip _____

We'll send you a voucher for $6.48 off any Insiders' Guide© and a list of available titles as soon as we get this card from you. Thanks for being an Insider!